Lecture Notes in Computer Science   8026

Commenced Publication in 1973
Founding and Former Series Editors:
Gerhard Goos, Juris Hartmanis, and Jan van Leeuwen

T0223893

Vincent G. Duffy (Ed.)

Digital Human Modeling and Applications in Health, Safety, Ergonomics, and Risk Management

Human Body Modeling and Ergonomics

4th International Conference, DHM 2013
Held as Part of HCI International 2013
Las Vegas, NV, USA, July 21-26, 2013
Proceedings, Part II

 Springer

Volume Editor

Vincent G. Duffy
Purdue University
College of Engineering
West Lafayette, IN 47907-2045, USA
E-mail: duffy@purdue.edu

ISSN 0302-9743   e-ISSN 1611-3349
ISBN 978-3-642-39181-1   e-ISBN 978-3-642-39182-8
DOI 10.1007/978-3-642-39182-8
Springer Heidelberg Dordrecht London New York

Library of Congress Control Number: 2013941252

CR Subject Classification (1998): H.5, J.2, H.3, H.1, I.6

LNCS Sublibrary: SL 3 – Information Systems and Application, incl. Internet/Web
and HCI

Typesetting: Camera-ready by author, data conversion by Scientific Publishing Services, Chennai, India

Printed on acid-free paper

Springer is part of Springer Science+Business Media (www.springer.com)

Foreword

The 15th International Conference on Human–Computer Interaction, HCI International 2013, was held in Las Vegas, Nevada, USA, 21–26 July 2013, incorporating 12 conferences / thematic areas:

Thematic areas:

- Human–Computer Interaction
- Human Interface and the Management of Information

Affiliated conferences:

- 10th International Conference on Engineering Psychology and Cognitive Ergonomics
- 7th International Conference on Universal Access in Human–Computer Interaction
- 5th International Conference on Virtual, Augmented and Mixed Reality
- 5th International Conference on Cross-Cultural Design
- 5th International Conference on Online Communities and Social Computing
- 7th International Conference on Augmented Cognition
- 4th International Conference on Digital Human Modeling and Applications in Health, Safety, Ergonomics and Risk Management
- 2nd International Conference on Design, User Experience and Usability
- 1st International Conference on Distributed, Ambient and Pervasive Interactions
- 1st International Conference on Human Aspects of Information Security, Privacy and Trust

A total of 5210 individuals from academia, research institutes, industry and governmental agencies from 70 countries submitted contributions, and 1666 papers and 303 posters were included in the program. These papers address the latest research and development efforts and highlight the human aspects of design and use of computing systems. The papers accepted for presentation thoroughly cover the entire field of Human–Computer Interaction, addressing major advances in knowledge and effective use of computers in a variety of application areas.

This volume, edited by Vincent G. Duffy, contains papers focusing on the thematic area of Digital Human Modeling and Applications in Health, Safety, Ergonomics and Risk Management, and addressing the following major topics:

- Digital Human Modeling and Ergonomics in Working Environments
- Ergonomics of Work with Computers
- Anthropometry, Posture and Motion Modeling

The remaining volumes of the HCI International 2013 proceedings are:

- Volume 1, LNCS 8004, Human–Computer Interaction: Human-Centred Design Approaches, Methods, Tools and Environments (Part I), edited by Masaaki Kurosu
- Volume 2, LNCS 8005, Human–Computer Interaction: Applications and Services (Part II), edited by Masaaki Kurosu
- Volume 3, LNCS 8006, Human–Computer Interaction: Users and Contexts of Use (Part III), edited by Masaaki Kurosu
- Volume 4, LNCS 8007, Human–Computer Interaction: Interaction Modalities and Techniques (Part IV), edited by Masaaki Kurosu
- Volume 5, LNCS 8008, Human–Computer Interaction: Towards Intelligent and Implicit Interaction (Part V), edited by Masaaki Kurosu
- Volume 6, LNCS 8009, Universal Access in Human–Computer Interaction: Design Methods, Tools and Interaction Techniques for eInclusion (Part I), edited by Constantine Stephanidis and Margherita Antona
- Volume 7, LNCS 8010, Universal Access in Human–Computer Interaction: User and Context Diversity (Part II), edited by Constantine Stephanidis and Margherita Antona
- Volume 8, LNCS 8011, Universal Access in Human–Computer Interaction: Applications and Services for Quality of Life (Part III), edited by Constantine Stephanidis and Margherita Antona
- Volume 9, LNCS 8012, Design, User Experience, and Usability: Design Philosophy, Methods and Tools (Part I), edited by Aaron Marcus
- Volume 10, LNCS 8013, Design, User Experience, and Usability: Health, Learning, Playing, Cultural, and Cross-Cultural User Experience (Part II), edited by Aaron Marcus
- Volume 11, LNCS 8014, Design, User Experience, and Usability: User Experience in Novel Technological Environments (Part III), edited by Aaron Marcus
- Volume 12, LNCS 8015, Design, User Experience, and Usability: Web, Mobile and Product Design (Part IV), edited by Aaron Marcus
- Volume 13, LNCS 8016, Human Interface and the Management of Information: Information and Interaction Design (Part I), edited by Sakae Yamamoto
- Volume 14, LNCS 8017, Human Interface and the Management of Information: Information and Interaction for Health, Safety, Mobility and Complex Environments (Part II), edited by Sakae Yamamoto
- Volume 15, LNCS 8018, Human Interface and the Management of Information: Information and Interaction for Learning, Culture, Collaboration and Business (Part III), edited by Sakae Yamamoto
- Volume 16, LNAI 8019, Engineering Psychology and Cognitive Ergonomics: Understanding Human Cognition (Part I), edited by Don Harris
- Volume 17, LNAI 8020, Engineering Psychology and Cognitive Ergonomics: Applications and Services (Part II), edited by Don Harris
- Volume 18, LNCS 8021, Virtual, Augmented and Mixed Reality: Designing and Developing Augmented and Virtual Environments (Part I), edited by Randall Shumaker

- Volume 19, LNCS 8022, Virtual, Augmented and Mixed Reality: Systems and Applications (Part II), edited by Randall Shumaker
- Volume 20, LNCS 8023, Cross-Cultural Design: Methods, Practice and Case Studies (Part I), edited by P.L. Patrick Rau
- Volume 21, LNCS 8024, Cross-Cultural Design: Cultural Differences in Everyday Life (Part II), edited by P.L. Patrick Rau
- Volume 22, LNCS 8025, Digital Human Modeling and Applications in Health, Safety, Ergonomics and Risk Management: Healthcare and Safety of the Environment and Transport (Part I), edited by Vincent G. Duffy
- Volume 23, LNCS 8026, Digital Human Modeling and Applications in Health, Safety, Ergonomics and Risk Management: Human Body Modeling and Ergonomics (Part II), edited by Vincent G. Duffy
- Volume 24, LNAI 8027, Foundations of Augmented Cognition, edited by Dylan D. Schmorrow and Cali M. Fidopiastis
- Volume 25, LNCS 8028, Distributed, Ambient and Pervasive Interactions, edited by Norbert Streitz and Constantine Stephanidis
- Volume 26, LNCS 8029, Online Communities and Social Computing, edited by A. Ant Ozok and Panayiotis Zaphiris
- Volume 27, LNCS 8030, Human Aspects of Information Security, Privacy and Trust, edited by Louis Marinos and Ioannis Askoxylakis
- Volume 28, CCIS 373, HCI International 2013 Posters Proceedings (Part I), edited by Constantine Stephanidis
- Volume 29, CCIS 374, HCI International 2013 Posters Proceedings (Part II), edited by Constantine Stephanidis

I would like to thank the Program Chairs and the members of the Program Boards of all affiliated conferences and thematic areas, listed below, for their contribution to the highest scientific quality and the overall success of the HCI International 2013 conference.

This conference could not have been possible without the continuous support and advice of the Founding Chair and Conference Scientific Advisor, Prof. Gavriel Salvendy, as well as the dedicated work and outstanding efforts of the Communications Chair and Editor of HCI International News, Abbas Moallem.

I would also like to thank for their contribution towards the smooth organization of the HCI International 2013 Conference the members of the Human–Computer Interaction Laboratory of ICS-FORTH, and in particular George Paparoulis, Maria Pitsoulaki, Stavroula Ntoa, Maria Bouhli and George Kapnas.

May 2013   Constantine Stephanidis
                              General Chair, HCI International 2013

Organization

Human–Computer Interaction

Program Chair: Masaaki Kurosu, Japan

Jose Abdelnour-Nocera, UK
Sebastiano Bagnara, Italy
Simone Barbosa, Brazil
Tomas Berns, Sweden
Nigel Bevan, UK
Simone Borsci, UK
Apala Lahiri Chavan, India
Sherry Chen, Taiwan
Kevin Clark, USA
Torkil Clemmensen, Denmark
Xiaowen Fang, USA
Shin'ichi Fukuzumi, Japan
Vicki Hanson, UK
Ayako Hashizume, Japan
Anzai Hiroyuki, Italy
Sheue-Ling Hwang, Taiwan
Wonil Hwang, South Korea
Minna Isomursu, Finland
Yong Gu Ji, South Korea
Esther Jun, USA
Mitsuhiko Karashima, Japan

Kyungdoh Kim, South Korea
Heidi Krömker, Germany
Chen Ling, USA
Yan Liu, USA
Zhengjie Liu, P.R. China
Loïc Martínez Normand, Spain
Chang S. Nam, USA
Naoko Okuizumi, Japan
Noriko Osaka, Japan
Philippe Palanque, France
Hans Persson, Sweden
Ling Rothrock, USA
Naoki Sakakibara, Japan
Dominique Scapin, France
Guangfeng Song, USA
Sanjay Tripathi, India
Chui Yin Wong, Malaysia
Toshiki Yamaoka, Japan
Kazuhiko Yamazaki, Japan
Ryoji Yoshitake, Japan
Silvia Zimmermann, Switzerland

Human Interface and the Management of Information

Program Chair: Sakae Yamamoto, Japan

Hans-Jorg Bullinger, Germany
Alan Chan, Hong Kong
Gilsoo Cho, South Korea
Jon R. Gunderson, USA
Shin'ichi Fukuzumi, Japan
Michitaka Hirose, Japan
Jhilmil Jain, USA
Yasufumi Kume, Japan

Mark Lehto, USA
Hiroyuki Miki, Japan
Hirohiko Mori, Japan
Fiona Fui-Hoon Nah, USA
Shogo Nishida, Japan
Robert Proctor, USA
Youngho Rhee, South Korea
Katsunori Shimohara, Japan

Michale Smith, USA
Tsutomu Tabe, Japan
Hiroshi Tsuji, Japan

Kim-Phuong Vu, USA
Tomio Watanabe, Japan
Hidekazu Yoshikawa, Japan

Engineering Psychology and Cognitive Ergonomics

Program Chair: Don Harris, UK

Guy Andre Boy, USA
Joakim Dahlman, Sweden
Trevor Dobbins, UK
Mike Feary, USA
Shan Fu, P.R. China
Michaela Heese, Austria
Hung-Sying Jing, Taiwan
Wen-Chin Li, Taiwan
Mark A. Neerincx, The Netherlands
Jan M. Noyes, UK
Taezoon Park, Singapore

Paul Salmon, Australia
Axel Schulte, Germany
Siraj Shaikh, UK
Sarah C. Sharples, UK
Anthony Smoker, UK
Neville A. Stanton, UK
Alex Stedmon, UK
Xianghong Sun, P.R. China
Andrew Thatcher, South Africa
Matthew J.W. Thomas, Australia
Rolf Zon, The Netherlands

Universal Access in Human–Computer Interaction

Program Chairs: Constantine Stephanidis, Greece, and Margherita Antona, Greece

Julio Abascal, Spain
Ray Adams, UK
Gisela Susanne Bahr, USA
Margit Betke, USA
Christian Bühler, Germany
Stefan Carmien, Spain
Jerzy Charytonowicz, Poland
Carlos Duarte, Portugal
Pier Luigi Emiliani, Italy
Qin Gao, P.R. China
Andrina Granić, Croatia
Andreas Holzinger, Austria
Josette Jones, USA
Simeon Keates, UK

Georgios Kouroupetroglou, Greece
Patrick Langdon, UK
Seongil Lee, Korea
Ana Isabel B.B. Paraguay, Brazil
Helen Petrie, UK
Michael Pieper, Germany
Enrico Pontelli, USA
Jaime Sanchez, Chile
Anthony Savidis, Greece
Christian Stary, Austria
Hirotada Ueda, Japan
Gerhard Weber, Germany
Harald Weber, Germany

Virtual, Augmented and Mixed Reality

Program Chair: Randall Shumaker, USA

Waymon Armstrong, USA
Juan Cendan, USA
Rudy Darken, USA
Cali M. Fidopiastis, USA
Charles Hughes, USA
David Kaber, USA
Hirokazu Kato, Japan
Denis Laurendeau, Canada
Fotis Liarokapis, UK

Mark Livingston, USA
Michael Macedonia, USA
Gordon Mair, UK
Jose San Martin, Spain
Jacquelyn Morie, USA
Albert "Skip" Rizzo, USA
Kay Stanney, USA
Christopher Stapleton, USA
Gregory Welch, USA

Cross-Cultural Design

Program Chair: P.L. Patrick Rau, P.R. China

Pilsung Choe, P.R. China
Henry Been-Lirn Duh, Singapore
Vanessa Evers, The Netherlands
Paul Fu, USA
Zhiyong Fu, P.R. China
Fu Guo, P.R. China
Sung H. Han, Korea
Toshikazu Kato, Japan
Dyi-Yih Michael Lin, Taiwan
Rungtai Lin, Taiwan

Sheau-Farn Max Liang, Taiwan
Liang Ma, P.R. China
Alexander Mädche, Germany
Katsuhiko Ogawa, Japan
Tom Plocher, USA
Kerstin Röse, Germany
Supriya Singh, Australia
Hsiu-Ping Yueh, Taiwan
Liang (Leon) Zeng, USA
Chen Zhao, USA

Online Communities and Social Computing

Program Chairs: A. Ant Ozok, USA, and Panayiotis Zaphiris, Cyprus

Areej Al-Wabil, Saudi Arabia
Leonelo Almeida, Brazil
Bjørn Andersen, Norway
Chee Siang Ang, UK
Aneesha Bakharia, Australia
Ania Bobrowicz, UK
Paul Cairns, UK
Farzin Deravi, UK
Andri Ioannou, Cyprus
Slava Kisilevich, Germany

Niki Lambropoulos, Greece
Effie Law, Switzerland
Soo Ling Lim, UK
Fernando Loizides, Cyprus
Gabriele Meiselwitz, USA
Anthony Norcio, USA
Elaine Raybourn, USA
Panote Siriaraya, UK
David Stuart, UK
June Wei, USA

Augmented Cognition

Program Chairs: Dylan D. Schmorrow, USA, and Cali M. Fidopiastis, USA

Robert Arrabito, Canada
Richard Backs, USA
Chris Berka, USA
Joseph Cohn, USA
Martha E. Crosby, USA
Julie Drexler, USA
Ivy Estabrooke, USA
Chris Forsythe, USA
Wai Tat Fu, USA
Rodolphe Gentili, USA
Marc Grootjen, The Netherlands
Jefferson Grubb, USA
Ming Hou, Canada

Santosh Mathan, USA
Rob Matthews, Australia
Dennis McBride, USA
Jeff Morrison, USA
Mark A. Neerincx, The Netherlands
Denise Nicholson, USA
Banu Onaral, USA
Lee Sciarini, USA
Kay Stanney, USA
Roy Stripling, USA
Rob Taylor, UK
Karl van Orden, USA

Digital Human Modeling and Applications in Health, Safety, Ergonomics and Risk Management

Program Chair: Vincent G. Duffy, USA and Russia

Karim Abdel-Malek, USA
Giuseppe Andreoni, Italy
Daniel Carruth, USA
Eliza Yingzi Du, USA
Enda Fallon, Ireland
Afzal Godil, USA
Ravindra Goonetilleke, Hong Kong
Bo Hoege, Germany
Waldemar Karwowski, USA
Zhizhong Li, P.R. China

Kang Li, USA
Tim Marler, USA
Michelle Robertson, USA
Matthias Rötting, Germany
Peter Vink, The Netherlands
Mao-Jiun Wang, Taiwan
Xuguang Wang, France
Jingzhou (James) Yang, USA
Xiugan Yuan, P.R. China
Gülcin Yücel Hoge, Germany

Design, User Experience, and Usability

Program Chair: Aaron Marcus, USA

Sisira Adikari, Australia
Ronald Baecker, Canada
Arne Berger, Germany
Jamie Blustein, Canada

Ana Boa-Ventura, USA
Jan Brejcha, Czech Republic
Lorenzo Cantoni, Switzerland
Maximilian Eibl, Germany

Anthony Faiola, USA
Emilie Gould, USA
Zelda Harrison, USA
Rüdiger Heimgärtner, Germany
Brigitte Herrmann, Germany
Steffen Hess, Germany
Kaleem Khan, Canada

Jennifer McGinn, USA
Francisco Rebelo, Portugal
Michael Renner, Switzerland
Kerem Rızvanoğlu, Turkey
Marcelo Soares, Brazil
Christian Sturm, Germany
Michele Visciola, Italy

Distributed, Ambient and Pervasive Interactions

Program Chairs: Norbert Streitz, Germany, and Constantine Stephanidis, Greece

Emile Aarts, The Netherlands
Adnan Abu-Dayya, Qatar
Juan Carlos Augusto, UK
Boris de Ruyter, The Netherlands
Anind Dey, USA
Dimitris Grammenos, Greece
Nuno M. Guimaraes, Portugal
Shin'ichi Konomi, Japan
Carsten Magerkurth, Switzerland

Christian Müller-Tomfelde, Australia
Fabio Paternó, Italy
Gilles Privat, France
Harald Reiterer, Germany
Carsten Röcker, Germany
Reiner Wichert, Germany
Woontack Woo, South Korea
Xenophon Zabulis, Greece

Human Aspects of Information Security, Privacy and Trust

Program Chairs: Louis Marinos, ENISA EU, and Ioannis Askoxylakis, Greece

Claudio Agostino Ardagna, Italy
Zinaida Benenson, Germany
Daniele Catteddu, Italy
Raoul Chiesa, Italy
Bryan Cline, USA
Sadie Creese, UK
Jorge Cuellar, Germany
Marc Dacier, USA
Dieter Gollmann, Germany
Kirstie Hawkey, Canada
Jaap-Henk Hoepman, The Netherlands
Cagatay Karabat, Turkey
Angelos Keromytis, USA
Ayako Komatsu, Japan

Ronald Leenes, The Netherlands
Javier Lopez, Spain
Steve Marsh, Canada
Gregorio Martinez, Spain
Emilio Mordini, Italy
Yuko Murayama, Japan
Masakatsu Nishigaki, Japan
Aljosa Pasic, Spain
Milan Petković, The Netherlands
Joachim Posegga, Germany
Jean-Jacques Quisquater, Belgium
Damien Sauveron, France
George Spanoudakis, UK
Kerry-Lynn Thomson, South Africa

Julien Touzeau, France
Theo Tryfonas, UK
João Vilela, Portugal

Claire Vishik, UK
Melanie Volkamer, Germany

External Reviewers

Maysoon Abulkhair, Saudi Arabia
Ilia Adami, Greece
Vishal Barot, UK
Stephan Böhm, Germany
Vassilis Charissis, UK
Francisco Cipolla-Ficarra, Spain
Maria De Marsico, Italy
Marc Fabri, UK
David Fonseca, Spain
Linda Harley, USA
Yasushi Ikei, Japan
Wei Ji, USA
Nouf Khashman, Canada
John Killilea, USA
Iosif Klironomos, Greece
Ute Klotz, Switzerland
Maria Korozi, Greece
Kentaro Kotani, Japan

Vassilis Kouroumalis, Greece
Stephanie Lackey, USA
Janelle LaMarche, USA
Asterios Leonidis, Greece
Nickolas Macchiarella, USA
George Margetis, Greece
Matthew Marraffino, USA
Joseph Mercado, USA
Claudia Mont'Alvão, Brazil
Yoichi Motomura, Japan
Karsten Nebe, Germany
Stavroula Ntoa, Greece
Martin Osen, Austria
Stephen Prior, UK
Farid Shirazi, Canada
Jan Stelovsky, USA
Sarah Swierenga, USA

HCI International 2014

The 16th International Conference on Human–Computer Interaction, HCI International 2014, will be held jointly with the affiliated conferences in the summer of 2014. It will cover a broad spectrum of themes related to Human–Computer Interaction, including theoretical issues, methods, tools, processes and case studies in HCI design, as well as novel interaction techniques, interfaces and applications. The proceedings will be published by Springer. More information about the topics, as well as the venue and dates of the conference, will be announced through the HCI International Conference series website: http://www.hci-international.org/

General Chair
Professor Constantine Stephanidis
University of Crete and ICS-FORTH
Heraklion, Crete, Greece
Email: cs@ics.forth.gr

Table of Contents – Part II

Digital Human Modeling and Ergonomics in Working Environments

Ergonomics of Work with Computers

Anthropometry, Posture and Motion Modeling

Table of Contents – Part I

Driving and Aviation Safety

Human Factors and Digital Human Modeling in Healthcare

Safety of the Human Environment

Part I

Digital Human Modeling and Ergonomics in Working Environments

A Knowledge Transfer Process: Establishing Training in New Technology for an Ageing Workforce

Conne Mara Bazley[1,*] and Denise Brooks[2]

[1] JimConna Inc., Colorado, USA
cbazley@jimconna.com
[2] ErgoWhat, Ohio, USA
ergowhat@ergowhat.com

Abstract. Learning new technology can transform the lives of older workers. Worldwide older workers remain in the workplace longer and continue to work for various personal and economic reasons. Some leave one workplace and take up a second or even a third career. The new technology training required for many industries is generally focused on younger workers already trained in new technology basics. Ideally, to keep a diverse workforce motivated and productive, training for younger and older workers is necessary. New technology training for older workers is designed differently than that of younger workers to address some of the physical and cognitive changes that occur with age. If older workers are given the appropriate training and help, there is evidence to show they are able to master the new technology.

Keywords: ageing, workforce, new technology, training.

1 Introduction

The workforce is aging and there are tremendous changes taking place in work environments and organizational structures. The introduction of new technology into working life has dramatically changed the nature of many jobs and work situations for many workers. Charness and Czaja [1] state that, "The continued reliance on computer-based technologies in the workplace increases the demand for knowledge, and skilled workers. To adapt to the changing workplace, all workers—including older workers—need to participate in worker training programs. This is particularly true for older adults who are less likely to have the technology skills needed in today's workplace".

Worldwide older workers continue to work beyond retirement age for various personal and economic reasons. Older workers remain in the workplace longer for various reasons. Some leave one workplace and take up a second or even a third career. Many older adults want to continue working because they're healthy. People are living longer and remain actively productive in some form. Some start a new job, maybe work part-time in a flexible work arrangement while others have to stay in the workforce because of need for healthcare benefits or economic reasons [2]. For many

V.G. Duffy (Ed.): DHM/HCII 2013, Part II, LNCS 8026, pp. 3–9, 2013.

older workers an ideal job is having the opportunity to work part-time on a flexible schedule, and the ability to obtain job training. AARP [3] found older workers need a flexible work schedule and have different needs and expectations with regard to work and giving back to the community.

2   New Technology Training for Older Workers

According to Charness and Czaja [1], today's global economy requires a trained and flexible workforce able to adapt quickly to new technology, changing methods of production, and evolving consumer demands. Not all employers, however, are convinced that older workers have what it takes to meet their needs in this new economy. In particular, they have reservations about older workers' technological competence and ability to learn new technology. The training required for many industries is generally focused on the idea that younger workers are already trained in new technology.

Ideally, to keep a diverse workforce motivated and productive, training for younger and older workers is necessary. New technology training for older workers is designed differently than that of younger workers to address some of the physical and cognitive changes that occur with age. Hence, ageing workers are significantly less likely to believe that they have career prospects when compared to prime age workers, and particularly so if they are undereducated, but there are no significant differences about fear of job loss [4].

3   Factors That Affect Older Workers

3.1   Stereotypes and Myths

Older workers don't fit one unique profile and differ from one another as much as anyone from any other age group in abilities, desires, and needs [5]. However, that being said negative stereotyping is often used against older workers and can have a serious effect on those who are being stereotyped as well as the rest of those that are not [6]. One of the most pervasive stereotypes of older workers is that they cannot learn "new tricks". The most frequently cited negative characteristic regarding older workers is related to difficulties in adjusting to change and technology [7]. Negative myths and stereotypes about older workers do exist and do impact on the workforce participation of such workers. Additionally, older workers may also hold similar ideas about their own abilities and believe the negative stereotypes.

3.2   Chronological Age and Lack of Confidence

Older workers indicate that they faced age discrimination in the workplace and that their age was a major impediment to continued employment. This result coincides with a recent report published by AARP [3] indicating that age discrimination is a serious concern and the single largest barrier confronted by people 50 years and older who wish to remain employed. Chronological age is a poor predictor of technical learning capacity; rather, the main factors affecting how older workers respond to technology and learning new skills are a combination of self-efficacy, self-belief and self-confidence, the perceived benefit in terms of time left in workforce, and the training approaches used [2]. Another challenge for older workers is lack of confidence. Many older people encountering new technology for the first time believe that it is far too difficult for them to make sense of it all at their age. This belief is reinforced by the attitude of many younger people. Czaja et al. [8] suggest that older adults' relationship with technology is much more complex than would be suggested by the stereotype of older adults simply being afraid and unwilling to use technology.

3.3   Psychology and Motivation

Two more factors that are often overlooked when discussing older workers are psychology and motivation. Experience Works [6] suggests that older people heavily weigh the benefits of whether or not to adopt new technology. Czaja et al. [8] found additional personal barriers to technology adoption: low self-efficacy regarding computer use and high anxiety for computer use.

3.4   Qualities Desired by Employers

Many businesses persist in believing stereotypes and myths about older workers and may discriminate against them even though the reputation of older workers is shown to be of high quality. Older workers exhibit many characteristics and attributes desired by employers and businesses [7]. Despite the stereotypes, employers affirm that, in general, older workers:

- have low turnover rates
- are flexible and open to change
- possess up-to-date skills
- are interested in learning new tasks
- do not experience transportation problems
- are willing to take on challenging tasks
- have low absentee rates
- have few on-the-job accidents

Another study, conducted by the Society for Human Resource Management (SHRM) in conjunction with the American Association of Retired Persons (AARP), confirmed the majority of these findings, and added several more [9]. Of the nearly 400 human resource professionals surveyed,

- 77% agreed that older workers have a higher level of commitment to the organization than younger workers   (only 5% disagreed)
- 68% concluded training older workers costs less or the same as training their younger counterparts (6% disagreed)

- 57% reported that age does not affect the amount of time required to train an employee (14% disagreed)
- 49% determined that older workers grasped new concepts as well as younger workers (18% disagreed)

However, the one area of concern expressed was how well older workers adapt to new technology. According to SHRM [9], "Sixty-six percent of the respondents agreed that older workers tend to be more fearful of technology than younger workers". On the other hand, other studies by Hall and Mirvis [10] report that older workers *are* trainable in "high technology skills" and are "comfortable" learning them. Hall and Mirvis [10] also found that with proper training, older workers are undaunted by technology eager to update their skills.

3.5   Lack of New Technology Skills

Other important obstacles reported by older workers with respect to finding a job include the lack of skills to compete in today's workforce and a tight job market. Older workers indicate that they have insufficient technology skills and need training for the new technology. These finding have implications with respect to training and imply that managers need training about aging to understand the value of the older worker to the organization. Older people are willing and able to learn new technology and use computers in various contexts but they consistently have more difficulty than younger users [11]. Additionally, older people need access to technology training programs that are designed to consider the learning limitations and preferred formats of older adults. Not all computer users are created equal, a fact that computer designers and software engineers have not always recognized. However, if older workers are given the appropriate help, there is evidence to show they are able to master the technology. On a positive note, older workers are generally enthusiasm about learning computer-based technologies and computer skills and are excited about returning to work. Managers that engage older workers and provide them with adequate job training and opportunities add an additional vital resource to their workforce.

4   New Technology Training for Older Workers

4.1   Older Worker Learning Preferences and Extra Time

In terms of learning preferences, older workers prefer active learning in group formats where there are opportunities to learn and share experiences with others. They also stress the importance of engaging in hands-on learning activities [12]. Additionally, participants indicated that access to feedback is important. This confirms results from a study by Sharit et al. [13]. There is a need for more feedback regarding the correctness of their responses. These results have implications for the design of training programs. According to Charness and Czaja [1] trainers should keep demands on working memory to a minimum, and where possible, capitalize on the learner's pre-existing knowledge base. If the task is complex, training demands can be reduced by using part-task training techniques such as providing practice on task components, and proceeding from simple to more complex aspects of the task.

Additionally, it is important to allow extra time for training an older adult (1.5 to 2 times the training time expected for a young adult), to ensure that help is available and easy to access (e.g., acquaint the person with sources of help), and to ensure that the training environment allows the individual to focus on the training materials [1].

4.2   Other Design Factors

The reading level of all instructions and manuals matches the abilities of the user and use simple support materials such as graphic aids or reminders of procedural steps minimizes the demands on working memory. It is important to match the instructional technique and the medium (e.g., text, voice, animation) to the type of material that is being presented. For example, "how to" information should be presented in a procedural step-by-step format and spatial tasks should be taught using a visual medium [1].

Charness and Czaja [1] also suggests allowing the learner to make errors, when safe, but provide immediate feedback regarding how to correct mistakes. The older adult should be actively involved in the learning process, and an engaging environment that captures the attention of the learner should be created.

Due to the rapid development of powerful technology tools multimedia programs are increasingly being used for education and training. Despite the significant use of multimedia in training, there has been very limited effort to evaluate the design of multimedia programs or the impact of this type of training format on user performance [14].

4.3   Strategies

It is important to develop strategies to encourage older workers to participate in training and retraining programs. Employers need to ensure that older adults are provided with access to training programs and incentives to invest in learning new skills. In general, people are more receptive to engaging in learning activities if they see a long-term benefit from the experience [8]. Additionally, consideration should be given to the scheduling and location of training programs.

To encourage the uptake of training opportunities, delivery methods need to be appropriate, such as self-paced and on-the-job formats that are relevant to the job, the job being undertaken, and teaching that relates to worker's previous experience [1].

5   Conclusion

Older people can learn to use new technology, given sensitive and effective teaching and support. New developments in this technology offer the possibility of considerably enhancing the lives of older people, in terms of productivity, communication, and support. In realizing these possibilities, attention paid to developing technology specifically for older people will not only bring social and economic dividends in itself, but will help in the design of technology which is more accessible for all of us.

Hence, to increase older adults' technology two approaches can be taken: 1) improve education about benefits for technologies that have not yet been adopted and 2) address computer self-efficacy and computer anxiety [11].

Currently there is little empirical knowledge to guide the developer of these applications. In addition, according to Charness, Fox and Mitchum [15] almost no research has been done with older adults. This issue is especially compelling given that multimedia formats place demands on cognitive processes that show age-related decline such as working memory and selective attention.

In conclusion, technology acceptance and adoption has implications for older adults and society as a whole. Therefore, as the aging population grows and technologies continue to develop it is imperative that we understand how to design technologies that support the needs and preferences of older adults [1]. The potential for new technology to transform the lives of older people in the workforce is ongoing and provides an opportunity for a rich and diverse workforce.

References

1. Charness, N., Czaja, S.J.: Older worker training: What we know and don't know. Technical report prepared for AARP (2005), http://www.aarp.org/research/work/issues/2006_22.worker.html
2. Czaja, S.J., Moen, P.: Technology and employment. In: Pew, R., Van Hamel, S. (eds.) Technology and Adaptive Aging, pp. 150–178. National Research Council, Washington, D.C (2004)
3. AARP: Perspectives of employers, workers, and policymakers in the G7 countries on the new demographic realities (2007), http://www.aarpinternational.org/usr_doc/intl_older_worker.pdf
4. Hedge, J.: Strategic human resource management and the older worker. Journal of Workplace and Behavioral Health 23(1/2), 109–123 (2008)
5. Cedefop, C.: The skill matching challenge; analyzing skill mismatch and policy Implications. Publications Office, Luxembourg (2010)
6. Fyock, D.: Get the Best: How to Recruit the People You Want. Business One Irwin, Homewood (1993)
7. Myths and Facts about Older Workers-Experience Works, www.experienceworks.org/Older_Worker_Myths_and _Realities
8. Czaja, S.J., Charness, N., Fisk, A.D., Hertzog, C., Nair, S.N., Rogers, W.A., Sharit, J.: Factors predicting the use of technology: Findings from the Center for Research and Education on Aging and Technology Enhancement (CREATE). Psychology and Aging 21, 333–352 (2006)
9. Society for Human Resource Management (SHRM), Many older worker myths are challenged by SHRM/AARP survey, press release, Alexandria, VA (May 15 (1998)

10. Hall, D., Mirvis, P.: Increasing the value of older workers: Flexible employment and lifelong learning. In: Auerbach, J.A. (ed.) Through a Glass Darkly: Building the New Workplace for the 21st Century, NPA Report #289, National Policy Association, Washington D.C (1998)
11. Czaja, S.J., Charness, N., Fisk, A.D., Hertzog, C., Nair, S.N., Rogers, W.A., Sharit, J.: Factors predicting the use of technology: Findings from the Center for Research and Education on Aging and Technology Enhancement (CREATE). Psychology and Aging 21, 333–352 (2006)
12. Czaja, S.J.: Ageing and the acquisition of computer skills. In: Rogers, W.A., Fisk, A.D., Walker, N. (eds.) Ageing and Skilled Performance. Lawrence Erlbaum, New Jersey (1996)
13. Sharit, J., Czaja, S.J., Hernandez, M., Yang, Y., Perdomo, D., Lewis, J.L., et al.: An evaluation of performance by older persons on a simulated telecom-muting task. Journal of Gerontology: Psychological Sciences 59B(6), 305–316 (2004)
14. Sutcliff, A.: Multimedia user interface design. In: Jacko, J.A., Sears, A. (eds.) The Handbook of Human Computer Interaction, pp. 245–262. Erlbaum, Mahwah (2002)
15. Charness, N., Fox, M., Mitchum, A.: Lifespan cognition and information technology. In: Fingerman, K., Berg, C., Antonnuci, T., Smith, J. (eds.) Handbook of Lifespan Psychology. Springer, New York (2010)

Towards Anthropomorphic Movements
for Industrial Robots

Christian Brecher[1], Simon Müller[1,*], Sinem Kuz[2], and Wolfram Lohse[1]

[1] Laboratory for Machine Tools and Production Engineering WZL, RWTH Aachen University
{c.brecher,s.mueller,w.lohse}@wzl.rwth-aachen.de
[2] Institute of Industrial Engineering and Ergonomics, RWTH Aachen University
s.kuz@iaw.rwth-aachen.de

Abstract. In order to increase productivity for processes that involve the interaction of human and robot, a promising approach is to increase the transparency of robot movements. Based on the hypothesis that anthropomorphic movements are more transparent to a human operator, this paper presents methodologies and techniques to generate humanlike movements for industrial robots.

Keywords: Anthropomorphic movements, industrial robot, movement parameters.

1 Introduction

To meet the increasing challenges in regard to production in high-wage countries, one of the approaches has been to automate assembly tasks using industrial robots. In today's production plants – in an increasing number of scenarios – these robots interact with human operators in cooperative environments. As the requirements regarding productivity increase, the naïve approach is to increase automation as well. According to the "law of diminishing returns", however, an increase in automation will likely not lead to a significant increase in productivity but can also have adverse effects. According to Kinkel the amount of process errors is in average significantly reduced by automation, but the severity of potential consequences of a single error increases disproportionately [1]. These "Ironies of Automation" which were identified by Lisanne Bainbridge can be considered as a vicious circle, where a function that was allocated to a human operator due to poor human reliability is automated [2]. Thus the automation results in higher function complexity, finally increasing the demands on the human operator for planning, teaching and monitoring, and hence leading to a more error-prone system.

In order to break cited vicious circle for assembly processes that involve the interaction of human and robot, a promising approach is to change the movement of the industrial robot, such that it resembles a human movement (anthropomorphic movements). This hypothesis is based on the findings by Kuz et al. towards the anticipation of a robot's movement characteristics by a human operator [3]. In the studies a virtual environment for the assembly in a predetermined working space was

V.G. Duffy (Ed.): DHM/HCII 2013, Part II, LNCS 8026, pp. 10–19, 2013.

setup and the expectation of the human operator was compared to the actual behavior of the robot. The foundations for the behavior of the virtual robot were movement trajectories of a human assembly operation that was acquired by a motion capture system. Due to the fact that it was a virtual scenario, the robot's control unit was able to control the robot in at every single point in time in all of the degrees of freedom.

The robot control unit of an industrial robot, however, provides only a limited set of predefined movement types, e.g. Point-To-Point (PTP) or Linear (LIN). In a fully automated scenario these types suffice to reach every point in the workspace of a robot from a predefined direction. The focus of these commands is on a specific objective like a certain speed or the shape of the path. The opportunities to vary the set of parameters for both speed and path are very limited. A human movement, however, is defined by a complex pattern for both speed and path throughout the motion from one point to another.

This paper presents methodology and techniques to transform human movement trajectories so that they can be executed by industrial robots. Chapter 2 describes the advantages of this methodology and the challenges of its application for industrial robots. The main model for the methodology is described in Chapter 3, followed by an outline of the application to a near-reality production environment in Chapter 4. The paper finishes with a description of first experimental results in Chapter 5 and concluding remarks in Chapter 6.

2   Human and Robot Movements

2.1   Anthropomorphic Movements

Research of the last years indicates that by transferring anthropomorphic features such as appearance to non-human entities, a higher user acceptance can be achieved [4-5]. Hence, especially research in the field of human-robot cooperation focusses increasingly on the design of robots with anthropomorphic characteristics to enable teamwork between man and machine. However the adaptation of human-like characteristics to an industrial robot is rarely investigated because efficiency and robustness are the most important aspects in industrial environments. Nevertheless, direct interaction between humans and robotic systems in industrial environments is a promising approach to combine the specific skills of the human and the robotic system and to increase the flexibility of the production system. Besides the aspect of physical safety, the level of trust of the human and the transparency of the system behavior are important factors for a successful collaboration. Hence, especially concerning complex automation systems, it might occur that the system behavior cannot always be anticipated by the human operator. Therefore, from a user centered point of view an important basic requirement for effective human-robot cooperation is to achieve conformity with operator expectations so that she/he can always understand the actions and intentions of the corresponding system. Thus, the advantages of anthropomorphism could also be applied for cooperative work of humans and robots in industrial environments. Accordingly, the question is whether augmenting industrial robot with anthropomorphic features would achieve a better anticipation of the robot's behavior by the human worker.

2.2   Robot Movement Commands

Most of the research in regard to anthropomorphic robots has been evaluated in scenarios involving custom made robots that provide open control structures. Industrial robot control units, however, usually offer only a limited set of predefined movement types, e.g. Point-To-Point (PTP) or Linear (LIN) (cp. Figure 1, left). The PTP command provides the fastest movement between two points but the trajectory is usually not a straight line between them. In a LIN movement, the trajectory is the straight-lined path between starting and target positions. For each of these movement types robot control units offer the possibility to set both the maximum velocity and maximum acceleration. If a movement is comprised of more than two points smoothing can be used to increase the overall speed for a movement (cp. Figure 1, right). If smoothing is enabled the robot does not need to reach the exact intermediate point but just needs to enter the smoothing area that is defined by the intermediate point and a maximum smoothing distance. In order to supply an industrial robot with the capability to move humanlike, the predefined movement types have to be utilized and parameterized to form a new movement command that resembles the pattern of a human movement.

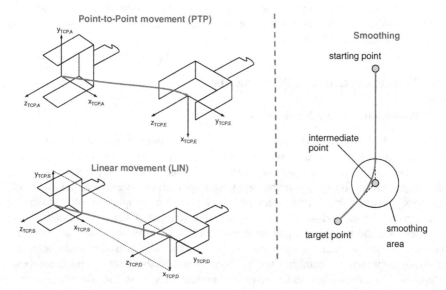

Fig. 1. Trajectories of robot movement commands PTP and LIN (left) and Smoothing (right)

3   Framework for Generating Human Like Movements

Figure 2 presents an overview of the framework that is used to create functions for anthropomorphic robot movement commands. In this context the term framework refers to a combination of methodologies and techniques as well as their concrete implementation in a technical system – hardware and software. The approach consists of three parts:

1. Human tracking and trajectory extraction
2. Robot movement generation and tracking
3. Robot trajectory optimization

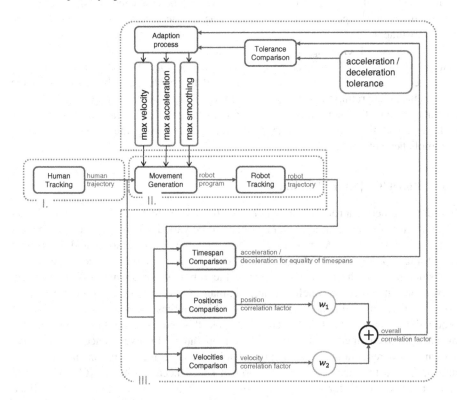

Fig. 2. Overview of framework to create anthropomorphic robot movements

3.1   Human Tracking and Trajectory Extraction

The first part deals with the requirement to acquire a technical representation of the human movement. In order apply anthropomorphic movement operations to an industrial robot, the trajectory of the human hand during the movement needs to be recorded. In regard to hardware, 3D markers and an optical motion capture system are utilized to record the position of the human wrist during the execution of the desired movement operation. The system captures hand trajectories as well as the duration to complete the operation. The human movement trajectories recorded by the motion tracking system – i.e. the x, y and z coordinates of the end-effector at every sampling instance – are stored in an XML file. Based on this information, the human movements are analyzed and information on speed and shape of the path are extracted.

3.2   Robot Movement Generation and Tracking

To find the set of movement commands that create an anthropomorphic movement for an industrial robot, different movement types have to be evaluated and the parameters for the movement types have to be varied. These trajectories form the basis for the robot movement.

The process of creating a robot program from the movement data has been automated using MATLAB. After importing a trajectory, the basic robot program structure is extended by the commands needed to enable the robot to perform the movements. Generating the robot program in MATLAB rather than by hand has many advantages, e.g. that corrections of motion tracking system measurement errors as well as adaptations of the number of data points along the trajectory can be accomplished automatically.

3.3   Robot Trajectory Optimization

In order to generate a robotic movement that resembles the human movement, the set of parameters for the robotic movement need to be varied. There are three parameters that can be modified: Maximum velocity, maximum acceleration and maximum smoothing (cp. Chapter 2). Due to the restrictions in maximum speed, acceleration and smoothing of the robotic movement, the robot is not always able to perform movements in the same timeframe as a human. Since industrial robots are usually used to perform value-adding activities, this implies a potential reduction of productivity. As described in the second chapter, this reduction might be compensated by an optimized interaction with a human operator. However, since studies have shown that a reduction in speed might lead to a false interpretation of movement information, a tolerance for the reduction in speed needs to be set [6]. In order to adapt the parameters for the robotic movement an optimization function is defined utilizing the correlation factor between the positions (ρ_{pos}) and velocities (ρ_{vel}) of the human movement and the robotic movement, respectively. For both correlation factors, the signals of the human movement is stretched in time to match the movement of the robot so that a correlation factor can be calculated. The optimization function thus results as:

$$\rho^* = \arg \max_{\{v \in \mathbb{R}|0 \leq v \leq 1\}, \{a \in \mathbb{R}|0 \leq a \leq 1\}, \{s \in \mathbb{N}|0 \leq s \leq 100\}} (\rho_{overall}(v, a, s))$$

$$= \arg \max_{\{v \in \mathbb{R}|0 \leq v \leq 1\}, \{a \in \mathbb{R}|0 \leq a \leq 1\}, \{s \in \mathbb{N}|0 \leq s \leq 100\}} (w_1 * \rho_{pos}(v, a, s) + w_2 * \rho_{vel}(v, a, s)),$$

$$w_1 + w_2 = 1, \{w_1 \in \mathbb{R}|0 \leq w_1 \leq 1\}, \{w_2 \in \mathbb{R}|0 \leq w_2 \leq 1\} \qquad (1)$$

The weighting factors w_1 and w_2 express a human's capability to recognize positions and velocities of movements. They are necessary due to the inherent conflict of objectives for achieving the exact positions and velocities as the human. For example, without smoothing enabled the trajectory of the robot is almost exactly the same as the humans. In regard to speed, however, there is little to no correlation between the two movements, since the robot stops at every intermediate point of the trajectory.

In the adaptation process the optimization is performed for those parameter combinations that fulfill the requirements regarding the timespan tolerance of the robotic movement.

The result of this model's application are functions for the robot control unit that provide the robot with a movement that is most similar to that of a human for a given operation. These functions can be utilized to further investigate on the perception of robotic movements from an operator's point of view. Thus, the framework comprises the basis for further laboratory tests in a near-reality production environment on a human operator's perception of anthropomorphic movements for industrial robots. Furthermore, the framework could be used to improve aspects of programming industrial robots e.g. in Programming-by-Demonstration based solutions [7].

4   Evaluation Scenario

4.1   Movement Recordings

In order to make use of the designed system in a production system, the evaluation is based on common pick and place movements. For the recording and tracking of the movements an infrared optical tracking system has been used in a scenario where 20 fields comprise a grid of possible target positions (cp. Figure 3). In a previous study the position data for all fields has been recorded, analyzed and transformed into a virtual scenario (see [3]). The gathered information is utilized for the generation of robot programs as well as the comparison in following steps. Since the target positions in the virtual scenario have a distance ranging between about 50mm and 400mm from the starting positions, they give a valid representation of real life pick and place operations in an industrial environment.

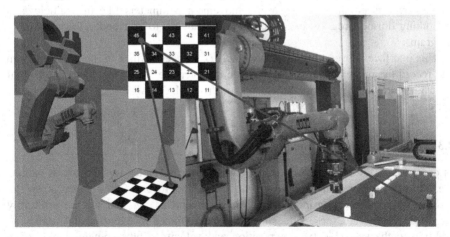

Fig. 3. Evaluation scenario in virtuality (left) and reality (right)

4.2   Robot Cell

To evaluate the designed framework in a near-reality production environment a validation scenario comprised of an industrial robot (KUKA KR 30 Jet) and a dexterous hand (SCHUNK Dexterous Hand 2) has been set up. This scenario is controlled by a system that is designed like the described framework and thus generates robot control programs utilizing different human movement patterns. When these programs are executed on the robot control unit, the system analyzes their resemblance to the human movement and adjusts the parameters of the used movement types according to possible differences.

Generally, robot control units such as the KUKA Robot Control (KRC) have only limited means to communicate with external systems, e.g. through digital or analogue inputs and outputs. This originates from their common use in highly automated environments where they perform predefined tasks. However, to analyze the robot movement trajectories, a link to an external PC is necessary.

For KUKA robots the Robot Sensor Interface (RSI) is an extension to the basic KUKA Robot Language (KRL), which offers the possibility to process sensor inputs in real-time, working with interlinked signal processing blocks. Moreover, it offers the means for communication with an external system. An XML string that contains information such as the tool center point position, orientation and the axis values is sent via TCP/IP from the KRC to an externals system every 12ms. The external system has to reply with an XML string of predefined structure within 4ms of reception. Hence, these XML strings can be used to send variable values in both directions.

A MATLAB interface for this XML communication has been designed that satisfies the used protocol and real-time constraints. Hereby it is possible to record the robot movement trajectories which are later compared to that of human movements. Moreover, it is possible to vary robot movement parameters like the velocity and smoothing during program execution, without having to edit and reload the robot program.

This interface is used to initiate movement sequences defined in the robot program and record the movement trajectory. While the interface also offers the possibility of controlling the TCP position and orientation from MATLAB, this is not desirable in our case.

4.3   Parameter Adaptation

In order to use the methodology from chapter 3, the variables w_1 and w_2 as well as the allowed acceleration need to be set. Since the focus of this paper is on the technical aspects of anthropomorphic robot movements, w_1 and w_2 are arbitrarily fixed to 0.5. In future, these values need to be determined by experimental studies. In addition to the two objectives – position and velocity – other potential objectives might result from these experimental studies, thus also increasing the number of weighting factors. For the acceleration tolerance no restrictions have been made in this scenario.

5   Experimental Results

Figure 4 presents an exemplary result for a robotic movement in PTP mode with a maximum acceleration of 80%, maximum velocity of 20% and a maximum smoothing of 20mm to the first row and first column grid in the scenario. The charts on the left hand side present the x, y and z coordinates of the robot's end effector and the human wrist over time, while the right hand side presents the velocities in x, y and z direction of the shared coordinate system. The execution time for the movements has already been adapted so that the correlation factors can be calculated. Given that the weighting factor w_1 and w_2 are set to 0.5 the chosen set of parameters achieves a high overall correlation factor – $\rho_{overall}(0.8, 0.2, 20) \approx 0.9171$ – for this movement operation.

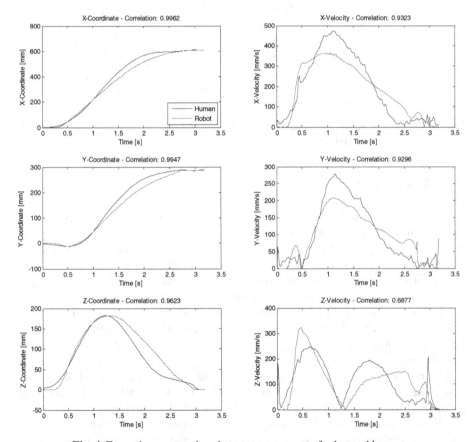

Fig. 4. Exemplary comparison between movement of robot and human

However, as Figure 5 indicates, this configuration (Max. Acceleration=80%, Max. Velocity=20%, Max. Smoothing=20mm – marked red) leads to a time for completion of a movement that is much higher than that of a human, i.e. the robot needs about 250% of the time that a human would need for that same movement.

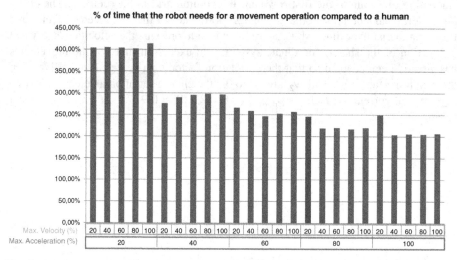

Fig. 5. Comparison between execution times of robot and human for movement to "Row4, Column5" with 20mm maximum smoothing

6   Conclusion

The presented methodology and techniques allow for the creation of robot movements based on arbitrary human movements. In order to imitate typical human movements in a production system, hand trajectories are obtained by a motion capture system. The recorded positions are extracted and a robot program is generated as well as executed on the respective industrial robot. The exact trajectory of the robot is logged and parameters for the robot motion are adapted in order to optimize that trajectory so that its correlation factor to the human movement increases. After several iterations and the accompanying adaptations, the parameters with the highest correlation between human and robot trajectory – with respect to given restrictions on timespans – are found.

The resulting parameters depend on multiple criteria. First of all the given restrictions in time pose a limit on the velocity, acceleration and smoothing parameter. Additionally the cost function is based on the correlation between robot and human position as well as velocity. For the current evaluation it has been assumed, that these two correlations are of equal importance in regard to the overall movement perception of a human observer. This assumption, however, needs to be verified in empirical studies.

Additionally, the hypothesis of this paper has been that if a robot moves in an anthropomorphic way, this leads to a better anticipation of the robot's trajectory by a human observer. In order to validate this hypothesis, the developed framework can be used in empirical studies to test the reaction of human operators for different movements.

Acknowledgements. The authors would like to thank the German Research Foundation DFG for the support of the depicted research within the Research Training Group 1491/2 "Ramp-Up Management: Development of Decision Models for the Production Ramp-Up" and the Cluster of Excellence "Integrative Production Technology for High-Wage Countries".

References

1. Bainbridge, L.: Ironies of automation. In: Rasmussen, J., Duncan, K., Leplat, J. (eds.) New Technology and Human Error, pp. 775–779. J. Wiley, Chichester (1987)
2. Kinkel, S.: Arbeiten in der Zukunft: Strukturen und Trends der Industriearbeit. Sigma, Berlin (2008)
3. Kuz, S., Heinicke, A., Schwichtenhövel, D., Mayer, M., Schlick, C.: The Effect of Anthropomorphic Movements of Assembly Robots on Human Prediction. In: Proceedings of the 4th International Conference on Applied Human Factors and Ergonomics (AHFE), pp. 1273–1281. USA Publishing, The Printing House, Stoughton (2012)
4. Kupferberg, A., Glasauer, S., Huber, M., Rickert, M., Knoll, A., Brandt, T.: Biological movement increases acceptance of humanoid robots as human partners in motor interaction. Journal of AI & Society 26(4), 339–345 (2011)
5. Duffy, B.: Anthropomorphism and The Social Robot. Special Issue on Socially Interactive Robots, Robotics and Autonomous Systems 42, 3–4 (2003)
6. Jokisch, D., Troje, N.: Die Wahrnehmung von absoluter Größe in biologischer Bewegung, Ruhr-Universität-Bochum (2001)
7. Göbel, M.: Verfahren zur intuitiven Programmierung von Industrierobotern durch Demonstration. In: Brecher, C., Klocke, F., Schmitt, R., Schuh, G. (eds.) Berichte aus der Produktionstechnik, Apprimus, Aachen (December 2012)

Ergonomic Assessment of Patient Barrow Lifting Technique Using Digital Human Modeling

Wen Cao, Meng Jiang, Ying Han, and Mohammad T. Khasawneh

Department of Systems Science and Industrial Engineering,
State University of New York at Binghamton, Binghamton, NY 13902, USA
mkhasawn@binghamton.edu

Abstract. Healthcare personnel involved in patient handling activities are often exposed to work-related musculoskeletal disorders (WMSDs). Therefore, the objective of this study is to conduct a comprehensive assessment of the Barrow lifting technique using digital human modeling (DHM). This study investigates the effects of patient weight and height (PWH), clinical staff weight and height (CSWH), clinical staff position (CSP) during lift, and clinical staff gender (CSG) on the clinical staff's low back compression force (LBCF). In addition, the impact of specific postural variables was evaluated using Comfort Assessment (CA). The results of this research showed that clinical staff in the larger weight and height percentiles that are male experienced higher LBCF. While the trunk of the clinical staff member was exposed to higher flexion angles that are still in the comfort range, the ratings associated with the trunk thigh and elbow were outside the comfort range. The results of this research are of paramount importance in designing lifting protocols and training programs with the ultimate goal being a reduction in the risk of developing low back injuries.

Keywords: Patient Barrow Lifting, Digital Human Modeling, Ergonomics.

1 Introduction

Work-related musculoskeletal disorders (WMSDs) are injuries to the soft tissues of human body, such as muscles, tendons, ligaments, and nerves after repeated exposure to work activities. Several factors, including lifting task parameters, awkward posture, and repetition, are listed by the National Institute for Occupational Safety and Health (NIOSH) as risk factors associated with WMSDs [1]. WMSDs could lead to uncomfortable feelings and even injuries that need surgeries, or even a termination of careers. This study focuses on WMSDs in the healthcare industry.

Healthcare staff members are impacted by WMSDs due to their involvement in many activities that involve risk factors, such as manual patient lifting, awkward position during patient care, and long working hours. In fact, nursing personnel have one of the highest rates of WMSDs based on a study by the U.S. Bureau of Labor Statistics [2]. The risk of nursing personnel developing WMSDs have been increasing during the recent years. In 2002, nursing aids ranked second and registered nurses

V.G. Duffy (Ed.): DHM/HCII 2013, Part II, LNCS 8026, pp. 20–29, 2013.

(RNs) ranked sixth in a list of at-risk occupations for strains and sprains [3]. In 2011, nursing aids ranked first and RNs ranked fifth, before construction workers who ranked seventh [2].

In addition to lost work time, a reduction in productivity, and possible career termination, WMSDs lead to an increase in the cost of medical care. In fact, about 12% of nurses leave the profession because of back injuries and 52% of them suffer from chronic back pain every year [4]. The facts that nurses leave their profession due to work-related injuries along with the shortage in this profession increase the workload for working nurses, making the working environment even more stressful.

Low back disorders (LBDs) have been found to be the most frequent WMSD, with an annual incident rate in the 30-60% range [5]. A variety of patient lifting tasks lead to LBDs [6]. For example, repeated patient lifting with outstretched arms and bent forward or even awkward postures could lead to injury. Preventive methods, such as lifting using devices, have been considered to assist nurses in those tasks, in an effort to reduce the risk of developing LBDs [7]. However, manual lifting is still widely used in healthcare facilities for various reasons, such as no adequate lifting devices and not enough awareness of safe or unsafe manual lifting [8].

Since nursing personnel are vulnerable to suffer from WMSDs, working posture analysis for patient lifting has been studied by many researchers. Traditional studies regarding patient lifting posture analysis are usually based on experimental studies using human subjects, which can be expensive and time-consuming. Therefore, this study chooses DHM to evaluate the ergonomics of the Barrow lifting technique, one the common manual patient lifting techniques. DHM helps address some of the limitations of traditional ergonomic assessment methods. The objective of this study is to analyze clinical staff's working posture during Barrow lifting. More specifically, this study evaluates the effect of patient characteristics (height and weight), clinical staff characteristics (gender, height and weight), and different positions and postures on lifting performance.

The remainder of this paper is organized as follows: Section 2 provides literature review about healthcare staff's working posture and patient lifting analyses. Section 3 illustrates the methodology used in this study. Section 4 presents the results and discussion. Finally, conclusions and future work are discussed in Section 5.

2   Literature Review

Most studies on patient lifting/handling were conducted using experimental methods or surveys [9]. The Ovako Working Posture Analysis System (OWAS) is one posture recording technique used in experimental studies. OWAS assigns a four-digit code to record the positions of various body segments. It can also reflect the level of risks. Hignett [10] adopted this system to evaluate nurses working postures for patient handling and non-patient handling tasks to record each observation by the position of the back, arms, legs, and estimated load. Statistical analysis was used to compare the results between patient handling tasks and non-patient handling tasks. The comparison showed that the percentage of risky working postures for patient handling activities was much higher than those of non-patient handling activities. The potential limitation associated with the OWAS system is that the coding approaches could only give broad range rather than accurate information of postures [11]. Other types of posture recording systems have also been developed; however, most of these techniques are limited in their ability to provide precise evaluation of body posture and cannot effectively assess WMSDs risk factors, such as vibration and repetition.

With the development in observational techniques, postures can be recorded using videotape or computerized methods. Winkelmolen et al. [12] conducted a laboratory-based study to evaluate five manual lifting techniques by using a video recording system with the help of markers attached to several parts on the human body. The five manual lifting techniques were: Australian lift, Orthodox lift, Barrow lift, Through-arm lift, and Under-arm lift, as shown in Fig. 1. Ten female volunteers were involved in the experiments and another two volunteers with different weight were recruited as patients. Posture evaluation, compressive forces at the lower back, and perceived stress were used as evaluation indicators. More specifically, several indicators were used for posture evaluation, both at the beginning and end of the lifting, including back rotation and lateral flexion. While the results showed that patient weight did not lead to significant difference on posture evaluation, the five lifting techniques did have impact on the evaluation measures [12]. The Barrow lift was identified with the most significant compressive force and both Barrow and Orthodox lifts were observed with more subjective stress than the other techniques. Even though this study laid a good foundation for future study of manual lifting techniques, several limitations in recording and collecting data can be found, such as the difficulties in recording all motions with the videotaping system and missing values [12].

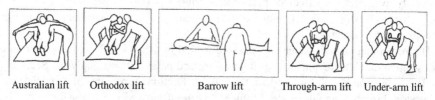

Australian lift   Orthodox lift   Barrow lift   Through-arm lift   Under-arm lift

Fig. 1. Five manual lifting techniques [12]

Freitag et al. [13] conducted a study to evaluate the stressful trunk postures of nurses by using computer-assisted recording and long-term analysis of musculoskeletal loads (CUELA) system, a computer-aided recording system. The system was attached to subjects with sensors on the joints to capture data about trunk and leg angles, as shown in Fig. 2. With the help of sensors, trunk movement can be assessed in 3D planes. The data was sent back to a computer that can re-construct the real body motions. The idea behind the ergonomic assessment was to investigate whether the joint positions deviated from neutral position severely. The higher the deviations from neutral position, the higher the risk of developing injuries.

Posture analysis can also be conducted using direct assessment methods, such as electric equipment that can output an electric signal related to human body's intersegmental displacement. The lumbar motion monitor (LMM), as an example of electro-goniometer, is used to provide 3D information about trunk position, as well as its velocity and acceleration. Electromyography (EMG) is another widely used tool that can indicate the levels of muscle activity by generating various signal amplitudes for further analysis. For example, Marras et al. [6] used EMG-assisted model to assess the spinal loading for several patient lifting techniques (single person lifting vs. team lifting) by attaching bi-polar electrodes at muscles of interest. The LMM was also applied to collect instantaneous 3D data as shown in Fig. 2.

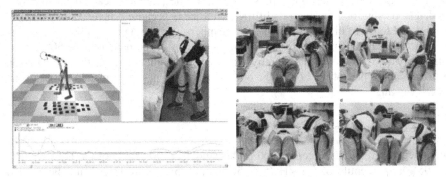

Fig. 2. CUELA measurement system, LMM and EMG systems in use [6], [13]

As stated earlier, there are several limitations for using experimental methods with human subjects, such as recruitment of subjects, workplace interruptions, the need for randomization, cost, convenience, etc. [14]. There is also the potential risk of exposing the subjects to risk or injury in experiments that involve lifting. Another approach for evaluating stresses on the human body or workload is survey analysis of self-reports, which can be in the form of rating scales through interviews or focused groups. Engels et al. [15] conducted a study to identify the risk factors associated with WMSDs for nurses using a questionnaire that was later analyzed using statistical analysis. The limitations of such methods include the subjective nature of the results, which may not be accurate or precise, as well as the lack of quantification of stresses caused by certain work postures.

In the past decade or so, digital human modeling has gained more interest in academia and industry [16-18]. Using virtual or computer-based environments, DHM allows for a wide range of applications including studies that involve crash simulations. In the healthcare domain, Samson [14] evaluated the ergonomics of patient lifting postures of paramedics using DHM. With the help of DHM, lower back stress was captured after analyzing different working postures while incorporating the anthropometric characteristics of paramedics and different lifting tools. Moreover, Salaskar [19] conducted an evaluation of laparoscopic surgery using DHM. The effects of laparoscopic monitor position, table height, and clinical staff's posture were measured using Rapid Upper Limb Assessment (RULA) score in the simulated environment. Finally, Cao [20] conducted a study to evaluate the sonography workplace and posture parameters using DHM. The sonography related work, such as typing and scanning were evaluated in an experimental design that includes percentile, gender, and posture using RULA, LBD and CA. In this research, the Barrow lifting technique is evaluated using digital human modeling.

3   Methodology

In this study, JACK 7.1 is used to develop a simulated model of the Barrow lifting technique. This research simulates the process in which two clinical staff members move one flat lying patient from a bed to another bed of the same height using Barrow lift. This technique requires the clinical staff to grasp each other's hand under the patient's waist [12]. More specifically, one person puts the other hand under patient's thighs, while the other person supports the patient's head by his/her free hand. The reason for choosing this lifting technique is because it involves asymmetric posture and load for the two clinical staff members. According to Winkelmolen et al. [12], the clinical staff member that lifts the lower part of the patient takes 60% of the patient's whole body weight, thereby experiencing higher loading than the person lifting the upper part of the body. The other person assumes the remaining 40% of the patient weight.

3.1   Experiment Design

The independent variables considered in this study are: percentile of PWH (5%, 50%, and 95%), percentile of CSWH (5%, 50%, and 95%), CSP (Head and Foot), and CSG (Male and Female). Therefore, there are 36 treatment combinations in this study. Throughout the study, a trunk flexion angle of 45° was maintained. Table 1 shows the combinations of all the experimental scenarios that have been simulated and tested in this research.

Table 1. Experimental combinations

Combin ation	PWH/CSWH/CSP/CSG	Combin ation	PWH/CSWH/CSP/CSG	Combin ation	PWH/CSWH/CSP/CSG
1	50th/5th/H/F	13	95th/95th/H/F	25	95th/50th/F/M
2	5th/50th/F/M	14	5th/50th/F/F	26	95th/50th/H/M
3	95th/5th/F/F	15	95th/95th/H/M	27	5th/50th/H/M
4	95th/50th/H/F	16	5th/95th/H/F	28	95th/50th/F/F
5	50th/95th/F/M	17	50th/95th/H/F	29	50th/50th/H/F
6	5th/50th/H/F	18	5th/5th/F/F	30	95th/95th/F/M
7	5th/5th/F/M	19	95th/95th/F/F	31	50th/5th/F/F
8	95th/5th/F/M	20	5th/95th/F/F	32	50th/5th/H/M
9	5th/95th/H/M	21	95th/5th/H/M	33	5th/5th/H/F
10	95th/5th/F/M	22	95th/5th/F/F	34	50th/50th/F/F
11	50th/50th/F/M	23	50th/50th/H/M	35	5th/5th/F/F
12	50th/95th/H/M	24	5th/95th/F/M	36	50th/5th/F/M

For each experimental scenario, data is collected on the L4/L5 force and comfort ratings for each person. For illustration purposes, Fig. 3 shows the simulated patient room, where two clinical staff members are lifting a patient from one bed to another using the Barrow lifting technique.

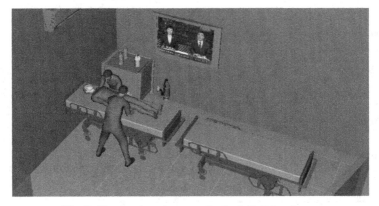

Fig. 3. Simulated environment in the Jack 7.1 software

3.2   Data Collection

The LBA and CA tools were used to evaluate the various treatment combinations, as shown in Fig. 4. LBA can measure the LBCF and compares the results with NOISH's compression action limits of 3400 N and maximum limits of 6400N. CA evaluates human posture parameters, limitations, and comfort ratings based on Porter's [21] database, which is already built in the Jack 7.1 software. In CA, green color indicates that the posture is located in the comfort zone and yellow color indicates that the posture located outside the comfort zone.

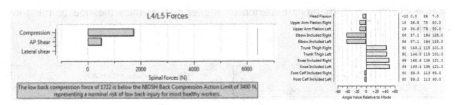

Fig. 4. LBA and CA analyses tools

4   Results

4.1   LBA

As shown in Fig. 5, out of the 36 combinations tested, only three have an LBCF that is lower than NIOSH's action limit of 3400N (safe region), indicating a nominal risk of low back injury for most healthy workers. A total of 31 combinations are above the 3400N action limit (but below the 6400N maximum limit), representing an increased risk of low back injury for some workers. The LBCF for the remaining two is above NIOSH's maximum limit of 6400N, representing an increased risk of low back injury for most workers, thereby requiring an immediate reengineering of the job.

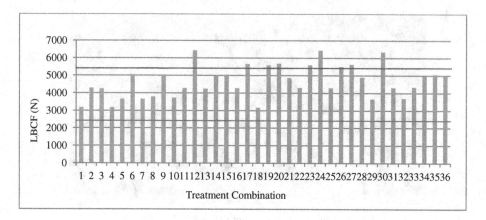

Fig. 5. LBCF analysis results

The ANOVA results in Table 2 show that the CSWH and CSG have significant impact on the LBCF at a 0.05 significance level. The results showed that the following interaction effects are significant: CSP*CSG, PWH*CSWH*CSP, and CSWH*CSP*CSG. The other interaction effects are not significant. As shown in Fig. 6, the LBCF increases when the percentile of CSWH increase. Fig. 6 also shows that males experience higher low back force than female clinical staff. However, the percentile of PWH and CSP do not have a significant effect on LBCF, which is consistent with the literature [12]. Furthermore, for a 95th percentile PWH, the head position clinical staff member experiences higher LBCF than the one at the foot position.

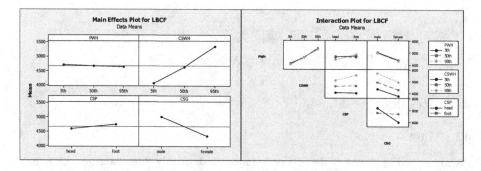

Fig. 6. Main and interaction effects plots for LBCF

Table 1. ANOVA results for LBCF

Source	DF	Seq SS	Adj SS	Adj MS	F	P
PWH	2	21484	21484	10742	0.07	0.935
CSWH	2	9918768	9918768	4959384	31.31	0.004
CSP	1	186480	186480	186480	1.18	0.339
CSG	1	3992670	3992670	3992670	25.21	0.007
PWH*CSWH	4	1637	1637	409	0	1
PWH*CSP	2	416321	416321	208161	1.31	0.364
PWH*CSG	2	2063	2063	1032	0.01	0.994
CSWH*CSP	2	387424	387424	193712	1.22	0.385
CSWH*CSG	2	53414	53414	26707	0.17	0.851
CSP*CSG	1	2798371	2798371	2798371	17.67	0.014
PWH*CSWH*CSP	4	7556981	7556981	1889245	11.93	0.017
PWH*CSWH*CSG	4	6262	6262	1566	0.01	1
PWH*CSP*CSG	2	264717	264717	132358	0.84	0.497
CSWH*CSP*CSG	2	2647028	2647028	1323514	8.36	0.037
Error	4	633586	633586	158397		
Total	35	28887207				

4.2   CA

The comfort rating depends on the output from major joints, including head flexion angle, head rotation angle, upper arm flexion, etc. In addition to the lower and upper bounds for the comfort rating, Jack 7.1 also provides the mode value, which represents the most comfortable angle. If the output is between the two limits, the posture is within the comfortable zone; if not, the posture is uncomfortable. The closer the output to the mode value for a specific joint, the more comfortable the posture associated with that posture. As shown in Fig. 7, the trunk thigh and knee are outside the comfort range. Fig. 7 also shows that the upper arm flexion and elbow included are in the comfort range. While the upper body experiences higher flexion angle that is near the comfort range's limit, the trunk thigh and elbow included are outside the comfort range.

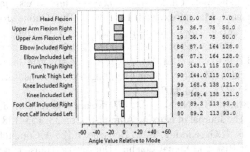

Fig. 7. Comfort ratings of 50th percentile male based on Porter's [21] database

5   Conclusions and Future Work

This study used DHM to assess the effect of percentile of CSWH, CSG, CSP during the lift, and the percentile of PWH when using the Barrow lifting technique. The impact of those variables on the LBCF on the L4/L5 of the clinical staff was investigated. With respect to position, there was no difference observed between the head and foot position clinical staff member, even though the person that lifts the patient's lower body experiences greater loading.

The results showed that the LBCF increases when the CSWH percentile increases. Also, male clinical staff members experience higher LBCF than females. The PWH percentile and the CSP have no significant impact on the LBCF. The head position clinical staff was observed to have slightly higher LBCF compared to that at the foot position. Even though three interaction effects were found to be significant, the interaction effect between CSP and CSG was the most visible (Fig. 6). Even though it remains in the comfort zone, the upper body of the clinical staff member experiences higher flexion angle. The trunk thigh and elbow included are outside the comfort range. Hence, keeping an appropriate distance between the clinical staff member and the patient bed, as well as avoiding significant bending of the upper body can keep the human body in the comfort zone.

Future work in this area will expand the modeling beyond having clinical staff members of the same percentile involved in the lifting process. In addition, since this study maintained a 45° trunk flexion angle, other angles can be considered in future studies. Furthermore, additional independent factors, such as patient body mass index, patient gender, and patient bed height can be considered in future research. Finally, the results of the Barrow lifting can be compared with other manual lifting techniques.

References

1. Bernard, B.P.: Musculoskeletal disorders and workplace factors (NIOSH Publication No. 97-141). National Institute for Occupational Safety and Health (NIOSH), Cincinnati (1997)
2. U.S. Bureau of Labor Statistics, http://www.bls.gov/news.release/osh2.t18.htm
3. de Castro, A.B.: Handle With Care®: The American Nurses Association's Campaign to Address Work-Related Musculoskeletal Disorders. The Online Journal of Issues in Nursing 9 (2004), http://www.nursingworld.org/MainMenuCategories/ANAMarketplace/ANAPeriodicals/OJIN/TableofContents/Volume92004/No3Sept04/HandleWithCare.aspx#deCastro
4. Motacki, K., Motacki, L.M.: Safe Patient Handling and Movement in a Pediatric Setting. Pediatric Nursing 35, 221–225 (2009)
5. Trinkoff, A.M., Brady, B., Nielsen, K.: Workplace Prevention and Musculoskeletal Injuries in Nurses. The Journal of Nursing Administration 33, 153–158 (2003)
6. Marras, W.S., Davis, K.G., Kirking, B.C., Bertsche, P.K.: A Comprehensive Analysis of Low-Back Disorder Risk and Spinal Loading During the Transferring and Repositioning of Patients Using Different Techniques. Ergonomics 42, 904–926 (1999)

7. Elford, W., Straker, L., Strauss, G.: Patient Handling With and Without Slings: an Analysis of the Risk of Injury to the Lumbar Spine. Applied Ergonomics 31, 185–200 (2000)
8. DuBose, T., Donahue, T.: Taking the Pain Out of Patient Handling. American Nurse Today 1, 37–43 (2006)
9. Li, G., Buckle, P.: Current Techniques for Assessing Physical Exposure to Work-Related Musculoskeletal Risks, with Emphasis on Posture-Based Methods. Ergonomics 42, 674–695 (1999)
10. Hignett, S.: Postural Analysis of Nursing Work. Applied Ergonomics 27, 171–176 (1996)
11. Keyserling, W.M.: Postural Analysis of the Trunk and Shoulders in Simulated Real Time. Ergonomics 29, 569–583 (1986)
12. Winkelmolen, G.H., Landeweerd, J.A., Drost, M.R.: An Evaluation of Patient Lifting Techniques. Ergonomics 37, 921–932 (1994)
13. Freitag, S., Ellegast, R., Dulon, M., Nienhaus, A.: Quantitative Measurement of Stressful Trunk Postures in Nursing Professions. The Annals of Occupational Hygiene 51, 385–395 (2007)
14. Samson, A.: Digital Human Modeling for Ergonomic Assessment of Patient Lifting by Paramedics. Master Thesis, Binghamton University (2009)
15. Engels, J.A., van der Gulden, J.W.J., Senden, T.F., van't Hof, B.: Work Related Risk Factors for Musculoskeletal Complaints in the Nursing Profession: Results of a Questionnaire Survey. Occupational and Environmental Medicine 53, 636–641 (1996)
16. Duffy, V.G.: Handbook of Digital Human Modeling: Research for Applied Ergonomics and Human Factors Engineering. CRC Press, Inc. (2008)
17. Li, K., Duffy, V.G., Zheng, L.: Universal Accessibility Assessments through Virtual Interactive Design. International Journal of Human Factors Modelling and Simulation 1(1), 52–68 (2006)
18. Demirel, H.O., Duffy, V.G.: Applications of Digital Human Modeling in Industry. In: Duffy, V.G. (ed.) HCII 2007 and DHM 2007. LNCS, vol. 4561, pp. 824–832. Springer, Heidelberg (2007)
19. Salaskar, S.: Digital Human Modeling for Ergonomics Evaluation of Laparoscopic Surgery. Master Thesis, Binghamton University (2010)
20. Cao, W.: Ergonomic Assessment of Sonography Workplace and Posture Parameters Using Digital Human Modeling. Master Thesis, Binghamton University (2012)
21. Porter, J.M., Gyi, D.E.: Exploring the Optimum Posture for Driver Comfort. International Journal of Vehicle Design 19(3) (1998)

An Interface Design Method for E-commerce Sites' Homepage Considering Users' Emotions

Fu Guo, Yaqin Cao, Meng Wang, Yi Ding, and Lin Wei Liu

Department of Management Science and Engineering, School of Business Administration,
Northeastern University, Shenyang, China, P.R.C.
fguo@mail.neu.edu.cn

Abstract. This paper proposes a useful method to understand the relationship between web design elements, Kansei evaluation and users' emotions based on Kansei Engineering, taking E-commerce sites for example. Firstly it establishes customers' evaluation image words through a survey of the web interface preference. Then it collects the data of Kansei evaluation and users' emotions to different websites by an emotion assessment test. Lastly it builds the relation models between web design elements, Kansei evaluation and users' emotions using the quantification theory I and partial least squares (PLS) method, and confirms the validity of the models.

Keywords: E-commerce, Emotion, Kansei engineering, Web design, PLS.

1   Introduction

According to the China Internet Network Information Center (CNNIC) 31th "China Internet Development Statistics Report" released in January 2013, Nearly 242 million Chinese people joined the online shopping army. As the netizens change their consuming habit, many businesses have to break away from the traditional mode of operation, using advanced network marketing model to pursue new growth points [1].

Online sales need the support of e-commerce sites. To enterprise, the interfaces of e-commerce sites are not only windows where the enterprises display their image, but also an important means to show the goods and help the user to complete the purchase. It has been an explosion of activity in recent years that how to design a web interface which can grab user's attention and make a better experience for the user.

Presently, study on the web interface design is focused on the following three aspects: usability research, aesthetic research and emotion research.

1.1   Usability Research in the Web Design

The ISO 9241 standard defines website usability as the "effectiveness, efficiency and satisfaction with which specified users achieve specified goals in particular environments [2]." Dr. Jakob Nielsen, a pioneer in the field of usability, proposed usability

V.G. Duffy (Ed.): DHM/HCII 2013, Part II, LNCS 8026, pp. 30–39, 2013.

guidelines in a book of his "usability engineering", which become the main reference for the later scholars to conduct usability studies [3]. Subsequent studies have mostly concentrated on the methods of website usability evaluation and testing. Currently, usability evaluation and testing methods are already quite mature. In general, there are two kinds of methods: One is the analysis or empirical approach [4], For example, Paper [5] verified the important indicators to make the website usable through an empirical approach. The other is evaluation method, including expert evaluation, user evaluation and model evaluation. [6].

1.2   Aesthetic Research in the Web Design

The early research on web design focused on objective indicators of efficiency, while ignoring the important role of the visual aesthetic elements in web design. The word "aesthetics" comes from the Greek Aesthesis, which original meaning is sensory feelings. Following Nielsen, many scholars discovered aesthetic factors can significantly affect the users' usability perception and satisfaction of website through empirical approach [7].

Users interact with the web mainly through some aesthetic elements (such as text and image) on the web, which should be organized according to visual hierarchy to guide users to browse web naturally [8]. Aesthetic element, such as animation, color, style of the text and position of the image, plays a meaningful role in the users' perception on the website [7].

1.3   Emotion Research

Emotion is mainly concern with people's psychological response to external stimuli, such as happy, anger, hate and so on [9,10,11]. The relationship between web page design elements and users' emotions is one of the hot topics which still hold numerous researchers' attention.

Which design elements will impact users' emotions? A lot of scholars has studied on this problem and drawn some valuable conclusions. Paper [12] examined the impact of four web site interface features (structure of information presentation, navigation, text, visual aspects) on the user's emotions. It found that structure of information presentation and navigation significantly influence the emotional state. In addition, the complexity of the web page is also important factors that affect the user's emotion [13]. Experimental study demonstrated that visual complexity of websites has multiple effects on human emotion [14].

For the quantitative relationship between the design elements and emotion, a small number of scholars have done some exploratory research. Paper [15] build a relationship model reflecting different design elements and users' Kansei evaluation of the e-commerce website by applying Kansei Engineering method. Paper [16] established a quantitative relationship between the design elements and Kansei evaluation with regression analysis. However, they could not explain the relationship between emotion and design elements, as well as why the two have relations. In addition, the results do not have a cross-cultural background.

To summarize, the following limitations exist in the current research:

1. Focusing on theory research and practical guidance in web design is far from sufficient. Currently research mainly concerned in clarifying the relationships among various design elements that affect the users' emotions. However, it rarely points out which specific design elements can induce what kind of emotion and put forward some methods to improve the web design. Furthermore, it is difficult to apply their findings to web design in China because of cultural differences.
2. Divide design elements into usability elements and aesthetic elements, and study its impact on emotion respectively. In fact, a lot of web design elements belong to the usability elements, and the aesthetic elements as well, such as the navigation bar and search box, where usability and aesthetics cannot be divided.

Based on Kansei Engineering, it establishes a Kansei evaluation scale for the evaluation of e-commerce sites suitable for the Chinese environment. Then, users' Kansei and emotional evaluation data is obtained in an experiment. With these results, it establishes the relation model between the Kansei words, emotional words and web design elements. It is organized as follows. In Section 2, a Kansei evaluation scale is established. In Section 3, an experiment is carried out to obtain Kansei and emotional evaluation data. In Section 4, a model reflecting the relationship of Kansei words and emotional words is proposed by PLS which is validated. In Section 5, the models reflecting the relationship between Kansei words, emotional words and design elements are proposed by PLS which are validated. A conclusion is given at the end of this paper.

2   Scale Building of User Kansei Evaluation

2.1   The Selection of Representative Websites

There are three important design factors affecting the users' emotion response on the appearance design of website in the research domain, that is layout, the whole color set and complexity of website [17-19]. So the representative websites are selected according to these factors.

1. A total of 80 websites were initially collected depending on some navigation websites such as hao123, hao360 etc. and the statistics of websites ranking.
2. A classification was made on these 80 websites. Three classes (i.e. corner style, up-down style and lane style) were determined for the difference of layout. Then light (white, cream-colored etc.) and deep colors (dark red, dark grey etc.) were classified according to the website's hue. Finally classification was made based on the complexity of websites (the size of homepage saved as picture). Three websites not used usually were chose as the representative websites to refrain from the effects of users' habit, that is, www.yifu.com, www.crucco.com and www.masamaso.com.

2.2   The Collection of Kansei Words

The Kansei words were selected according to web design guidebook, textbook of web visual design, survey reports and pertinent literatures, and have a high frequency of use. 14 words were determined after a preliminary investigation. And bipolar adjectives were used for accurate measure of users' Kansei evaluation on web interface, shown as table 1.

Table 1. Kansei Words for E-commerce Web Sites

No.	Kansei Words	No.	Kansei Words
V1	childish-mature	V8	stodgy-artistic
V2	disorder-concise	V9	rough-delicate
V3	neglected-impressive	V10	prim-lively
V4	classic-modern	V11	abrupt-coordinating
V5	dim-clear	V12	discourtesy-courtesy
V6	ordinary-creative	V13	dull-interesting
V7	complicated-simple	V14	feminine-manly

2.3   Questionnaire Design

100 undergraduate students (46 males, 54 females) from Northeastern University participated in the Kansei evaluation from 18 to 27 years. Participants were asked to browse and interact with webs selected in section 2.1 for simple tasks (e.g. find a product), then fill the 7-point questionnaire from -3 to 3 composed of 14 bipolar words shown as table 1.

2.4   The Establishment of Kansei Evaluation Scale

Correlation analysis was made between Kansei words, of which V1, V4, V7, and V14 were deleted for lack of correlation with the whole evaluation. Then reliability analysis indicates a high reliable of the scale with Cronbach alpha coefficient all above 0.8 for Kansei words and the whole evaluation. Two factors were extracted by factor analysis for verifying the structural validity of the scale. They are named as aesthetic factor (V3, V4, V8, V1, V5, V6) and Kansei factor (V7、V9、V2、V10).

3   The Experiment of Kansei and Emotion Evaluation on E-commerce Web

The goal of this experiment in this section is to collect Kansei evaluation and emotion values of users after browsing webs.

3.1   The Selection of Emotional Experience Scale

Basic emotions and emotion changes caused by cognition alternation from external stimuli are main emotions of human being according to emotional psychology. Emotion changes can be obtained by calculating the difference between user's whole emotion(measured by PAD)and component of emotion caused by user's disposition (measured by personality questionnaire FFM)when user' whole emotion is determined [20,21].

3.2   Experiment Design and Data Collection

9 modish e-commerce webs of apparel were selected as stimuli. 20 students (10 males, 10 females) from Northeastern University participated in the experiment. The subjects have prior experience of online shopping aging from 18 to 30. The major steps of this experiment are as follows: in the preliminary procedure, the subjects were required to fill the FFM several days before the experiment. Then the 9 webs were evenly divided into three groups. There are five minutes for relaxing before subjects browsing the first group webs. PAD and Kansei evaluation scale were filled by subjects when finish browsing one web. Then repeat the foregoing step until the three groups webs all browsed by subjects.

4   The Relation Modeling between Kansei Evaluation and Emotional Experience

4.1   Model Building Based on PLS Regression

A regression model with the free variable set X of Kansei words (from V1 to V10) and the dependent variable set Y of three emotional dimensions was built respectively. As shown in formula 1, 2 and 3.

$$P=2.0238-0.0393V1-0.0834V2+0.2180V3+0.1841V4+0.2992V5-0.0212V6-$$
$$0.2855V7+0.0672V8+0.2593V9+0.1262V10 \quad (1)$$

$$A=3.7194-0.0392V1-0.0699V2+0.1437V3+0.1247V4+0.2088V5-0.0284V6-$$
$$0.2190V7+0.0389V8+0.1671V9+0.0762V10 \quad (2)$$

$$D=5.9332-0.0277V1-0.0326V2+0.0091V3+0.0142V4+0.0351V5-0.0292V6-0.0722V7-$$
$$0.0077V8+0.0102V9-0.0084V10 \quad (3)$$

4.2   Model Verification

The predictive figure was made with the predictive values of pleasure, arousal and dominance as the abscissa and the observed values as ordinate to test the validity of models. There is little difference between predictive values and observed if all the points distributed evenly near the diagonal. The results are shown as fig.1.

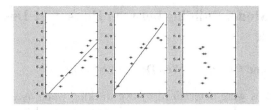

Fig. 1. The predictive result of PLS regression models

From Fig.1, the observed values of pleasure and arousal keep in line with the predictive according to PLS regression models, while the PLS model is invalid for the dominance. A survey was done to test the validity of models further. 10 questionnaires were issued to evaluate three webs randomly selected from the nine representatives, and the mean values of Kansei evaluation were used as inputs to the PLS models of pleasure and arousal. A comparison between predictive values from equations and observed indicates the difference was not statistically significant.

4.3   Interpretations of the Models

Kansei words can interpret pleasure and arousal well and have a consistency for them from the foregoing results. Pertinent literatures indicate that moderate intensity positive emotion is conducive to promote thinking and decision making, overstrain with high arousal and otherwise inadvertency when users browse webs not good for producing positive emotion. Hence there is a positive correlation between pleasure and arousal indicating that well designed webs using appropriate factors can keep balanced state of pleasure and arousal when users browse webs. Moreover Kansei words are hardly to interpret and predict dominance, used to describe users' feelings on web interface, while dominance is just an emotional experience during interactive with webs. So there is no obvious relation between them.

In detail, Kansei words such as V3, V4, V5, V7, and V9 can interpret users' emotion well, of which V3, V4, V5, and V9 have a positive effect indicating stronger pleasure and arousal with higher scores. V3, V4, and V5 belong to aesthetic factors meaning lively and bright colors (e.g. red), and innovative as well as artistic factors can bring pleasure to users and maintain a level of arousal to attract users' attention simultaneously. And V9 is one factor of sensory. Users will have better emotional experience when integrating emotion into product design according to Norman. Some design factors are required to bring users warmth and comfort and maintain users' pleasure and arousal. V7 has a negative effect on users' emotion for dynamic design factors in some webs. While these dynamic factors make users feel boring and distract users' attention as well such as products images change in some intervals and banner ads rotation.

The other Kansei words (i.e. V1, V2, V6, V8, and V10) are moderate words and have a stable level on pleasure and arousal. Take V1 for an example, it means that simple and refreshing webs make users pleasure. While users feel boring and have a low arousal when browsing webs with too simple contents.

5   Relation Model Building between Homepage Design and User Experience

5.1   Extraction and Coding of Web Design Elements

Major design features were determined by eye tracking when users browsing homepages of e-commerce websites. Categories of each item were obtained by comparison, analysis, filter and consult from designers based on the 80 webs' homepages determined in section 2.1.

Table 2. The Design Elements of E-commerce Web Sites' Homepage

Major design features	Item	Category			
The overall design features (A)	Color (A_1)	Light tone (A_{11})	Dark tone (A_{12})		
	Complexity (A_2)	Less than three (A_{21})	More than three (A_{22})		
	Layout (A_3)	Left-corner (A_{31})	Right-corner (A_{32})	Up-down (A_{33})	Three-column (A_{34})
	Ratio of text and picture (A_4)	Mainly by the text (A_{41})	Equally (A_{42})	Mainly by the picture (A_{43})	
Navigation (B)	Background color (B_1)	White (B_{11})	Red (B_{12})	Charcoal grey (B_{13})	
	Interactive effect (B_2)	Label (B_{21})	Drop-down (B_{22})	Ordinary link (B_{23})	
List of goods category (C)	Interactive effect (C_1)	Down-suspension (C_{11})	Ordinary link (C_{12})	Right-suspension box (C_{13})	
Banner (D)	Form (D_1)	Pictures (D_{11})	Pictures and texts (D_{12})		
	Dynamic effect (D_2)	Gradual change (D_{21})	Up-down (D_{22})		
Goods display system (E)	Way of display (E_1)	Static (E_{11})	Rotation display (E_{12})		
	Way of picture segmentation (E_2)	Boundary clear (E_{21})	Blank (E_{22})		
	Way of goods' compound mode (E_3)	Irregular (E_{31})	Uniform size (E_{32})	Matched (E_{33})	

Combined with the classification of variable in table 2, the 9 representatives were coded. Different items of one design elements are mutually exclusive in each web. So 0 and 1 were used to distinguish them, 0 represents no item in web design, and the opposite is the other way around.

5.2   Relation Model Building between Homepage Design and Kansei Evaluation

Model Building. Partial least square estimation was applied for insufficient samples with 31 design elements and only 9 representative samples to construct the relation model of Kansei words and design variables, the contribution rate of Kansei words of their corresponding design variables. Take "disorder-concise" as an example, the corresponding model is shown as formula 4.

$$
Y = 3.771 + \begin{pmatrix} 0.634A_{11} \\ -0.662A_{12} \end{pmatrix} + \begin{pmatrix} -0.274A_{21} \\ 0.246A_{22} \end{pmatrix} + \begin{pmatrix} -0.256A_{31} \\ 0.133A_{32} \\ 0.491A_{33} \\ -0.565B_{34} \end{pmatrix} + \begin{pmatrix} -0.614A_{41} \\ 0.157A_{42} \\ 0.352A_{43} \end{pmatrix} + \begin{pmatrix} 0.067B_{11} \\ 0.740B_{12} \\ -0.748B_{13} \end{pmatrix}
$$

$$
+ \begin{pmatrix} -0.267B_{21} \\ 0.086B_{22} \\ 0.157B_{23} \end{pmatrix} + \begin{pmatrix} 0.157C_{11} \\ 0.342C_{12} \\ -0.614C_{13} \end{pmatrix} + \begin{pmatrix} -0.118D_{11} \\ 0.095D_{12} \end{pmatrix} + \begin{pmatrix} 0.277D_{21} \\ -0.3D_{22} \end{pmatrix} + \begin{pmatrix} 0.114E_{11} \\ -0.142E_{12} \end{pmatrix} + \begin{pmatrix} -0.368E_{21} \\ 0.345E_{22} \end{pmatrix} + \begin{pmatrix} 0.009E_{31} \\ -0.165E_{32} \\ 0.106E_{33} \end{pmatrix} \quad (4)
$$

As can be seen from formula 4, the first level of navigation has the highest contribution rate while banner lowest indicating that background color of navigation must be red to satisfy users and the deploying style of banner has no effect on users. There are 11 coefficients of design variables below zero. These variables will make the web disorder, of which four design variables have the worst effect i.e. dark grey background used for navigation, deep color background applied for the whole web, three-column layout or left corner and text dominant.

The following design solution is made to obtain a concise web from foregoing analysis. Firstly the color of the overall web should be light and has a layout not more than 3 columns. And up-down style should be made with pictures dominant. The background color of navigation should be red. Ordinary link should be used for interaction and category list, banners with text and picture of gradient color and static style for products deploying, leaving blank between pictures and same size pictures for product portfolio.

Model Test. Data from section 3 and "disorder-concise" were used for model test. 4 webs were selected randomly from the 9 representatives. A comparison was did between the predictive value obtain from regression models and scores of Kansei words obtained via questionnaires. Paired sample test was did indicating insignificant difference between predictive values and observed and the models are valid.

5.3   The Relation Model between Homepage Design and User Emotion

Model Building. Similar regression equations can be determined by applying PLS regression analysis to construct the relation between homepage design variables and user emotion. The formulas are 5 and 6.

$$
\bar{P} = 4.9387 + \begin{pmatrix} 0.2922A_{11} \\ -0.1141A_{12} \end{pmatrix} + \begin{pmatrix} 0.3046A_{21} \\ -0.1283A_{22} \end{pmatrix} + \begin{pmatrix} -0.1512A_{31} \\ -0.2768A_{32} \\ 0.3722A_{33} \\ 0.2926B_{34} \end{pmatrix} + \begin{pmatrix} -0.0999A_{41} \\ 0.2268A_{42} \\ 0.0623A_{43} \end{pmatrix} + \begin{pmatrix} 0.0983B_{11} \\ 0.2627B_{12} \\ -0.2372B_{13} \end{pmatrix}
$$

$$
+ \begin{pmatrix} -0.064B_{21} \\ 0.017B_{22} \\ -0.2372B_{23} \end{pmatrix} + \begin{pmatrix} 0.2194C_{11} \\ -0.2489C_{12} \\ 0.2268C_{13} \end{pmatrix} + \begin{pmatrix} 0.1298D_{11} \\ 0.0192D_{12} \end{pmatrix} + \begin{pmatrix} -0.61D_{21} \\ 0.21D_{22} \end{pmatrix} + \begin{pmatrix} -0.2275E_{11} \\ 0.4056E_{12} \end{pmatrix} + \begin{pmatrix} 0.0034E_{21} \\ 0.1456E_{22} \end{pmatrix} + \begin{pmatrix} 0.0498E_{31} \\ 0.132E_{32} \\ -0.0087E_{33} \end{pmatrix} \quad (5)
$$

$$\bar{A} = 5.282 + \begin{pmatrix} 0.2767A_{11} \\ -0.1187A_{12} \end{pmatrix} + \begin{pmatrix} 0.2726A_{21} \\ -0.1146A_{22} \end{pmatrix} + \begin{pmatrix} -0.1424A_{31} \\ 0.2368A_{32} \\ 0.3171A_{33} \\ 0.2768B_{34} \end{pmatrix} + \begin{pmatrix} -1.016A_{41} \\ 0.2193A_{42} \\ 0.053A_{43} \end{pmatrix} + \begin{pmatrix} 0.079B_{11} \\ 0.2529B_{12} \\ -0.2232B_{13} \end{pmatrix}$$
$$+ \begin{pmatrix} 0.0406B_{21} \\ 0.065B_{22} \\ 0.1734B_{23} \end{pmatrix} + \begin{pmatrix} 0.1734C_{11} \\ -0.2158C_{12} \\ 0.2193C_{13} \end{pmatrix} + \begin{pmatrix} 0.1089D_{11} \\ 0.0233D_{12} \end{pmatrix} + \begin{pmatrix} -0.0446D_{21} \\ 0.1768D_{22} \end{pmatrix} + \begin{pmatrix} -0.191E_{11} \\ 0.349E_{12} \end{pmatrix} + \begin{pmatrix} 0.0185E_{21} \\ 0.1136E_{22} \end{pmatrix} + \begin{pmatrix} 0.0567E_{31} \\ 0.0976E_{32} \\ -0.0033E_{33} \end{pmatrix} \tag{6}$$

The following design solution should be made to obtain a pleasure and arousal web from formulas 5 and 6. Firstly the color of the overall web should be light tone and has a layout not more than 3 columns with an up-down style. And the content of webs should keep a balance between text and pictures, the background color of navigation should be red with an ordinary link, the category list should be played with a right-suspending box style, banners with combination in a up-down style, leaving blank between pictures and keeping the same size of pictures for product portfolio in a rotation display style.

Model Test. 4 webs were selected randomly from the 9 representatives based on the data obtained from emotion evaluation in section 3. Paired sample test was did indicating insignificant difference between predictive values and observed of pleasure and arousal and the models are valid.

6   Conclusion

Based on e-commerce website as the research object, it established a Kansei evaluation scale, extracted key web design elements, and obtained user's Kansei and emotional evaluation data of 9 typical website through an experiment of Kansei and emotional evaluation on e-commerce web. It established the relation model between the Kansei words, emotional words and web design elements using PLS and verified the validity of the models. The results demonstrated that design elements of e-commerce website can be selected according to users' pleasure and arousal .That is, the website can be can be designed according to users' Kansei words to meet users' emotional needs. Research methods and conclusions provide reference for web designers to design website according to the user's emotional needs.

There are still some deficiencies of this study. Firstly, it is need improve the method of selecting the design elements of the website. Representative design elements of website were selected through eye tracking in this study, which was timesaver but could not include all the design elements. Secondly, using the real website in the experiment couldn't avoid the impact of other factors (such as the kinds of goods) on user's Kansei and emotional evaluation. Future research should design website to control the variety of design elements to examine the impact of different design elements on the user's Kansei evaluation and emotional experience.

Acknowledgments. The author would like to acknowledge the national natural science foundation for its contribution to the research in this paper. National natural science foundation: 71171041.

References

1. China International Network Information Center, http://www.cnnic.net.cn
2. ISO 9241-11: Ergonomic requirements for office work with visual display terminals (VDTs)-Part II: Guidance on usability, International Organization for Standardization (1998)
3. Nielesn, J.: Usability Engineering. Morgan Kaufmann, San Francisco (1994)
4. Spool, J.M.: Web Site Usability: A Designer's Guide. Morgan Kaufmann, San Francisco (1999)
5. Roy, M.C., Dewit, O., Aubert, B.A.: The impact of interface usability on trust in web retailer. Internet Research 11(5), 388–398 (2001)
6. Hartson, H.R., Andre, T.S., Williges, R.C.: Criteria for evaluating usability evaluation methods. International Journal of Human-Computer Interaction 15(1), 145–181 (2003)
7. Schenkman, B.N., Jonsson, F.U.: Aesthetics and preferences of web pages. Behavior and Information Technology 19(5), 367–377 (2000)
8. Faraday, P.: Visually Critiquing Web Pages. In: Proceedings of the Eurographics Workshop in Milano, Italy, pp. 155–166 (2000)
9. Johnson-Laird, P.N., Oatley, K.: The language of emotions: An analysis of a semantic field. Cognition and Emotion 3(2), 81–123 (1989)
10. Ortony, A., Clore, G.L., Collins, A.: The cognitive structure of emotions. Cambridge University Press (1990)
11. Frijda, N.H.: The emotions. Cambridge University Press (1986)
12. Ethier, J., Hadaya, P., Talbot, J., Cadieux, J.: Interface design and emotions experienced on B2C Web sites: Empirical testing of a research model. Computers in Human Behavior 24(6), 2771–2791 (2008)
13. Tuch, A.N., Bargas-Avila, J.A., Opwis, K., Wilhelm, F.H.: Visual complexity of websites: Effects on users' experience, physiology, performance, and memory. International Journal of Human-Computer Studies 67(9), 703–715 (2009)
14. Deng, L., Poole, M.S.: Affect in web Interfaces-A Study of the impacts of Web Page Visual Complexity and Order. MIS Quarterly 34(4), 711–730 (2010)
15. Lokman, A.M., Noor, N.L.M., Nagamachi, M.: ExpertKanseiWeb: A Tool to Design Kansei Website. In: Filipe, J., Cordeiro, J. (eds.) ICEIS 2009. LNBIP, vol. 24, pp. 894–905. Springer, Heidelberg (2009)
16. Kim, J., Lee, J., Choi, D.: Designing emotionally evocative homepages: an empirical study of the quantitative relations between design factors and emotional dimensions. International Journal of Human-Computer Studies 59(6), 899–940 (2003)
17. Porat, T., Liss, R., Tractinsky, N.: E-Stores Design: The Influence of E-Store Design and Product Type on Consumers' Emotions and Attitudes. In: Jacko, J.A. (ed.) HCI 2007. LNCS, vol. 4553, pp. 712–721. Springer, Heidelberg (2007)
18. van Schaik, P., Ling, J.: The effects of frame layout and differential background contrast on visual search performance in Web pages. Interacting with Computers 13(5), 513–525 (2001)
19. Ling, J., van Schaik, P.: The effect of text and background colour on visual search of web pages. Displays 23(5), 223–230 (2002)
20. Wiggins, J.S.: The Five-factor Model of Personality: Theoretical Perspective, New York (1996)
21. Li, Y.M., Fu, X.L., Deng, G.F.: Prelim inary Application of the Abbreviated PAD Emotion Scale to Chinese Undergraduates. Chinese Mental Health Journal 22(5), 327–329 (2008)

Safety and Health at Work through Persuasive Assistance Systems

Matthias Hartwig and Armin Windel

Federal Institute for Occupational Safety and Health - Division
"Products and Work Systems", Friedrich Henkel 1-25 D-44149 Dortmund, Germany
{hartwig.matthias,windel.armin}@baua.bund.de

Abstract. In working environments, violations against safety regulations like the use of personal protective equipment pose a significant threat to well-being and health of working people. A laboratory study investigated the potential of different computer generated feedback forms encouraging users to wear protective equipment (PPE), even when this PPE hinders their primary work task, thus threatening their financial compensation. The results show a substantial increase in usage of PPE when being confronted with a persuasive designed feedback like a traffic light or an emotional expression of a virtual avatar. In contrast, solely informative feedback showed no significant impact of safety behavior. In summary, the findings indicate a potential of persuasive technology for occupational safety affairs and underline the importance of the outward appearance of computer generated persuasive messages.

Keywords: Adaptive Work Assistance Systems, Chances and Risks, Evaluative Feedback, Persuasion, Safety and Health.

1 Theory

By now, there is extensive knowledge about safe and healthy behavior at work: Education, information, rules and regulations are used to ensure this behavior in operational practice, for example the use of personal protective equipment (PPE). The effectiveness of these measures varies substantially, depending on the field of application. In sum however safe and healthy behavior is often neglected in practice. This suggests a substantial deficit in the perceived necessity of such behavior, in spite of all existing threats of penalty.

On organizational level, conscious infringements against safety regulations are often driven by economical motives. On individual level, reasons are divergent. Reason [1] classifies "unsafe acts" into unintentional errors like slips and mistakes, and intentional violations, which are based on a conscious decision to act against the regulation. These conscious violations often pose an especially high risk, because they commonly form a habit and will most likely be repeated in every similar situation. As a result, the individual risks for an accident to happen add up over time. Motives for these intended violations can be twofold: Firstly, the person could consider the safety behavior to be inappropriate or useless and has no intention to perform it, which

V.G. Duffy (Ed.): DHM/HCII 2013, Part II, LNCS 8026, pp. 40–49, 2013.

means the person has a negative attitude towards the respective behavior. Secondly, the person could consider the safety behavior per se to be useful, but its negative aspects outweigh the stimulus for acting or are more salient in the specific situation. These aspects can range from additional effort, slower working progress to less thrilling experiences at work. In this case, the person has a positive attitude towards the behavior itself, but in the specific situation, it is not strong or salient enough to activate the associated behavior. The second constellation is very relevant in every day life, because the prevention of accidents is rarely perceived as the primary goal of work, and so the risk and the subjective relevance of safety behavior are pushed to the background in the mind of the working person. The probability for violations is therefore especially high, when safety behavior is perceived as hindering for the working goals. To counteract these tendencies, a solution might be to remind the user of the relevant safety behavior and encourage it, preferably in the very moment the behavior is indicated.

Modern man-machine systems have the potential to provide such assistance, particularly those oriented to the technology vision of ambient intelligence. This technology paradigm is based on the idea of "ubiquitous computing" by Marc Weiser [2] and is characterized by Aarts [3] by the central features context awareness, personalization, adaptive behavior) and anticipation. In the working environment, these are called adaptive work assisting systems (AWAS,[4]) Applied to the described scenario, these properties enable the system to reduce violations by (1) being aware of the behavior of the user, (2) evaluating it autonomously regarding violations and (3) presenting evaluative feedback that changes the users behavior. Computer interfaces, purposely designed to change the behavior of the user, can be subsumed under the term persuasive technology [5]. While there are numerous approaches in field of persuasive technologies to investigate the applications for e-commerce, environmental protection or private healthcare, there are only few efforts made on how persuasive technology can be applied in the working environment. Furthermore, it is still unclear whether the outward appearance of feedbacks is critical for the persuasion. Two approaches are particularly relevant for the described scenario: (a) forms that are already associated with action stimuli from everyday life such as traffic lights, and (b) anthropomorphic interfaces such as animated virtual agents. Reeves and Nash [6] were able to show that users involuntarily attribute human characteristics to computer interfaces with human-like appearances. Therefore, computers can provide similar social cues as human do. The question, if this implies similar effects and action mechanisms as in social persuasion, is subject of an ongoing debate (for examples see [7, 8]).

The German Federal Institute for Occupational Safety and Health (BAuA) therefore conducted a laboratory experiment to investigate the potential of those different persuasive feedback forms to facilitate the use of personal protective equipment. The study is part of its current research focal point Ambient Intelligence (AmI), evaluating chances and risks of new adaptive technologies in the working environment. Testing the effects of persuasive feedback for safety and health behavior requires a setting that meets certain requirements. Participants should be able to accomplish the task without special knowledge, the need for PPE should be easily comprehensible without exposing participants to real hazards and the setting should be static, so the feedback on a monitor can always be seen by the participants. Taking these aspects into account, a simulation of a simple electrical engineering task was chosen as working task, while usage of isolating gloves was selected as corresponding safety behavior.

2   Procedure and Materials

All participants were given detailed standardized instructions on their task to manually build ten electronic circuits correctly and as quickly as possible according to a step by step guide on the monitor. They were also informed that during certain working steps there is a risk of an electric shock (which was in fact not the case). The subjects were instructed to wear insulated gloves as PPE in these operations. Usage of these gloves was the primary dependent variable of the experiment. The thick and stiff work gloves impaired and slowed down the filigree task of building the circuits significantly, creating a conflict between the two objectives given.

This conflict was exacerbated by two means. First, a bonus of 5 Euro (~ $6) for task completion in less than the average time was promised. This average time was not specified to the subjects; in fact, all participants received this "bonus". In contrast, use of gloves was not explicitly taken into account for payment. Secondly, after 30% of the circuits have been built, all subjects received a computer generated message, stating that they are about 2 Minutes slower than the average so far (regardless of their actual speed) and that their current working speed would therefore not be sufficient to receive the bonus.

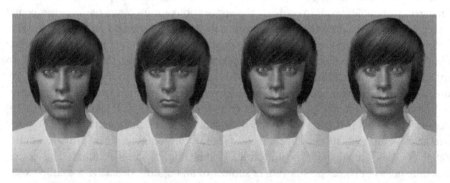

Fig. 1. Two different negative (left) and positive (right) Avatar feedbacks

In the control group, the subjects worked on these tasks without additional information on their PPE use. In the three other experimental groups, different forms of feedback on their use of gloves appeared on one half of the instruction monitor at each corresponding step. All feedbacks were accompanied by a very short bell sound, to make sure that they were recognized. In the experimental group "text" a short, purely informative held writing appeared, either "gloves used" as positive feedback, or "Please wear gloves" as negative feedback. In the experimental group "traffic light" the same text was presented, accompanied by a picture of a traffic light, displaying either green (positive) or red (negative) light. Finally, in the experimental group "virtual agent" an anthropomorphic virtual agent was shown, which presented either one of two positive predefined expressions (joy) or one of two negative (anger or sadness, all four different expressions are shown in Figure 1). To make the agent-based feedback more vivid and natural, in this experimental group the accompanying text was not held constant, but varied randomly between ten positive - affirmative (e.g. "very good, Gloves used") or negative - prompting messages ("forgetting something?"). The study was designed as a between-subject experiment; each subject took part in only one of these experimental conditions. The feedback was realized by the experimenter using the Wizard of Oz- technique. During the study, the experimenter - invisible to the subjects – recorded the "violations", which is the number of working steps were gloves were not use although the subject was supposed to. Other dependent variables were speed and quality of task performance, measured by the time the participants needed to complete the circuits and the number of correctly reconstructed circuit boards. As part of a manipulation check, a questionnaire asked (1) for the general perceived time pressure, as well as (2) how hindering the gloves were. Other questions asked (3) as how necessary the gloves were perceived, (4) how helpful the feedback was during the task and (5) whether the feedback had an impact on the participants' decision, to wear or not to wear the gloves. These items were used to understand the psychological mechanisms of action of the different feedback forms. Psychological acceptance was measured by the items (6) "I would not comply with such a feedback on principle", (7) "I could imagine an automated feedback system on daily work" and (8) "I could imagine an automated feedback system during training time". All Items were answered based on 5 point Likert scale (ranging from 1 = "does not apply at all" to 5 = "applies completely"). Participants answered the Neo-FFI [9] in its German translation [10], a personality questionnaire on the big five to rule out the influence of personality traits on experimental behavior.

2.1 Participants

The total sample of external subjects consisted of eighty persons. Five participants were ruled out from the statistical analyses. Two did not meet the internal time limit of the experiment, one was unable to use the gloves due to a bandaged hand and two persons were no native speakers and had an insufficient language ability to understand the instructions on the screen. Resulting seventy-five subjects (38 females, 37 males; age 25,75; SD 4,26) in the final sample were randomly assigned to one of four experimental conditions (feedback in form of an virtual avatar ($n= 19$), a traffic light ($n= 18$), a text message ($n=18$) or no feedback at all ($n= 20$). All subjects were mainly recruited on the internet and through announcements at nearby universities. All resulting participants were native German speakers. The experiment lasted between 120 and 150 Minutes, for which the participants were paid 25 € (approximately $ 32 US at the time the study was conducted).

Fig. 2. Experimental work station with gloves (left), circuit board (bottom) and instruction monitor (center)

2.2   Hypotheses

Based on the theoretical considerations, it was hypothesized that the feedback in general has an impact on safety behavior, resulting in the experimental groups differing significantly in terms of glove use (hypothesis 1). More specifically, it was assumed that the informative text-based feedback increases the salience of safety behavior, thus increasing the probability of occurrence (hypothesis 2a). The same effect should be achieved by the persuasive designed feedback forms so we assumed that the Traffic Light and Virtual Avatar – groups perform fewer violations than the control group (hypothesis 2b). In addition, it was hypothesized that the effect of persuasive feedback was greater than the one of a purely informative feedback. This should result in more violations in the text group than in traffic light and virtual avatar group (hypothesis 3). Finally, it was assumed that the effects of the two persuasive feedbacks to be based on different psychological mechanisms, reflected in different impacts (hypothesis 4). The questionnaire was designed in order to give information on these different mechanisms.

3   Results

3.1   Descriptive Statistics and Tests on Normal Distribution

The safety behavior was operationalized by counting the number of operations where the participant was not wearing gloves although supposed to (called "violation"). Before the message, out of 11 possible violations, participants score an average of 2,19 (*SD* 3,486, Range 0-11). After the message, the average number of performed violations was 6,43 (*SD* 9,54, Range 0-23) out of 23 possible violations. 41

participants scored zero violations, always wearing the gloves during the corresponding steps. A Kolmogorov-Smirnov test therefore showed an in-normal distribution of violations ($p. = 0.000$), skewed to the right.

Concerning working speed, it took the participants on average 3509 seconds (SD 747 sec. Range 1928-5550 sec.) to complete all ten circuits. After the manipulated working speed report between boards three and four, average time to complete the remaining seven boards was 2182 sec. (*SD* 537 sec., Range 1219-3697 sec.). Both curves were normally distributed (KS-test, $p > .05$). The quality of work was measured by counting the correct assembled and working circuits for each participant. The average number of working circuits was 6,36 (*SD* 1,73, Range 2-10).

In the questionnaire, participants reported a mediocre time pressure (mean 3,68, on a scale between 1-5, *SD* 0,774). As intended, the gloves were stated as very hindering for the task at hand (mean 4,41, *SD* 1,25) and not necessary (1,96, *SD* 1,27). In all feedback-groups, it was reported as being mediocre useful (3,00 *SD* 1,09) and disturbing (2,80 *SD* 1,41), as well as having a mediocre effect on the participants behavior (3,13 *SD* 1,39. Conscious reactance (Item 6, "I would not comply with such a feedback on principle") was stated relatively low with a mean of 1,75 (*SD* 9,89), while acceptance for use in daily work/training time was reported relatively high (mean of 3,87 *SD* 0,89 and 4,24 *SD* 0,816 respectively).

3.2   Manipulation Check: Conflict

First, it was checked whether the intended conflict between working speed and safety is reflected in the data. To test this, working speed and violations were correlated. Kendall's-Tau coefficient was used the because of the in-normal distribution of violations. Confirming our intentions, the test showed a significant negative correlation (-.244, $p. < .05$) between total working time and violations, which means using gloves led to increased working time.

3.3   Performance and Safety Behavior

The **Hypothesis 1** states that text-based, purely informative feedback would lead to fewer violations than in the control group without any feedback. To test this, violations before and after the manipulated working speed message were submitted to a Univariate Analyses of Variance (ANOVA) each, with Feedback Form as independent variable. ANOVA was chosen due to its error-robustness, though the in-normal distribution of violations infringes its mathematical preconditions. The Welch-Value was calculated additionally in order to rule out distortion caused by deviating variances. and ensure the results.

After the message, the experimental groups differed significantly from each other regarding glove usage. (ANOVA: $F = 3,445$, $p = 0,021$). The additionally conducted Welch Test revealed a significant difference as well ($F = 3,286$, $p = 0,031$). The average score of violations in the experimental groups are shown in Figure 3.

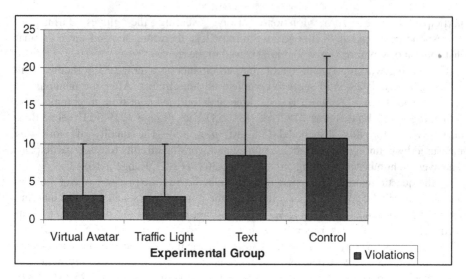

Fig. 3. Average violations and standard deviations for the experimental groups

On account of the floor effect concerning the distribution of violations, the *F* values are comparatively low for the given percental discrepancy of incidents (e.g. in the control group, roughly three times more violations occurred compared to the Virtual Agent group). No post-hoc pair comparisons show significant results. After balancing out contentual relevance and formal statistical aspects, it was decided to calculate the paired comparisons between the experimental groups with t-Tests. In order to avoid a summation of alpha-errors, we tested only those pairs which are part of the hypotheses.

Hypothesis 2a states that fewer violations occur in the textual feedback group compared to the control group. A one tailed t-test results in a $p = 0,516$ ($t = -0,656$), so the hypothesis is not confirmed.

Hypothesis 2b postulates that fewer violations occur in the persuasive feedback groups compared to the control group. A one tailed t-test reveals a significant difference ($t = 2,252$, $p = 0,002$) between the averages, confirming the hypothesis.

In **Hypothesis 3**, it was assumed that the persuasive feedback groups have fewer violations compared to the textual feedback group. The respective one tailed t-test shows a significant difference as well ($t = 2,252$, $p = 0,028$), so hypothesis 3 is confirmed.

Hypothesis 4 assumed the two kinds of persuasive Feedback to have a different impact on violations as well. A two tailed t-test reveals no significant result though ($t = 0,093$ $p = 0,926$), leaving hypothesis 4 unconfirmed.

To gain insight about the psychological impact forms, the questionnaire ratings were analyzed for the two persuasive designed feedback forms via t-tests. On three items, the two feedback groups showed significant discrepancies. The gloves were rated as significantly more hindering when confronted with feedback by traffic lights ($t = -2,444$, $p = 0,025$). In the virtual agent group, feedback was assessed as more disturbing ($t = 2,081$, $p = 0,045$). Finally, participants rated the traffic light as more acceptable as a feedback system during training time ($t = -2,794$ $p = 0,008$). Two more items showed noticeable results: feedback by a virtual avatar was numerically rated having a greater impact on safety behavior, while in the traffic light group, the glove itself were assessed as more necessary. In both items however, the two groups did not differ significantly by a small margin ($t = 1,825$, $p = 0,078$ and $t = -1,931$, $p = 0,064$, respectively). Concerning work speed and work quality, ANOVAS revealed no significant differences between the experimental groups regarding working time and number of working circuits, neither before nor after the interim message.

4   Discussion

The study presented investigates the influence of different feedback forms on safety violations. A dynamic feedback on safety behavior based on persuasion was expected to reduce the number of safety violations, even when this means acting against ones own financial interests. In a laboratory study, participants performed an electric task, building electronic circuits. They worked under time pressure, being told that fast performance would grant them a financial bonus, and asked to simultaneously use unhandy gloves as personal protective equipment on specific operations, slowing down the working process. While working on the task, they either received no evaluating feedback on their PPE use, a purely informative text message, a picture of a traffic light or the picture of a virtual avatar showing an emotional expression. Safety behavior was measured, counting the numbers of actual PPE-use during relevant operations. Additionally, working speed and quality of work were recorded, while a questionnaire gauged various attitudes concerning task, feedback and safety behavior. Taking quality of work and speed into account, no significant differences between the experimental groups were found, suggesting that such forms of feedback on safety behavior have no substantial impact on the primary task. Concerning safety behavior, displaying feedback per se is not sufficient to significantly reduce safety violations. However persuasive designed feedback, either in form of a traffic light or a virtual avatar showing an emotional expression, had not only a statistically significant but also a substantial impact on safety behavior, reducing the violations occurring in the absence of any feedback by roughly 60 %.

The results of the presented study suggest that purely informative feedback on safety behavior is not sufficient to reliably prevent violations, even when it is presented at the most relevant moment. Instead, the appearance of the feedback seems to be a crucial factor when it comes to impact on user behavior. Intriguingly, in this study the feedback did not only change behavior of the participants, but it successfully persuaded them to act directly against their own financial interests. This strongly suggests that persuasive designed feedback does not only work as reminder that triggers a behavior to which people are motivated anyway, but can act as a factor of its own in decision making. For occupational practice, these results strongly advocate to consider the human psychology when using signs and guidelines to ensure safety behavior. It may not be enough to make sure these signs are readable and understandable. On the contrary, the actual impact on the behavior might depend on its outward appearance, especially when there is no thread of punishment or it is perceived as unlikely to happen. Since the persuasive feedback in this study had an impact on behavior, without being bolstered by the thread of sanctions, one can assume that persuasive technology can be used even where certain safety behaviors are desirable, but prohibitions or sanctions are inappropriate. This was considered to be especially important because presently, there are only few "gentle" methods available to support safety behavior without using prohibitions and sentences. At the same time the results imply that a responsible application of persuasive technology is mandatory. Because of its impact on behavior, this kind of technology works somewhere in between assisting the users and manipulating them. Future research efforts should evaluate this continuum and define the terms of an ethical action guiding versus an unacceptable violation of autonomy.

When comparing the two persuasive designed feedback forms (traffic light and virtual avatar) with each other, no significant difference were found concerning direct impact on safety behavior. The questionnaire however, indicates that there were substantial differences concerning how the feedback influences the user psychologically. Participants rated anthropomorphic feedback significantly more disturbing, but also as having a larger impact on decision making, while the traffic light feedback is rated as more acceptable during vocational adjustment. Finally, presentation of traffic light feedback leads to more negative rating of the safety behavior itself. Taken together, these findings might suggest that anthropomorphic feedback is experienced as more intrusive and draws more attention, while the traffic light triggers a well known association (red – "dangerous", green – "ok") without much thought about the traffic light itself.

It remains unclear however, if these differing subjective measures reflect distinct psychological mechanisms of behavior change. If so, the different feedback forms might show distinctive impact on behavior under different circumstances, for instance longer working time, higher cognitive demands of the primary task, or regarding persistence of behavior change. The last aspect is considered of particular importance. All forms of feedback scored a substantially higher acceptance rate for training period than for permanent use, which advocates a temporary use, where achieving a permanent behavior change would be mandatory. One could assume hypothetical explanations for the superiority of both feedback types. On the one hand, the observed better (in this case: less hindering) assessment of the safety behavior when confronted with the virtual avatar could lead to fewer violations, even after the feedback is no longer presented. However, it is not clear how continual this assessment would be. On the other hand, the anthropomorphic feedback, being perceived as more disturbing and having more impact, might represent a consciously perceived external motivation. If so, the increase of safety behavior would be displayed to receive the positive feedback, and would therefore go back when the external reward ceases. It might even have an effect of undermining intrinsic motivation [11]. As a result, a planned follow up study will focus on more accurate insights (1) on the psychological mechanisms how different forms of automatic feedback influence user and (2) the stability of behavior changes.

Acknowledgements. We would like to thank the laboratory unit and especially Ulrich Hold and Nina Schelter for invaluable assistance and support during the realization and implementation of the study.

References

1. Reason, J.: The Human Contribution. Unsafe Acts, Accidents and Heroic Recoveries. Ashgate Publishing (2008)
2. Weiser, M.: The computer for the twenty-first century. Scientific American 265(3), 94–104 (1991)
3. Aarts, E.H.L., Harwig, H., Schuurmans, M.: Ambient Intelligence. In: Denning, J. (ed.) The Invisible Future, pp. 235–250. McGraw Hill, New York (2001)
4. Windel, A., Hartwig, M.: New Forms of Work Assistance by Ambient Intelligence. In: Paternò, F., de Ruyter, B., Markopoulos, P., Santoro, C., van Loenen, E., Luyten, K. (eds.) AmI 2012. LNCS, vol. 7683, pp. 348–355. Springer, Heidelberg (2012)
5. Fogg, B.J.: Persuasive Technology: Using Computers to Change What We Think and Do. Morgan Kaufmann (2003)
6. Reeves, B., Nass, C.: The Media Equation: how people treat computers, television, and new media like real people and places. University Press, Cambridge (1996)
7. Roubroeks, M.A.J., Ham, J., Midden, C.J.H.: When artificial social agents try to persuade people: The role of social agency on the occurrence of psychological reactance. Social Robotics 3(2), 155–165 (2011)
8. Schulman, D., Bickmore, T.: Persuading Users through Counseling Dialogue with a Conversational Agent. In: Proceedings of Persuasive Technology 2009, Claremont (2009)
9. Costa, P.T., McCrae, R.R.: Normal personality assessment in clinical practice: The NEO Personality Inventory. Psychological Assessment 4(1), 5–13 (1992)
10. Borkenau, P., Ostendorf, F.: NEO-Fünf-Faktoren-Inventar (NEO-FFI) nach Costa und McCrae (S. 5-10, 27-28). Hogrefe, Göttingen (1993)
11. Deci, E.L., Koestner, R., Ryan, R.M.: A Meta-Analytic Review of Experiments Examining the Effects of Extrinsic Rewards on Intrinsic Motivation. Psychological Bulletin 147, 627–688 (1999)

Evaluating Ergonomics Risks for Digital Radiologists

Alan Hedge

Cornell University, Dept. Design and Environmental Analysis, Ithaca NY 14853, U.S.A.
ah29@cornell.edu

Abstract. Modern radiology is digital and the work of the radiologist now shares many features with that of other high technology computer work. Many digital reading rooms are poorly designed in terms of ergonomics and how they accommodate computer technology. Lighting is typically inadequate resulting in visual health problems of eyestrain and headaches and inadequate lighting also adversely affects image reading performance. The prevalence of musculoskeletal symptoms among radiologists often exceeds levels seen among other computer workers. An innovative reading room design is briefly described that incorporates some ergonomic design features and this has resulted in high levels of workplace satisfaction. Finally, the Cornell Digital Reading Room Ergonomic Checklist is presented which aims to give guidance on the ergonomic design of future reading rooms.

Keywords: Digital radiology, Ergonomics checklist, Innovative Reading Room, Musculoskeletal symptoms, Visual health.

1 Introduction

Radiology was one of the first medical specializations to undergo rapid technological change as film-based reading rooms were replaced by computer-based picture archiving and communication systems (PACS). The first installation of a PACS was at the University of Kansas in 1982, and more widespread development and use of PACS began in the 1990s [1]. The widespread introduction of digital medical imaging technology in the past twenty years has dramatically changed the nature of the work of the radiologist, and changed the design of the work environment to support this work. Film based radiology reading rooms often required the radiologist to stand and look at x-ray film on a light box reader, moving from physical image film to physical image film to assess a case. However, PACS allows for more sophisticated analysis and precise diagnosis, and electronic sharing of the x-ray image. In the digital world, images can be easily manipulated, allowing the radiologist to move around the image, zoom in and out, annotate the image, and in some systems even see the image in color and 3D. Advocates for the transition to PACS argued that this would result in significant improvement in workflow [2]. Modern computer-based reading rooms now resemble high-technology offices in many respects, and reading x-rays has is now much more sedentary work than in the past. As such, users of these reading rooms report a variety of issues comparable to those found in other computer work

V.G. Duffy (Ed.): DHM/HCII 2013, Part II, LNCS 8026, pp. 50–58, 2013.

environments. In general, these concerns have to do with the reading room environment such as the lighting, acoustics and air quality, the layout of the reading room, and the poor ergonomic design of the workstation, [3-5]. Some of these factors are examined below.

2   Digital Reading Room: Lighting and Visual Health

Designing appropriate lighting for a digital reading room remains a concern, especially with the move from film to cathode ray tube (CRT) display to liquid crystal display (LCD). Research has shown that typical office lighting designs and levels can reduce the efficacy of radiologic diagnoses when compared with lower levels of ambient lighting. A study [6] tested whether five ambient light levels (480, 100, 40, 25, and 7 lux: 44.6 fc, 9.3 fc, 3.7 fc, 2.3 fc, 0.7 fc) affected the decisions of 79 experienced radiologists reading 30 posteroanterior wrist images and determining whether or not a fracture was present. Reading images at 40 and 25 lux resulted in fewer false-positives and false-negatives compared with 480, 100 lux or 7 lux. Radiologists specializing in reading musculoskeletal trauma images were only partly able to compensate for inappropriate lighting levels.

In part agreement with the previous study, when four chest radiologists read 100 radiographs (50 normal and 50 containing a subtle nodule) under two different ambient light levels: low illuminance of 1 lx (0.1 fc) and elevated illuminance of 50 lx (4.65 fc), there was no statistically significant performance difference, although there was a trend for faster average selection times, for decreased false positive identification times (35.4 ± 18.8 to 26.2 ± 14.9s) and for true positive identification times (29.7 ± 18.3 to 24.5 ± 15.5s) at 50 lx [7].

A rise in the prevalence of visual health symptoms may be expected as the work of radiologists increasing becomes near work involving long periods staring at one or more computer screens. A study of 3 radiologists and 3 radiology residents, who worked at a computer an average of 5.7 hours per day, assessed the accommodative ability of the eyes at the start and end of the workday [8]. Results showed that accommodation ability is significantly reduced after a day of radiology near work on a computer screen, with readers becoming more myopic, and the duration of reading correlated with reports of headache, eyestrain, difficulty focusing, and blurry vision. Long workdays have also been shown to significantly reduce accommodation accuracy, increase visual fatigue and oculomotor strain, and reduce the ability to detect fractures [9]. The prevalence of headaches among Swedish radiologists and nurses in one hospital increased from around 25% to over 60% after the construction of a new PACS reading room, and remained high at around 70% in another hospital after renovation of the reading room to accommodate PACS workstations [10].

3   Digital Reading Room: Workstation Ergonomics and Musculoskeletal Disorders

Within radiology there are subspecialties with higher risks of developing occupational musculoskeletal injuries associated with maintaining poor postures over long periods, with the added load of wearing protective apparel [11] and with the poor ergonomic design of the radiology reading room [12].

A study of 12 radiologists in a department of some 40 people at the Tripler Army Medical Center, Honolulu, found that the incidence rate of carpal tunnel syndrome was 8.3%, which is around double the normal incidence rates in administrative and clerical staff, and 33% were clinically symptomatic with either carpal tunnel syndrome or cubital tunnel syndrome [14]. Significant deficiencies were observed in all areas of the radiology department and an occupational hygienist made 93 recommendations for work area improvements. There was limited availability of keyboard or mouse trays, the chairs used were only height adjustable and provided limited arm support, workstations were a standard size and were not adjustable. The symptomatic radiologists were found to spend more time on computers and they experienced their symptoms when using the PACS workstations.

The impact of introducing PACS in 2 large Stockholm hospitals was investigated [10]. In one hospital 27 radiologists and 68 nurses were surveyed before-and-after moving to a new building with a new PACS. The % of their sedentary work (>50% of workday seated) increased from ~50% to 80% of the work day. In another hospital 42 radiologists and 81 nurses were surveyed who remained in existing but renovated radiology space. When a PACS was implemented the prevalence of their seated work postures for >50% of the day increased, especially among radiologists, from around 70% to over 90%of the day. In both hospitals there was a high prevalence (>60%) of very frequent neck/cervical spine, shoulder, upper arm and lower back musculoskeletal pain associated with reading activities. The prevalence of musculoskeletal symptoms among radiologists was studied for a sample of 30 radiologists from the Henry Ford hospital in Detroit [15]. For diagnostic radiology work all radiologists worked at shared computer workstations with the same equipment, set-up and adjustment capabilities. Results showed that 67% reported neck discomfort from the computer screen position, 50% had wrist problems from use of their computer mouse, 43% complained of neck and low back discomfort from their chair, and 40% experienced headaches when reading images. Discomfort ratings were not associated with the frequency of adjustments but rather the work postures of the radiologists.

Researchers at Massachusetts General Hospital randomly surveyed 28 radiologists and found that only 7.2% were free of musculoskeletal symptoms, whereas 70% had seen a physician for a musculoskeletal injury associated with PACS use, and some radiologists experienced multiple symptoms. Neck pain was reported by 43%, low back pain by 39%, shoulder pain by 32%, headache by 32%, and 17% did not adjust their chairs and these individuals experienced 3 or more symptoms [16].

A survey of 107 faculty members, fellows, and residents working in a PACS-based radiology department found that 68% reported working more than 8 hours per day at a personal computer or PACS monitor, and 58% reported musculoskeletal symptoms [17]. Fifty four people subsequently received ergonomic chairs and 70% reported improvements in their musculoskeletal symptoms. Fifty five people subsequently received an ergonomic workstations and 80% of them reported improvements. Twenty people underwent ergonomic training and 80% of them also reported improvements. The researchers concluded that although there is a high prevalence of musculoskeletal symptoms among radiologists working in a PACS-based environment, these symptoms are responsive to ergonomic interventions and ergonomic initiatives to reduce the risk for musculoskeletal injuries in radiology departments.

4   Innovative Digital Reading Room Evaluation

The previous sections have shown how digital reading room design can have a major impact on the health and performance of radiologists. A study of an innovative digital reading room design evaluated radiologists' satisfaction with the ergonomic furniture and workstation design, lighting, and collaborative spaces [19]. The innovative reading room incorporated ergonomic workstation design features, such as easily adjustable multi-screen flat panels PACS displays, multiple CPU's in holders, adjustable height work surfaces, negative tilt adjustable height keyboard trays with a mouse platform, wire management, sound absorbing panels between and above stations, textured sound absorbing walls, music and white noise systems for speech privacy, and variable lighting. Results for all aspects showed high levels of satisfaction with the reading room design, especially for the furniture and ergonomic workstations (Table 1).

Table 1. Satisfaction Levels with Digital Reading Room Components [18] *(1 - very dissatisfied; 2 - dissatisfied; 3 - neutral; 4 - satisfied; 5 - very satisfied)

Furniture and Workspace Questions	Average Satisfaction Rating*
Adequacy of Desk space	3.73
LCD Monitor Placement	3.89
Keyboard & Mouse Placement	3.45
Dictation Microphone Placement	3.55
Adjustability of Desk	3.7
Chair Comfort	4.1
Sufficient space for personal belongings	2.93
Fabric portable dividers between workstations	3.6
Open floor layout of reading room	3.66
Layout encourages collaboration between radiologist	3.57
Amount of space in reading room	3.93
Ease of access to reading room coordinators spaces	4
Reading room testbed enhances radiology workflow	3.64
Overall comfort of workspace	3.8

5 Cornell Digital Reading Room Ergonomics Checklist

Digital reading rooms that are designed in accordance with ergonomic principles for intensive computer workplaces seem to be the exception rather than the rule. In part this may be a consequence of simply replacing film in a reading room with PACS workstations without changing lighting or furniture. Partly it may be a result of a lack of ergonomic knowledge. In the design of many socio-technical systems, ergonomists develop checklists to assist the designers and to help provide them with guidance on important ergonomic design considerations. Consequently, the Cornell Digital

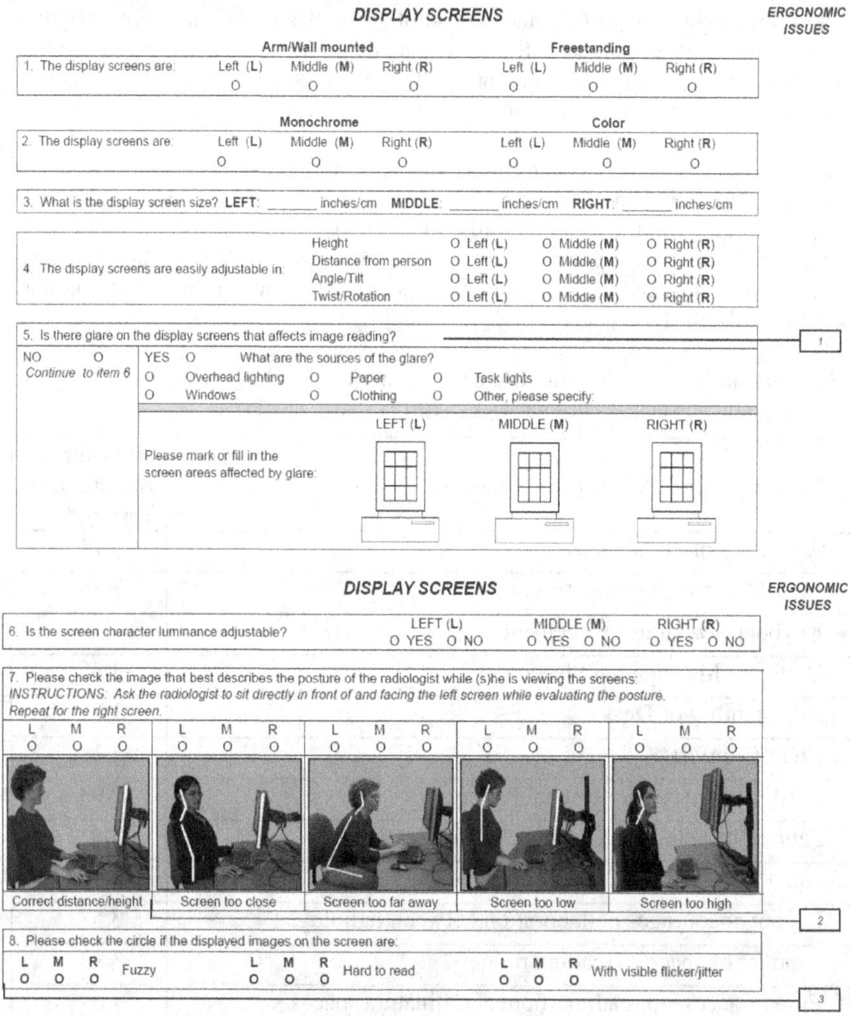
DISPLAY SCREENS

ERGONOMIC ISSUES

	Arm/Wall mounted			Freestanding		
1. The display screens are:	Left (L) O	Middle (M) O	Right (R) O	Left (L) O	Middle (M) O	Right (R) O

	Monochrome			Color		
2. The display screens are:	Left (L) O	Middle (M) O	Right (R) O	Left (L) O	Middle (M) O	Right (R) O

3. What is the display screen size? **LEFT**: ______ inches/cm **MIDDLE**: ______ inches/cm **RIGHT**: ______ inches/cm

4. The display screens are easily adjustable in:				
	Height	O Left (L)	O Middle (M)	O Right (R)
	Distance from person	O Left (L)	O Middle (M)	O Right (R)
	Angle/Tilt	O Left (L)	O Middle (M)	O Right (R)
	Twist/Rotation	O Left (L)	O Middle (M)	O Right (R)

5. Is there glare on the display screens that affects image reading? — 1

NO O *Continue to item 6*

YES O What are the sources of the glare?
O Overhead lighting O Paper O Task lights
O Windows O Clothing O Other, please specify:

Please mark or fill in the screen areas affected by glare: LEFT (L) MIDDLE (M) RIGHT (R)

DISPLAY SCREENS

ERGONOMIC ISSUES

6. Is the screen character luminance adjustable? LEFT (L) O YES O NO MIDDLE (M) O YES O NO RIGHT (R) O YES O NO

7. Please check the image that best describes the posture of the radiologist while (s)he is viewing the screens:
INSTRUCTIONS: Ask the radiologist to sit directly in front of and facing the left screen while evaluating the posture. Repeat for the right screen.

L M R O O O	L M R O O O	L M R O O O	L M R O O O	L M R O O O
Correct distance/height	Screen too close	Screen too far away	Screen too low	Screen too high

— 2

8. Please check the circle if the displayed images on the screen are:
L M R O O O Fuzzy L M R O O O Hard to read L M R O O O With visible flicker/jitter — 3

Fig. 1 a. Cornell Digital Reading Room Ergonomics Checklist [19]

INPUT DEVICES

9. What is the wrist angle? Please check the image that fits the posture:

If the workstation has a keyboard tray:

If the workstation keyboard is placed on the desk:

| Neutral wrist angle | Wrist Flexion | Wrist Extension | Neutral wrist angle | Wrist Flexion | Wrist Extension |

`4`

10. Check the circle if the mouse designed for: O Right handed use only   O Left handed use only   O Use with either hand

11. Where is the mouse used?   O On platform over keyboard   O Platform adjacent to keyboard   O On desk

12. What is the wrist position? Please check the image that fits the posture:

| Neutral wrist | Radial Deviation | Ulnar deviation |

`5`

13. Please check any other hand operated input devices used at the workstation that put the hand or arm in an awkward posture:
O Trackball   O Touchpad   O Touchpoint   O Joystick   O Lightpen   O Other: _____

`6`

14. Is voice recognition used?
     O NO   O A hands-free headset   O A free standing microphone   O A hand-held microphone

WORKSTATION & WORKSTATION ACCESSORIES

15. Does the work surface look cluttered?   O NO   O YES Desktop size: Width: _____ inches. Depth: _____ inches

`7`

16. Does the workstation have any sharp edges that could cause compression to either hands or arms?   O NO   O YES

`8`

17. Does the radiologist have sufficient clearance underneath the desk?   O YES   O NO _____

`9`

18. Can the angle of the workstation surface be changed?   O YES   O NO

19. Can the desk height be adjusted to accommodated for seated work as well as standing work?   O YES   O NO

Depth at knee level: _____ inches   Desk width: _____ inches
Depth at foot level: _____ inches   Desk height: _____ inches

20. Does the work require a document holder for paper?

O NO	O YES	Is there a stable document holder at the workstation? O YES O NO	`10`
Continue to item 21	Is the document placed at the same height as the screen? O YES O NO		`11`
	Is the document placed at the same distance as the screen? O YES O NO	
	Height of document holder: _____ Distance from person: _____	

21. Does the radiologist need to use a telephone while reading images?

O NO	O YES	
Continue to item 22	Is the telephone used with the head upright and shoulders relaxed? O YES O NO	`12`
	Please check the circle that best describes the phone usage	
	O Hands free / Headset (cell/regular phone)	O Shoulder cradle (regular phone)	O Regular phone w/o accessories	O Cell phone w/o accessories

22. Does the workstation have a footrest?   O YES   O NO

`13`

Fig. 1b. Cornell Digital Reading Room Ergonomics Checklist [19]

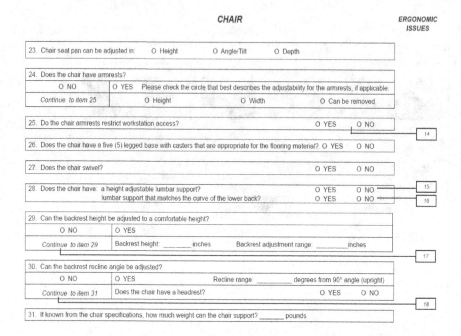

Fig. 1c. Cornell Digital Reading Room Ergonomics Checklist [19]

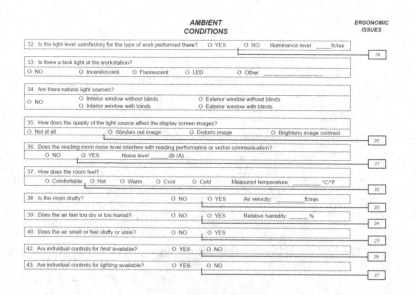

Fig.1d. Cornell Digital Reading Room Ergonomics Checklist [19]

Reading Room Ergonomics Checklist (CDRREC) was developed, based on questionnaire items found in thirteen checklists and educational materials published by the U.S. government, independent researchers and furniture makers, and based on empirical observation studies of reading rooms in both the U.S.A. and Iceland [19-20]. The CDRREC is intended as a tool for the quick evaluation of the working environment for radiologists who work with digital medical images. The checklist can be used to document the conditions for one radiologist or several radiologists. The checklist has five sections: Display Screens; Input devices; Workstation and Workstation accessories; Chair; Ambient Environment (Figure 1). Each section asks questions about the physical environment (such as the height of the desk or the temperature of the room) and the users (such as the posture of the radiologist and how s/he uses the equipment).

6   Conclusions

Designing a successful digital reading room requires consideration of the varied tasks that must be undertaken to encourage and enhance the performance of radiologists and facilitate interactions between clinicians and radiologists. As digital imaging technology improves so the design of reading room facilities should focus on encouraging clinical collaboration, enhancing patient care, and ultimately improving radiologists' job satisfaction and productivity. Above all else, digital reading room design needs to pay attention to ergonomics to optimize the work, comfort and health of radiologists.

References

1. Huang, H.K.: Short history of PACS. Part I: USA. Eur. J. Radiol. 78(2), 163–176 (2011)
2. Reiner, B.I., Siegel, E.L.: The Cutting Edge: Strategies to Enhance Radiologist Workflow in a Filmless/Paperless Imaging Department. J. Digit. Imaging 15(3), 178–190 (2002)
3. Harisinghani, M.G., Blake, M.A., Saksena, M., Hahn, P.F., Gervais, D., Zalis, M., Fernandes, L.S.D., Mueller, P.R.: Importance and Effects of Altered Workplace Ergonomics in Modern Radiology Suites. Radiographics 24(2), 615–627 (2004)
4. Siegel, E.L., Reiner, B.I.: Radiology reading room design: The next generation. App. Radiol. Online 31(4), 1 (2002), http://www.appliedradiology.com/Issues/2002/04/Articles/Radiology-reading-room-design-The-next-generation.aspx
5. Horii, S.C., Horii, H.N., Mun, S.K., Benson, H.R., Zeman, R.K.: Environmental Designs for Reading from Imaging Workstations: Ergonomic and Architectural Features. J. Digit. Imaging 16(1), 124–131 (2003)
6. Brennan, P.C., McEntee, M., Evanoff, M., Phillips, P., O'Connor, W.T., Manning, D.J.: Ambient Lighting: Effect of Illumination on Soft-Copy Viewing of Radiographs of the Wrist. AJR 188(2), W177-W180 (2007)
7. Pollard, B.J., Samei, E., Chawla, A.S., Beam, C., Heyneman, L.E., Koweek, L.M., Martinez-Jimenez, S., Washington, L., Hashimoto, N., McAdams, H.P.: The effects of ambient lighting in chest radiology reading rooms. J. Digit. Imaging 25(4), 520–526 (2012)

8. Krupinski, E.A., Berbaum, K.S.: Measurement of Visual Strain in Radiologists. Acad. Radiol. 16(8), 947–950 (2009)
9. Krupinski, E.A., Berbaum, K.S., Caldwell, R.T., Schartz, K.M., Kim, J.: Long Radiology Workdays Reduce Detection and Accommodation Accuracy. J. Am. Coll. Radiol. 7(9), 698–704 (2010)
10. Pinto, A., Brunese, L.: Spectrum of diagnostic errors in radiology. World J. Radiol. 2(10), 377–383 (2010)
11. Lindbeck, L., Höglund, U.: Ergonomic evaluation of picture archiving and communication system implementations in two X-ray departments. Ergonomics 51(2), 98–124 (2008)
12. García-Lallana, A., Viteri-Ramírez, G., Saiz-Mendiguren, R., Broncano, J., Dámaso Aquerreta, J.: Ergonomics of the workplace in radiology. Radiologia. 53(6), 507–515 (2011)
13. Moan, R.: Poor ergonomic design plagues reading rooms. Diagnostic Imaging 32(5) (2010), http://www.diagnosticimaging.com/practice-management/content/article/113619/1575035
14. Ruess, L., O'Connor, S.C., Cho, K.H., Slaughter, R., Husain, F.H., Hedge, A.: Carpal tunnel syndrome and cubital tunnel syndrome: musculoskeletal disorders in four symptomatic radiologists. AJR 181, 37–42 (2003)
15. Agarwal, A., Belk, A., Boothroyd, K., Hedge, A.: Radiology Workplace Assessment (2007), http://ergo.human.cornell.edu/ErgoPROJECTS/2007projects/Radiology%20FINAL.pdf
16. Ridley, E.L.: Radiologists be prone to work-related injuries (2010), http://www.auntminnie.com/index.aspx?sec=prtf&sub=def&pag=dis&itemId=90475&printpage=true&fsec=ser&fsub=def
17. Boiselle, P.M., Levine, D., Horwich, P.J., Barbaras, L., Siegal, D., Shillue, K., Affeln, D.: Repetitive stress symptoms in radiology: prevalence and response to ergonomic interventions. J. Am. Coll. Radiol. 5(8), 919–923 (2008)
18. Hugine, A., Guerlain, S., Hedge, A.: User evaluation of an innovative digital reading room. J. Digit. Imaging 25(3), 337–346 (2012)
19. Brynjarsdóttir, H., Hedge, A.: Cornell Digital Reading Room Ergonomics Checklist (2006), http://ergo.human.cornell.edu/CDRREC.htm
20. Brynjarsdóttir, H.: The Cornell Digital Reading Room Ergonomics Checklist: Development and Evaluation. M.S. Thesis, Cornell University, Ithaca, NY, USA (2007)

A Study of the Effect of the Shape, the Color, and the Texture of Ikebana on a Brain Activity

Yuki Ikenobo[1,2], Yoshiyuki Kida[2], Noriaki Kuwahara[2], Akihiko Goto[3], and Akio Kimura[4]

[1] Ikenobo Society of Floral Art, Kyoto, Japan
[2] Kyoto Institute of Technology, Kyoto, Japan
[3] Osaka Sangyo University, Osaka, Japan
[4] Digital Medic Inc., Kyoto. Japan
info@ikenobo.jp, {kida,nkuwahar}@kit.ac.jp
gotoh@ise.osaka-sandai.ac.jp, kimura@digital-medic.com

Abstract. A study was performed on the difference between beginners and experts of Ikebana. The brain activity measurement results showed that for beginners, the incidence of α wave increased with time both during the planning and the production of the arrangement. However, for experts, the incidence of α wave decreased with time during the planning and increased during the production of the arrangement. This result indicated that the experts concentrate the mind more during the planning through the course of the arrangement, and relaxes more during the production of the arrangement. Also, the result of questionnaire survey showed that beginners were unable to recognize the formal beauty of an Ikebana arrangement, while experts were able to evaluate it correctly. It indicates that the experts have the special criteria of the formal beauty of Ikebana cultivated through the long-term training.

1 Introduction

Ikebana, along with the tea ceremony, is a traditional culture that represents Japan. It originates from the Buddhist tradition of flower offertories for the deceased and possesses a 1500-year history.

Unlike western flower arrangement, Ikebana is distinct because it finds the light of life not only in beautiful flowers but also in wilted or rotten flowers. Another characteristic is how emphasis is given not only to the structural form, but also to the arrangement process and the mental focus and unity during the arrangement. Ikebana's adherence to Taoist concepts, as seen in its other name "Kadou," is derived from these features. However, there is marginal to no research on Ikebana that focuses on the act of arranging and the arrangements themselves. Hence, it is difficult to say whether the essence of Ikebana arrangements is sufficiently understood [1, 2].

It is necessary to maintain a constant level of competence and to establish the most rational, scientific, data-driven training method by scientifically clarifying the act of and the actual arrangement of Ikebana. Such a rational training method developed on the basis of data should result in the most effective, universal method for teaching Ikebana, which will enable the worldwide expansion of Ikebana, regardless of nationality or cultural environment.

V.G. Duffy (Ed.): DHM/HCII 2013, Part II, LNCS 8026, pp. 59–65, 2013.

2   Methods

2.1   Purpose

The purpose of the experiment was to measure and to compare the brain activities of experts and beginners during the planning of and production of an actual Ikebana arrangement by having experts and beginners produce an Ikebana arrangement. Then, by having other experts and beginners view the arrangements, an impression evaluation survey was conducted, and a comparison of the results was presented.

2.2   Ikebana Style

Shouka is selected as the best style of Ikebana for these experiments, because it involves standardized technique and both experts and beginners are able to produce.

2.3   Materials

Five red willow branches and two chrysanthemums were used to make a total of seven materials of Ikebana for this experiment. As red willow branches can be bent by force to make an ideal shape, and because bending them requires a certain touch, they are a material that effectively reflects the Ikebana experience.

2.4   Participants

Two participants were selected for brain activity measurement: a female with 63 years of experience as an Ikebana artist and 51 years of training experience (Participant A, age 72) and a male with 4 years of experience (Participant B, age 27).

Three participants were selected for the impression evaluation survey: a male with 20 years of Ikebana experience, whose occupation is the production of Ikebana arrangements (Participant C, age 42), a female with two years of Ikebana experience (Participant D, age 25), and a male student of the Kyoto Institute of Technology with no previous Ikebana experience (Participant E, age 24).

2.5   Experimental Method

(1) Brain Activity Measurement
The experiment site was a conference room that is approximately 5 m in width and 15 m in depth, surrounded by white walls apart from a south-facing window. One corner was surrounded by partitions and used as the experimental space. To enable participants to focus on the experiment, the experimental space was separated from the rest of the room by three partitions, with the wall being the fourth side. A table 1 m in width and 0.6 m in depth with a chair was placed inside. This space was designated as the production of and viewing location for the Ikebana arrangements as shown Fig. 1.

In the experiment, one participant at a time produced an arrangement, while wearing an electroencephalogram (EEG) monitor. A chair and table were placed, and the participant arranged the Ikebana in a seated position. As shown in Fig. 2, after the arrangement of one material, the participants were refrained from physically changing the arrangement for 20 s, which was the time designated for planning. This pause for planning was repeated after every act of arrangement. Brain activity was measured throughout the process. The planning time of 20 seconds was also maintained before the final adjustments during completion, and an additional time of 20 seconds was provided for viewing after the completion of the arrangement.

The brain activities were measured by a portable EEG monitor, developed and distributed by Digital Medic Inc. This EEG monitor obtained a correlation coefficient of 0.94 in a comparative study of measurement results with a medical EEG monitor (NEC San'ei Synafit 1000).

(2) Impression Evaluation Survey
An impression evaluation experiment was conducted following the completion of the expert's and beginner's arrangements.

The evaluation experiment was conducted on one participant at a time. The arrangements were replaced after each viewing to prevent the simultaneous viewing of the arrangements of Participant A and B. The participants recorded their evaluation results on the questionnaire survey sheet during viewing.

Using the items employed in the plant impression evaluation research [3-6] as reference, 32 pairs of adjectives (e.g., "peaceful–not peaceful") were selected as survey items and were evaluated on a 7-point scale.

Fig. 1. Production of an Ikebana arrangement (wearing of an EEG)

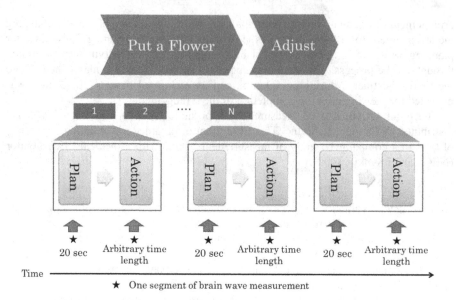

Fig. 2. Flow of brain activity measurements during an Ikebana arrangement

3   Results

3.1   Brain Activity Measurements of Ikebana Artists during Planning and Arranging

Fig. 3 shows the brain activity measurement results of Participant A (Expert). The vertical axis shows the incidence rate of α wave, and the horizontal axis shows the brain activity measurement points. Fig. 3(a) shows the changes in brain activity during planning before arranging the materials, and Fig. 3(b) shows the changes in brain activity during the act of arranging the materials.

Fig. 4 shows the brain activity measurement results of Participant B (Beginner). As shown in Fig. 3, the vertical axis shows the incidence rate of α waves, and the horizontal axis shows the brain activity measurement points (★) shown in Fig.2, Fig. 4(a) shows changes in the brain activity during the planning before arranging the materials, and Fig. 4(b) shows changes in the brain activity during the process of arranging the materials.

A negative correlation (-0.68, $p < 0.05$) was observed between the incidence of α waves and measurement points for the expert during planning, while a positive correlation (0.70, $p < 0.05$) was observed between the incidence of α waves and measurement points during the process of arrangement. Conversely, a positive correlation (0.48, $p < 0.1$) was observed between the incidence of α waves and measurement points for the beginner during planning, while a positive correlation (0.60, $p < 0.05$) was observed between the incidence of α waves and measurement points during the act of arrangement.

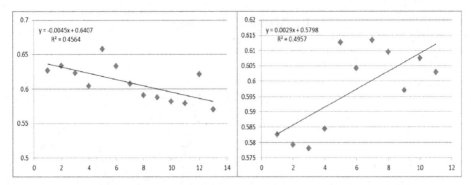

(a) Change in α wave incidence during arrangement

(b) Change in α wave incidence during act of planning

Fig. 3. Brain activity measurement of the expert

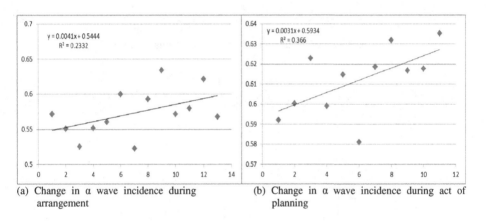

(a) Change in α wave incidence during arrangement

(b) Change in α wave incidence during act of planning

Fig. 4. Brain Activity Measurements of the Beginner

3.2 Results of the Impression Evaluation of Ikebana

As an example, Fig. 5 shows the profile of the beginner's impression evaluation results. As show in Fig. 5, the beginner could not recognise the difference of the formal beauty between expert's and beginner's Ikebana. The inexperience is almost the same as the beginner. However, expert's profile shows completely deferent pattern.

In proof of this, the average absolute value of the difference of every survey item between expert's and beginner's Ikebana were calculated and compared. The results are shown in Fig. 6. The differences in the evaluation values show a major trend, from the largest to the smallest, in the order of the expert, beginner, and inexperienced person. While there is an average difference of two points in the evaluation values for the expert, the average difference was about 0.3 points for the inexperienced person, who barely noticed any difference between the expert's and beginner's arrangements. Also, the one-way analysis of variance showed a significant difference in the evaluation, based on differing years of experience ($F(2, 92) = 16.35$, $p < 0.01$).

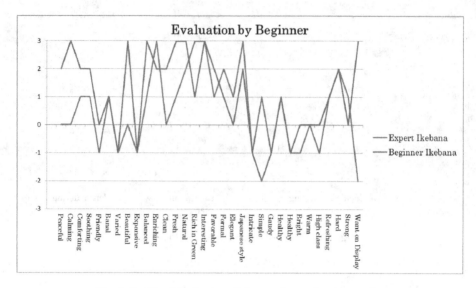

Fig. 5. Profile of the beginner's impression evaluation results

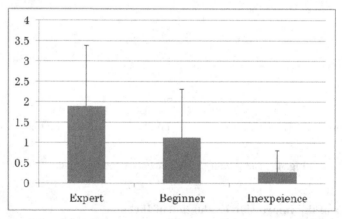

Fig. 6. Comparison of the difference in evaluation values (absolute values) of the expert, beginner, and inexperienced person

4   Summary and Future Work

The expert's incidence of α wave during planning decreased with time in the process of production. It was believed that this occurred because of an increase in the expert's mental concentration level. On the other hand, the incidence of α wave during arrangement increased with time in the process of production. This was believed be an indication that the expert was entering a deeper relaxed state as the process of production progressed. This result suggests that the Ikebana expert was alternatingly experiencing concentration and relaxation during production. It is inferred that this is connected to the mental discipline, as displayed in the concepts of Kadou. The beginner's incidence of α wave during planning increased with time in the process of production. This indicates the reason for why the beginner lost the degree of concentration in the process of production.

Among the viewers of the arrangement, Participant C (expert) displayed a clear difference in the evaluation of Participant A (expert)'s arrangement and Participant B (beginner)'s arrangement. Participant D (beginner) and Participant E (inexperienced person)'s graphs of impression evaluation results show that the distribution of evaluation values for both arrangements was very similar, suggesting that they could not distinguish the differences between the arrangements. Further research will address the factors that divide the evaluation results between experts and beginners/inexperienced people and the origins of these divisions.

References

1. Okamoto, H., Mukai, N.: A Study on Improvement of Learning Effect for an Ikebana Simulator. Institute of Electronics, Information, and Communication. Technical Report Educ. Technol. 111(237), 7–12 (2011)
2. Takara, S., Mukai, N., Kosugi, M.: Ikebana Training System. ITE Technical Report 32(54), 25–30 (2008)
3. Kim, E., Fujii, E.: A Fundamental Study of the Physio-psychological Effects of the Color of Plant. J. Jpn. Inst. Landscape Architect. 58(5), 141–144 (1995)
4. Hideyuki, A., Nishina, H., Namba, R., Masui, Y., Hashimoto, Y.: Evaluation of the Impression of Ornamental Foliage Plants and Psychological Rating of Rooms with Ornamental Foliage Plants by Means of Semantic Differential Method. Shokubutsu Kojo Gakkaishi. Journal of Shita 7(1), 34–45 (1995)
5. Hasegawa, S., Takashi, S.: Comparison of Psychological Effects on Workers between a Small Interior Plant and a Large Interior Plant. Journal of the Japanese Society of Revegetation Technology 36(1), 63–68 (2010)
6. Hasegawa, S., Takashi, S.: Influences of the Plants' Shape, Size, and Distance to the Estimator on the Impression Evaluation of the Indoor Plant. Landscape Research (online collection) 4, 24–32 (2011)

Application and Future Developments
of EMA in Digital Production Planning and Ergonomics

Benjamin Illmann, Lars Fritzsche, Wolfgang Leidholdt, Sebastian Bauer,
and Markus Dietrich

imk Automotive GmbH, Annaberger Str. 73, 09111 Chemnitz, Germany
info@imk-automotive.com

Abstract. The Editor for Manual Work Activities (EMA), a planning method
based on a 3D digital human model, addresses the need for realistic and holistic
assessment of time and ergonomics in an early phase of product, process and
resource planning. Since the first introduction of EMA in 2011 practical
applications have triggered several improvements driven by the requirements of
various industrial customers. Experiences in different branches called for a wide
focus of new developments that now allow a broader application. This paper
illustrates the connection between practical requirements and technical
improvements of EMA within the past years. It also demonstrates how EMA
may contribute to cost-efficient and accurate planning in different phases of the
product development cycle. Finally, some of the future developments are
illustrated.

Keywords: Digital Human Modeling, Production Planning, Ergonomics.

1 Introduction

Demographic change is one of the widely used keywords for reasoning investments
on the field of ergonomics. Fact is that the ageing of the workforce – mostly caused
by extended life expectation and decreasing fertility – has become a major
productivity risk, especially in manual assembly tasks. Causing already almost one
third of all sick leaves, musculoskeletal disorders (MSD) show a significant higher
prevalence at a higher age [1][2]. The urgency for ergonomic countermeasures
increases thusly.

It is well known that the later these countermeasures are taken, the less impact they
have and the more it will cost. Therefore cost-efficiency will be highest in early
phases of production planning [3][4]. Once series production has started costs of
changes may easily outnumber the benefits retrieved from improvement of
ergonomics. As a consequence, production planners have a high responsibility not
only to assure good ergonomics, but also other aspects of "good work" such as
efficiency and feasibility. In order to meet these objectives appropriate methods for
digital production planning are needed. Simulating the interaction between products
(car body, part etc.), work processes (assembly tasks) and equipment (tools,
machinery) with human resources is a promising holistic approach for validation and
evaluation purposes in early planning phases. Yet, simulation methods themselves

V.G. Duffy (Ed.): DHM/HCII 2013, Part II, LNCS 8026, pp. 66–75, 2013.

need to be efficient and intuitively applicable in order to conduct digital evaluations in a timely manner.

In regard to preventive ergonomic work design during pre-production planning, digital human models (DHM) have been considered a very promising method [5], however most DHM suffer from a time-consuming simulation and inefficient adaption and variation with regard to illustrating design alternatives. The reasons are manifold, but they can often be found in static posture generation through inverse kinematics. Especially when it comes to dynamic simulation and human motion generation conventional methods lack precision, validity and variability.

This paper introduces EMA (Editor for Manual Work Activities), a software-based planning method that resolves most deficiencies of current DHM tools. Main focus of this paper is to present practical applications of EMA and to give an outlook on future developments.

2   Rediscovering EMA

2.1   The Definition of EMA

In 2011 EMA was introduced by Fritzsche et al. as a software tool "[…] that reduces the effort for preparing simulations of human work and, at the same time, improves the accuracy of simulations" [6]. Through practical application and continuous improvement in the past years it has become more than a software tool – it is now considered as a software-based planning method, which uses 3D-DHM simulations and established "process languages". This method allows a holistic and realistic assessment of human work in regard to time efficiency, feasibility and ergonomics through the fast and variable simulation of human motion.

There are several advantages that distinguish EMA from other planning methods / DHM application tools:

— Easy to use by drag and drop handling metaphors
— Use of typical planning language suitable for manufacturing applications ("pick part A, place in appliance B, use tool C to fixate")
— Self-initiated motion generation
— Use of object references
— MTM-based standard-time calculation
— EAWS-based ergonomic assessment of full-shift physical strain

EMA's key to efficient human motion simulation is the continuous use of object references and the self-initiated motion generation, which is based on motion-capturing studies with real production worker. Once the task is described in very simple language ("pick part A, place …") and specified by certain parameters (which part and location etc.), EMA will generate human motion without further ado, thus being fast and realistic. Using relative object references EMA will always find the specified object, no matter how often it has been moved in the 3D-environment. This enables the user to generate alternative design and planning scenarios in a very short time just by moving the referenced object to another location or by changing certain object preferences, such as shape, size, or weight. Unlike other DHM nothing else within the simulation needs to be adapted to create such an alternative scenario. Multiple planning solutions can be tested in a cost-efficient way by using this method for a fast variation of processes (order of tasks etc.), products (weight and dimensions etc.) and resources (5th%ile vs. 95th%ile etc.)[7]. Moreover, the most relevant planning objectives – production time, physical workload and geometric feasibility – can be evaluated and objectively compared based on the produced reports on standard assessment methods (MTM-time and EAWS-ergonomics).

For ergonomic risk assessment the EAWS (Ergonomic Assessment Worksheet [8]) has been implemented. It is the only commonly used holistic method that allows the evaluation of physical workload throughout the entire work process. Additional analysis functions of EMA can be used to avoid waste (in reference to the Toyota Production System); for instance, by illustrating ergonomic strains, long walking distances, and double handling of parts and tools.

In summary, these EMA report tools enable the production planner to compare alternatives of product and process design by means of objective quantitative analyses of efficiency and ergonomics based on human simulations.

2.2   From Software Implementation to Stand-Alone-Software

When EMA was first introduced in 2011 it was only available as a plug-in for Dassault Systèmes' Delmia V5 software suite that is now called "EMA-V5". In the meantime, EMA is also available as a stand-alone system that could be incorporated in nearly all PLM/PDM systems. It offers the same scope of services but appears as a more flexible and lean system with more data interfaces and modular expandability. The figure below shows the new EMA interface.

Fig. 1. EMA user interface

The main difference between EMA as a standalone software and EMA-V5 is the integrated 3D graphic engine and the advanced human model. EMA-V5 still offers the same user interface and functions, but shows the simulation in the DELMIA window using the "Delmia Human Builder" manikin as human model.

This evolution of EMA to a stand-alone-software widens the area of application because it allows an even more customer-specific adaption of the software and better usability. Especially SMEs should be interested in using a lean system without having to purchase a costly full PLM-system, yet still have the same benefits. Generally, EMA is a very flexible system that allows companies to incorporate the software in their own specific IT-landscape. In the past several company-specific methods were integrated, such as an individual ergonomic assessment tool of a large automotive OEM.

Since 2011 the performance and efficiency of EMA has increased significantly. By now, simulations can be generated using less complex operations and thus, in a much quicker manner. For example, EMA is now able to automatically calculate the shortest walkway and the best relative position for picking and placing objects.

Also the validation of human motion through motion-capturing was continued, thus creating even more realistic human motion in regard to execution and duration. Both of these factors are very important for increasing the accuracy of ergonomic assessment and time prediction. Field studies that were conducted at VOLKSWAGEN, one of the most prominent EMA users, compared ergonomic assessments with EAWS in paper-pencil and EMA demonstrating significant correlations between the conventional scores and the results calculated with EMA [9]. Internal studies about MTM-1 analysis and EMA production time have shown deviations of less than 5 %, thus being sufficiently accurate for planning purposes.

In order to increase the timely accuracy of EMA and ensure a full translation of EMA process languages into MTM-codes, the EMA-family will grow by a full integration in MTM's standard software system for time analysis called "TiCon". As a long-term result EMA will be able to generate MTM-codes out of the simulation and vice-versa [10].

3   Practical Application of EMA

The industrial application of EMA has been a key element to further improvement of the planning method and the DHM. Especially the wide range of industries and tasks has offered significant inputs for improving motion generation, software usability and analysis functions. Most partners are OEM's in automotive industry, like Audi, BMW, Daimler and Volkswagen. However especially applications in other industries, such as aviation industry (Airbus), textile machinery (Karl Mayer Textilmaschinenfabrik) and white goods, ensure a broad development of EMA driven by the very diverse requirements of each industry.

The following paragraphs specify areas of application in the product development cycle and illustrate three examples of EMA application describing their contribution to further development.

3.1   Areas of Application

EMA can and certainly should be used during the entire product development process. The earlier EMA is used in product conception and production planning, the more costs for re-design can be saved; however, EMA can be applied in all phases, from concept design, to pre-production planning, pre-series production trails and series production.

During the concept phase the focus is certainly put on buildability and plausibility checks. Ergonomics and time can only be assessed rudimentarily due to the lack of process descriptions, but the simulation and analysis functions offer an early estimation of bottle-neck-processes in regard to physical workload and manufacturing time. These early assessments have a strong product-reference; however they should also be used to evaluate concepts for facilities, equipment, and production layout in general.

The definition of standard working sequences should be the result of pre-production planning. The planning method EMA can be used for compilation and validation of optimal work processes and product specification, while various alternatives are assessed and visualized within the 3D environment. This phase has a strong process focus and lays the foundation for the following pre-series planning. The ergonomic assessment and time analysis now requires greater detail and, for the first time in the product development cycle, focuses on the whole cycle or shift.

Pre-series production offers a last chance to optimize product, process and resource before series production starts. This requires simulations and analysis to be very detailed and accurate. If the simulation with EMA has been gradually build up throughout the product development process only minor adjustments need to be made and last changes can be virtually assessed without expensive tryouts. Similarly EMA could be used to support the continuous improvement process during series production. Hereby mostly the integration of new concepts in regard to product, process and resource is of importance. Again, a simulation and analysis with EMA avoids the interruption of the production process for costly try-outs. In that phase EMA may also be used for qualification matters. The simulation videos illustrate standard working procedures that newly hired workers need to learn before they can be deployed at the running production line. In that sense, EMA may also serve to support communication between planning and production because it shows the ideal process just as it was intended to run.

After start of production, EMA is particularly useful to investigate layout optimization and the integration of new tools or machinery in running production lines, before they actually exist. Within the 3D environment the available space of the workplace becomes visible and illustrates the future work process without physical tryouts or interruptions of the running production.

3.2   Industrial Application I

An early scenario of EMA application consisted of multiple picking tasks in the logistics supermarket area for an automobile assembly line (Fig. 2). At first, EMA had several problems simulating material handling tasks. For example, until that date it was not possible to operate multiple parts. Therefore the whole operation of material handling needed to be remodeled, so several parts could be grabbed and released by the DHM at different times. Furthermore the operation for pushing and pulling trolleys and carts needed to be implemented. More structural elements for subcategorizing tasks needed to be created for a correct ergonomic assessment with EAWS (pushing includes grabbing, connecting, walking and releasing). The implementation of another structural level however also helped organizing the tasks into operation sequences, which are often used in larger companies as structural elements within their PLM-system. Therefore EMA could now also inherit the structure of tasks used in most companies. For instance, the tasks "pick up lid", "walk to car body" and "place lid in appliance" can now be merged in the operation sequence "install front lid".

Fig. 2. Pushing and pulling during consignment tasks in EMA V5

Another focus of this application was the mapping of EMA standard time with MTM-time. Before, the deviations of the time simulated by EMA and MTM-1-time were significant for certain tasks and movements. Based on this example, however, the timely accuracy of EMA was tremendously increased by conducting a step-by-step comparison of movements and MTM-1 modules.

3.3   Industrial Application II

Another very interesting application at a textile machinery plant (Karl Mayer Textilmaschinenfabrik) showed that EMA can be used in a wide range of areas. The main focus was design improvement in regard to maintenance tasks. These can be

Fig. 3. Different possible postures of EMA

very time-consuming due to large machinery and odd postures and movements that need to be executed in order to reach certain maintenance accesses. Such movements consist of crawling, kneeling, sliding and lying as well as motions to and from these postures. In this example, EMA was used in order to get an accurate estimation of accessibility and time need for certain maintenance tasks, (Fig. 3). Besides that, also typical applications in manual assembly tasks, especially in the automotive industry, benefit from this specific development: In-car motion such as sliding from one side to another can now be simulated and assigned with a standard planning time based on MTM-1.

3.4   Industrial Application III

Tool handling has been another big issue during the development of EMA. In order to be effective and accurate in creating the simulation, tools need to be handled by EMA without further information-input by the planner. Applications at Daimler (Mercedes-Benz Manufacturing Hungary) and Volkswagen (Kaluga plant in Russia) have offered a variety of scenarios to use specific tools. Particularly, the use of welding tongs and different pistol-grip tools have shown the most important determinants for tool handling. Firstly a tool-center point (TCP) needed to be defined, which describes the place and orientation of the application point. Secondly each tool needed a special gripping point to ensure correct hand-wrist-orientation. Thirdly, specific body movements had to be created depending on the tool trajectory; EMA nowadays automatically follows the tool step by step and always finds the optimal posture in reference to the place of application (Fig. 4). In the near future the tool-objects will inherit more information about the process, such as involved body forces and necessary movements. This way, manual and automatic tools will automatically cause a different execution of a task.

Fig. 4. Tool-based positioning of EMA (white goods example)

4   Future Developments

Triggered by the continuous input and requirements of customers as well as general trends within the industry, the future development of EMA will ensure that the planning process with EMA constantly improves in efficiency and accuracy. Currently the possible extensions seem endless; however some are certainly of more concern. The most important ones that are going to be implemented in the near future are presented in the following.

Currently object constraints can only be realized within the 3D-Layout, since creating constraints during tasks of the DHM is especially challenging. This is necessary if an object needs to be assembled and then handled again as a single object. However this feature will be implemented shortly. A related topic is working in and on moving objects, which exists quite often especially in assembly lines. No currently available DHM or production planning systems allows this kind of simulation, yet the consequent use of object reference in EMA creates the ability to always find its objects within the 3D environment, thus allowing working in and on place-unsteady objects.

Another constant subject of further development is the reduction of user commands. More automatic algorithms for situation-based motion generation are required to reduce the number of user interactions and finally, increase the efficiency of EMA simulations. One example is the context-based walking target selection, which eliminates the need to specify walking patterns, thus reducing the number of commands needed. Walking targets may differ in reference to the geometry of objects that are picked and placed.

Another key to reduced commands is a detailed collision control. Currently, collision control is implemented only for lower extremities. The more the DHM automatically generates correct human motion, the fewer tasks need to be specified. The long-term objective is a full collision control, which will be implemented gradually. At the moment, a major drawback of full collision control is that system performance is strongly impeded. Despite being a very lean system, EMA constantly needs performance optimization in order to realize such computationally intensive operations. Shape-based parameterizations are closely related to collision control. Behind this bulky expression one can find features like automatic grip-point definition at complex objects. EMA will then always find the optimal grip-point, for example the handle of a can.

Beside the improvement of the simulation in terms of efficiency and accuracy, also the analysis functions will be enhanced. For example, the so-called Ergo-Optimizer will not only allow an assessment of risks, but also aid the planner to systematically reduce ergonomic risks by taking the most effectives countermeasures in a certain situation.

One last development is the further extension of PLM-system-interfaces. Currently Collada and JT are defined as standard data-formats, but in addition to improving JT-data handling a new set of extensions and applications may be accessible with advanced data-handling procedures. Future applications may range from automatic data import from construction data management systems to a full implementation of (company-specific) library data elements (tools, anthropometry data, standard racks etc.).

5   Conclusions

In the past years EMA has evolved from a planning tool that uses an innovative approach for human motion generation to a full grown planning method. This paper has shown that industrial applications have greatly contributed to the improvement of movement-accuracy and planning-efficiency. A main focus was put on motion generation as the core competence, however also the performance of different assessment methods, such as EAWS for ergonomic assessment and MTM for time analysis, greatly benefited from the requirements that were defined by EMA customers. Through the use of EMA in the automotive industry, aviation industry, white goods and other industries the range of possible tasks and the system performance vastly increased and created many ideas for future developments. Especially in terms of data exchange of the software and interaction with the surrounding 3D-environment of the DHM, EMA will soon allow a broader and more efficient applicability in all phases of the product development process.

References

1. European Agency for Safety and Health at work: Podniece, Z.: Work-related musculoskeletal disorders: prevention report, A European campaign on musculoskeletal disorders, Office for Official Publications of the European Communities (2008), https://osha.europa.eu/en/publications/reports/en_TE8107132ENC.pdf

2. Betriebskrankenkasse [BKK]: Gesundheitsreport 2012 – Gesundheit fördern – Krankheit versorgen – mit Krankheit leben. BKK Bundesverband, Essen (2012)
3. Ilmarinen, J.E.: The ageing workforce – Challenges for occupational health. Occupational Medicine 56, 362–364 (2006)
4. Fritzsche, L.: Ergonomics risk assessment with digital human Models in car assembly: Simulation versus real-life. Human Factors and Ergonomics in Manufacturing & Service Industries 20, 287–299 (2010)
5. Duffy, V.G.: Handbook of Digital Human Modeling. In: Research for Applied Ergonomics and Human Factors Engineering, pp. 3-1–3-30. CRC Press, Taylor & Francis Group, Boca Raton (2009)
6. Fritzsche, L., Jendrusch, R., Leidholdt, W., Bauer, S., Jäckel, T., Pirger, A.: Introducing ema (Editor for Manual Work Activities) – A New Tool for Enhancing Accuracy and Efficiency of Human Simulations in Digital Production Planning. In: Duffy, V.G. (ed.) ICDHM 2011. LNCS, vol. 6777, pp. 272–281. Springer, Heidelberg (2011)
7. Illmann, B., Finsterbusch, T.: Beschreibung menschlicher Arbeit in einer Prozesssprache. Die Zukunft der Mensch-Simulation in der Produktion. In: Arbeitswissenschaft, G.F. (ed.) Gestaltung nachhaltiger Arbeitssysteme - Wege zur gesunden, effizienten und sicheren Arbeit, Kongress der Gesellschaft für Arbeitswissenschaft, vol. 58, pp. 127–130. GfA-Press, Dortmund (2012)
8. Schaub, K., Caragnano, G., Britzke, B., Bruder, R.: The European assembly worksheet. Theoretical Issues in Ergonomics Science (1) (April 27, 2012)
9. Schönherr, R., Fritzsche, L., Schmickartz, S.: Praxis digitaler Arbeitsplanung – Validierungsstudie zum Einsatz des Editors menschlicher Arbeit (ema). In: Arbeitswissenschaft, G.F. (ed.) Gesellschaft für Arbeitswissenschaft, 59. Kongress der Gesellschaft für Arbeitswissenschaft (2013)
10. Illmann, B., Fritzsche, L.: Erweiterung der ema-Prozesssprache zur ganzheitlichen Simulation und Ergonomiebewertung. In: Arbeitswissenschaft, G.F. (ed.) Gesellschaft für Arbeitswissenschaft, 59. Kongress der Gesellschaft für Arbeitswissenschaft (2013)

Using Anthropomorphism to Improve
the Human-Machine Interaction
in Industrial Environments (Part I)

Sinem Kuz[1], Marcel Ph. Mayer[1], Simon Müller[2], and Christopher M. Schlick[1]

[1] Institute of Industrial Engineering and Ergonomics, RWTH Aachen University
{s.kuz,m.mayer,c.schlick}@iaw.rwth-aachen.de
[2] Laboratory for Machine Tools and Production Engineering WZL, RWTH Aachen University
s.mueller@wzl.rwth-aachen.de

Abstract. The concept of socio-technical systems emphasizes the mutual interrelationship between humans and technical system considering the human operator as an integral part of the system. However, to use the full potential of this idea the technical system has to be perceived and accepted as a team-partner. Anthropomorphism is a promising approach to improve the acceptance of a robotic system as a team-partner. In the first part of this joint contribution we introduce a study focusing on the effect of anthropomorphism in industrial environments. A virtual environment consisting of a robotized assembly cell was utilized to conduct a prediction experiment with 24 participants comparing anthropomorphic movements and trajectories based on linear and angular kinematics of an articulated robot. The task was to predict the target position during movement. The corresponding reaction value and the prediction accuracy were analyzed.

Keywords: Human-robot interaction, anthropomorphism, socio-technical system, prediction, self-optimization.

1   Introduction

Increasing globalization and the resulting cost pressure require a flexible adaptation of manufacturers to market conditions in order to meet the demand for diversity or short product life cycles. The necessary flexibility cannot be achieved by fully automated systems. Therefore, investigating the possibilities for increasing flexibility of production systems is an important issue. The integration of the human operator and the cooperation with robotic systems seems to be a promising approach to enable the optimal combination of different capabilities of humans and robots and thereby results in more flexible and agile.

When considering the coexistence of robotic systems with humans, it is necessary to ensure the occupational safety of people. Besides this aspect, when working with a robotic co-worker, the level of stress, comfort and trust of the human operator during the interaction is also a decisive factor for an effective collaboration [1], [2]. Therefore; the analysis of factors influencing the human acceptance of the robot as a

V.G. Duffy (Ed.): DHM/HCII 2013, Part II, LNCS 8026, pp. 76–85, 2013.

partner is a central issue. For this reason, current work in the field of human-robot interaction focuses on the idea of anthropomorphism, i.e. the simulation of human characteristics by non-human agents. By transferring anthropomorphic features such as appearance on robotic systems, a higher level of safety and user acceptance can be achieved [3].

Anthropomorphism is an approach that is already used in the area of social or humanoid robotics because there is almost no physical separation between humans and robots. The simulation of human behavior by an industrial robot is rarely investigated because the focus in manufacturing environments lies more on the design of fully automated systems that should operate robustly and efficiently without human interaction or cooperation. Nonetheless, depending on the market situation, these systems quickly reach their limits in rapidly changing manufacturing environments and the integration of the human operator becomes more and more important. Focusing on scenarios with human-robot interaction or even cooperation, anthropomorphism might be an important design principle in order to achieve a safe, effective, and efficient cooperation between humans and robots in industrial environments. Especially with regard to self-optimizing production systems the ability to plan and execute a process autonomously raises the complexity of these systems so that the system behavior cannot always be anticipated by the human operator. Therefore, within a sub-project of the Cluster of Excellence "Integrative Production Technology for High-Wage Countries" at the RWTH Aachen University the interaction between human and a cognitively automated robotic system is investigated. In order to guarantee an effective teamwork between man and machine within such environments in terms of a socio-technical concept, the system behavior should be understandable and predictable to ensure transparency. In other words, the human has to be able to understand and trust the system as well as associate it with intelligence. For this purpose, Krach et al. [4] proved a positive correlation between the degree of human likeness and the perceived level of intelligence of a non-human entity.

The empirical study that will be presented within this work focuses on the effect of anthropomorphism in assembly environments, in particular in motion behavior of an assembly robot. This idea is mainly based on the scientific evidences concerning the neural activity of the brain when watching someone performing an action. These special brain areas (mirror neurons) in humans and non-human primates are activated both by action generation and observation of other humans' actions [5], [6]. Researchers claim, that mirror neurons may explain a variety of social cognitive functions such as the action and intention recognition of others. Based on these results, Gazzola et al. [7] have investigated human mirror neurons during the observation of simple robotic actions and reported a significant activation of these special brain areas. Hence, the research question focuses on how movement trajectories (anthropomorphic vs. conventional movements) of a gantry robot might affect the predictability of its behavior. The paper is divided into two parts. In the first part the results of the first empirical study on the research question are presented. The second part of the paper concentrates on the deeper analysis and discussion of the findings of the first study and the results of a subsequent study related to this issue [8].

2   Anthropomorphism in Industrial Environments

Recent research has repeatedly shown that anthropomorphism is an interesting concept to improve the human-robot interaction [9]. Concerning industrial environments a subarea of the European research project ROSETTA focuses also on human like design of industrial robot systems in order to increase the acceptance of human when cooperating with such systems. The investigation focused on an anthropomorphic model of the kinematic control of an industrial robot during manipulation tasks. For each position of the end effector the anthropomorphic posture of the elbow joint can be calculated by a human inspired movement pattern algorithm. The study could empirically prove that by applying the kinematic control on a 7-degree-of-freedom (7-DOF) anthropomorphic manipulator, a reduction of the stress level of the humans working side by side with the robot can be achieved [10].

Huber et al. [11] also investigated how human cooperation characteristics can be transferred to human-robot cooperation scenarios. In this case a handover process was used, in which the human-human, human-robot and human-humanoid cooperation were compared to each other. They used a human-inspired trajectory that was modeled after the maxim of a free flow as smoothly as possible and compared it to a trajectory that resulted from a trapezoidal velocity profile. Results of this analysis have shown that reaction times of the humans concerning human-inspired trajectories were lower than the trapezoidal case. Findings concerning anthropomorphic characteristics in appearance could also prove shorter reaction times. Because of the results concerning the appearance, the hypothesis was generated that human trajectories as opposed to trajectories based on simple inverse kinematics could lead to a further improvement of the reaction times.

Moreover, in contrast to traditional approaches in industrial robotics, there are an increasing number of new concepts for automation solutions with human-like characteristics such as two-armed robots [12], [13]. Accordingly based on these findings, augmenting the movements of an industrial robot with anthropomorphic features might be a promising approach to improve safety.

3   Method

To address the aforementioned research question, a first study with a repeated measures design and three within-participants factors (perspective, movement type, and position) was conducted by means of a virtual simulation environment consisting of an assembly robot and its workplace. A C++ simulation program which was already utilized in different empirical studies within the Cluster of Excellence was adapted and employed as testing environment [14]. The simulation scene comprises a six-axis gantry robot that could be regarded as a real human arm in a real "placing" situation. A black and white grid with 20 fields was used to illustrate the working area of the robot. Within the study the focus lies on how movement trajectories (anthropomorphic vs. conventional movements) of an assembly robot might affect the predictability of its behavior. The movement type (anthropomorphic vs. robotic), the field position and the perspective (frontal vs. lateral) were considered as independent variables, whereas the reaction time, the relative reaction way and the prediction accuracy were the dependent variables. The prediction accuracy was analyzed in terms of correct, incorrect and missing predictions. The reaction time describes the elapsed time from the beginning of a movement sequence until the prediction of the participant and the relative reaction way is the percental part of the presented movement trajectory that was tracked from the start of a movement until the subject predicted a target field. Furthermore the sequence of the testing conditions to be passed was permuted to avoid order effects. For the evaluation process the virtual working area of the assembly robot was divided into rows and columns in order to be able to make further analysis regarding the incorrect predictions (see Fig. 2).

3.1   Pre-study: Generation of the Human Motion Data

In order to generate the movement data for the main empirical study, a preliminary experiment was conducted using an infrared optical tracking system. Therefore, human motion trajectories during placing an object were recorded and analyzed. For the execution, the participant was standing in front of a table, where black plastic discs were mounted at regular intervals for placing a cylindrical object (see Fig. 1). As depicted in the figure, the participant always started in the same posture in front of the table and placed the cylinder with markers in the black marked area on the grid without changing the posture of the body. The data recorded by the motion tracking system represent the trajectory of the human wrist during the execution of the placing movements. In addition to the cartesian coordinates, the duration of the complete movement from the start position until placing the object was also computed. Figure 1 represents on the right side the human and the conventional point-to- point robot trajectories for the same starting point and end points in comparison.

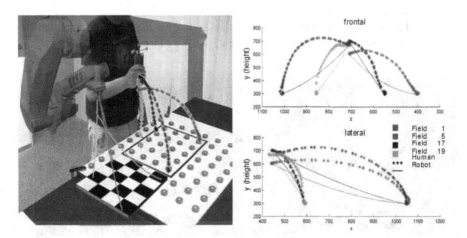

Fig. 1. The experimental setting for motion tracking in comparison to the virtual environment with the corresponding robotic and the human movement trajectories (left) and the acquired trajectories (right)

The trajectory of the robot proceeds on a relatively straight course, whereas the recorded human movements appear more curved. Afterwards, the human motion data were adapted to control the articulated robot in the simulation environment.

3.2   Procedure

The main study can be divided into three different phases. Within the first phase the personal data of the participants were collected, e.g. age, profession, experiences with 3D simulation environments (e.g. computer games) as well as with robotic systems. Afterwards, a visual acuity test, a stereo vision test, and a color vision test were carried out to control intervening variables related to visual perception. After completing these pretests, the participants were seated in front of a TFT LCD 28" monitor, and were asked to observe the virtual articulated robot while performing different pick and place operations on the grid. To avoid order effects, the study started with the frontal perspective for the one half of the participants and with the lateral perspective for the other half (see Fig. 2). During the observation part of the study, the virtual robot placed the cylinder on every field of the grid. Each of these 20 fields was approached by both the human trajectories and the conventional point-to-point robotic movements whereby the order of the motion sequences was permuted before each experiment. The participants should monitor each of these 40 motion sequences per perspective and predict the target field as early as possible within the duration of the presented movement trajectory by using a computer mouse. After all 40 motion sequences have been executed within the first perspective, the view changed and the same motion sequences were again presented from the other perspective. After marking a field the simulation was interrupted and the next motion sequence could be started by the participants. During the experiment the corresponding reaction time, the relative reaction way and the prediction accuracy were collected for later examinations.

Within the last phase the participants were asked to give their opinion about which perspective has improved the predictability best.

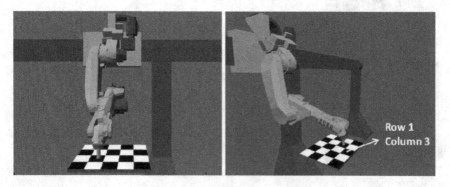

Fig. 2. The virtual scene presented from the frontal (left) and the lateral perspective (right)

3.3   Participants

A total number of 24 male subjects, who are either taking part in an engineering bachelor/master program or have just graduated, participated in the study. The participants were aged between 20 and 33 years (mean 25.21 years, SD 3.799). 83% of the participants had already experience with 3D simulation environments. Almost 38% of the subjects had worked with robotic environments and even 33% of them for several months. All of the participants passed the visual acuity test, the stereo vision test, and the color vision test.

4   Results

A total of 1920 predictions were carried out by the participants. According to the experimental setup, each cell was approached four times (two different profiles combined with two perspectives).

In 216 presented movement trajectories the selection of the target field by the participants was not done within the movement duration. The distinction between the movement types shows a much higher value of 82.41% for the conventional robot movements than for the human trajectories, where participants could not answer in 17.59% of the cases in a timely manner. 51.85% of the missing predictions are within the frontal perspective and about 48.15% are within the lateral one.

The number of correct predictions, i.e. the matches between the approached target position by the robot and the subjects marked field, is only 112 for both perspectives. 78.57% of the correct predictions are within the frontal and 21.43% within the lateral perspective. This small number of correct predictions shows that the experimental task was quite difficult and stressful so that it was in general not easy for the participant to recognize the right target area. This might be caused due to the lack of depth information in the visualization, which was also remarked by the subjects during the study.

Furthermore, we analyzed the absolute row and column distance between the predicted field of the participant and the correct target position. The average column distances were in general very small, and for both perspectives nearly the same. Analyses show that the minimum of the average column distances between the predicted field and the correct target position are close to zero and the maximum is less than 0.6. The average row distances are in contrast to the column distances much higher. Results for the lateral view show that compared to the conventional robot trajectories, human movements lead in the first two rows (the upper section of the work area from the standpoint of the assembly robot) to higher average deviations from the target field (see Fig. 3). This effect is reversed for rows 3 and 4. The row distances concerning the frontal view are similar to the ones for the lateral view so that the same applies here: the row distances in the front areas of the virtual workplace are lower for human motion trajectories than for the robotic ones.

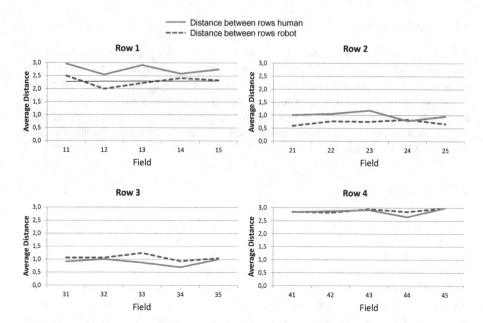

Fig. 3. Average values for row distances between the prediction and the target field (lateral view)

Regarding the reaction time inferential statistics did not show any significant effects neither for the perspective nor for the movement type. Only the field position has a significant effect on the reaction time, which is not examined in detail within this work. Afterwards the different perspectives were analyzed separately, but the analysis of variance did not reveal any significant effects of the movement type on the absolute reaction time.

Concerning the relative reaction way the analysis of variance again could not reveal any significant effects neither for the movement type nor for the perspective. However, the statistical analysis of the different perspectives showed significant results regarding the lateral perspective. The analysis shows that both the type of movement $(F(1, 23) = 6.647, p = 0.017)$ as well as the position $(F(19, 437) = 7.449, p <0.001)$ have a significant effect on this variable. There is also a disordinal interaction effect between the movement type and the position $(F(19, 209.683) = 7.036, p <0.001)$, whereby the main effects could not be interpreted separately. Nevertheless, on closer examination of the means of the relative reaction way for the different rows on the grid, the already mentioned tendencies are confirmed. The comparison shows that the reaction way for fields that are closer to the virtual robot (row 3 and 4) are shorter for anthropomorphic movements than for robotic ones (see Fig. 4).

At the end of the experiment the participants were asked to indicate which perspective they would prefer concerning the prediction and about 70% stated that they would intuitively favor the lateral view.

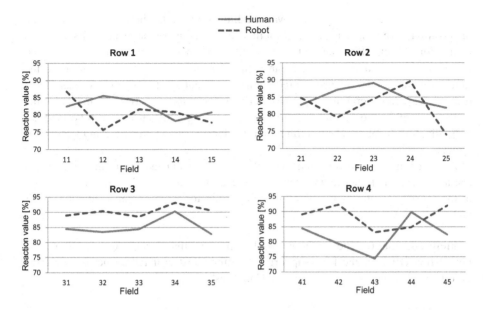

Fig. 4. The relative reaction ways [%] in comparison for different rows on the virtual work area (lateral view)

5   Summary and Outlook

The goal of this paper was to present the results of the first experimental study in which the impact of human-like motion patterns of an industrial robot on human prediction of target positions of placing movements were examined. A laboratory study was conducted, where anthropomorphic movements were compared to conventional robotic trajectories by means of a simulation environment. Therefore, pick and place movements of the human were tracked by an optical motion capture system. The captured data were analyzed and adapted to control the articulated robot in the simulation software. The prediction accuracy, the reaction time and the relative reaction way were analyzed as dependent variables during the evaluation process.

The prediction accuracy was divided into the missing, the correct and the incorrect predictions. Results concerning the missing predictions show that within both the frontal and the lateral perspective the participants more often failed to mark a target field concerning the conventional robot trajectories than the human movements. The number of correct predictions was very small. The probable reason for this might be the lack of depth information of the visualization of the simulation environment. The incorrect predictions were investigated by means of the absolute row and column distances between the prediction field of the participant and the correct target position. Results concerning the average row distances show in both perspectives that compared to the human movements the conventional robot trajectories lead in rows 3 and 4 to higher average distances from the target field. For rows 1 and 2 the average row distances were higher for the anthropomorphic trajectories.

Concerning the relative reaction way, findings showed that both the movement and the position have a significant effect on this variable. Due to the disordinal significant interaction effects, the interpretation of the two main effects was not possible. Nevertheless, the comparison of mean values for the different rows on the grid, the same effect as for the incorrect predictions is evident for the average values of the reaction way. In general this value was better at short distances (rows 3 and 4) for the anthropomorphic movement trajectories and at longer distances for robotic ones. Regarding the absolute reaction time inferential statistics did not show any significant effects.

A clear limitation of this study was that it was conducted by means of a virtual testing environment; hence an interesting avenue for future work is the investigation of the impact of anthropomorphic movement trajectories on human prediction under real conditions.

Acknowledgement. The authors would like to thank the German Research Foundation DFG for the kind support within the Cluster of Excellence "Integrative Production Technology for High-Wage Countries".

References

1. Oleson, K.E., Billings, B.R., Kocsis, V., Chen, J.Y.C., Hancock, P.A.: Antescendents of Trust in Human-Robot Collaboration (2011)
2. Billings, D.R., Schaefer, K.E., Chen, J.Y.C., Hancock, P.A.: Human-robot interaction: developing trust in robots. In: Proceedings of the 7th ACM/IEEE International Conference on Human-Robot Interaction, Boston, Massachusetts, USA, pp. 109–110 (2012)
3. Duffy, B.: Anthropomorphism and The Social Robot. Special Issue on Socially Interactive Robots. Robotics and Autonomous Systems 42(3-4) (2003)
4. Krach, S., Hegel, F., Wrede, B., Sagerer, G., Binkofski, F., Kircher, T.: Can machines think? Interaction and perspective taking with robots investigated via fMRI. PLoS ONE 3(7), e2597 (2008)
5. Rizzolatti, G., Fadiga, L., Gallese, V., Fogassi, L.: Premotor cortex and the recognition of motor actions. Cognitive Brain Research 3, 131–141 (1996)
6. Rizzolatti, G., Fadiga, L., Matelli, M., Bettinardi, V., Paulesu, E., Perani, D., Fazio, F.: Localization of grasp representations in humans by PET: 1. Observation versus execution Experimental Brain Research 111, 246–252 (1996)
7. Gazzola, V., Rizzolatti, G., Wicker, B., Keysers, C.: The anthropomorphic brain: The mirror neuron system responds to human and robotic actions. Journal of Neuroimage 35(4), 1674–1684 (2007)
8. Kuz, S., Mayer, M.P., Müller, S., Schlick, C.M.: Using Anthropomorphism to Improve the Human-Machine Interaction in Industrial Environments-Part I. In: The Proceedings of the 4th International Conference on Digital Human Modeling and applications in Health, Safety, Ergonomics and Risk Management, Las Vegas, NV, USA (2013)
9. Eyssel, F., Kuchenbrandt, D., Bobinger, S., De Ruiter, L., Hegel, F.: If You Sound Like Me, You Must Be More Human':On the Interplay of Robot and User Features on Human-Robot Acceptance and Anthropomorphism. In: Proceedings of the Seventh Annual ACM/IEEE International Conference on Human-Robot Interaction, pp. 125–126 (2012)

10. Zanchettin, A.M.: Human-centric behavior of redundant manipulators under kinematic control, PhD Thesis, Politecnico di Milano (2012)
11. Huber, M., Rickert, M., Knoll, A., Brandt, T., Glausauer, S.: Robot and Human Interactive Communication. In: The 17th IEEE International Symposium on RO-MAN 2008, Munich, Germany, pp. 107–112 (2008)
12. Baxter's Capabilities: A unique robot with unique features,
    `http://www.rethinkrobotics.com/index.php/products/baxter/`
13. ABB concept robot for small parts assembly applications (FRIDA), `http://www.abb.de/`
    `cawp/abbzh254/8657f5e05ede6ac5c1257861002c8ed2.aspx`
14. Odenthal, B., Mayer, M., Ph., K.W., Kausch, B., Schlick, C.M.: Investigation of Error Detection in Assembled Workpieces Using an Augmented Vision System. In: Proceedings of the IEA 17th World Congress on Ergonomics (CD-ROM), Beijing, China, pp. 1–9 (2009)

Changes in Heart Rate Variability during Manual Controlled Rendezvous and Docking with Task Complexity

Pengjie Li[1,3], Bin Wu[1,3], Yijing Zhang[2,3], Zhi Yao[3], Weifen Huang[3], and Xiang Zhang[3]

[1] State Key Laboratory of Space Medicine Fundamentals and Application, Beijing, 100094, P.R. China
[2] National Key Laboratory of Human Factors Engineering, Beijing, 100094, P.R. China
[3] China Astronaut Research and Training Center, Beijing, 100094, P.R. China
wubinacc@sina.com, zyj.acc@gmail.com

Abstract. This research aims to study how HRV parameters change with task complexity during manual controlled Rendezvous and Docking (RVD). One one-factor experiment was conducted. The experiment task was manual controlled Rendezvous and Docking (RVD) operation and the factor was task complexity which was divided into three levels. Eight male volunteers participated in this experiment, which consisted of three trials, and each of which consisted of ten operation units containing three complexity levels. The dependent variables were main performance parameters and HRV parameters. Results showed that operation time and fuel consumption changed significantly with different complexity levels. Besides, there were significant differences on partial HRV parameters. It can be inferred that some HRV parameters are useful for mental workload evaluation. However, the relationship between the insignificant parameters and complexity levels needs to be validated and the way how HRV should be used for mental workload evaluation deserves further study.

Keywords: Heart rate variability, Rendezvous and Docking, Task complexity, Mental workload.

1 Introduction

Manual controlled RVD is a task that is full of continuous operations in a dynamic environment. It requires that the astronauts have excellent operation skills and reaction capacity, make a good distribution of attention capacity, keep the eye-hand coordination and ensure the operations on the six degrees of freedom. Owing to these high demands, astronauts used to bear a heavy mental workload when executing the task [1].

In recent years, some research has shown that heart rate variability (HRV) has a remarkable correlation with mental workload in different fields, such as aviation and

V.G. Duffy (Ed.): DHM/HCII 2013, Part II, LNCS 8026, pp. 86–92, 2013.

driving. It is a sample, measurable and real-time index to reflect the activity of sympathetic and parasympathetic nervous system and their coordination [2], and it will decrease with the increase of mental workload[3,4,5]. However, HRV still remains to be controversial when measurement is made on workload of different strength and type [6]. The evaluation of mental workload during manual controlled RVD has been studied in the previous work in our laboratory, and skin temperature was found to be a sensitive index [7]. This research aims to study how HRV parameters change with task complexity during manual controlled Rendezvous and Docking (RVD).

2   Method

2.1   Volunteers

Eight male right-handed volunteers, aged between 21 and 26, were recruited for the experiment. They all have bachelor degree or above, some astronautic knowledge backgrounds and no experience in manual controlled RVD operation. In addition, they had passed the psychological and ability tests in the selection link by using DXC-6 Psychological Assessment Instrument (developed by the Fourth Military Medical University, Xi'an, China). These tests included velocity estimate test, rotation test and both-hand coordination ability test. All the requirements above ensured the similarity of astronauts to some extent. The experiment plan had been reviewed by the ethics committee of Astronaut Center of China. Besides, all the volunteers had signed the informed consent.

2.2   Experiment Task and Variable Design

The experiment task was manual RVD operation in which the operators judged the relative position and attitude of the two spacecraft through the monitoring interfaces and then manipulated the chaser spacecraft using the two controllers. This procedure started from the location where two spacecrafts were apart from each other for 140 meters, and continued until they successfully docked or when time limit expired.

One one-factor experiment was designed in this research. The independent variable was task complexity which depended on the deviation of the relative position, attitude, velocity and angle velocity of two spacecrafts. Three complexity levels named as low, middle and high complexity levels were defined in the study according to the engineering requirements of RVD. The less deviation meant that manual RVD had lower task complexity. The dependent variables were main performance parameters and HRV parameters. The two performance parameters were operation time and fuel consumption. The HRV parameters were standard deviation of the RR intervals between normal beats (SDNN), root mean square of successive differences (RMSSD) as time domain features and very low frequency (VLF), low frequency (LF), high frequency (HF), the ratio of LF to HF (LF/HF), normalized LF (LFNU), and normalized HF (HFNU) components as frequency domain features [8].

2.3   Experiment Equipment

The experiment was implemented in the manual controlled RVD simulator, in which the operating data throughout the whole docking procedure was recorded and stored, including the final performance data. The electrocardiography of the volunteers was recorded by a physiological indices recording detector called KF2, which was worn on the chest by every volunteer.

2.4   Experiment Process

Before the start of the experiment, the volunteers were taught the basic knowledge and scientific disciplines of manual RVD techniques. The experiment consisted of three trials, each of which was composed of ten operation units that were classified into three complexity levels. The average time for one trial was about 2 hours, and the time interval between the two adjacent trials was 2-4 days. In order to avoid memory and learning effects for the same unit, the settings of the same complexity level were different in different trials. The volunteers were told to keep in rest state for at least 3 minutes before the operation in each trial.

2.5   Data Analysis

Both the performance and HRV parameters analyzed were the average values of the three trials. The internal for the processing of HRV basic data was 3 minutes. The difference among three complexity levels was analyzed by using one-way ANOVA, while the difference with one other was analyzed by using paired T test. The data processing software was SPSS 16.0, and the level of significance test was set by $p < 0.05$.

3   Result

3.1   The Difference of Main Performance Parameters at Different Complexity Levels

Operation time and fuel consumption were chosen as the main performance parameters, and the result of the analysis are shown in Table 1.

Table 1. The effects of complexity level on the main performance parameters ($\bar{x} \pm s, n = 8$)

performance parameters	complexity level		
	low	middle	high
operation time(s)	491.43±35.14	520.23±43.54	567.14±61.48*#
fuel consumption(Kg)	7.32±1.83	8.74±1.33**	10.51±1.85**#

Note: * $p < 0.05$, ** $p < 0.01$, as compared with the low complexity level by using paired T test; # $p < 0.05$, as compared with the middle complexity level by using paired T test.

The result shows that both operation time and fuel consumption increased significantly with the growth of complexity level. The result of ANOVA for operation time and fuel consumption (p values were 0.023 and 0.027 respectively) also showed statistically significant effects of complexity level.

3.2   The Difference of HRV Parameters at Different Complexity Levels

The HRV parameters extracted in the rest state before the operation in each trial were analyzed. It was verified that all HRV parameters had no significant difference between different trials, and it can be inferred that each volunteer's physiological status was stable during the experimental period. The effects of complexity level on HRV parameters during the operation is shown in Table 2.

Table 2. The effects of complexity level on HRV parameters ($\overline{x} \pm s, n = 8$)

HRV parameters	complexity level		
	low	middle	high
SDNN(ms)	41.32±18.45	43.81±20.37	47.42±16.39
RMSSD(ms)	28.40±21.37	30.74±20.57	31.49±22.83
VLF(ms^2)	262.47±110.81	255.71±115.32	271.52±109.71
LF(ms^2)	260.32±224.71	275.52±235.88	292.38±242.26*
HF(ms^2)	172.71±143.37	140.51±133.71*	128.42±124.63*
LF/HF	2.40±1.21	3.48±1.75	4.83±2.07*#
LFNU	63.57±12.52	73.72±13.87*	77.36±11.02*
HFNU	38.74±10.94	29.37±12.77*	26.32±11.73*

Note: * $p<0.05$, as compared with the low complexity level by using paired T test; # $p<0.05$, as compared with the middle complexity level by using paired T test.

The result shows that there are statistically significant differences between different complexity levels for the parameters of LF, HF, LF/HF, LFNU and HFNU. LF, LF/HF and LFNU rose significantly (p values were 0.029, 0.048 and 0.031 respectively by ANOVA) with the increase of complexity levels. HF and HFNU declined significantly (p values were 0.046 and 0.033 respectively by ANOVA) with the increase of complexity levels. While other parameters show no significant difference (p values were 0.213, 0.492 and 0.334 for SDNN, RMSSD, and VLF respectively by ANOVA) between different complexity levels.

4   Discussion

This study was designed according to the practice of astronaut training, in which theoretical training was conducted before operation and the operation units were classified into three complexity levels. It is found that the complexity level had significant effects on the HRV parameters. The results of the main performance parameters showed that operation time and fuel consumption rose significantly with the increase of the complexity level. The validity of the complexity level design was further verified according to the research results of Park and our laboratory concerning the measurement of operation complexity [9,10], with the addition of engineering requirements and the facts in astronaut training.

The fact has been proved in many studies that HRV parameters are related to mental workload to a certain extent. In quiet situations, pneumogastric excitability dominates in the autonomic nerve system, and the variation of heart rate is adjusted by the pneumogastric nerve system. While, in the situations of sports, strain and high pressure, sympathetic excitability becomes dominated, and the variation of heart rate is adjusted by the sympathetic nerve system. The activity of sympathetic nerve system can be reflected by the low frequency component (LF, 0.04Hz~0.15Hz) of HRV. Meanwhile, The activity of pneumogastric nerve system can be reflected by the high frequency component (HF, 0.15Hz ~ 0.40Hz) of HRV. When operator's mental workload increases, the value of LF will increase and HF will decrease. Besides, it has a good sensitivity. So, HRV is thought to be a physiological index reflecting mental workload [3,4,5]. In this study, only partial HRV parameters showed a significant difference between different complexity levels. The values of LF, LFNU and LF/HF increased significantly with the increase of the complexity level, while the HF and HFNU decreased. An inference may be made that the increase of the complexity level will make the activity of operator's sympathetic nerve system enhanced, thus making the operator's mental workload increase. Therefore, there is a positive correlation between mental workload and complexity level, which can be represented by partial HRV parameters.

The experiment results showed that the parameters of LF, HF, LF/HF, LFNU and HFNU were sensitive to the complexity level and the others were not. There might be two reasons: First, the other parameters themselves are not sensitive to the complexity level; Second, the differences between the designed complexity levels are not high enough to make these parameters clearly show their sensitivity. The results agree well with what were found in some previous studies, but there are still some controversies. Because HRV is vulnerable to many factors, such as experiment environment, mood and mental state, the characteristics of these parameters still need to be further verified.

Nowadays, mental workload is still hard to be defined concordantly. However, the measurement and application of mental workload have been studied for many years in different fields. Physiological method is a kind of popular and critical approach to measure mental workload arising from the characteristics of objectivity, measurability and instantaneity among other methods. The sensibility of different methods and indexes is correlated to certain tasks and environment to some extent. Therefore, the research concerning the measurement of mental workload is usually set on a certain task and certain environment. The correlation of HRV with mental workload was researched in this study. The results indicated the availability of HRV parameters to measure mental workload during manual controlled RVD. Since the operation performance is the only critical index to evaluate the effect of training now, operators who obtain the same performance results can be scored the same. However, it would not be reasonable enough if they have made different efforts. Therefore, the inclusion of mental workload measured by HRV would be helpful to make a more objective, reasonable and comprehensive evaluation.

5   Conclusion

This study showed that operation complexity had significant effects on partial HRV parameters, and the HRV parameters could be used as effective indexes for mental workload evaluation in manual controlled RVD training. The validity of the operation complexity was further verified, which corresponded to the result of previous study on spaceflight operation complexity in our laboratory [11]. The influencing factors of HRV parameters were diverse, and conclusions of researches concerning the variation of HRV parameters were also not concordant. Therefore, the application and variation trend of HRV parameters in mental workload evaluation should be researched and verified in further studies. This study may also provide scientific basis for the design of astronaut manual controlled RVD training methods, comprehensive evaluation of mental workload and training effect evaluation in future. It could also provide some theoretical guidance for the researches on mental workload in other fields, such as nuclear power plant and driving.

Acknowledgements. The volunteers' cooperation and the attentive guidance from Wu Bin and Zhang Yijing are highly appreciated. This study is also supported by National Natural Science Fund project (71001092) and National Basic Research Program of China (2011CB711000)and the foundation of National Key Laboratory of Human Factors Engineering (HF2011Z-ZB-04).

References

1. Renzhang, Z.: Rendezvous and docking technology of Spacecraft. National Defense industry Press, Beijing (2005)
2. Kim, D., Seo, Y:, Kim, S.H., Jung, S.: Short Term Analysis of Long Term Patterns of Heart Rate Variability in Subjects under Mental Stress. In: International Conference on BioMedical Engineering and Informatics, pp. 487–491 (2008)
3. Wilson, G.: Air to groud training mission: a psychophysiological workload analysis. J. Ergonomics. 36(9), 1071–1087 (1993)
4. Veltman, J.A.: A comparative study of psychophysiological reactions during simulator and real flight. The International Journal of Aviation Psychology 12(1), 33–48 (2002)
5. Kai, C., Linyan, S., Linhui, S., et al.: The effectiveness of heart rate variability to measure mental workload. Industrial Engineering and Management 3, 56–63 (2008)

6. Baucsein, W., Backs, R.W.: Engineering psychophysiology as a discipline: Historical and theoretical aspects. In: Engineering Psychophysiology: Issues and Application, Mahwah, NJ, pp. 3–29 (2000)
7. Wu, B., Hou, F., Yao, Z., Niu, J., Huang, W.: Using physiological parameters to evaluate operator's workload in manual controlled rendezvous and docking(RVD). In: Duffy, V.G. (ed.) ICDHM 2011. LNCS, vol. 6777, pp. 426–435. Springer, Heidelberg (2011)
8. Henelius, A., Hirvonen, K., Holm, A., Korpela, J., Muller, K.: Mental Workload Classification using Heart Rate Metrics. In: Proceedings of 31st Annual International Conference of the IEEE EMBS, Minneapolis, Minnesota, USA, pp. 2–6 (2009)
9. Park, J., Jung, W., Ha, J.: Development of the step complexity measure for emergency operating procedures using entropy concepts. Reliability Engineering and System Safety 71(2), 115–130 (2001)
10. Yijing, Z., Bin, W., zhizhong, L., et al.: Research on the complexity measurement of spacecraft emergency operation procedure. Acta Astronautica 30(2), 384–390 (2009)
11. Jinwu, Z., Yijing, Z., Xiang, Z., et al.: The effect of training on the correlation between difficulty of space operation task and operation time. Space Medicine and Medical Engineering 25(2), 98–101 (2012)

Using Anthropomorphism to Improve
the Human-Machine Interaction
in Industrial Environments (Part II)

Marcel Ph. Mayer, Sinem Kuz, and Christopher M. Schlick

Chair and Institute of Industrial Engineering and Ergonomics of RWTH Aachen University
{m.mayer,s.kuz,c.schlick}@iaw.rwth-aachen.de

Abstract. The idea of socio-technical systems emphasizes the mutual interrelationship between humans and technical system considering the human operator as an integral part of the system. However, to use the full potential of this idea the technical system has to be perceived and accepted as a team-partner. Anthropomorphism is a promising approach to improve the acceptance of non-human entities as team-partners. In the second part of this joint contribution we present a revised experimental setup of the studies presented in the first part. A virtual environment consisting of a robotized assembly cell was utilized to conduct a prediction experiment with nine subjects comparing anthropomorphic and robotic speed profiles on a gantry robot. As in the first part the task of the participants was to predict the target position during movement. The results show significant effects towards shorter prediction time and less errors when using anthropomorphic speed profiles.

Keywords: Human-robot interaction, anthropomorphism, socio-technical system, prediction, self-optimization.

1   Introduction

Anthropomorphism, which can be derived from the Greek ἄνϑρωπος (anthropos) for man and μορφή (morphē) meaning form or appearance, describes "the attribution of human characteristics or behavior to a god, animal, or object" (Oxford Dictionary 2012). Anthropomorphisms can be found throughout the history of man such as historic figurines or in fairy tales e.g. the Aesopian fables which can be dated to about 600 B.C. In everyday life anthropomorphisms are omnipresent and used in advertisements suggesting us something is as intuitive as it is to use natural language.

But how come we are concerning anthropomorphism in industrial environments, especially in the field of industrial robotics? The reason is at hand: Manufacturers like Motoman®, ABB® and KUKA® are introducing robotic systems that are anthropomorphic and might be introduced into future production systems to directly cooperate with humans in pulsed assembly lines.

Therefore, from a human factors point of view it is crucial to consider anthropomorphism as a possible design factor for joint cognitive systems. Especially when regarding production systems with simulated cognitive functions such as self-optimizing assembly systems that can plan autonomously ([2], [3], [4]) and might therefore be even more difficult to monitor and intervene.

V.G. Duffy (Ed.): DHM/HCII 2013, Part II, LNCS 8026, pp. 93–100, 2013.

We decided to present our research in two parts. The first part of our research on anthropomorphism in human-robot interaction provides an explorative approach [5]. The second part can be considered as lessons learned resulting in a revised method, focused on one particular aspect research hypothesis.

Our goal was to investigate whether anthropomorphic movement of a gantry robot will have an advantage compared to conventional robotic trajectories such as classic point-to-point. As an experimental setup we chose a self-developed simulation environment which was presented to the subject on a regular screen. In the first part we investigated different influencing factors such as the orientation of the subject to the robot, the type of movement as well as the position.

2   Motion as a Source of Information

The idea to draw information from motion is not new. Detailed analysis on the basis of cyclographic pictures were carried out by Gilbreth as early as 1913 [6] and can be regarded as the foundation to systems of predetermined times such as MTM, Work Factor and many more. In later years Rhomert and Ruthenfranz used a similar approach based on cyclographic analysis to distinguish whether a worker using a hatchet was tired or not ([7], see figure 1). Even though, in the case of cyclographic analysis the motion is decoupled from time we can draw information out of the particular form of the motion patterns.

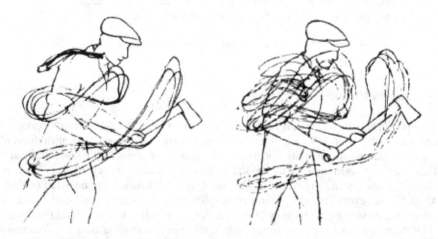

Fig. 1. Cyclographic analysis of a worker using a hatchet (left: not tired; right: tired)

Looking at motions that are really "in motion" in terms of a spatial-temporally continuous movement of a man, it is possible to retrieve more information. Even in the case of a heavily reduced representation of a human body by just using dots for major joints, it is possible to determine the direction of motion, the gender, basics about the state of mind (happy or sad) just to mention a view. For more information about this work please refer to [8].

The basic principle behind this is rooted in our brain. Areas that normally would be active in case we actually perform a task also fire if we observe such a task. These regions called mirror neurons were discovered by Rizolatti in 1996 in a study with monkeys [9]. There have been discussions about whether mirror neurons can be activated if observing non-living things such as robots [10]. However, in later works it could be shown that mirror neurons are not limited to living beings but can also fire in case of a robot performing tasks [11].

In case we want to transform motion patterns that are normal to a certain entity to another entity we have to regard the study carried out by Saygin et al. [12]. Theis study deals with the combination of movements typical for a robot and a human appearance. To do this kind of investigation three sorts of videos were recorded. The first one was a female person waving. The second was a robot that was designed to be a very precise optical imitation of that particular woman. However, the robot was not designed to reproduce typical human motion patterns and therefore moves like a robot. The third combination was the robot stripped to its bare mechanical components doing the same motion as in the second video. As a result of MRT-studies, the findings of Gazzola et al. [11] could be proven right. In the case of the second combination that "should not be", a significant raise in mirror neuron activity could be observed, which Saygin et al. [12] take as a hint for the uncanny valley that will be described in the next paragraph in more detail.

3   The Uncanny Valley

The uncanny valley as presented by Mori in 1970 [13], describes a paradox in the acceptance of technical, nonverbal behavior of artificial figures like robots. The most common presentation of this paradox is the version as depicted in figure 2 with familiarity on the ordinate and human-likeness on the abscissa. Mori states a higher effect when objects are actually moving compared to standing still.

The effect can be explained by the expectations of the person observing animated characters. Be the expectation that of a human being e.g. due to appearance or other influences, missing human features will diminish familiarity and can change to eeriness. In the case of a technical expectation however, additional human-likeness can lead to more familiarity with the system. Approaching the uncanny valley from the technical side, the drop in familiarity might be caused by a shift in expectations.

Despite the logic behind Mori's uncanny valley, the model lacks an empirical validation base is and is based mainly on Mori's thoughts. According to Gellar [14] *"[Mori] drew it as a graph, and that made it seem more scientific."*

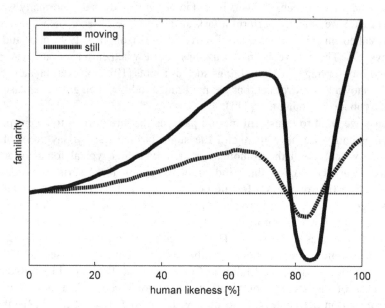

Fig. 2. The relation of human likeness and familiarity known as the uncanny valley

A few studies exist that underpin Mori's model with empirical data such as MacDorman [15]. However, one must say that only the uncanny valley itself was in the focus of this particular study. More generally speaking the main focus of research related to Mori's model tries to explain and thus to avoid or minimize the valley when approaching it from 100% human likeness.

From a scientific point of view the more interesting approach is to focus on what we call the canny hill. It is the area left of the uncanny valley where the expectation of the human observer is of mainly technical nature. The introduction of human like features is little compared to the amount of human likeness that would make expectations shift to human. Hence, with the experiments introduced in the first part of this two part publication as well as the experiment presented in the following, we introduce human motion patterns as an additional feature of an industrial gantry robot to improve safety, efficiency and job satisfaction in a manufacturing environment.

4   Revising the Method

The results presented in the first part of our contribution did not show main effects that can be interpreted right away. We did not see a significant difference in prediction time comparing robotic movement to human movement. Regarding the trajectories for human motion and robotic point-to-point movement, we see a large difference in the trajectories which might have lead to the observed results, for the classic point-to-point trajectories tend to converge faster with the target position and from the very start, whereas for human trajectories convergence occurs later and slower. Additionally, we see a difference for target positions that are closer to the robot (left side (x ca. 600), figure 3) compared to positions further away (right side (x ca. 1050), figure 3). In case we look at the relative length of the trajectory that was performed until the prediction, we find tendencies in the data, that for target positions that are close to the robot and therefore have similar trajectories, the results for prediction time and relative length of human and robotic movement is comparable, despite the later and slower convergence of human motion with the target position.

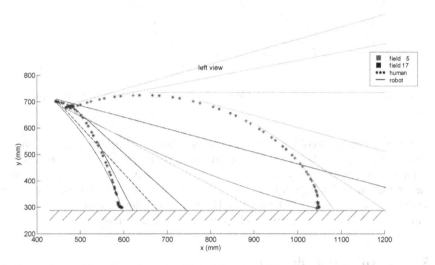

Fig. 3. Comparison of human trajectories (dotted lines) to point-to-point robotic movements (solid lines) regarding convergence (depicted as tangents) with near to the robot target positions (left) and positions further away (right)

Since a detailed description of the method and the experimental setup can be found in the first part of the contribution (see Kuz et al. [5]) we want to focus more on the changes made to the experiment. The task of the participants of the study, to predict the target position of a robot performing a pick-and-place operation, was adjusted in three points. 1) Compared to the first study, the motion now covers full pick-and-place trajectories starting on the same height as the target position. 2) We chose the lateral view for the second study, since regarding the subjective ratings of the subjects the lateral view was perceived better compared to the frontal view [5]. 3) There is only one trajectory per target position based on a human movement but with different speed profiles as shown in figure 4. The level for the constant speed profile equals the mean speed of the anthropomorphic profile to assure identical times for the approaching of each field.

At this point, we can only present results of nine subjects which participated in the study so far. As in the first experiment, all subjects are male and either taking part in an engineering bachelor/master program or have finished their studies. The age is comparable to the first group of subjects (mean 26.11 years, SD 4.43).

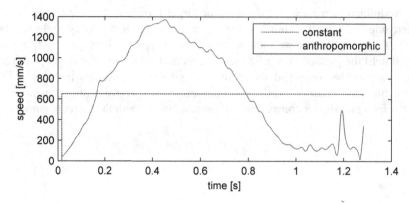

Fig. 4. Comparison of the speed profiles used in the second experiment (exemplary for one particular field)

The independent variables are the field position as in the first part and the speed profile that distinguishes between human and constant profile as in classic point-to-point robotic movement. As dependent variable the elapsed time between the start of the animation and the prediction of the target position was chosen. For statistical analysis a version of the Scheirer Ray Hare Test adjusted to repeated measures was carried out. A detailed description of the test can be found in Mayer [16].

5   Results and Discussion

The statistical results show a significant effect for the field ($p<0.001$) as well as for the speed profile ($p=0.006$). For the significant interaction ($p=0.001$) is ordinal, the main effects can be interpreted individually.

Table 1. Results of the adjusted Scheirer Ray Hare Test

	Sum.Sq	d.f.	H	p
field	1.87E+06	19	135.52	<0.001
error	4.90E+05	152		
speed profile	6.38E+05	1	7.61	0.006
error	1.16E+05	8		
interaction	1.59E+05	19	43.09	0.001
error	4.73E+05	152		

Regarding the fields, the experiments show longer prediction times for fields that are further away from the robot than compared to close fields. Since the trajectories used in the experiment all started and ended at the same height and had comparable shapes, the effect mainly can be explained by the specific time for reaching a particular field.

Comparing human speed profile to constant speed profile, we see shorter prediction times under the human condition. The only difference is the speed profile on an identical trajectory for each field. Hence, the effect clearly shows a timely advantage in predicting a target position when using anthropomorphic speed profiles compared to constant speed. Additionally, we see less false predictions under that condition. Hence, a speed accuracy trade-off does not occur.

6   Summary

Using anthropomorphism in industrial robotics is not an uncommon approach, since manufacturers are offering industrial robots with at least slight anthropomorphic features. Despite this development, little research has been carried out focusing on industrial applications yet, the majority of research work aims at humanoid robotics. From an ergonomic point of view, we see the necessity to address the topic of how to improve human-machine interaction especially in industrial robotics using anthropomorphism as a "natural" way of interaction.

In the two parts of this joint publication we introduced an experimental setup to investigate the influence of anthropomorphism in human-machine interaction for the special application of industrial robots. The task for the subjects in the experiment was to predict the final position of an animated robot during the performance of a pick-and-place task by indicating the expected target field. The results clearly show that anthropomorphic characteristics embedded into the motion of industrial robots can have positive effects on the prediction time of the subjects involved as well as the accuracy of the prediction.

Since the experiments have been carried out on the basis of a simulation, the next step will be to validate the experiment in a realistic scenario. Therefore, the assembly cell as presented by Brecher et al. [3] will be used as the next experimental setup.

Acknowledgments. The authors would like to thank the German Research Foundation DFG for the kind support within the Cluster of Excellence "Integrative Production Technology for High-Wage Countries".

References

1. Oxford Dictionary anthropomorphism (2010), http://oxforddictionaries.com/definition/english/ (February 16, 2013)
2. Mayer, M., Schlick, C., Ewert, D., Behnen, D., Kuz, S., Odenthal, B., Kausch, B.: Automation of robotic assembly processes on the basis of an architecture of human cognition. Production Engineering Research and Development 5(4), 423–431 (2011)
3. Brecher, C., Müller, S., Kuz, S., Lohse, W.: Towards Anthropomorphic Movements for Industrial Robots. In: The Proceedings of the 4th International Conference on Digital Human Modeling and Applications in Health, Safety, Ergonomics and Risk Management (a Volume of the Combined Proceedings of HCI International 2013), Las Vegas, NV, USA (2013)

4. Faber, M., Kuz, S., Mayer, M., Schlick, C.: Design and Implementation of a CognitiveSimulation Model for Robotic Assembly Cells. In: The Proceedings of the 4th International Conference on Digital Human Modeling and Applications in Health, Safety, Ergonomics and Risk Management (a Volume of the Combined Proceedings of HCI International 2013), Las Vegas, NV, USA (2013)

5. Kuz, S., Mayer, M., Müller, S., Schlick, C.: Using Anthropomorphism to Improve the Human-Machine Interaction in Industrial Environments (Part 1). In: The Proceedings of the 4th International Conference on Digital Human Modeling and Applications in Health, Safety, Ergonomics and Risk Management (a Volume of the Combined Proceedings of HCI International 2013), Las Vegas, NV, USA (2013)

6. Gilbreth, F.B., Gilbreth, L.M.: Applied Motion Study: A Collection of Papers on the efficientMethod to industrial Preparedness. Macmillan, New York (1919)

7. Rohmert, W., Rutenfranz, J. (eds.): Praktische Arbeitsphysiologie. Thieme, Stuttgart (1983) (in German)

8. http://www.biomotionlab.ca

9. Rizzolatti, G., Fadiga, L., Gallese, V., Fogassi, L.: Premotor cortex and the recognition of motor actions. Cognitive Brain Research 3, 131–141 (1996)

10. Tai, Y.F., Scherfler, C., Brooks, D.J., Sawamoto, N., Castiello, U.: The Human Premotor Cortex is "Mirror" Only for Biological Actions. Current Biology 14, 117–120 (2004)

11. Gazzola, V., Rizzolatti, G., Wicker, B., Keysers, C.: The anthropomorphic brain: The mirrorneuron system responds to human and robotic actions. NeuroImage 35, 1674–1684 (2007)

12. Saygin, A.P., Chaminade, T., Ishiguro, H., Driver, J., Frith, C.: The thing that should not be: predictive coding and the uncanny valley in perceiving human and humanoid robot actions. Social Cognitive and Affective Neuroscience (advance access published April 22, 2011)

13. Mori, M.: The Uncanny Valley. Energy 7(4), 33–35 (1970); (translated by MacDorman, K.F., Minato, T.)

14. Geller, T.: Overcoming the Uncanny Valley. IEEE Computer Graphics and Applications (July/August:11-17, 2008)

15. MacDorman, K.F.: Subjective ratings of robot video clips for human likeness, familiarity, and eeriness: An exploration of the uncanny (2006)

16. Mayer, M.: Entwicklung eines kognitionsergonomischen Konzeptes und eines Simulationssystems für die robotergestützte Montage. Dissertation der Rheinisch-Westfälischen Technischen Hochschule Aachen. Shaker, Aachen (2012) (in German)

Numerical Reconstruction of the Real-Life Fatal Accident at Work: A Case Study

Marcin Milanowicz and Paweł Budziszewski

Central Institute for Labour Protection – National Research Institute (CIOP-PIB),
ul. Czerniakowska 16; 00-701 Warszawa, Poland
{marmi,pabud}@ciop.pl

Abstract. Every year about 2.8 million people are injured in accidents at work in Europe. The resulting high costs are incurred by the victims themselves, their families, employers, and the society. A numerical simulation can be used to reconstruct accidents and to provide information about the course and cause of those accidents. This knowledge is crucial in developing successful safety systems and safety procedures.

This paper presents a multi-body approach to reconstructing a real-life fatal accident of a forklift that overturned with its operator. A reconstruction took place to find out why forklift overturned. This study consisted of about 700 simulations. Their results were compared to data from the real accident. The path of simulated wheels and the location of the model of a forklift after the accident corresponded to the real tire tracks and the final location of the real machine. The location and position of the computer model of the operator was similar, too. The injury criteria obtained in the simulation exceeded the critical values for the head and neck, which corresponded to the operator's injuries: numerous fractures of the skull and cervical spine fracture with dislocation. Thus, speeding and a sudden turning maneuver caused the accident.

Keywords: accident reconstruction, computer simulation, multi-body, MADYMO, human model.

1 Introduction

In spite of increasing accident prevention the number of accidents at work is still very high. In EU 27[1] in 2009, 2.8 million people were injured in accidents at work [1]. In Poland, 90 000 people per annum are injured as a result of those accidents [2]. In 2002, according to some estimates, the total cost of all accidents at work in Poland incurred by the victims, their families, employers, and the society was approximately 2 200 million PLN (740 million USD). Thus, a reduction in the number of accidents at work can have high social as well as economic benefits. A proper understanding of the course and cause of accidents is a major factor in accident prevention. This knowledge is crucial in developing systems and procedures that are to be successful.

---

[1] EU 27 – Twenty seven is the number of member states in the European Union.

V.G. Duffy (Ed.): DHM/HCII 2013, Part II, LNCS 8026, pp. 101–110, 2013.

However, it is often hard to identify the precise course of events on the basis of the evidence at the site of an accident. In such cases a numerical simulation can help reconstruct accident-related events. Computer simulations can improve safety; they can also help in establishing responsibility in court.

For years, numerical simulation has been successfully used in reconstructing road accidents. These analyses simulate the dynamics of vehicles, the behavior of their occupants, and their injuries. Advanced simulation software, e.g., PC Crash[2] and MADYMO [3], is used for this purpose. Road accidents can be reconstructed with either of two main numerical simulation methods, the finite element method or the multi-body dynamics method. In addition to accidents involving cars only, collisions of cars and motorcycles [4] or pedestrians [5] are reconstructed, too. The analyses focus then on evaluating injuries. Adapting the methodology of reconstructing road accidents to reconstructing accidents at work is not easy. There are fewer configurations of car accidents, for example. Moreover, the occupants of cars are usually in their seats restrained with safety belts; even the configuration of the cars involved is often typical. On the other hand, each accident at work can be configured differently. Hence, each case requires an individual approach. In spite of those problems, or possibly because of them, researchers work on reconstructing accidents other than car-related. O'Riordain [6] used multi-body modeling software to reconstruct real-life head injury accidents resulting from falls. Their aim was to compare simulation output with sustained injuries. Doorly [7] used the MADYMO Pedestrian model with an adapted finite element brain model to reconstruct real-life accidents with injuries resulting from falls.

The aim of this study was to reconstruct a real-life fatal accident at work on the basis of numerical simulations. The accident involved a forklift that overturned with its operator. The study was carried out at the Central Institute for Labour Protection – National Research Institute (CIOP-PIB).

2   Methods

2.1   Overview

Method of reconstructing accidents at work with numerical simulations can be used to reconstruct accidents related to mechanical hazards: falls, overturns, or impact by objects. The sequence of events that led to an accident is determined with equations describing the mechanical properties of real objects. This task requires computer models of all objects and persons involved in the accident and defined initial conditions. The reconstruction will be accurate if the initial models and conditions are faithful; this is relevant for the quality of data describing an accident and its site. These data are usually incomplete, sometimes inaccurate or even contradictory. In the reconstruction such data must be considered multiple variants of the initial conditions. Simulating each variant leads to identifying the most probable one. This methodology

---

[2] MEA Forensic Engineers & Scientist. Retrieved January 28, 2013, from:
http://www.pc-crash.com

is successful for road accidents. For accidents at work it has to be altered. These accidents are very diverse, each one has to be reconstructed individually. Even so, some steps in the procedure of the reconstruction are the same.

2.2 Numerical Simulation and Software

Accidents at work differ from road accidents. There are numerous possible scenarios such as falling, being crushed or being hit with parts of machinery. In these accidents, attention should be focused on the behavior of the human body. Kinematics and dynamics of the human body can be modeled with numerical simulation using multi-body (MB) and finite element (FE) methods. The reconstruction analysis described in this paper was done with MADYMO crash simulation software [3], with the MB method.

MADYMO combines two types of solvers in one simulation program: the MB module for simulating the motion of the body and its systems, and FE methods for simulating the motion of deformable structures. The MB model consists of a chain of rigid bodies connected with joints. Loads, contacts, and restraints (such as friction in joints or spring-dampers) can be defined to simulate real conditions. Differential equations describe motion, they are solved with numerical integration, which results in displacements, velocities, and accelerations of rigid bodies. These data, together with masses and moments of inertia, are used to calculate forces and moments. The FE model is deformable; the deformation depends on the properties of the material. The motion of the body can be defined with initial velocity, a prescribed motion, or an acceleration field. Contact interaction between any surfaces can be defined. In MB, contact between planes, ellipsoids, cylinders, and FE models can be defined. Moreover, physical parameters like damping or friction can be incorporated in contact definitions. For both MB and FE contact forces prevent surfaces from going through each other and if a deformable structure is used, it is deformed in accordance with the properties of the material. Loads and constraints can be applied on every deformable structure [3].

2.3 Injury Evaluation

Numerical simulation can be used to evaluate probable injuries. This is done with so-called injury criteria; they provide correlation between physical quantities such as resultant accelerations, forces, or moments of force measured at the time of impact, and the probability of a body subjected to the same strain sustaining an injury. There are different injury criteria for injuries in different parts of body. Injury criteria are not all-purpose, they are limited by the range of cases for which they were validated. These criteria do not provide detailed information on injuries but they do provide the probable level of the injury according to a predefined scale. Abbreviated injury scale (AIS) describes most injury criteria; it ranges from 1 (minor injuries) and to 6 (virtually unsurvivable) [8].

3   Reconstructing Real Accidents

One real-life example of a fatal accident of a forklift overturning with its operator will illustrate the method of reconstructing accidents at work. Because there were no eyewitnesses, the cause of the accident could only be inferred from tire tracks. The most probable sequence of events that led to the accident and its cause were established on the basis of a reconstruction.

3.1   Description of Accident

The accident happened in front of a warehouse. The operator was driving a forklift around the square and loading pallets onto a delivery truck. All other workers had their lunch break. While they were inside a building, they heard a loud noise. They immediately ran outside, where they saw the overturned forklift. The frame of the forklift crushed the operator; it had pinned his neck to the ground. He died on the spot. He had not fastened his seat belt. There were tire tracks close to the forklift.

Because there were no eyewitnesses, it was crucial to determine the cause of the accident. It was necessary to find out whether a forklift could make a turning maneuver that would result in its overturning. A computer simulation would make it possible to determine the initial speed of the forklift and to describe the turning maneuver.

3.2   Simulation Models

Forklift Model. A computer model of the forklift was created on the basis of the technical specifications of the real forklift. Table 1 lists data that defined the model.

Table 1. Technical specifications of the forklift

Characteristics		
Curb weight	3485	(kg)
Load center	500	(mm)
Width/Height	1150/2110	(mm)
Turning radius	2190	(mm)
Wheel base	1650	(mm)
Front tires diameter/Width	672/192	(mm)
Rear tires diameter/Width	540/160	(mm)

There is no information on the maximum speed of this kind of forklift in the technical specifications. So, for the purpose of this simulation, the maximum speed of the forklift was defined as 25 km/h (such speed can be reached by similar types of forklifts). On the basis of the turning radius, the maximum angle of the wheels was calculated as 40°. The forklift model consisted of rigid bodies with masses and moments of inertia. Ellipsoids described the outer surface. Interaction between the forklift and the ground was simulated with an elastic contact model. In MADYMO, it is possible to define contact interaction between a master surface and a slave surface, and contacting surfaces can penetrate each other. Penetration of the surfaces depends on the elastic contact force. This dependency can be defined as the force-penetration characteristic [3]. The first contact was defined between the ellipsoids describing the wheels and the plane describing the ground. The friction coefficient was a variable parameter. The second contact was defined between the ellipsoids describing the body of the forklift and the ground. The friction coefficient was set to 0.4. In both contacts the force-penetration characteristics were set according to data obtained from the MADYMO model database. The movement of the forklift was simulated with linear velocity set on the forklift and angular velocity set on the wheels. The turning of the forklift was defined with a function that changed the angle of the wheels during the simulation. In four-wheel vehicles the angle of turning for the outside wheel is different from for the inside wheel, and this is so because of the kinematics of such vehicles. The angle of each turning wheel was calculated separately on the basis on this function. The function of the turning of wheels was defined on the basis of two parameters describing this maneuver: the maximal angle of the wheels and the time necessary to reach that angle. The maximal possible angle was set to 47.8° for the inside and 34° for the outside wheel on the curve of the road and the time to reach those angles was set between 0.5 and 2 seconds.

Model of Tire Tracks. Three tire tracks were identified as traces of three wheels of the forklift sliding on the ground. Photogrammetry [9] based on photographs taken at the site of the accident was used. Photogrammetry consists in drawing a grid on the photo that is based on a reference pattern. Any object with known dimensions can be used as a pattern. In this case it was a paving block. The procedure was as follows: the grid was applied onto the photo and matched to the pattern of paving blocks; the image with the grid was turned into an orthogonal projection; the projection was used to create a 3D model of the tires tracks.

Human Model. A computer model of a human is the most critical aspect of reconstructing an accident. We selected one of the many types of dummies and human models in the MADYMO database: the Pedestrian (Fig. 1). The Pedestrian was developed with the MB method; it consisted of 52 rigid bodies with defined mass, center of gravity, and moments of inertia. Ellipsoids described the geometry of the model. Bodies are connected via different types of joints. These joints are restrained by functions describing parameters such as friction and damping in order to simulate human joints. The Pedestrian has 11 contact interactions between the following parts of the body defined by default: head and torso, lower extremities, upper extremities, and thorax and pelvis. These are elastic contact models with force-penetration characteristics and parameters defined on the basis of biomechanical research on the human body [10]. Moreover, for the purpose of the simulation, contact interactions human – forklift and human – ground were defined. The Pedestrian made the following outputs possible: animation with the kinematics of the body, forces that had been recorded, moments of force, displacements, positions, velocities, and accelerations of body segments.

Fig. 1. The Pedestrian from MADYMO database (left) in a standing posture and (right) seated in the forklift

3.3   Simulation Analysis

The simulation focused on finding a set of initial conditions that would make the simulation result as close to the accident result as possible. The comparison focused on the shape of the tire tracks and the place where the forklift was located at the end of the accident. The analysis had two phases. First, the ranges of parameters for which it was possible for the forklift to overturn were determined. Then, those parameters were modified—within those ranges—to match the tire tracks.

Identifying the Initial Conditions Leading to the Accident. Four parameters were considered as variables in this phase: speed at the beginning of the curve, maximal angle of the wheels, time to reach the maximal angle of the wheels, and the coefficient of friction between the road and the tires. The simulations aimed to establish ranges of those parameters for which the forklift could overturn. To do this parameters were changed as follows. Initially the parameters were set to maximal (speed, angle of the wheels, and friction coefficient) or minimal (time to reach the angle of the wheels) values for this type of forklift. The model of the forklift overturned in those initial conditions. Next, the parameters were changed in pre-determined steps until the forklift no longer overturned. Initially, the maximal speed of the forklift was set to 25 km/h, then it decreased by 0.5 km/h. The maximal angle of the wheels was set to 40°. This angle was reduced in one-degree steps. The speed of turning the steering wheel was defined as a function of time. The time to reach the maximal angle was 0.5–2.0 s. The friction coefficient corresponded to friction between rubber and dry concrete. It was changed in the range of 0.25–1 [11]. Table 2 lists the obtained ranges of parameters leading to the forklift overturning.

Table 2. Parameters of the simulation models leading to the forklift overturning

Speed (km/h)	Maximal angle of wheels (°)	Time to reach maximal angle (s)	Coefficient of friction between tire and ground (–)
18	40	0.5–2	1
19	31–40	0.5–2	0.85–1
20–25	31–40	0.5–2	0.85–1

Matching Simulated Wheels Path to the Tire Tracks. This phase determined values of variables in such a way that the path of the simulated wheels would match the tracks from the accident site. The results were considered positive if the simulated wheels moved inside a 180-mm wide corridor around the tracks.

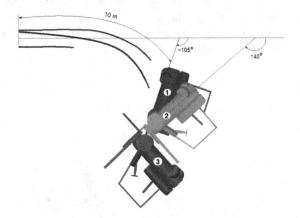

Fig. 2. Rotation of forklift at the end of accident: 1 – rotation of real forklift; 2 – borderline acceptable rotation of simulated forklift (140°); 3 – unacceptable rotation (>140°)

The simulation was successful if speed was set to 22–25 km/h, whereas the angle of the wheels to 38–40° and friction coefficient to 0.9-0.95. Although in these cases the path of simulated wheels was inside the corridors, the final location of the overturned forklift was sometimes drastically different than in the accident. Two problems were identified. Firstly, sometimes the forklift drove much further before it hit the ground. According to the tracks from the site of the accident, the rear left wheel covered 10 m from the beginning of the tracks to the place where they stopped moving. To eliminate this problem, results where this distance was approximately 10 m were considered only. Secondly, the final rotation of the overturned forklift was sometimes much higher than in the accident. In the actual accident it was around 105° (Fig. 2, position 1), whereas in the simulation it sometimes exceeded 180° (Fig. 2, position 3).

This problem, however, strongly depends on the definition of contact between the side of the vehicle and the ground. This contact was difficult to simulate because of insufficient data and the complicated shape of the forklift. So, all results where this angle was not greater than 140° were considered correct (Fig. 2, position 2). The fit of the tire tracks was best with the friction coefficient of 0.9 but in that case the location of the overturned forklift was outside the acceptable area. This could be so because real ground was not smooth; paving blocks covered it and during the slip, a tire could catch on the edge of blocks. To simulate such a situation, the friction coefficient was changed during the slip of the tire from 0.9 to 1.7.

4   Results

4.1   Position of the Forklift and the Operator

After about 700 simulations, a set of parameters was found for which the forklift overturned in an acceptable area. The speed at the beginning of the curve was 23 km/h, the wheels were at 39°, the time necessary to reach that angle was 2 s, and the coefficient of friction between the road and the tire was 0.9, increasing at the end to 1.7. Figure 3 illustrates the position of the forklift.

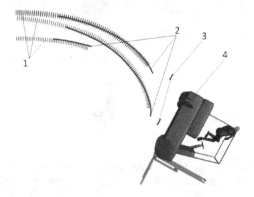

Fig. 3. Position of oveturned forklift with simulated reference tire tracks. 1 – simulated path of wheels; 2 – tire tracks of real forklift; 3 – position of real wheels; 4 – position of simulated forklift.

The results follow:

- The path of the simulated wheels was inside a 180-mm-wide corridor outside the tire tracks.
- The path of the simulated wheels ended before the tire tracks (i.e., before the place where the tires lost contact with the ground). The difference was 0.2–0.3 m.
- The final position of the simulated forklift was about 0.6 m further than real tracks indicated.
- The rotation of the overturned forklift was 118° (as opposed to 105° in the actual accident).
- The driver fell off his seat during the accident. The frame of the forklift hit his neck and pinned him to the ground.

4.2   Injuries

The autopsy report listed serious head (abrasions, bruises, and numerous skull fractures) and neck (cervical spine fracture with dislocation) injuries. That is why the acceleration of the head and forces in the neck were measured during the simulation. Thus it was possible to evaluate the injuries on the basis of the head and neck injury criteria.

Table 3. Values of injury criteria for the head and the neck

Body part	Injury criterion	Value	Critical value	AIS
Head	HIC 15 ms	20 859	>1800 (severe life endangering fracture) [12]	4–5
Neck	For- & rearward shear force Fx (N)	14 285		
	Lateral shear force Fy (N)	7377	>3300 (major neck rupture and dislocation) [13]	4–6
	Axial force Fz (N)	4407		

Notes. AIS – abbreviated injury scale [8], HIC – head injury criterion [14].

Head injuries were evaluated with HIC. This injury criterion was calculated by MADYMO software on the basis of resultant acceleration of the head's center of gravity. Neck injuries were evaluated on the basis of shear and axial forces measured in the neck segment; they were then compared with critical values. The measurement of these forces was possible because the Pedestrian model has virtual load cells implemented in most parts of the body including the neck segment. The results indicated that the injuries for both the head and the neck were critical (Table 3).

5   Conclusion

By changing initial conditions it was possible to match simulated paths of the wheels to the tire tracks from the site of the accident. The simulated wheels moved in a 180-mm-wide corridor, which was comparable to the width of the tires. The operator's injuries estimated with injury criteria matched the autopsy report. Moreover, the final position of the overturned forklift matched tracks in the actual accident. Any differences could have been caused by the simulated contact between the frame of the forklift and the pavement. Real contact was much more complex and should be modeled more precisely. According to the description of the actual accident, after the forklift overturned, the operator was in a sitting position with the frame of the machine pressing his head to the ground. As a result of the simulation, the human model, ejected by the centrifugal force, was pinned to the ground, with the frame of the forklift pressing on its neck. That was exactly how the accident had been described. The configuration of his extremities was different, though. This may have been caused by the operator's movements, which were not simulated. Another conclusion can be drawn, too: the operator's behavior in the last phase of the accident did not have much influence on the overall result. A comparison of the simulation results with the values for the injury criteria of the head and neck shows that both the head and the neck exceeded the critical values, which means life-threatening skull fracture and serious fracture with dislocation of the cervical spine. According to the description of the accident, that is exactly what happened to the operator of the forklift. An analysis of the results shows that speeding and a sudden turning maneuver were the causes of the accident.

Acknowledgements. This paper has been based on the results of a research task carried out within the scope of the second stage of the National Programme "Improvement of safety and working conditions" partly supported in 2011–2013 — within the scope of research and development — by the Ministry of Science and Higher Education/National Centre for Research and Development. The Central Institute for Labour Protection – National Research Institute is the Programme's main co-ordinator.

References

1. Eurostat, Health and safety at work statistics (2009), http://epp.eurostat.ec.europa.eu/statistics_explained/index.php/Health_and_safety_at_work_statistics#Database (retrieved January 28, 2013)
2. Główny Urząd Statystyczny (GUS), Wypadki Przy Pracy w 2010 r., (Accidents at work in 2010), GUS, Warszawa, Poland (2010) (in Polish)
3. TASS, MADYMO Theory Manual Release 7.3, TASS, Rijswijk, The Netherlands (2010)
4. Lei, G., Xian-Long, J., Xiao-Yun, Z., Jie, S., Yi-Jiu, C., Jian-Guo, C.: Study of injuries combining computer simulation in motorcycle–car collision accidents. Forensic. Sci. Int. 177(2-3), 90–96 (2008)
5. Weng, Y., Jin, X., Zhao, Z., Zhang, X.: Car-to-pedestrian collision reconstruction with injury as an evaluation index. Accid. Anal. Prev. 42(4), 1320–1325 (2010)
6. O'Riordain, K., Thomas, P.M., Phillips, J.P., Gilchrist, M.D.: Reconstruction of real world head injury accidents resulting from falls using multibody dynamics. Clin. Biomech. 18(7), 590–600 (2003)
7. Doorly, M.C., Horgan, T.J., Gilchrist, M.D.: Reconstruction of head injury cases arising from falls using the UCD brain trauma model. In: Gilchrist, M.D. (ed.) IUTAM Symposium on Impact Biomechanics: From Fundamental Insights to Applications Solid Mechanics and Its Applications, vol. 124, pp. 431–440. Springer, Dordrecht (2005)
8. Günay, Y., Yavuz, M.F., Eşiyok, B.: Comparison of Turkish Injury Scale (TIS) with the Abbreviated Injury Scale (AIS). Forensic. Sci. Int. 132(1), 1–4 (2003)
9. Du, X., Jin, X., Zhang, X., Shen, J., Hou, X.: Geometry features measurement of traffic accident for reconstruction based on close-range photogrammetry. Adv. Eng. Soft. 40(7), 497–505 (2009)
10. TASS, MADYMO Human Models Manual Release 7.3, TASS, Rijswijk, The Netherlands (2010)
11. Villagra, J., d'Andréa-Novel, B., Fliess, M., Mounier, H.: A diagnosis-based approach for tire–road forces and maximum friction estimation. Control Eng. Pract. 19(2), 174–184 (2011)
12. Occupant Protection & Egress in Rail Systems (OPERAS), Proposed HIC tolerance levels correlated to skull fracture (Table 15) (2001), http://www.eurailsafe.net/subsites/operas/HTML/appendix/Table15.htm (retrieved January 28, 2013)
13. Occupant Protection & Egress in Rail Systems (OPERAS), Neck injury criteria tolerance levels (Table 22) (2001), http://www.eurailsafe.net/subsites/operas/HTML/appendix/Table22.htm (retrieved January 28, 2013)
14. Hutchinson, J., Kaiser, M.J., Lankarani, H.M.: The Head Injury Criterion (HIC) functional. Appl. Math. Comput. 96(1), 1–16 (1998)

The Relationship between Nursing Students' Attitudes towards Learning and Effects of Self-learning System Using Kinect

Mitsuhiro Nakamura[1], Yasuko Kitajima[1], Jun Ota[2], Taiki Ogata[2], Zhifeng Huang[2], Ayanori Nagata[2], Kyoko Aida[1], Noriaki Kuwahara[3], Jukai Maeda[1], and Masako Kanai-Pak[1]

[1] Faculty of Nursing, Tokyo Ariake University of Medical and Health Sciences,
2-9-1 Ariake, Koto-ku, Tokyo 135-0063, Japan
{m-nakamura,kitajima,k-aida,jukai,p-kanai}@tau.ac.jp
[2] Research into Artifacts Center for Engineering (RACE), The University of Tokyo,
5-1-5 Kashiwanoha, Kashiwa-shi, Chiba 277-8568, Japan
{ota,ogata,zhifeng,nagata}@race.u-tokyo.ac.jp
[3] Department of Advanced Fibro-Science, Kyoto Institute of Technology,
Matsugasaki, Sakyo-ku, Kyoto 606-8585, Japan
nkuwahar@kit.ac.jp

Abstract. The purpose of this study is to clarify the relationship between nursing students' attitudes towards learning and effects of Kinect self-learning system for skill acquisition. Five students received feedback after each performance from the Kinect self-learning system. The students' performance was evaluated before (pre-test) and after (post-test) using 21 checkpoints. In order to investigate the students' attitudes towards learning, a survey questionnaire was distributed before the study. Based on the score, each student's attitudes towards learning were identified as either "active" or "passive". The difference between the pre-test and post-test scores for each student was calculated. Pearson product-moment correlation coefficients were calculated of the difference in the number of learning characteristics. There was a strong negative correlation between learning characteristic (Passive learning attitude) and the difference of score ($r=-.80$ $p=.11$). From this study, it is recommended that the Kinect self-learning system is not effective for skill acquisition for students whose attitudes were passive.

Keywords: Kinect, Medical Error & Simulation, Nursing Student, Nursing skill, Nursing Education.

1 Introduction

Nursing education is always challenging because it covers three domains of learning such as cognitive, psychomotor, and affective. In nursing programs, students have to spend many hours in lab and clinical practicum in order to acquire

V.G. Duffy (Ed.): DHM/HCII 2013, Part II, LNCS 8026, pp. 111–116, 2013.

nursing skills to give appropriate care for clients. Nursing skills such as giving injections, taking vital signs, and giving bed bath require fine physical coordination of care givers. For nursing students, teachers design effective and efficient ways of teaching nursing skills. Contrary to faculty's device, new graduates indicated only four skills which they have confidence to perform out of 104 skills expected to acquire [1].

In current clinical practice, demand for new graduates has become higher due to development of high technology, increase numbers of elderly clients, and increase high acuity level of inpatiens. Compare to the past, chances of giving direct patient care by nursing students have become limited because of patient safety reasons and of high demand from patients. This would be one of the reasons for less confident among new graduates when giving care.

There is a need for strengthening students' skill during course work not only in clinical practicum but also in lab rooms on campus. Nursing students have to learn many nursing care skills in the limited time period. In classroom settings, the average hours for each student to learn one skill under faculty's supervision is 9.4 minutes [2]. In order for students to acquire skills, they have to spend a quite amount of time in the lab room. Students practice nursing care skills with other students in the lab rooms in which faculty members may not always attend. Whiles students practice skills by trail and errors, they receive feedback from other students. The feedback, however, may not always be correct [3].

One of the ideal teaching methods for skill acquisition is to teach man-to-man method. The study indicated that the students acquired the skills with using this method [4]. This method, however, is not feasible due to the limited time and numbers of faculty.

For the past four years, the researchers have been investigating how nursing students acquire nursing care skills effectively and efficiently. The first study was conducted using accelerometers. Out of 14 nursing care items, transfer skills were identified by accelerometers [5]. Using accelerometers, a model performance of transfer a patient from bed to wheelchair was investigated. The visual patterns of a model performance of this transfer skill were identified. The data collection of this transfer skill was conducted using 10 nursing students. It was obvious that the visual patterns of this performance by nursing students were deviated from the patterns of the model performance. If nursing students can visualize the differences in patterns of the performance in lab rooms, they are able to acquire skills efficiently. Based on these studies, the self-learning system with accelerometers was developed.

The researchers investigated the effect of accelerometers for nursing students. An experimental study was conducted for a transfer skill using 10 nursing students (5 for experiment group and 5 for control group). For the experimental group, the students received feedback after the performance based on the results of patterns of the performance. For the control group, the students practice a transfer skill in a traditional way such as watching the video and practicing in the lab room. The result indicated that the students in the experimental group improved the transfer skill compared with those in the control group (p<.05) [6].

One of the weaknesses of using accelerometers is inconvenience. It takes time to put accelerometers in certain areas of the body. The researchers used Kinect instead of accelerometers. The study for investigating the effect of Kinect was conducted. Using a Kinect system, an experimental study was carried out. The nursing students in the experimental group significantly improved the transfer skill [7]. Although the average score of the experimental group was statistically higher (p<.05), a student did not improve the skill. The researchers speculated the reasons for this result. One of the reasons could be students' attitudes towards using a Kinect system. It is necessary to investigate reasons.

2   Purpose

The purpose of this study is to clarify the relationship between nursing students' atti-tudes towards learning and effects of Kinect self-learning system for skill acquisition.

3   Methods

Five freshman students participated in the study. The skill which the students had to learn was transferring a patient from the bed to wheelchair.

The Kinect self-learning system with which the students received feedback after each performance. The students were allowed to spend 20 minutes to practice using the system. The students' performance was evaluated before (pre-test) and after (post-test) using 21 checkpoints (Table 1). Each checkpoint was allocated as one point. The total points were summed.

To check the statistical significance, the calculation of Student's t-test carried out by the difference in the number of Pre-test and Post-test for each student.

In order to investigate the students' attitudes towards learning, a survey questionnaire was distributed at the beginning of the study (Table 2). Students were asked to answered each question with a five-point Likert scale. The quesionnaire consists of two different attitudes towards learing: „active" and „passive". The scores were summed separately in „active" and „passive" for each student. The students were identifid as either „active learning attitude" and „passive learning attitude" based on the scores [9].

The difference between the pre-test and post-test scores for each student was calculated. Pearson product-moment correlation coefficients were calculated and the differ-ence in the number of learning characteristics.

Table 1. Evaluation items for transferring a patient from the bed to wheelchair

No.	Evaluation Items
1-a	Set wheelchair at the side of the bed with 20 to 30-degree angle
1-b	Place wheelchair close to the patient
2	Apply brakes
3-a	Place nurse's left feet forward and right leg backward when bringing the patient close to the edge of the bed
3-b	Place nurse's left leg between patient's legs
4-a	Support patient's hip
4-b	When bringing the patient close to the edge of the bed, move the patient's center of the gravity to right and left
5	Bring patient's heels close to the bed
6	Place patient's both arms around nurse's shoulder
7	Support patient's waist
8-a	Place nurse's left feet forward and right leg backward when patient stands up
8-b	Place nurse's foot between patient's legs
9-a	Bend nurse's knees
9-b	Patient stands up like bowing
10	Turn patient toward the wheelchair
11-a	Nurse bends the knees while placing the patient in the wheelchair
11-b	Patient sits down in the wheelchair like bowing
12	Hold patient's forearm from behind the patient and the patient's both the side
13	Bring the patient's buttocks towards the back of the wheelchair while placing patient's head lower
14-a	Bring down footrest of the wheelchair
14-b	Place patient's feet on the footrest

Table 2. Questionnaire items of students' attitudes towards learning

items	Attitudes
A better way of learning at college is that students devise themselves.	active
A better way of learning at college is that students are taught by faculty in classrooms.	passive
I prefer to take courses which I am interested in though it might be difficult to earn credits.	active
I prefer to take courses which are easy to earn credits.	passive
It is preferable that students actively involve with study in the classroom.	active
It is preferable that students listen to the lectures in classrooms.	passive

4   Results

The average pre-test score was 8.6 with the range between 3 and 13 (SD 4.34). The average post-test score was 17 with the range between 14 and 21 (SD 2.55) (Fig. 1). There was a statistically significant difference in the Pre-test score and Post-test score (t=-4.39 p=.01).

There was a strong negative correlation between learning characteristic (Passive learning attitude) and the difference of score (r=-.80 p=.11).

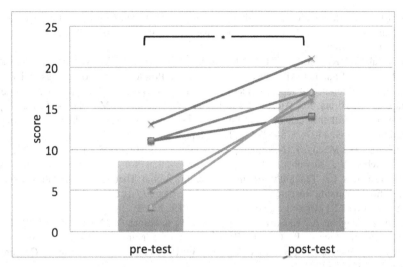

Fig. 1. Correlation of Score (Pre-test and Post-test). Line graph are total score of students. Bar chart is average pre-test and post-test score. Student's t-test *P<.05.

5   Discussion

Based on this study, effect of using Kinect is directly related to learners' attitudes towards Kinect. The learners' attitudes could be affected by the environment. For this data collection in the experimental group, the students were surrounded by many devices and several people operating the devices. This environment might create a feeling of pressure and threats to some students. The researchers' goal is to develop the Kinect self-learning system built in the room so that learners would not be surrounded by many devices and people. Using the Kinect self-learning system, students are able to practice as many times as they wish. Moreover, they receive feedback from the system so that they can assess their weaknesses immediately after their performance.

Faculty's challenge for investigating effective and efficient teaching/learning methods for nursing care skills acquisition continues as higher demands for nurses in clinical settings.

The limitation of this study is the numbers of subjects. In order to generalize the result, replication of the study is essential.

References

1. Japanese Nursing Association: Survey of basic nursing skills of freshman nurses (2002) (in Japanese)
2. Nakamura, M.: Building the foundation for a new nursing skill education system based on patient moving. Handout, Special Interest Group of Nonverbal Interface, Human Interface Society (2011)

3. Kanai-Pak, M.: Innovation in Collaborative Research between Nursing and Engineering: A new Approach for Skill Acquisition. The Japanese Journal of Nursing Research 44(6), 554–558 (2011) (in Japanese)
4. Kanai-Pak, M., Kitajima, Y., Hirata, M., Aida, K., Takabatake, Y., Nakamura, M., Maeda, J.: The effect of nursing skill education our ideal and Problems. In: Proceedings of The 30th Academic Conference of Japan Academy of Nursing Science, p. 243 (2010) (in Japanese)
5. Kitajima, Y., Hirata, M., Aida, K., Takabatake, Y., Nakamura, M., Maeda, J., Kanai-Pak, M.: Nursing skill that can be identified by acceleration sensor. The Japanese Journal of Nursing Research 44(6), 575–582 (2011) (in Japanese)
6. Kanai-Pak, M., Maeda, J., Nakamura, M., Kitajima, Y., Hirata, M., Takabatake, Y., Aida, K., Takebe, Y., Kuwahara, N., Ota, J.: Innovation for Nursing Education: Using Accelerometers for Teaching Nursing Skills. In: Sigma Theta Tau International's 22nd International Nursing Research Congress (2011), http://stti.confex.com/stti/congrs11/webprogram/Paper47479.html
7. Huang, Z., Nagata, A., Kanai-Pak, M., Maeda, J., Kitajima, Y., Nakamura, M., Aida, K., Kuwahara, N., Ogata, T., Ota, J.: Development of a Nursing Self-training System for Transferring Patient from Bed to Wheelchair. In: Proceedings of SICE Annual Conference 2012, pp. 246–254 (2012)
8. Nakamura, M., Maeda, J., Kitajima, Y., Aida, K., Kanai-Pak, M.: Possibility of nursing skills self-learning and the effect of evaluation system. In: Proceedings of the 31nd Academic Conference of Japan Academy of Nursing Science, p. 260 (2011) (in Japanese)
9. Benesse Educational Research and Development Center WWW site (February 22, 2013), http://benesse.jp/berd/center/open/report/daigaku_jittai/hon/pdf/data_08.pdf (in Japanese)

Extending Global Education
through Remote Laboratory Access

Uwe Reischl[1] and Scott Harris[2]

[1] Boise State University, Boise, Idaho, USA
ureischl@boisestate.edu
[2] Apriori LLC, Boise, Idaho, USA
sharris@reach-in.com

Abstract. Advanced software technologies that are integrated with physical laboratories now allow students and researchers to access laboratory equipment and instruments remotely through the Internet. While this capability has been used in engineering and science education successfully for some time, application of this approach to human factors engineering and ergonomics education is new. The development of a remote ergonomics laboratory based on such an Internet technology is described. The focus of this new laboratory is to provide a method of evaluating protective clothing heat stress using a thermal manikin technology. The laboratory has generated global interest and created international collaboration in teaching and research.

Keywords: Remote laboratory, ergonomics education, thermal manikin, international collaboration.

1 Introduction

The rapid expansion of the Internet and its growing popularity worldwide has had a significant impact on education. This technology offers new tools for a broad range of engineering and science disciplines. The technology also offers the opportunity to promote the development of new teaching strategies such as interactive experimentation, simulation, etc. (1). Broadband access and data compression support the delivery of audio and video streaming of lectures on the Internet. Computer and Internet based learning has become an important part of education internationally.

A special challenge for online education in the engineering, science, and technology fields is how to extend the traditional hands-on laboratory settings over the Internet. Hands-on laboratories have been an integral part of engineering programs (2). Concepts presented in lectures are often complemented with laboratory experimentation. Hands-on education allows students to experience the "backbone" of engineering and science by conducting experiments, observing dynamic phenomena, testing hypotheses, learning from their mistakes, and reaching their own conclusions (3). With the rapid advances in microprocessor and communication technologies, more and more equipment can now be reconfigured and controlled

V.G. Duffy (Ed.): DHM/HCII 2013, Part II, LNCS 8026, pp. 117–123, 2013.

remotely. These developments have made hands-on training via the internet possible. Currently, there are two approaches to conducting labs online. These include virtual labs and remote labs

- Virtual laboratories are based on software to simulate the lab environment and are especially useful when equipment is too expensive, unsafe, or unavailable.
- Virtual labs allow students to repeat an experiment multiple times, giving them the chance to see how changed parameters and settings can affect the outcome. Students can learn from failures without causing real damage.
- Remote laboratories are facilities used to conduct experiments that are controlled remotely through the Internet. The experiments use real components and instruments at a different location from where they are being controlled from. The logistics of developing a real laboratory is often a significant problem for educational institutions because the availability of space is frequently limited, availability of funding for instrumentation and supporting equipment is limited, and the availability of technical support staff is also limited.

To promote student access to hands-on learning in the fields of ergonomics and human factors engineering, not only at the local level but also regionally and internationally, an existing thermal manikin laboratory at Boise State University was reconfigured to accommodate an Internet-based remote control technology. The laboratory now serves as an educational platform for academic partner institutions regionally and internationally.

2   Laboratory Implementation

The Ergonomics Laboratory is equipped with a thermal manikin system capable of assessing the heat exchange characteristics of protective clothing worn under controlled environmental conditions. Equipment includes a manikin air pressure system, manikin air heating system, environmental ventilators, infrared radiators, and digital thermometers measuring manikin input and output temperatures needed to compute the manikin heat gain or heat loss.

- Before the facility is ready for use as a remote laboratory, the IT infrastructure as it relates to the remote connections had to be solved. Factors such as network firewall policy or which software was going to be used for the connection and interface had to be resolved.
- Initiating a remote laboratory experiment required that all of the supporting staff as well as the students were fully aware of the experimental procedures, knowledgeable in using the remote controls properly and safely, and were aware of the time requirements associated in collecting accurate data.
- Assessing the learning outcome or value of the remote laboratory assignment required the collection and evaluation of feedback from the student users. This information was used to correct deficiencies and was used to modify the laboratory experience.

3   Remote Controls

The Internet platform serving the Remote Laboratory is provided by Apriori, LLC through its "Reach-In" browser technology which allows novice Internet users, i.e. users with no special computer skills, the ability to control mechanical devices through the internet using nothing more than their everyday computer and their everyday home Internet connections.   This functionality is possible in any geographical location in the world that has Internet access. This technology platform provides major advantages for international collaboration in the following ways:

- The software reduces latency to less than 1 second based on the current Internet infrastructure.
- The software works in all major browsers without the need for special downloads.
- The software can control any hardware component over the web.
- The technology allows many users to interact on one site without compromising the quality for the user in control.
- A queuing methodology allows for global users to join a queue from anywhere on the Internet. This architecture accounts for every person in line and dynamically adjusts for variances in line positioning.

Any student or researcher with sufficient connection speed can log onto the remote laboratory website and control all of the assigned laboratory devices from anywhere in the worlds without a time delay. The user has the ability to control a camera, pan up and down, and zoom in and out on every instrument located in the laboratory. At a click of their mouse, a user can control up to 12 mechanical devices at any one time.

4   System Architecture

The key feature of this system lies in its architecture which minimizes the latency time of the hardware components and the latency of the software that controls the devices. A main server acts as a hub for all information transfer. A dedicated replication server is included that handles the video stream separately since the video stream represents the largest amount of data transfer. A camera is connected to an on-site control box. The mechanical devices in the laboratory are connected to motherboard located inside the control box which converts the digital data signals into voltage outputs. The voltage outputs act as the driving force to articulate the geared camera hardware back and forth, up and down, on, and of, etc. A kernel of software is located on the control box that communicates with the main servers providing an "IsAlive" beacon. Service technicians can respond if the "IsAlive" beacon does not check-in within 15 seconds.

5   Laboratory Set-Up

The ergonomics laboratory contains an inflatable thermal manikin system designed to measure the heat transfer characteristics of clothing systems. The technical design features are illustrated in Figure 1. While the manikin needs to be clothed by a staff member, all controls required to operate the system can be manipulated remotely via the Internet. A student, or a researcher, logs on to the laboratory website and sees the laboratory "live" through a camera that is in the "ON" position 24/7 (Fig. 2). The user can then engage the manikin sub systems consisting of the manikin air pressure system and the manikin internal air heating system activated through by the power control relays (Fig. 3). This provides the "start-up" operating configuration for the manikin. The manikin must reach thermal equilibrium with the laboratory environment prior to testing. The user can then operate the laboratory IR exposure lamps and the laboratory cooling fans to change the manikin exposure conditions. Using the camera's directional controls and the "zoom" feature, the user can monitor the digital thermometers that display the manikin input air temperature as well as the manikin output air temperature (Fig. 4). These values are then used to calculate the heat loss or heat gain exhibited by the manikin during exposure to different environmental conditions or clothing configurations. The laboratory remote control schematic illustrating the relationship between the key components and the sub-systems of the laboratory are illustrated in Fig 5.

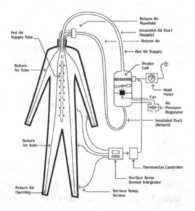

Fig. 1. Illustration of the inflatable thermal manikin system

Fig. 2. Remote controlled internet camera allowing un-interrupted visual access to the laboratory

Fig. 3. Remote control relays used in activating power to thermal manikin sub-systems

Fig. 4. Temperature monitors showing manikin input air temperature and manikin output air temperature values which are needed to compute manikin heat loss values

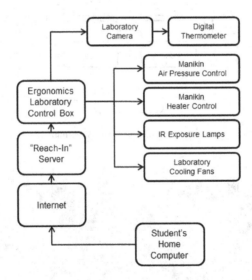

Fig. 5. Layout for of the laboratory remote control system

6   Conducting an Experiment

To determine the heat transfer characteristics of a garment requires the student or researcher to perform two measurement conditions sequentially using the following steps as illustrated schematically in Fig.6:

- The thermal manikin must first reach thermal equilibrium in a "semi-nude" configuration (wearing short pants only). This serves as the "control" configuration (Fig. 7A).
- The temperature difference between output air and input air is observed and recorded and entered into a standard energy loss calculation.
- Once thermal equilibrium is reached, heat radiation exposures or wind conditions can be added. Again, the manikin input and output temperature values are recorded at equilibrium.
- To measure the thermal characteristics of clothing systems, the procedures used for the "control" conditions are repeated with the exception that the manikin is now clothed (Fig. 7B)
- The energy loss values are then compared to the "control" conditions. This provides the student or researcher accurate values for the thermal properties of the clothing system.

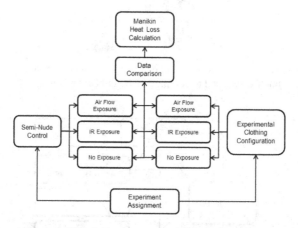

Fig. 6. Testing protocol schematic

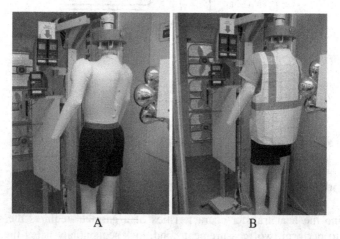

Fig. 7. Illustration of thermal manikin in a semi-nude "Control" configuration (A) and in the "Experimental" configuration (B)

7   Use of Laboratory

Access to the remote thermal laboratory is currently open to the global Internet community. Visitors are permitted to operate the equipment "at-will" to observe the technical functions of the key manikin equipment. User tracking has shown that persons from all continents around the world have accessed the facility either as a viewer or as an active "player" operating the various manikin sub-systems. Although the current features appear to offer visitors a video-game "entertainment" opportunity, the goal of the open access policy is to promote interest in ergonomics research. However, when experiments are being conducted locally or "in-house", the remote controls are disabled. This allows the researchers to eliminate outside interference or interruptions. However, the camera continues to remain "on" during experiments which allows visitors anywhere in the world to view these activities 24/7.

8   International Collaboration

International use of the remote thermal manikin laboratory as a research facility developed after visiting researchers successfully conducted in-house studies using the thermal manikin technology and wanted to continue with their experiments after returning home. The collaborations have now expanded from Boise State University in the USA to the University of Zagreb in Croatia and the Hong Kong University of Science and Technology. Preliminary collaborations are being explored with universities in Brazil and in Peru. Although the advantage of using the remote laboratory increases with distance, differences in the East-West time-zones can make real-time communications regarding experimental problems and set-up requirements difficult. Nevertheless, as academic resources become scarcer, collaborative use of laboratory resources locally, regionally, and internationally will be helpful. Remote laboratories will undoubtedly play an important role in promoting collaboration.

References

1. Selmer, A., Kraft, M., Moros, R., Colton, C.: Weblabs in Chemical Engineering Education. Education for Chemical Engineers 2, 38–45 (2007)
2. Feisel, L., Rosa, A.: The Role of the Laboratory in Undergraduate Engineering Education. Journal of Engineering Education 94, 121–130 (2005)
3. Tompkins, P.A., Pingen, G.: Real-Time Experimentation Across the Internet. Physics on the Internet 40(1), 408–410 (2002)

Combining Motion Capture and Digital Human Modeling for Creating Instructions in Industrial Settings

Ulrike Schmuntzsch, Ulas Yilmaz, and Matthias Rötting

TU Berlin, Department of Psychology and Ergonomics, Chair of Human-Machine Systems
Marchstr. 23, 10587 Berlin, Germany
{usc,uyi,roetting}@mms.tu-berlin.de

Abstract. In this paper, a hybrid framework for creating an instruction video by means of motion capture technologies will be explained. In this video an animated pedagogical agent named *Anastasia* (<u>an</u>imated <u>as</u>sistant for <u>tas</u>ks in <u>i</u>ndustrial <u>a</u>pplications) provides human operators with assistance while performing maintenance tasks in IPS^2. Firstly, the paper contains a description of the creation process of an animated pedagogical agent which will be illustrated step by step on *Anastasia*. Secondly, the motion capture technology in form of a data glove will be presented. Thirdly, the concept and implementation how to improve realism of *Anastasia* by using the data glove will be introduced.

Keywords: animated pedagogical agent, instruction video, human modeling, motion capturing, data glove, wearable computing technologies, smart clothes.

1 Introduction

The growing global competition with emerging BRICS nations forces internationally operating industrial companies to work out a unique selling point and to gain a competitive edge. To keep up, high technology companies develop extremely customized industry solutions combining products and services. These, so called Industrial Product-Service Systems (IPS^2) are characterized by a variety of different users, contexts of usage and highly specialized products and services. Human operators working in these settings are in charge of the "supervisory control", which includes monitoring the system process and performing tasks that cannot be automated efficiently such as maintenance or overhaul (Sheridan in [12]). This constellation oftentimes forces human operators to unexpected and unpracticed interventions which could be risky for man, machine and environment (Reason in [9]).

As to the initially illustrated situation, an urgent need of coherent and understandable user support exists by taking different user populations and contexts into account (Uhlmann et.al. in [17] and Schmuntzsch in [13]). This project focuses on the design of multimodal instructions in IPS2 so that the given user support for human operators provides practical and intuitive information on actions, technical

V.G. Duffy (Ed.): DHM/HCII 2013, Part II, LNCS 8026, pp. 124–133, 2013.

processes and potential hazards. A prominent and successful method, used for instance in online markets and computer games, is to provide instructions to a multitude of different users by an animated character. However, there are only few examples when it comes to technical contexts (Ziegler and Zülke in [21]). One important reason might be the complexity and great adaptability in industrial settings which makes it difficult as well as time and cost consuming to apply animated characters for industrial tasks. However, through huge technical progress and reduced prices, motion capture technologies, traditionally applied in film and gaming industry and ergonomics research, nowadays are increasingly used in further areas (Bergler in [1], Brodie et.al. in [2] and Xsens in [20]). These increased opportunities are used in our project to combine the motion capture technology with the modeling of an animated pedagogical agent, who demonstrates how to perform a maintenance task in an instruction video. The realism of finger movements is a key to more realistic instruction videos. That's why, in this study, the focus is on increasing the realism of hand in the instruction video by integrating a motion capture system into the design.

The article is organized as follows. Hereafter in Section 2, the design process of the animated character and the therefore used software tools are presented. Section 3 gives insides how the finger movements are captured using the data glove. The mapping procedure and the overall framework are clarified in Section 4. The article concludes with a discussion of the main experiences and challenges of the realization process.

2   Animated Characters

2.1   Theoretical Classification

The enormous variety of animated characters can be subdivided into two basic categories: humanoid and nonhumanoid types. For the first group, the humanoid characters, exist numerous terminologies, such as virtual human (Rickel in [10]) or digital human (Lopiccolo in [7]), digital actor or synthetic actor (Thalmann in [16]), animated pedagogical agent or virtual (interface) agent (Rickel and Johnson in [11]). Even though they all seem similar, slightly different meanings are noticeable. For the purpose of this work, an animated pedagogical agent seems appropriate. Due to having sufficient knowledge about the content and reacting properly towards user inputs, animated pedagogical agents are used to facilitate the learning processes (Lester in [6]). Apart from that group, virtual (interface) agents also suggest an interesting alternative. These characters can be split into avatars, assistants and actors. Relevant to us are especially actors because they represent a computer-based human acting in a virtual setting whose behavior cannot be influenced by the user (Mase in [8]). Functioning as instructor, advisor, motivator or companion, animated characters are widely used in different application fields, mainly in computer games and entertainment, e-commerce and learning environments. There, they not only support users by giving stepwise instructions, but also by evoking the feeling not to be left alone with a problem (Fröhlich and Plate in [3]). In several user studies, it has been shown that humanoid characters can increase user satisfaction and entertainment value (Lester in [6]). Furthermore, it has also been found out that a true-to-life representation of a virtual character leads to an increased user motivation and readiness to work (Johnson et.al. in [5]). Thus, one can state that its mere presence creates a pleasant working atmosphere for users. Working in technical contexts means learning oftentimes complex factual as well as practical knowledge. For these kinds of settings, there is much less examples for user support (Ziegler and Zülke in [21]). A relatively well known example is the animated pedagogical agent *Steve* who functions as tutor teaching students how to use or overhaul complex machines (Rickel and Johnson in [11]). Particularly for such industrial tasks, animated pedagogical agents provide many advantages. For instance, the interactive demonstrations make it possible to teach users how to perform physical tasks such as repairing equipment. That way, different sequences of events, which have to be carried out to fulfill a task, can be reproduced stepwise. Another important factor, as to Rickel in [10], is the agent's gaze and gestures. Due to their familiarity and human likeness they seem to be very suitable as attention guides. Further advantages of animated pedagogical agents are their expressed emotions and personality as well as the associated story and character. This helps to increase the learning motivation as well as to capture and to hold attention. All the mentioned aspects can be seen as key factors to trigger user's emotions and to gain a better understanding of the required technical procedures and knowledge.

2.2   The Creation Process of *Anastasia* and Her Technical Equipment

As to the above mentioned advantages of using animated pedagogical agents especially for teaching technical procedures, in the project it was decided to model a female character and to name her *Anastasia* which also stands for animated assistant for tasks in industrial applications (Schmuntzsch et.al. in [14] and [15]). This acronym indicates the function and the field of application of *Anastasia*, as well.

In order to finally realize the instruction video in its present form several steps had to be carried out. This meant to realize various 3D concepts, to acquire data from the data glove, to send remote animation scripts over network, and to integrate all the existing software components. Here, a mixture of different software tools such as *MakeHuman*, *Autodesk Inventor* and *Blender* had to be used. *MakeHuman* is free software for the modeling of three dimensional humanoid characters. It is released under an open source license and available for various operating systems such as *Windows*, *Mac OS X* and Linux (www.makehuman.org). *Autodesk Inventor* is 3D mechanical solid modeling design software for creating 3D digital prototypes used in the design, visualization and simulation of products (usa.autodesk.com/autodesk-inventor). Finally, *Blender* is a free and open source 3D computer graphics software product used for creating animated films, visual effects, interactive 3D applications and video games (www.blender.org). Creating *Anastasia* the first step was to design a model of an animated assistant with the software tool *MakeHuman 1.0 alpha 6.0* as shown in Figure 1a. Then, the created model was exported as so called "Blender Exchange" in mhx file format.

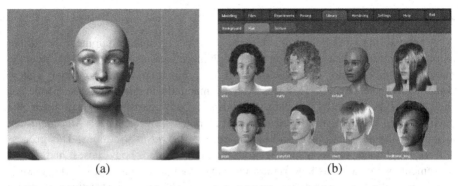

(a)   (b)

Fig. 1. (a) The human model of *Anastasia* in *MakeHuman* and (b) various hair options

For various reasons, such as inter-software inconsistencies, nonstandard file format definitions, and integration challenges, creation of the hair of Anastasia requires special attention. Thus, the hair of Anastasia was also created in MakeHuman using one of the hair templates provided within the software as shown in Figure 1b. It was then exported as Wavefront file in obj file format with some manual settings and several small adaptations in hair and clothing, in order to make the animated assistant look natural and familiar. The human operator interacts at the workstation with several other technical components, such as machine equipment and tools. Modeling these components was also an essential part of the creation process of the instruction video. Thus, a model of the real micro milling machine (see Figure 2a) was created in Autodesk Inventor 2012 and adapted to Blender as shown in Figure 2c. Tools, such as the Allen key and the jaw spanner were also designed with the same program and adapted to Blender. During the adaption process, the created models were first exported as CAD models in stl file format, and then modified parts were combined in Blender, so that the final model could be colorized and animated realistically.

(a)   (b)   (c)

Fig. 2. (a) Real micro milling machine; (b) micro milling machine designed in *Inventor* and (c) imported into *Blender*

Further technical equipment used in the instruction video, such as power supply, operating computer, spindle box, laptop, tables and backgrounds, were directly designed in *Blender*.

2.3   Animating *Anastasia*

After creating the virtual character *Anastasia* and her technical equipment the further animation process of the instruction video took place in two steps. In the first step, the main body movements of *Anastasia* and the animation regarding other system components were created. This was realized manually in *Blender* "Pose Mode" as shown in Figure 3a by moving *Anastasia*'s body parts and position in the environment. Whereas in the second step, finger movements of *Anastasia* are acquired using the data glove, and integrated into *Anastasia*'s motions. This process will be explained in detail in Section 3. Both created body poses and finger movements were saved as key frames. Oral explanations synchronous to *Anastasia*'s actions are integrated as third person narration, and finally the instruction video was exported as a video file, a screenshot of which is shown in Figure 3b.

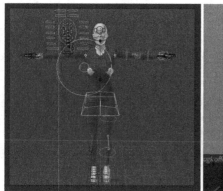

Fig. 3. (a) *MakeHuman* model imported into *Blender* and shown in "Pose Mode" where possible body movements are illustrated; (b) beginning of the instruction video

3   Motion Capture

Motion capture technologies are being used in ergonomic research and in the film industry for quite a long time (Bergler in [1], Brodie et.al. in [2] and Xsens in [20]). IPS^2, on the other hand, is a rather new field of application. Growing product complexity and increasing heterogeneity of users and contexts highlight the importance of understandable and illustrative user support such as instruction videos. Creating these videos, one can make use of motion capturing in order to increase realism, as it is widely done in film industry. However, most of the time, the focus in such videos, is on the hand, respectively on the fingers. The more realistic are the fingers modeled the more realistic is the instruction video. That's why, the focus of the study is on increasing the realism of hand in the instruction video by using a data glove to capture finger movements of the human operators. In the following two subsections, the data glove used in the study will be described. Furthermore, it will be explained in detail, how the calibration for increasing realism was managed.

3.1   Data Glove

Depending on the sensors being used, the data glove systems available on the market can be grouped into four categories: optical, mechanical, inertial and bend (VRealities in [18] and Inition in [4]). Each system has its advantages and disadvantages. For instance, optical systems are relatively cheap, but the occlusion problem is inevitable. Mechanical systems are relatively robust, but they are ergonomically hard to use. Inertial systems are precise, yet considerably expensive and very sensitive to magnetic interference. Our working environment has high magnetic interference and as the human operator moves around freely, system components are being continuously occluded. Consequently, the cheapest easy-to-use system that fits our working environment was the *X-IST Wireless DataGlove* that has bend sensors on fingers (X-IST in [19]). The data glove and the micro milling machine while the human operator is replacing the spindle are as shown in Figure 4a.

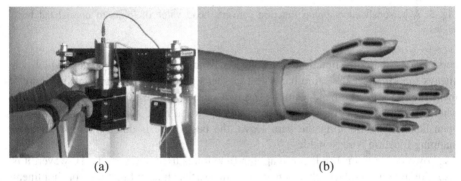

(a)   (b)

Fig. 4. (a) The micro milling machine and the data glove while the operator is replacing the spindle; (b) the distribution of bend sensors on finger joints

In *X-IST Wireless DataGlove* the sensors are located on finger joints as shown in Figure 4b; two sensors being on the thumb and three on each of the rest. Each sensor delivers a 10 bit value that corresponds to the relative bend of the finger bone at that instance. The working frequency is 60 Hertz. Note that, with *X-IST Wireless DataGlove* hand rotation is poorly captured through inertial sensors and finger spread is not to be acquired at all.

3.2   Calibration

The data glove delivers the maximum bend values, when the hand is open, and the minimum values, when it is closed to an ideal fist. However, not everyone's finger joints form a perfect line when the hand is open, or they form a 90 degrees angle when the person makes a fist. So, depending on some anatomical and the habitual differences, these bend values differ for the same hand gesture of different operators. In order to normalize bend data, an interactive interface through which the human operator calibrates the data glove was implemented. With that, it is possible to get a

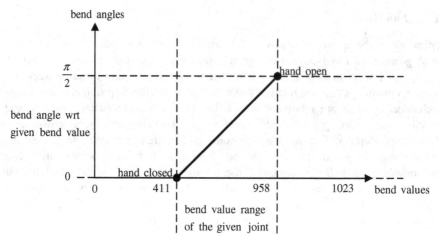

Fig. 5. A personalized mapping function converts bend value of joints to normalized bend angles

personalized mapping function that converts bend values to bend angles, which are always the same for the same hand gesture. This procedure is illustrated in Figure 5 for a single joint. The bend values occupy a portion of the possible bend spectrum, where the minimum bend value corresponds to closed hand and the maximum to the open hand. By calibrating the data glove, the best range is determined, so that the mapping function is reasonable.

As shown in Equation 1, a linear mapping function is used in the study. However, it is also possible to replace this function with partial linear functions or nonlinear functions for a better performance with different data gloves.

$$angle(v) = \begin{cases} 0 & v < v_{min} \\ \pi/2 & v > v_{max} \\ \dfrac{v - v_{min}}{v_{max} - v_{min}} \pi/2 & otherwise \end{cases} \qquad (1)$$

Through the developed interface, vmin and vmax can be set manually. Furthermore, the following calibration methods are also implemented in the designed interface. Thereby, one can first perform an automated calibration and then manually refine the extracted calibration parameters.

- Greedy range extraction
- Distribution analysis
- Gesture based calibration

In greedy range extraction the human operator is asked to make possible hand gestures, which are supposed to be done during the specified instructions. This is recorded for a given amount of time. At the end, the minimum value and the maximum value, which occur in the data set, are extracted to be the v_{min} and the v_{max}, respectively. In order to avoid outliers, a median filter can be applied to the data by selecting the nth extremes instead of the first ones. In distribution analysis method, human operator is asked to open and close his hand continuously for a given amount of time. Then, the minimum and the maximum value, which lie in some predefined standard deviations of the mean, are extracted to be the v_{min} and the v_{max}, respectively. In gesture based calibration the human operator is asked to make some specific hand gestures, such as open hand, fist, holding a specific tool, etc. The statistical mode of bend values is recorded during each gesture. At the end, the minimum and the maximum of these recorded values are selected to be the v_{min} and the v_{max}, respectively.

4   Mapping Process and the Making-of of the Instruction Video

4.1   Mapping Process

The designed interactive interface reads bend values from data glove using the serial connection and converts these values into bend angles which can be used with the *MakeHuman* model of *Anastasia*. Most of *Anastasia*'s movements regarding the instruction video are already prepared in *Blender*. Hence, a *Blender* plug-in was written, in order to connect our interface with *Anastasia* over TCP/IP. An illustration of this flow is shown in Figure 6.

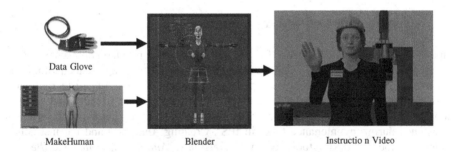

Data Glove

MakeHuman   Blender   Instructio n Video

Fig. 6. System overview of capturing hand movements from serial port to *Anastasia*

The plug-in can connect to any server that provides proper Python scripts which can be used for animating mhx models in *Blender*. The designed interface, naturally, provides Python scripts for animating the right hand of *Anastasia*. Once the connection is established, bend angles of the right hand are read over TCP/IP and shown directly on the model. The user captures the motion and inserts the key frame online to the preferred position in the instruction video as shown in Figure 7a.

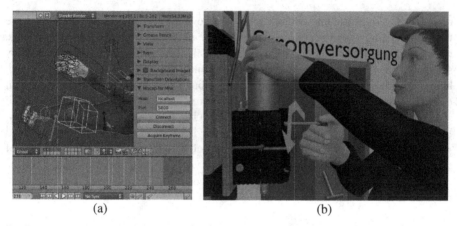

(a)   (b)

Fig. 7. (a) The user inserts a new keyframe using the plug-in and (b) the effect of the inserted keyframe shown while *Anastasia* is using Allen key on the micro milling machine

4.2   Instruction Video

The instruction consists of many work stages. So, the entire animation was exported in several short avi video sequences (codec H.264, audio codec: mp3, resolution: 1280x800) to assist the user at its specific problem. As an example for one instruction video, a screenshot of *Anastasia* using Allen key on the micro milling machine, is shown in Figure 7b.

5   Conclusions and Future Ongoing

In this paper, a hybrid framework for creating an instruction video is presented. Here, the realism of a pedagogical agent was increased using motion capture technologies in form of a data glove. The created pedagogical agent named *Anastasia* (animated assistant for tasks in industrial applications) is used to create friendly and realistic looking instruction videos in order to provide human operators with efficient assistance during maintenance tasks in IPS^2. Creating *Anastasia* and the instruction videos, various 3D design tools such as *MakeHuman*, *Autodesk Inventor* and *Blender*, as well as our own software were used to acquire data from the data glove, to send remote animation scripts over network, and to integrate all the existing software components. Even though motion capture technologies are already in use in entertainment industry and ergonomics research, IPS^2 is rather a new field of application. Growing product complexity and increasing heterogeneity of users and contexts in this field underlines the importance of realistic and illustrative user support, such as instruction videos. Currently, the focus is on the realism of finger movements in the instruction videos, since the realism of these limbs seems to be the most important issue in the application area. However, for future development it is planned to use a motion suit by which full body motion can be acquired, and virtual reality techniques through which one can improve realism in creating instruction videos in maintenance tasks.

Acknowledgments. We thank the German Research Foundation (DFG, Deutsche Forschungsgemeinschaft) for funding this research within the Transregional Collaborative Research Project TRR 29 on Industrial Product-Service Systems – dynamic interdependencies of products and services in production area.

References

1. Bergler, C.: Motion capture technology for entertainment. IEEE Signal Processing Magazine 24(6), 158–160 (2007)
2. Brodie, M., Walmsley, A., Page, W.: Fusion motion capture: a prototype system using inertial measurement units and GPS for the biomechanical analysis of ski racing. Sports Technologies 1(1), 17–28 (2008)
3. Fröhlich, B., Plate, J.: The cubic mouse: A new device for three-dimensional input. In: CHI, pp. 526–531. ACM Press (2000)
4. Inition: Hand motion capture (2012), http://www.inition.co.uk/3D-Technologies/productsection/43
5. Johnson, W.L., Rickel, J.W., Lester, J.C.: Animated pedagogical agents: Face-to-face interaction in interactive learning environments. International Journal of Artificial Intelligence in Education 11, 47–78 (2000)
6. Lester, J.C.: The persona effect: Affective impact of animated pedagogical agents. In: Human Factors in Computing Systems, pp. 359–366 (1997)
7. Lopiccolo, P.: What are 'veople' for? Computer Graphics World 25(11), 4–5 (2002)
8. Mase, K.: Aspects of interface agents: Avatar, assistant and actor. International Joint Conferences on Artificial Intelligence. In: Workshop on Animated Interface Agents, pp. 33–37 (1997)
9. Reason, J.: Human Error, 2nd edn. Cambridge University Press (2003)
10. Rickel, J.W.: Intelligent virtual agents for education and training: Opportunities and challenges. In: International Conference on Intelligent Virtual Agents, pp. 15–22 (2001)
11. Rickel, J.W., Johnson, W.L.: Animated agents for procedural training in virtual reality: Perception, cognition, and motor control. Applied Artificial Intelligence 13, 343–382 (1999)
12. Sheridan, T.B.: Telerobotics, Automation and Human Supervisory Control. MIT Press, Cambridge (1992)
13. Schmuntzsch, U., Rötting, M.: Multimodal user interfaces in IPS^2. In: International Conference on Digital Human Modeling in the Context of HCI International, pp. 347–356 (2011)
14. Schmuntzsch, U., Sturm, C., Reichmuth, R., Rötting, M.: Virtual agent assistance for maintenance tasks in IPS^2. Advances in Ergonomics in Manufacturing, 221 – 231 (2012)
15. Schmuntzsch, U., Yılmaz, U., Reichmuth, R., Rötting, M.: A first approach to generate hybrid animations for maintenance tasks in IPS^2. In: Intern. Conf. on Cognitive Modeling (2012)
16. Thalmann, D.: Autonomy and task-level control for virtual actors. Programming and Computer Software 21(4), 202–211 (1995)
17. Uhlmann, E., Meier, H., Stelzer, C., Geisert, C., Bochnig, H., Sadek, K.: Design of PSS based on customer requirements. In: First International Seminar on PSS, Bochum (2008)
18. VRealities: Data gloves (2012), http://www.vrealities.com/glove.html
19. X-IST: Dataglove wireless (2009), http://www.vrealities.com/x-ist.html
20. XSENS: MVN customer examples (2012), http://www.xsens.com/xsens-mvn-examples
21. Ziegler, D., Zühlke, D.: Emotional user interfaces and humanoid avatars in industrial environments. In: IFAC World Congress (2005)

Digital Human Modeling for Physiological Factors Evaluation in Work System Design

Lingyan Wang and Henry Y.K. Lau

Department of Industrial and Manufacturing Systems Engineering,
The University of Hong Kong, Hong Kong, P.R. China
{lywang,hyklau}@hku.hk

Abstract. This paper aims to develop a theoretical framework for physiological factors evaluation in work system design, and the goal has been achieved by combining principles and techniques derived from Digital Human Modeling (DHM). In more specific terms, geometrical, biomechanical, and graphical models are constructed to realize the simulation of worker's physical status in the virtual working environment, then to detect and evaluate work-related musculoskeletal disorders (WMSDs) which have a great potential of causing occupational impairment and disability. Furthermore, the ultimate object of this proposed framework is to fit the work system to the worker, and prevent the WMSDs from the original design phase.

Keywords: Work-related Musculoskeletal Disorders, Digital Human Modeling, Work System Design.

1 Introduction

Despite the fact that automatic operation plays a predominant role in industrial production, manual operation still accounts for a large proportion in virtue of the agility, flexibility and dexterity of human being. However, manual workers are easily exposed to a variety of hazardous work environment factors which have been the causes of negative effects upon the workers' physical health status and the work system performance from time to time.

WMSDs are heterogeneous group of chronic injuries or disorders of the body parts and tissues like muscles, nerves, tendons, ligaments, joints, or bones which develop over time due to work-related awkward and static postures, frequent and highly repetitive activities, forceful exertion, long duration as well as short cycle operations, they are serious occupational safety and health problems that closely related to a broad range of manual workers' physiological discomfort, fatigue, pain, injury and disability during work or at rest. Normally, there is no doubt that these common health risks can adversely affect a significant scale of workers' performance either through increasing the error rates or decreasing the workload which has been recognized as the reason of compromising the value of work system output and even the profits of company.

V.G. Duffy (Ed.): DHM/HCII 2013, Part II, LNCS 8026, pp. 134–142, 2013.

The structure of this paper is illustrated as follows: firstly, an overview of WMSDs and DHM is given to make the background clear and transparent; secondly, geometrical model, biomechanical model, and graphical model are introduced to represent the DHM tool; thirdly, a theoretical framework is developed to lay out the strategy of using DHM to demonstrate the work functions and evaluate the physiological factors, and this simulation method is performed to assess work postures and motions, then prevent the occupational hazards; finally, effects of the proposed framework, either positive or negative, are discussed in the context of a systemic analysis, and the feasible future work is presented for research continuity.

2   Background

2.1   Work-Related Musculoskeletal Disorders

The musculoskeletal system which is made up of bones, muscles, joints, tendons, ligaments, and other connective tissues consists of two interrelated systems, one is the skeletal system that provides a structure for physical support of the body, gives protection for the internal organs and fragile body tissues, realizes principal function of body movement, stores minerals, produces blood cells, and regulates incretion, the other is the muscular system that maintains posture, causes motion, stabilizes joints, circulates blood, and generates heat.

WMSDs describe disorders and diseases of this musculoskeletal system which are suspected to have been caused and exacerbated by a wide extent of work-related risk factors such as abominable work conditions, disorganized working process, shift work and long work hours, excessive force and sustained postures, etc. These disorders include degenerative and inflammatory syndromes of the muscles, skeleton and related tissues like tendons, joints, ligaments, bursae, cartilages, blood vessels, and peripheral nerves, for instance, myalgia, arthritis, osteoarthrosis, tenosynovitis, sciatica, bursitis, and so forth [1].

Disorders of the skeletal system contain sprain, luxation, and fracture. A sprain is an injury to the ligament or tissues around a joint that caused by a sudden fall or twist. A luxation is a joint dislocation occurs when bones are forced out of the right position in a joint. A traumatic bone fracture means the bone is completely or partially broken or cracked while an intense physical force is being exerted to it accidentally, and a pathological bone fracture is a bone lesion that arises from some underlying diseases.

Common muscular system injuries include strain, contusion, and cramp. A strain occurs when the muscle and adjacent tissues are extremely stretched or possibly ripped by a severe tension force. A contusion is a relatively minor hematoma of skin, subcutaneous tissue, and muscle that caused by a strong compression force. A cramp is a painful, sustained, and involuntary contraction of the skeletal muscle due to muscle fatigue and rigidity.

2.2   Digital Human Modeling

DHM is a simulation tool that provides a virtual representation of human beings in the simulated working environment for assessing the biomechanical attributes of human bodies with rapid computational efficiency, the skeleton structure and graphical appearance of virtual human are set up to realize the dimensional and physical properties from the interior to the exterior, thus to predict potential occupational fatigue and disorder risk. In general, the core of DHM is that it investigates multiple aspects of human postures and calculates the anthropometric elements quickly and objectively by replicating the on-going operation of complex work systems based on the database of recorded real human postures and motions.

The specific DHM tools like Ramsis, Siemens NX Human Modeling, Ergoman, Santos, CATIA, and DELMIA have been extensively utilized as proactive and available approaches to visualize and evaluate the interaction of workers and work systems from ergonomic aspects like visibility, functionality, scalability, and comfort in the fields of manufacturing, automobile, aerospace, military, healthcare, etc [2]. Hu et al. used five indices to assess the impact of ergonomic measurements feedback via a simulated drilling task operated by male manufacturing workers in the virtual environment [3]. Chang and Wang applied a visual workplace evaluation method to assess automobile assembly tasks by integrating dynamic digital environment simulation and biomechanical posture analysis [4]. Tian and Duffy implemented a DHM based Job Risk Classification Model to dynamically evaluate the corresponding task risk via calculating velocity and angular velocity of specified body segments/joints, in addition, they also analyzed potential errors to test the validity and reliability of this upgraded model [5]. Jung et al. combined the DHM with a commercial CAD system to implement the knowledge-based parametric modeling function of vehicles, and this integrated framework was carried out to gain optimized interior design parameters for ergonomic evaluations of various human-vehicle interactions [6]. Hanson et al. modified a DHM tool and utilized it to illustrate the cost efficiency and user-centered design processes of a health care bathing product. In this DHM working process scenario, joint range of motion and preferred bathing postures were defined, then description and appearance of the manikin was customized to fit the requirements [7].

2.3   Objective

The general objective of this research is to propose a theoretical framework associated with the digital human tool under which different aspects of human elements and data can be simultaneously integrated and simulated to realistically visualize the complex task oriented motion and interaction of real worker and workstation for multivariate assessment of physiological factors at the early stage of work system design, in order to concurrently evaluate biomechanical discomfort and analyze potential WMSDs exposures for identifying workplace and work task problems, then establish the adjustment of work environment to accommodate the workers for preventing them rapidly and economically.

3   Methodology

3.1   Geometrical Human Modeling

Geometrical human modeling is a modeling tool and technology of generating data structures and defined functions for presenting the finite dimensions, angles, and such characteristics of a desired human body shape as realistically as possible, and it focuses on the adequate numerical acquisition, simulation, and representation of the anthropometric features in order to quantize the numeric values of physiological factors in detail. Moreover, it provides fast visualization and parameterization of the body as well as defines these two or three-dimensional (3D) shapes efficiently by estimating the geometrical constraints of body joints and performing the mathematical calculations of human actions.

This geometrical approach is widely used in various computer-based application fields such as product design, mechanical engineering, animation design, medical image, etc. Wang proposed a feature based parameterization algorithm for parametric mannequin design according to the semantic feature extraction technique and symmetric detail mesh surface of the human body in fashion industry [8]. Wang et al. gave a detailed survey on existing parameterized 3D human body modeling and skin deformations methods which are primitive construction methods named rod-like model, surface model, volume model, and composite multi-layer model, model reconstruction methods based on 3D body scanning, contour data, and image, as well as sample interpolation synthesis methods [9]. Volkau et al. formulated a suitable 3D geometric venous segmentation algorithm of the human intracranial vasculature system for education and clinical applications by proposing three geometrical models based on circular, elliptic, and free-shape cross sections [10].

3.2   Biomechanical Human Modeling

Biomechanical human modeling studies the properties of the muscle, skeleton, and soft tissue when human performs physical activities like static postures or dynamic motions from the perspective of physiological kinematics that muscles generate tension through connective soft tissues which transfer it to move bones around joints. It is a valuable tool for ergonomic evaluations not only because of understanding musculoskeletal system capabilities, but also due to providing testable hypotheses of mechanical behavior variation and predicting the posture and trajectory of human body.

The muscle model is used to simulate the actual molecular structure and internal functioning of a muscle which represents the mechanical response of muscle contraction by emulating three primary relationships named force-length, force-velocity, and stimulus-tension curves when muscle fibers generate tension. The skeleton model is formulated in terms of an articulated multi-body dynamic system which takes into account the parameters of joint moment strengths, joint torques, and joint movement ranges, it aims at contributing to describing the posture, velocity, and acceleration of human motions by a set of dynamic equations. The soft tissue model represents the physically-based deformations of soft tissues via proposing the exponential strain energy functions for real-time computation of deformability which exhibits mechanical characteristics like nonlinear stress-strain behavior, anisotropy, and linear viscoelasticity.

3.3   Graphical Human Modeling

Graphical human modeling is central to the visual representation of biomechanical human body structure, and it typically consists of two basic components: realistic modeling of articulated skeleton structure and graphical appearance of virtual body. The skeletal model is composed of a suitable kinematic tree based revolute joints with various degree of freedom, and along with bones as rigid links at the articulation sites, this linear and angular displacements of the whole body is divided into 12 joints named neck, shoulder, elbow, wrist, hip, knee, and ankle, as well as 14 segments named head, body, upper arm, forearm, hand, thigh, shank, and foot. The visual model provides the visual feedback component which includes multi-planar interactive image display of human body to get approximate shape, size and relative proportions of real human.

The graphical human model encompasses the kinematic properties and visual features of human behavior as the foundation for shape initialization, pose estimation and motion detection, this vision-based interpretation is performed consistent with human factors principles and practices. Shape initialization is obtained by utilizing a scatter data interpolation model to deform the average shape, pose estimation is a process of pose configuration evaluation from single monocular images, in addition, motion detection refers to monitoring the change in position of an object with respect to its surroundings.

4   Framework

A DHM based theoretical model is formulated to simulate the biomechanical attributes of manual handling operators and investigate working postures and activities while the workers performing the tasks in order to predict potential WMSDs and adjust the workplace and work practices. The center of this Physiological Evaluation Framework is a simulation structure along with the computational estimation, as shown in Figure 1.

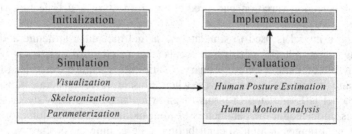

Fig. 1. Physiological Evaluation Framework

4.1   Initialization

The initialization step presented in this paper can be formulated as the process of providing a conventional model approximating the size, shape, appearance, kinematic structure to obtain an initial hypothesis about the pose and position of the worker, and to define the boundary conditions under which the proactive gestures and motions can take place for interpreting and tracking body behavior. This initial hypothesis deals with a better extraction and representation of body motion by initializing various values of the geometric and dynamic properties, as well as biologic characteristics which will be synthesized in an effort to anticipate and evaluate physical body intentions before they occur. It is a fundamental and key channel to bring in prior knowledge and data source about familiar body configuration and reconstruction which can help to constrain and prevent the production of unrealistic body acquisition and pose estimation due to the high dimensional pose state space.

4.2   Simulation

The simulation step enables a rapid and virtual representation of human bodies to facilitate assessing multiple aspects of physical work-related features which are commonly cited as risk factors for WMSDs. It includes three essential phases named visualization, skeletonization, and parameterization, as depicted in Figure 2.

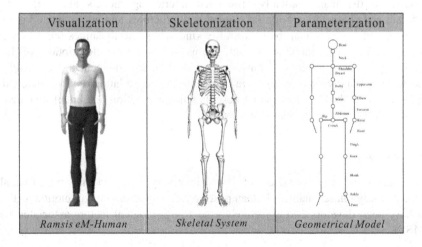

Fig. 2. Simulated Human Model

Visualization. Human body visualization implies the immersive image acquisition progress through computer graphics and image processing to achieve digitally constructed transformation, selection, and representation of a real object. It focuses on converting nonobjective human data into concrete imagery, so as to present visual information, communicate graphical messages, and explore the implicit or explicit understanding of these data. In particular, the realistic visualization of human body can be broken down into two successive procedures, the first one disposes rigid skeleton structure of the body, and the second one deals with rendering of muscles, skin, and such non-rigid tissue system. Generally, the visualization phase aims at recognition and tracking of human gestures and actions in a suite of image sequences.

Skeletonization. Human body skeletonization is a common preprocessing operation in pattern to vector conversion, and it is aimed to extract the central path based shape features which give an illustrative definition of the skeleton, and represent the general form of a body with all soft tissue eliminated. The skeleton extraction provides a simple and real-time way of implementing layer by layer erosion and distance transformation for the purposes of detecting boundaries extracted as the representative descriptor of human posture and creating an accurate description of bodily motion. It is articulated in three stages named silhouette detection, mass center to extremities calculation, and structural pattern recognition for the full body skeleton articulation and trajectory measurement in relation to their original properties of the shape such as length, width, position, orientation, etc.

Parameterization. Human body parameterization represents the numerical implementation of biomechanical human posture features creation and modeling, it comprises geometric information extraction together with topological motion translation for parameterized transformation of the static and dynamic body system. In other words, mathematically articulated interacting models are proposed to formulate and characterize both the geometrical structures and approximated motion movements of a real human body from the kinematics and dynamics point of view. The exploration of kinematic model begins with concise description of links parameters as well as joints constraints, and it is complemented by means of concatenating state vectors in a general mathematical formulation of static states. It is emphasized that the dynamic model describes linear position and angular velocities evolution of the motion vector system over time.

4.3   Evaluation

The evaluation step consists of two relatively independent but mutually complementary phases, namely human posture estimation and human motion analysis that have been developed to objectively assess physiological factors associated with WMSDs.

Human Posture Estimation. Human posture estimation intends to provide a representative method for assessing the degree of suitability between the work environment parameters and the anthropometric dimensions of the worker, as well as evaluating postural load which depends on the specific operational context during working time, in order to prevent discomfort, fatigue, and injury caused by awkward working postures of trunk, arms, and legs which place their joints away from the natural position for a long time. The Ovako Working Posture Analysis System (OWAS) is an analytical and quantitative method which enables calculating worker's posture load and time expenditure for each activity at workstation by means of analyzing the postural data, and it is heuristically implemented to obtain the improvement of problematic working postures negative for workers. Additionally, OWAS categorizes the whole body posture into four major body segments named trunk, arms, legs, and head/neck based on a systematic classification combined with observations of work tasks, it is described and measured by a four classes posture ranking system in which normal posture means no intervention required, slightly harmful posture should be corrected in near future, distinctly harmful posture needs corrective action as soon as possible, and extremely harmful posture must be improved immediately.

Human Motion Analysis. Human motion states the continuous movement or change in body position with respect to time, motion analysis is critical in the field of WMSDs prevention, and it is divided into three processes: motion recognition, motion segmentation, and motion evaluation. Human motion recognition describes the basic elements of human activities in terms of position, direction, angle, trajectory, velocity, acceleration, time, duration, and so forth. Human motion segmentation decomposes human activities into a sequence of actions, and it is a preprocessing stage for capturing the univariate or multivariate motion data before and after an operation, then analyzing the computational human motion model with high spatial and temporal accuracy. Human motion evaluation presents the detailed foundation, principle, and procedure for coherent clusters of working actions assessments. Specifically, it acquires motion captured parameters as indices to indicate the worker's physiological capacity level, then elucidates the desirable motion features and estimates these parameters in a hierarchical order based on experimental investigations, the difficulty of this process derives directly from complexity of and diversity of human movement.

4.4   Implementation

The implementation step provides guidance regarding how to realize all the modification requirements obtained during the previous steps, and execute specific improvement progresses based on essential features of operational work system. It is viewed as a vital system development process that continually seeks to make adjustments to workplaces, embed better workflows, as well as monitor achievements against objectives, for the purpose of creating smarter work system to accommodate worker's needs. The key focus is to properly carry out the modification and execution stages, systematic modification stage analyzes and determines if the proposed adjustments are appropriate for reducing the level of WMSDs risk, deliberate execution stage is performed to meet work system design demands until the result is acceptable. This dynamically optimized step is required to be used as a fundamental element in turning work system mission, vision, and values into reality.

5   Conclusion

In conclusion, this paper introduces a theoretical approach to illustrate how a modified DHM tool is utilized to assess worker's physiological factors within the context of interactive visualization environments. Graphical, biomechanical, and geometrical models are used in the simulation of work postures and activities, thus to furnish a basis for evaluating the WMSDs which have negative consequences both for the worker and work system performance, and then adjust the relevant work system elements to prevent risks. Future research will concentrate on providing experimental intervention and mathematical evaluation for multifactorial muscular system and skeletal system disorders measurement of human postures and motions, for the sake of confirming the feasibility of this theoretical framework as integrating DHM into physiological factors evaluation in work system design. In addition, the disparity between simulation results and real practice performances will be demonstrated to represent the reliability and accuracy of simulated human model.

References

1. Punnett, L., Wegman, D.H.: Work-related Musculoskeletal Disorders: the Epidemiologic Evidence and the Debate. Journal of Electromyography and Kinesiology 14, 13–23 (2004)
2. Duffy, V.G.: Handbook of Digital Human Modeling: Research for Applied Ergonomics and Human Factors Engineering. CRC Press, Boca Raton (2008)
3. Hu, B., Zhang, W., Salvendy, G.: Impact of Multimodal Feedback on Simulated Ergonomic Measurements in a Virtual Environment: A Case Study with Manufacturing Workers. Human Factors and Ergonomics in Manufacturing & Service Industries 22, 145–155 (2012)
4. Chang, S.W., Wang, M.J.J.: Digital Human Modeling and Workplace Evaluation: Using an Automobile Assembly Task as an Example. Human Factors and Ergonomics in Manufacturing & Service Industries 17, 445–455 (2007)
5. Tian, R., Duffy, V.G.: Computerized Task Risk Assessment using Digital Human Modeling based Job Risk Classification Model. Computers & Industrial Engineering 61, 1044–1052 (2011)
6. Jung, M., Cho, H., Roh, T., Lee, K.: Integrated Framework for Vehicle Interior Design Using Digital Human Model. Journal of Computer Science and Technology 24, 1149–1161 (2009)
7. Hanson, L., Högberg, D., Lundström, D., Wårell, M.: Application of Human Modelling in Health Care Industry. In: Proceedings of the 2nd International Conference on Digital Human Modeling, San Diego, USA, pp. 521–530 (2009)
8. Wang, C.C.L.: Parameterization and Parametric Design of Mannequins. Computer-Aided Design 37, 83–98 (2005)
9. Wang, H., Sun, S., Shu, T., Shi, F., Wu, J.: Survey: Parameterized 3d Human Body Modeling and Geometric Deformation Technology. In: Proceedings of IEEE 10th International Conference on Computer Aided Industrial Design & Conceptual Design, Wenzhou, China, pp. 1486–1493 (2009)
10. Volkau, I., Ng, T.T., Marchenko, Y., Nowinski, W.L.: On Geometric Modeling of the Human Intracranial Venous System. IEEE Transactions on Medical Imaging 27, 745–751 (2008)

Cognitive Behavior Modeling of Manual Rendezvous and Docking Based on the ACT-R Cognitive Architecture[*]

Chunhui Wang[2], Yu Tian[2], Yanfei Liu[1], Shanguang Chen[2], Zhiqiang Tian[2], and Junsong Li[1]

[1] Zhejiang Sci-Tech University, Hangzhou, 310018, China
[2] National Key Laboratory of Human Factors Engineering, Astronaut Research and Training Center of China, Beijing, China 100094
chunhui_89@yahoo.com.cn, cctian@126.com, yliu@zju.edu.cn, tianzhiqiang2000@163.com, ljscg@sina.com

Abstract. Astronauts are exposed to numerous stressors during spaceflights, to reduce the faulty operations and improve human performance in manually controlled rendezvous and docking (manual RVD) of space vehicles, a method, which applies sophisticated cognitive architecture Adaptive control of thought–rational (ACT-R) to model astronaut's cognitive behaviors and investigate the cognitive components influencing human performance, is proposed in this paper . To model the cognitive behaviors in completing manual RVD task, the declarative knowledge of the cognitive processes was obtained from experiments, the procedural knowledge was acquired by analyzing the relationship between cognitive processes and behaviors, and the model parameters were set up according to the boundary conditions and task characteristics. Manual RVD cognitive behavior model is then built up based on the declarative knowledge, the procedural knowledge and the model parameters. Comparisons of model running results and manual control results were performed to test the model's validation. ACT-R control panel tool was also used to analyze the process of model's running and manual control behaviors. Results of the comparisons indicate that the ACT-R model proposed in this paper is in accordance with human cognitive behaviors.

Keywords: ACT-R, manually controlled Rendezvous and docking task, cognitive behavior modeling, model's validation.

1 Introduction

Cognitive models are appearing in all fields of cognition at a rapidly increasing rate, ranging from perception to memory to problem solving and decision-making. A large

---

[*] This work is supported by 973 Program of China under Grant No. 2011CB711000, Zhejiang Provincial Natural Science Foundation under Grant No. LY12C09005, Y1110477, and National Natural Science Foundation of China under Grant No.61100183.
[**] Corresponding author.

percent of the articles appearing in major theoretical journals of Cognitive Science involve cognitive modeling. Furthermore, applications of cognitive modeling are beginning to spill over into other fields including human factors, clinical psychology, cognitive neuroscience, agent based modeling in economics, and many more [1]. As an effective research method for human's cognition, cognitive modeling is well accepted and widely studied recently, such as Anderson and Fincham(2012) track problem-solving using brain imaging[2], Janssen and Gray(2012) Reinforce Learning based Models of Cognition[3], Kennedy and Ritter(2012) address the topics related to cognitive modeling of beyond-rational cognition[4], Gunzelmann (2011) elaborate a variety of disciplines and methodologies on Modeling Spatial Cognition[5], and Borst and Taatgen (2011) perform model-based fMRI analyses by using high-level symbolic cognitive models to enable fine-grained exploratory fMRI research[6] etc. Thus cognitive modeling is becoming an essential tool for Cognitive Science in particular and the Social Sciences in general.

As one of the most typical and widely used cognitive architecture and a unified theory of cognition [7], ACT-R aims at using software to simulate a full range of cognitive tasks, has been used to construct models to simulate human's task performing and cognitive process, such as Beckmann and Yilmaz(2012) introduce a realization of a more complicated interactive warning framework to avoid operator mistakes during maintenance[8], Kennedy and Patterson (2102) present an ACT-R model to predict the development of intuitive decision-making in humans[9] etc. In addition, ACT-R has been used to access and improve human's performance in complex and adaptive system such as aircraft operations, nuclear power operations and supervisory control. Gunzelmann and Moore (2012) tries to account for the function of a particular brain area and raises questions for understanding cognitive performance [10], Wayne and David discuss how to use cognitive modeling to access human(pilot, computer user, and car driver) performance[11-12], and Gunzelmann et .al use cognitive modeling to study impaired performance due to sleep deprivation [13-14].

Manual RVD is a complex and difficult task for astronauts. During manual RVD, due to human's capability in observation, analysis, judgment, decision-making and handling, the astronauts can make judgment and decision timely for the system's fault and can improve probability of success for manual RVD task. However, Astronauts are exposed to numerous stressors during spaceflights, such as microgravity, confinement, and radiation, all of which may impair human cognitive capabilities. In some critical operations for spaceflight, such as operating the mechanical arms, extravehicular activities, and driving the spacecraft, etc., fault operation may cause serious disasters. Moreover, due to limitations for test conditions, uncertainty and poor features of experimental results in the study of human cognitive behavior for spaceflight, experimental researches are difficult to implement in reality. As a cognitive modeling tools, The ACT-R provide studies helps for astronauts' performance on orbit.

2   Data Acquisition and Knowledge Extraction

2.1   Data Acquisition Experiment

To obtain the knowledge and model parameter for manual RVD task's cognitive behavior model, manual RVD experiment is designed and implemented to collect the raw data. For convenience, the experiment only consider the situation that manual RVD operation start from distance 20 meters of two space vehicles to the manual RVD task being finished, longitudinal speed maintains 2m/s and remains unchangeable, the initial displacement in the horizontal and vertical direction of two vehicles are both 2 meters, there is no initial velocity in the direction of horizon and vertical, and there is no posture (rotation, pitch and yaw) operation during the whole manual RVD task. That is to say that there is only three dimensions' moving operation being considered in the designed experiment.

During experiment of operator's manual RVD task, the operator's behavior and vehicle's status are recorded. Table 1 shows the snippet of the recorded information as examples.

Table 1. Cognitive behavior for manual RVD task

| Distance / Time | Vision | Information processing | | | | Manual control | |
	Vehicle's status	Attention	Memory	Judgment	Decision making	Move op.	Time elapse
0'0"(20m)	Q1, N	RU	Lo, Po	RU	O:S	NULL	
0'0"-0'1"	Q1,R	RU	Lo,Po	RU	O:L	L,1	0.5'
...							

In Table 1, Q1 - Quadrant I, N - No motion trend, RU-Right upper corner location, O-Operation, R-Right (in Vehicle status column represent right moving, and in Decision making column and Move op. column represent for right operation), Lo-Location, Po - Posture, S -Start operation, L - Left, and 1 - 1 time.

2.2   Knowledge Extraction and Model's Parameters

The most important thing in ACT-R is extraction for declarative knowledge, procedural knowledge and model's parameter. The declarative knowledge is some conceptions definition for the task or some facts, such as the operations, the vehicle's status and the relationship between drone's size and vehicle's distance etc. The procedural knowledge is rules for decision-making of the model, and procedural knowledge is acquired by analyzing the relationship between cognitive processes and behaviors. Typical procedural knowledge such as determining operation behavior according the vehicle's location or determining the vehicle's distance according to the drone's size can be extracted from the experimental data recorded in Table 1. The model parameters are set up according to the boundary conditions, some custom constants predefinition and the task's characteristics, such as the vehicle's maximum speed, maximum contact speed and the maximum allowable deviations etc.

2.3   Manual RVD Cognitive Behavior Modeling

The cognitive model on ACT-R architecture platform is programed in lisp programming language and composed of two main parts, the first part is the manual controlling part for user's manual controlling GUI, and another part is the model part. The manual controlling part implement the functions for dealing of user's operation input, vehicle's movement and related information display in GUI.   The model part includes the chunk type's definition, declarative knowledge, first goal of the model and all the procedural knowledge.

3   Model's Running and Validation

The model can be run either in manual controlling or automatic mode. As in the manual controlling mode, the operator implement manual RVD task by controlling the vehicle's movement according the vehicle's moving status, and vehicle's running status and operations are recorded by model. When model running in automatic mode, the model start running according to model's first goal, and then it fires productions circularly along with the model's new goal. The model will end as there is no any production fit the goal of the goal buffer and being trigged.

The comparison method for model running results and manual control process is used to test the model's validation, and also ACT-R control panel tool is used to analysis the process of model's running and manual control behavior. Figure 1 show the time period comparison for manual operation result and model's running result.

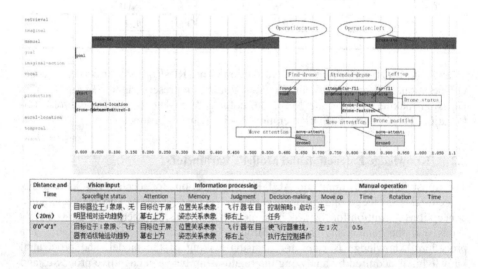

Distance and Time	Vision input		Information processing				Manual operation			
	Spaceflight status	Attention	Memory	Judgment	Decision-making	Move op	Time	Rotation	Time
0'0" (20m)	目标器位于I象限、无明显相对运动趋势	目标位于屏幕右上方	位置关系表象姿态关系表象	飞行器在目标右上	控制策略：启动任务	无			
0'0"-0'1"	目标位于I象限、飞行器有沿纵轴运动趋势	目标位于屏幕右上方	位置关系表象姿态关系表象	飞行器在目标右上	使飞行器靠近，执行左控制操作	左1次	0.5s		

Fig. 1. Behavior Comparison results for manual operation and model's running

The upper half section of the figure 1 is the cognitive procedure when model running and displayed in ACT-R control panel tool. On the left of this section we see the names of all the buffers and along the bottom we see the time. For each buffer there are boxes displayed which correspond to the actions which occurred related to that buffer. The boxes in the production row show the names of the productions which fired, but for the other buffers they display the chunk-type of the request which was made at the top of the box and the name of the resulting chunk (if there was one) along the bottom. The lower half part is the operator's behavior procedure as the manual RVD experiment being conducted. From the figure we can find the model's results are is quite up to the manual control operations.

The comparison of vehicle location for manual control and model's automatic running in the procedure of manual RVD tasks are implemented. Fig. 2 shows the comparison results for the horizontal and vertical direction.

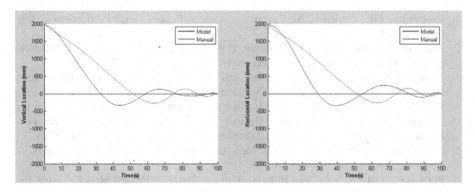

Fig. 2. The location's comparison results for manual operation and model's running

The figures show that the model's running procedure is in accordance with the moving trend of manual control procedure in manual RVD task.

4   Discussion

To get the model to fit the manual cognitive behavior requires not only writing a plausible set of productions which can accomplish the task, but also setting the ACT-R parameters that control the behavior as described in the equations governing the operation of declarative memory. This paper only describes the model running result with the default values for the parameters and hence the model's result shows some of the general trends in figure 2. There are lots of parameters in ACT-R that reflects human's characteristic such as base-level-activation, retrieve threshold and latency factor, etc. By adjusting the model's parameter, the manual RVD task's performance is not investigated here.

5   Conclusion

ACT-R is a developing theory and architecture, on the one hand it is complex both in theory and architecture, on the other hand it has been developed very quickly recently. Cognitive model of a simple task is developed in this paper and lots of simplifications have been made. There is much work to do in developing models for sophisticated manual RVD tasks and assessing difference behavioral performance with parameter's tuning in the model.

The contribution of this paper is that a method for analyzing the human cognitive behavior is proposed. Comparisons of both the cognition procedures and vehicle's locations were performed to validate the cognitive model. The analyzing result shows that the model based on the ACT-R cognitive architecture is effective in modeling astronaut's cognitive behavior in the manual RVD task.

References

1. Busemeyer, J.R., Diederich, A.: Cognitive modeling, Pages 1. Sage Publications (2009) (incorporated)
2. Anderson, J.R., Fincham, J.M., Schneider, D.W., Yang, J.: Using brain imaging to track problem-solving in a complex state space. NeuroImage 60, 633–643 (2012)
3. Janssen, C.P., Gray, W.D.: When, What, and How Much to Reward in Reinforcement Learning based Models of Cognition. Cognitive Science 36(2), 333–358 (2012)
4. Kennedy, W.G., Ritter, F.E., Juvina, I., Gratch, J., Young, R.M.: ICCM Symposium on Cognitive Modeling of Processes "Beyond Rational". In: Proceedings of the 11th International Conference on Cognitive Modeling, Berlin, Germany, April 12-15 (2012)
5. Gunzelmann, G.: Introduction to the Topic on Modeling Spatial Cognition. Topics in Cognitive Science 3(4), 628–631 (2011)
6. Borst, J.P., Taatgen, N.A., Van Rijn, H.: Using a Symbolic Process Model as input for Model-Based fMRI Analysis: Locating the Neural Correlates of Problem State Replacements. NeuroImage 58(1), 137–147 (2011)
7. Beckmann, M., Yilmaz, U., Pöhler, G., Wegerich, A.: A framework for task accomplishment using an ACT-R simulation. In: Proceedings of the 11th International Conference on Cognitive Modeling. Universitaetsverlag der TU Berlin, Berlin (2012)
8. Kennedy, W.G., Patterson, R.E.: Modeling Intuitive Decision Making in ACT-R. In: Proceedings of the 11th International Conference on Cognitive Modeling, Berlin, Germany, April 12-15 (2012)
9. Gunzelmann, G., Moore, L.R.: Evaluating the relationship between neuropsychological function and cognitive performance. In: Proceedings of the Thirty-Fourth Annual Meeting of the Cognitive Science Society, pp. 414–419 (2012)
10. Wayne, G., David, K., Guk-Ho, G., Sang-Hwan, K., Ben-Asher, N., Joachim, M., Shi, C., Yili, L., Cleotilde, G., Glenn, G., Kevin, G.: Symposium on Human Performance Modeling. In: Proceedings of the 11th International Conference on Cognitive Modeling, Berlin, Germany, pp. 324–327 (April 2012)
11. Schoelles, M., Gray, W.D.: SimPilot: An exploration of modeling a highly interactive task with delayed feedback in a multitasking environment. In: Proceedings of the 11th International Conference on Cognitive Modeling, Berlin, Germany, vol. 66 (2012)
12. Gunzelmann, G., Gluck, K.A., Moore, L.R., Dinges, D.F.: Impaired performance due to sleep deprivation: A role for diminished knowledge access. Cognitive Systems Research 13(1), 1–11 (2012)
13. Gunzelmann, G., Moore, L.R., Salvucci, D.D., Gluck, K.A.: Sleep loss and driver performance: Quantitative predictions with zero free parameters. Cognitive Systems Research 12(2), 154–163 (2011)
14. Anderson, J.R., Bothell, D., Byrne, M.D., Douglass, S., Lebiere, C., Qin, Y.: An integrated theory of the mind. Psychological Review 111(4), 1036–1060 (2004)

Serious Gaming Used as Management Intervention to Prevent Work-Related Stress and Raise Work–Engagement among Workers

Noortje Wiezer[1], Maartje Bakhuys Roozeboom[1], and Esther Oprins[2]

[1] TNO, Work & Health, Hoofddorp, The Netherlands
[2] TNO, Training and Performance Innovation, Soesterberg, The Netherlands
{noortje.wiezer,maartje.bakhuysroozeboom}@tno.nl,
esther.oprins@tno.nl

Abstract. Work-related stress is a large occupational risks in the Netherlands but interventions to reduce this risk are not implemented in organizations. The characteristics of a serious game make it a useful training tool for managers to raise awareness on their role in stimulating work engagement and managing work-related stress. In this research project a serious game for managers is developed and implemented and will be evaluated as an intervention to reduce work-related stress and raise work-engagement among employees. The evaluation will be done in a longitudinal case-control study, using a generic, standardized evaluation framework for validation of serious games. Focus of the evaluation will be on the direct effects of playing the game and on long-term effects, cf. transfer of training. In this paper the development of the game and the design for the evaluation study will be described.

Keywords: work-related stress intervention, management intervention, work-engagement, serious gaming.

1   Introduction

Work related stress is one of the largest occupational risks in the Netherlands. Over 13% of the employees in the Netherlands report mental fatigue due to work, and this percentage is increasing (Koppes et.al 2010). Developments like the increase of restructuring, the growing amount of information an employee has to process, the individualization of society, increase the risk of work related stress even more. Work related stress is an important cause for mental health problems, absenteeism and early retirement. Research of the OECD showes that employees with 'mental health complains', are less productive, score higher on presenteeïsm, are more careless than employees without complains and therefor create risks for colleagues (OECD 2012). For all these reasons, costs of work related stress are high. In the Netherlands the costs of sick leave due to mental illness, partly caused by work related stress is estimated at 2,7 billion Euro (de Graaf et al, 2010). Nevertheless, interventions to

V.G. Duffy (Ed.): DHM/HCII 2013, Part II, LNCS 8026, pp. 149–158, 2013.
© Springer-Verlag Berlin Heidelberg 2013

reduce or prevent work related stress are not implemented in organizations. Results of an annual survey among employees in the Netherlands (N= 22.742) show that 40% of the respondents indicate that measures to reduce work related stress are necessary but not sufficiently or not at all taken in their company (Koppes et. al 2010). Annual research among employers shows similar results. Although 49% of the employers indicate that work pressure (imbalance between job demands and job resources) is one of the major occupational health risks in their company, more than a quarter (26%) does not take any measures to improve occupational health and safety, let alone measures to reduce work related stress (Oeij et. al 2008). The Netherlands are not an exception in Europe. Results of an EU-OSHA study (2012) on the ESENER-data show that although on average almost 40% of the companies indicate that stress is a major concern, only 24% has procedures in place to deal with work-related stress. In this same study factors are examined that make dealing with psychosocial risks difficult. Sensitivity of the issue and a lack of awareness are the most important reasons for management not to deal with psychosocial risks. Lack of training and experience and the culture within the establishment are other important reasons (EU-OSHA, 2012). Houtman et.al (2012) looked at the reasons for Dutch companies not to take measures, even if they are scientifically proven to be effective. The results of their research is similar to the results of the ESENER study. Company (or sector) culture hinders interventions on this sensitive topic. Work related stress is not a topic that is easily discussed in most companies. The unawareness of the risks and lack of insight in the consequences of the risks are barriers to act on reducing these risks. Lack of awareness of the problem and the consequences hinders commitment of management to deal with psychosocial risks. Not only does this affect the willingness of management to take measures, it also affects the success of interventions. For interventions on psychosocial risks to be successful management commitment is very important. Individual managers indicate that they 'don't know how to recognize stress signals, and also have little confidence in the impact of their own actions on the work related stress of their employees' (Wiezer et. Al. 2012). Houtman et. al. (2012) also looked at reasons for companies to do take measure. Past positive experiences with interventions, own experiences or experiences from colleagues, increase the willingness for managers to work on decreasing risks.

The intervention we aim at therefore has three goals. First, it should create a sense of urgency among managers to deal with psychosocial risks. Second, the intervention should increase the self-efficacy of managers to deal with these issues. Third, the intervention should contribute to an actual change in the behavior of managers to deal with these issues.

Serious Gaming: In this project we are looking for an intervention that eventually will change managers' behavior concerning psychosocial risks. In often used behavior changes models several key elements are defined that increase the intention of a person to change its behavior (see for example the I-change model, Brug et al 2007). Outcome expectations' (what will be the benefits or the effects of the preferred behavior), 'risk perception' (what will happen if I don't change my behavior), feedback (am I doing alright? What can I do to improve), task-efficacy' (the confidence in your ability to show the preferred behavior), and performance skills (needed to show the preferred behavior) are among the important ones. A serious game could be an effective and appropriate mean to reach behavioral change.

Serious games are often defined as games that serve other goals than entertainment (Harteveld 2011, 2012). A well-developed serious game has a number of features. For a serious game to be effective fidelity is important. The virtual world should be as authentic, realistic and convincing as possible, although it is sometimes necessary to simplify reality in order for the player to be able to understand the game rules. This not only applies to the visible representation of the game world, but also to the scenario's and the behavior of the characters in the game. According to Graesser, Chipman, Leeming and Bid Bach, (in Ritter Field, Cody & Vorderer, 2009) a well-developed serious game matches the interests and perceptions of the player, and provides the player with the opportunity to actively play the game and try and experiment with different approaches which lead to alternative game situations. The difficulty of the game should be well balanced. The game is challenging enough to keep players motivated to play and improve the score. The players are able to experience success in their game. Success experiences creates self-efficacy (Lepper and Woolverton, 2002). In a well-developed game there will be feedback on actions. This affects the commitment, effort and self-efficacy of the player (e.g. Jackson & Greasser, 2007). A storyline in the game makes the gaming experience more memorable. Finally, a good serious game is fun to play (Vorderer, Klimmt & Ritterfeld, 2004). When a game is fun, a player is motivated to continue and replay the game. A serious game containing these features will offer players the opportunity to experiment in a safe environment and to learn by experiencing. Serious games have the advantage that effects of interventions can be scaled, not only short term but also medium and long term effects can be shown and experienced during the game. This will provide outcome expectations but will also increase the risk perception. Players can try different styles, behavior or interventions without fearing negative consequences. In this sense, a serious game on psychosocial risks looks like a promising tool. The topic is complex and outcome expectations and risk perception are not easily met. A game will help players to increase the awareness on psychosocial risks, to understand their role in managing these risks and to increase their self-efficacy in doing so. Psychosocial risks is also a very sensitive topic, sharing experiences on this topic is not easily done by managers. A game will provide a fun and safe way of dealing with this topic.

There has been research done on the effectiveness of serious games (see the recent reviews by Sitzmann (2011) and Connoly, Boyle, MacArthur, Hainey & Boyle (2012). Computer games and serious games are linked to perceptual, cognitive, affective, motivational and behavioral outcomes. Most evidence is found on the effects of serious games on learning. By playing a (well-developed) game, people experience flow, which increases the motivation to keep on playing and thus practicing and learning. Spending time on learning and practicing also increases the self-efficacy, which in turn help reaching the learning objectives of the game (Sitzmann, 2011). In this paper we describe the development of a serious game for psychosocial risk management and the research design for validating this game.

2   Work Related Stress and Engagement

Fidelity is important for a game to be effective. It is therefore important to base the development of the game on an evidenced based theoretical model. The Engagement game is a serious game, that can be used as a training tool for managers to raise awareness on their role in stimulating work engagement and managing work-related stress. Work-related stress and work engagement are the two most important (learning) objectives in this game. For the Engagement game, described in this paper we combined the theoretical models of work related stress and work engagement.

A lot of research has been done into the topic of work-related stress. A number of models are developed and several definitions exist for the concept. For the Engagement game we used a definition that is widely used in research, but can also easily be translated into game rules. Work-related stress is defined as: *a state, which is accompanied by physical, psychological or social complaints (sometimes expressed in behavior) that is caused by an imbalance between requirements and expectations at work and the ability of a person to meet these requirements and expectations.* An individual is well adapted to cope with short term exposure to stress, but has great difficulty coping with prolonged exposure to intensive stress.

Work engagement fits into the tradition of positive psychology. In this tradition the focus is not on negative outcomes or states but on the positive ones (Seligman & Csikszentmihalyi, 2000). What increases mental health and well-being (even for people that are already relatively healthy and happy), is the central question. For work-engagement we used the definition developed by Schaufeli and Bakker (2001): *Work engagement is a positive work-related state of fulfillment that is characterized by vigor, dedication and absorption.*

Almost all recent models on work related stress define stressors: factors that can evoke stress reactions (for example high job demands), and moderators: factors that can reduce, or increase if they are absent, the effect of stressors (for example organizational of personal resources like autonomy, social support, learning and development opportunities). In all models the balance between stressors and resources is important. If there is a good balance between stressors and resources, work related stress will not occur. If there are not enough resources to meet the stressors, than work related stress will occur. A proper balance between job demands and resources, which are motivational in nature, may also lead to positive outcomes such as work engagement. The more recent Job Demands Control model (Bakker, Schaufeli & Demerouti, 1999 and Bakker & Demerouti, 2007) complement the work related stress models and additionally focus on the positive aspects of well-being (engagement). The model used in the Engagementgame is based on the Job Demands Control Model.

Figure 1 shows the model used in the game. An imbalance between job demands and organizational and personal resources increases work related stress, which in turn has a negative effect on for example health and productivity of employees. Organizational and personal resources increase work engagement. This is even more the case if organizational and personal resources are combined with challenging job demands. Work engagement in turn has a positive effect on organizational outcomes such as health and productivity.

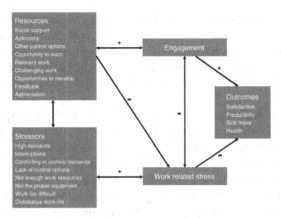

Fig. 1. The theoretical model used in the Engagement game

3   The Development of the Engagement Game

The development of the Engagement game was a collaboration of four parties: A large health and safety consultancy firm, a large bank, a game developer and a research institute. All parties had a different role. The scientific background for the game was provided by the research institute. Together with the game developer they translated the theoretical models into game rules and scenarios. The game developer build the game. The participants from the consultancy firm and the bank provided the 'reality check', from their experience with day to day practices in companies and helped develop the scenarios. The bank incorporated the Engagement game in the leadership training program for their own managers and the consultancy firm developed a training for leadership and engagement of which the Engagement game is an important element.

The project to develop the Engagement game was divided into three work packages. In the first package the theoretical model was developed, which is described in the previous paragraph. A literature review into empirical evidence for the described relationships was conducted. At the time of this review not many longitudinal studies were published on the (relatively new) topic of work engagement. Where empirical evidence was not found, relative strength of relations were estimated by experts in the field of work-related stress and work engagement, that were consulted. In the second work package the theoretical model is formalized and translated into game rules and scenarios. For this step we first had to determine what the 'learning goals' were we wanted to reach with our game. What is the message we want to bring across? For this message to be clear, and for the player to be able to understand the message it was necessary to simplify the model into a working model that contains only the most essential and important relationships. It took several meetings with experts in the field to develop this working model. In the third package the game was build. For building the game an 'agile approach' was used, the theoretical model was translated into game rules and game specifications and functionalities in little steps. After each step there was a feedback round and the last steps contained feedback from end users as well. We were constantly testing whether the scenarios and the game rules were authentic, realistic and convincing, whether different learning styles were used (visual, active, reflective, experimental), whether different playing styles could be used (more pragmatic, more theoretical), and whether the game was challenging enough so players would stay in a flow while playing it.

For the Engagement game we used the story of the manager of a Mexican restaurant. We chose for this metaphor because we would never succeed in building an exact copy of the work situation and work processes of the player (for instance a manager in a bank). If we suggested an exact copy of the work of the player, every deviation of that would disturb the flow of the player. We chose for a restaurant because this is a situation most players can relate to. As player you are the manager of this restaurant and you are assigned to increase the financial results. You have to manage six employees. These employees have tasks with job demands and they have resources, competences and ambitions. The balance between their job demands and their resources influences their work engagement and stress level. The work engagement and stress level of the employees in the restaurant influences the quality of their work and that influences the number of customers and thus the returns of the restaurant. Interventions of the manager (the player) changes the job demands or the resources and have an impact on the engagement and stress of the employees. To gather information you can talk to your employees (pull) and sometimes they come to you for a talk (push). Besides that they 'send tweets' to comment on your interventions (feedback). Customers also tweet, on their experiences in your restaurant. While you try to manage your restaurant all kind of events take place on which you have to react. And of course, measures taken to react on events also influence the work engagement and work related stress of your employees. We developed two scenario's, the second being more challenging than the first. Both scenarios can be played in twenty minutes and at the end feedback is provided on the reasons you did or did not reach the targets. The game is usually played in couples to stimulate discussion on the decisions, and as part of a training. After playing the game the results of all couples are discussed in the group. If the game is played 'stand-alone' (not as part of a training) a reflection form is added to stimulate the player to translate the game-experience into their own day to day practice.

4   Evaluation of the Engagement Game

Besides the development of the game, the evaluation of the effectiveness of the game is part of the project as well (fourth work package). The central research question of this evaluation study is 'is this serious game an effective intervention to decrease work related stress and increase work engagement in companies?' The Engagement game is effective if managers are better able to reduce work related stress and increase work engagement of their own employees after playing the Engagement game as part of a training. The effect of the Engagement game will therefore be examined on two levels: the level of the manager (the player) and the level of the employees of the manager. We are not only interested in the effects of the game itself, but also in the process: which elements influence the effectiveness of the Engagement game.

For the evaluation the following research questions will be answered:

1. Did the manager learn from playing the game?

- Is he better able to recognize determinants of work related stress and work engagement?
- Has his sense of urgency related to work related stress and work engagement increased?
- Did the intervention (playing the game as part of a training) change the behavior of the manager? (long term transfer of training)

2. Did this intervention reduces work related stress and increased work involvement among employees?

- Did the participation of the manager in the training program with the Engagement game increase the amount of resources for employees and/or decrease the amount of stressors?
- Did the participation of the manager in the training program with Engagement game reduce work related stress and increase work engagement among the employees of the manager?
- Did the participation of the manager in the training program with Engagement game lead to better organizational outcomes (reduced sick leave, better productivity)?

3. What are the success and fail factors for the effectiveness of Engagement game and why are these factors important?

- Factors that relate to the game design and learning experience (gaming mechanisms)
- Factors that relate to the implementation of the game and the training (process)

The evaluation will be done in a longitudinal case-control study, using a generic, standardized evaluation framework for validation of serious games developed by TNO and applied for other games (Oprins 2011). This evaluation framework consists of indicators, methods and instruments (questionnaires, checklists, data logging methods) with which the effectiveness of a serious game can be evaluated. The framework consists of more generic process measure aimed at learning and more domain specific outcome measures (specific content or specific competencies, in case of this study: understanding of stress and engagement theory). These measures can show a short term effect (right after playing the game) or a long term effect (transfer of training). The clustering of the case-control study is on the level of the workgroups. Two groups will be distinguished: an intervention group and a control group. The managers of the intervention group will receive a training with the Engagement game, the managers of the control group will receive a regular training without a serious game. To be able to show an effect on our primary outcome measure (work engagement of the employees), the number of managers we need in our research is 94. In addition, we need ten employees of each participating manager to be part of this research as well. For the effect and process evaluation a questionnaire will be filled out by managers and employees of both groups at three moments in time: before the intervention, right after the intervention and four months after the intervention. Semi structured interviews will be held with the managers of the intervention group. Multilevel analyses will be conducted on the data to determine if changes in the outcome measure differ for the intervention group and the control group.

In preparation of the evaluation study we organized a number of workshops for managers, in which the game is played. The first results of these workshops are described in the next paragraph.

5   First Results

The first results of the workshops are promising. Managers evaluated the game positively. There was a lot of laughter during the workshops. The fun factor was mentioned as one of the positive aspects of the game. This motivated the managers to play the game. They recognized the situations in the game and thought the speed of the game was good. The engagement of managers to the game was high. There was also a lot of discussion during the game and after the game, when results of the groups were presented. The discussion with colleagues was also one of the aspects that managers evaluated positively. Managers discussed interventions to decrease work related stress and increase engagement in their own work situation using examples and characters from the game. They were able to make the translation from the game world to their actual work situation. The game and the game story gave them 'words and examples' to talk about their own experiences. They indicated that after playing the game they had more understanding of the theory of work related stress and work engagement. They also experienced the role a manager could have in managing these risks. For some managers it was an eye-opener to see the effect of work engagement on the results of the restaurant.

Most players indicated that they would have liked to have more opportunities to intervene in the game. In the game players can choose between a limited number of 'standard' interventions (and this number increases if information is gathered by 'talking' to employees). Managers would have liked to be able to formulate their own interventions. They would also have liked to be able to have a 'real' conversation with the characters in the game, instead of just being able to select standard questions or remarks. To be able to experiment with more styles and types of behavior would have increased the perception of the influence a player has on the outcomes of the game.

6   Discussion and Conclusion

Work related stress is an important occupational risk in the Netherlands, and it is not dealt with enough by management in companies. This can be explained by unawareness of the risks and consequences, and lack of insight in the possible interventions and self- efficacy. Culture in companies often hinders to talk about this sensitive topic. The first results of our project suggest that playing the Engagement game increases the insight in the topic and provides a 'safe environment' to experiment with this sensitive topic. These findings are supported by research into the development of serious games (Graesser, Chipman, Leeming and Bid Bach, (in Ritter Field, Cody & Vorderer, 2009).

The first experiences also show that although the game is important, the training in which the game is imbedded (the big game) is also very important. The link from experience (in the game) to understanding can only be made when there is a well-developed translation phase after playing the game. The effect of the game will also depend on the quality of the training in which the game is imbedded. This finding is supported by studies into the effectiveness of serious games as a tool for learning and training (see for example Sitzmann, 2011).

Our ambition is to show the effect of the Engagement game on the knowledge, competences and awareness of the players, on their self- efficacy to deal with topic and also on their behavior related to this topic. The hypothesis in this research is that the changed behavior of the manager will change the resources and stressors of the employees and thus change their levels of stress and engagement. This will affect the outcomes of the organization. Resources and stressors of employees can also be affected by other determinants than the behavior of the manager and that is even more the case for outcomes of the organization. Although the intervention group and the control group will be matched carefully, this could influence the results of this study.

There is a need for effective interventions, not only to manage psychosocial risks, but to manage all occupational safety and health risks. And not only is there a need for effective interventions, company management should also be convinced to work on these risks. If the Engagement game proves to be effective in increasing a players' awareness and sense of urgency to deal with risks, in changing their self- efficacy in dealing with the risks and in changing their behavior, this might be an indication that serious gaming is a promising new way of dealing with health and safety risks in general.

References

1. Bakker, A.B., Demerouti, E.: The job-demands resources model: state of the art. Journal of Managerial Psychology 22, 309–328 (2007)
2. Bakker, A.B., Schaufeli, W.B., Demerouti, E.: Werkstressoren, energiebronnen en burnout: het WEB model. In: Winnubst, J., Schuur, F., Dam, J. (eds.) Praktijkboek Gezond Werken, vol. II(3.2), pp. 1–19. Elsevier, Maarssen (1999)
3. Brug, J., van Assema, P., Lechner, L.: Gezondheidsvoorlichting en Gedragsverandering. van Gorcum, Assen (2007)
4. Connoly, T.M., Boyle, E.A., MacArthur, E., Hainey, T., Boyle, J.M.: A systematic literature review of empirical evidence on computer games and serious games. Computers & Education 59, 661–686 (2012)

5. European Agency for Health and Safety at Work. EU-OSHA, European Agency for Safety and Health at Work, Drivers and barriers for psychosocial risk management: an analysis of the findings of the European Survey of Enterprises on New and Emerging Risks (ESENER), Office for Official Publications of the European Communities, Luxembourg (2012)
6. de Graaf, R., ten Have, M., van Dorsselear, S.: De psychische gezondheid van de Nederlandse Bevolking [The Mental Health of the Dutch population]. Trimbos-Instituut, Utrecht (2010)
7. Graesser, A., Chipman, P., Leeming, F., Biedenback, S.: Deep Learning and Emotion in Serious Games. In: Ritterfeld, U., Cody, M., Vorderer, P. (eds.) Serious Games: Mechanisms and Effects, pp. 83–102. Routledge, New York (2009)
8. Harteveld, C.: Triadic game design: Balancing reality, meaning and play. Springer, London (2011)
9. Harteveld, C.: Making sense of Virtual Risks: a Quasi-Experimental Investigation into Game-Based Training. IOS Press, Amsterdam (2012)
10. Houtman, I., Kok, L., Klauw, M., van, d.L.M., Janssen, Y., Ginkel, W.: van.: Waarom werkgevers bewezen effectieve maatregelen wel of niet nemen [Why employers do or do not take proven effective measures]. TNO, Hoofddorp (2012)
11. Jackson, G.T., Greasser, A.C.: Content matters: An investigation of feedback categories within an ITS. In: Lucking, R., Koedinger, K., Greer, J. (eds.) Artificial Intelligence in Educattion: Building Technology Rich Learning Context That Work, pp. 127–134. IOS Press, Amsterdam (2007)
12. Koppes, L.L.J., de Vroome, E.M.M., van den Bossche, S.N.J.: The Netherlands Working Conditions Cohort Study. TNO, Hoofddorp (2010)
13. Lepper, M.R., Woolverton, M.: The wisdom of practice: Lessons learned from the study of highly effective tutors. In: Aronson, J. (ed.) Improving Academic Achievement: Contributions of Social Psychologie, pp. 133–156. Academic Press, Orlando (2002)
14. OECD, Sick on the job? Myths and Realities about Mental Health and Work. Mental Health at Work. OECD Publishing (2012)
15. Oeij, P.R.A., de Vroome, E.M.M., Sanders, J.M.A.F., van den Bossche, S.N.J.: Werkgevers Enquête Arbeid [Empoyers Working Conditions Survey]. TNO, Hoofddorp (2008)
16. Oprins, E.: Evaluatieraamwerk voor het evalueren van Serious Games, onderzoeksvoorstel (researchproposal). TNO, Soesterberg (2011)
17. Schaufeli, W.B., Bakker, A.B.: Job demands, job resources, and their relationship with burnout and engagement: a multi-sample study. Journal of Organizational Behavior 25, 293–315 (2004)
18. Seligman, M.E.P., Csikszentmihalyi, M.: Positive psychology: An introduction. American Psychologist 55, 5–14 (2000)
19. Sitzzmann, T.: A Meta-analytic Examination of the instructional effectiveness of computer-based simulation games. Personnel Psychology 64, 489–528 (2011)
20. Vorderer, P., Klimmt, C., Ritterfeld, U.: Enjoyment: At the heart of media entertainment. Communication Theory 14, 388–408 (2004)
21. Wiezer, N., Schelvis, R., van Zwieten, M., Kraan, K., van der Klauw, M., Houtman, I., Bakhuys Roozeboom, M., Kwantes, J.: Werkdruk. TNO, Hoofddorp (2012)

Validation of an Integrated Biomechanical Modeling Approach to the Ergonomic Evaluation of Drywall Installation

Lu Yuan

Department of Computer Science and Industrial Technology, Southeastern Louisiana
University, SLU 10847 Hammond, LA 70402 USA
Lu.Yuan@selu.edu

Abstract. The present study validated an integrated biomechanical modeling approach that the researcher has previously developed to study the physical demands for drywall installers. In particular, a sensitivity analysis was conducted to examine the impact of some quantitative assumptions that have been made to facilitate the modeling approach. Through setting up null hypothesis for each assumption and changing one parameter at a time, the new model output values were compared to the original ones. Using student t-tests to evaluate the statistical differences of the mean values, the sensitivity analysis was achieved by determining if any assumption or parameter has significant impact on the model. The results indicated that the modeling approach seemed to be the most sensitive to both the distribution of work cycles for a typical 8-hour workday and the distribution and values of Euler angles that are used to determine the "shoulder rhythm." Whereas other assumptions including the distribution of trunk postures did not appear to have significant impact on the model output values. It was concluded that the integrated approach might provide an applicable examination of exposure variability particularly reflected by the non-routine feature of the work.

Keywords: Biomechanical Modeling, Sensitivity Analysis.

1 Introduction

Construction workers who perform drywall installation are at a high risk of various musculoskeletal injuries and disorders, especially to the low back and shoulder areas (Chiou et al., 2000; Hsiao and Stanevich, 1996; Lemasters et al., 1998; Lipscomb et al., 1997, 2000). Previous biomechanical analyses of drywall installation examined the physical stress and postural stability during lifting of the drywall panels (Pan and Chiou, 1999; Pan et al., 2002/2003). The authors were aware of many practical limitations to conducting accurate, non-invasive and reasonably priced ergonomic assessments at the worksite due to the dynamic nature of construction activities. Therefore, more reliable and cost-effective ergonomic exposure assessment methods are warranted.

V.G. Duffy (Ed.): DHM/HCII 2013, Part II, LNCS 8026, pp. 159–168, 2013.
© Springer-Verlag Berlin Heidelberg 2013

With the development and application of PATH (Posture, Activity, Tools, and Handling), an observational work sampling-based approach to direct observation (Buchholz et al., 1996), it has become practical to quantify the percent of time that construction workers are exposed to awkward postures, various tasks and activities, and manual handling (Buchholz et al., 2003; Forde and Buchholz, 2004; Paquet et al., 1999, 2001, 2005; Rosenberg et al., 2006). PATH has also been used in other industrial sectors that involve non-repetitive job activities including retail, agriculture, and healthcare industries (Earle-Richardson et al., 2005; Pan et al., 1999; Park et al., 2009).

The joint angle and load ranges that are represented by the PATH data are categorical rather than continuous. However, the Monte-Carlo simulation method, which is used to generate random numbers from a defined distribution, can be utilized to extract discrete values from the categorical PATH data for biomechanical analysis of the low back and shoulder (Tak et al., 2007). The Monte-Carlo method has also been successfully used both to capture the trunk muscle activity during torso bending (Mirka and Marras, 1993) and to simulate variability in muscle moment arms and physiological cross-sectional areas for prediction of shoulder muscle force (Chang et al., 2000; Hughes, 1997).

The researcher has previously explored a hybrid model integrating work sampling, computer simulation, and biomechanical modeling to conduct the ergonomic analysis of drywall installation (Yuan, 2006; Yuan et al., 2007). Since it is often infeasible to conduct direct measurements of ergonomic exposure assessment particularly within the construction industry, such a method has provided a reasonable alternative to estimate the physical demands during drywall installation. The present study was designed to demonstrate the validity and utility of this modeling approach, so that the impact of drywall storage position and size on the physical demands for drywall installers could be evaluated later. In particular, a sensitivity analysis was conducted to examine the impact of some quantitative assumptions that have been made to facilitate the modeling approach.

2   Methods

The integrated modeling approach started with the PATH methodology which provided the basic characterization of drywall installation work by quantifying the percent of time that the drywall installers were conducting different activities with different body segment (trunk, arm, and leg) postures. The relative frequencies of key activities, recorded over two hours, were used to construct the eight-hour-workday activity series using Monte-Carlo simulation. The biomechanical model input variables, including anthropometric data, joint angles, external load force and position vectors, and internal muscle parameters, were then generated for the analyses of the low back and shoulder. Utilizing different optimization programs in MATLAB (The MathWorks, Natick, MA, USA), the three-dimensional static equilibrium equations were solved and the biomechanical model output variables of muscle contraction forces and joint reaction forces at the low back and shoulder were computed.

Seven main activities which represent a typical drywall installation task were examined in this study, including: 1. cut/measure; 2. lift; 3. carry; 4. hold/place; 5. screw; 6. in between; and 7. other. It was determined from the field observations that there were 12 possible work cycles, with 4 occurring during installation of a whole sheet and 8 denoting installation processes for a partial piece. The probability of each work cycle was calculated by multiplying the probability of every single activity during that cycle (Yuan, 2006). As studied by Pan and Chiou (1999), the drywall lifting method in which the worker used one hand to support the horizontal drywall sheet at its bottom and the other hand to grasp the sheet at its top produced the highest L4/L5 disc compression forces and therefore appeared to be the most stressful. It was assumed that the drywall installers in this study exclusively used such a lifting method as a demonstration of the worst case scenario. Activity 6 (in between) denoted exclusively loading/adjusting the screw guns and it always followed activity 5 (screw). Activity 7 (other) included climb/descend, communicate, mark/draw, and other miscellaneous job activities.

The drywall sheets studied in this project were Sheetrock® Brand Gypsum Panel from CGC Inc., with bulk density of 881 kg/m^3 (55 lb/ft^3). Summary statistics for subject weight, height, trunk widths and depths are acquired from Marras et al. (2001), because subject anthropometry was not obtained when the original PATH data were collected. The present study assumes subject height and weight follow a normal distribution because height and weight are generally known to be normally distributed (Roebuck et al., 1975). This assumption has been validated by Jung et al. (2009) using the 1988 US Army data (Gordon et al., 1988).

The relationships between subject trunk muscle parameters and anthropometric characteristics, such as subject height and weight, body mass index, and trunk width and depth at the planes of muscle origins and insertions, were determined by Marras et al. (2001). The regression equations with higher R squares were chosen in this study to represent those relationships. The weight percentages of different body segments of the whole body and the distance coefficients between the body segment center of mass and the proximal joint were calculated based on information from Drillis and Contini (1966) and Dempster (1955), respectively.

To conduct the sensitivity analysis, a list of the important quantitative assumptions that have been made to facilitate modeling was first created. These assumptions include, but are not limited to, the following:

1. The overall probabilities of the possible work cycles for a typical drywall installation task follow the general discrete distribution.
2. For a right-handed person, the trunk tends to lean toward the left side and twist counterclockwise for 80% of time during manual work (Tak et al., 2007).
3. Trunk flexion angles follow a lognormal distribution, whereas trunk lateral bend and twist angles both have normal distributions.
4. Values of the external load position on the Z-axis (directed upwards when the subject is standing erect) are dependent on the trunk flexion angles and show a normal distribution.

5. Shoulder flexion angles display a normal distribution, and other motions of the shoulder, elbow, and wrist all have triangular distributions.
6. Values of Euler angles that are used to determine the "shoulder rhythm" (Högfors et al., 1991) have a normal distribution.

From this list, the researcher selected a small number of those assumptions (e.g., the probability of distribution type for trunk flexion angles) which are likely to have the biggest impact on the results for further examination. Through setting up the following null hypotheses for each assumption and changing one parameter at a time, the new model output values were compared to the original ones.

- **Hypothesis 1:** The distribution of work cycles for a typical 8-hour workday has significant impact on the low back model.
- **Hypothesis 2:** The probability of the trunk tending to lean toward the left side and twist counterclockwise for a right-handed person during manual work has significant impact on the low back model.
- **Hypothesis 3:** The distribution of trunk flexion angles has significant impact on the low back model.
- **Hypothesis 4:** The ranges of PATH trunk posture categories have significant impact on the low back model.
- **Hypothesis 5:** The distribution and values of Euler angles that are used to determine the "shoulder rhythm" have significant impact on the shoulder model.

Using student t-tests ($p < 0.05$) to evaluate the statistical differences of the means of major model input and output values including joint angles, muscle forces and joint reaction forces for the low back and shoulder for an average subject working on a typical 8-hour workday, the sensitivity analysis was achieved by determining if the model is sensitive to any assumption or parameter.

It should be noted that there is no gold standard for validation of the average muscle forces and joint reaction forces for a typical eight-hour workday. However, the results from a previous research study (Yuan, 2006) suggested that 1) the Monte Carlo simulation did generate the same activity distribution as the PATH observations; and 2) the output for the low back model gives similar results to the 3DSSPP (The University of Michigan, 1999).

3   Results

3.1   Hypothesis 1: The Distribution of Work Cycles for a Typical 8-Hour Workday Has Significant Impact on the Low Back Model

In the original model, the overall probabilities of the possible (12) work cycles for a typical 8-hour workday of drywall installation were assumed to follow the general discrete distribution. The present study examined the following two new assumptions and compared them with the original one:

1. The 12 work cycles had equal probability; in other words, they follow the uniform distribution. And
2. The 4 work cycles for whole-sheet installation and the 8 work cycles for partial-sheet installation had equal probability. This means that there is 1/8 probability for each cycle of whole-sheet installation and 1/16 probability for each cycle of partial-sheet installation, respectively.

The comparison between the first assumption and the original one indicated that:

1. The ratio of activity 1 (cut/measure) over activity 2 (lift) was higher, which means that there were more work cycles of partial-sheet installation and the 8-hour workday tends to be less strenuous. However, the total work productivity (measured by the square foot of installation) might be reduced.
2. The angles of trunk flexion, lateral bending, and twisting were the same.
3. The MMCI (Maximum Muscle Contraction Intensity) and the forces of two major paired trunk muscles (Erector Spinae and Latissimus Dorsi) were statistically significantly smaller.
4. The absolute values of the L4/L5 joint reaction forces (disc compression, lateral shear, and anterior-posterior shear) were statistically significantly smaller ($t = 5.715$, $p < 0.0001$; $t = 2.414$, $p = 0.008$; and $t = 5.705$, $p < 0.0001$, respectively).

The comparison between the second assumption and the original one indicated that:

1. The frequency of the seven activities for a typical 8-hour workday appeared to be similar to that of the original model. And as a result,
2. There were no statistically significant differences among the joint angles, MMCI, muscle forces, and joint reaction forces.

Based on these findings, it appears that Hypothesis 1 could not be rejected. In other words, the distribution of work cycles for a typical 8-hour workday determines the frequency of the seven activities that were examined in this study; and consequently, has significant impact on the low back model output values.

3.2   Hypothesis 2: The Probability of the Trunk Tending to Lean toward the Left Side and Twist Counterclockwise for a Right-Handed Person during Manual Work Has Significant Impact on the Low Back Model

In the original model, it was assumed that "For a right-handed person, the trunk tends to lean toward the left side and twist counterclockwise for 80% of time during manual work." The present study changed such a probability to 50%, 75%, and 85%, respectively. The comparisons between these probabilities and the original one indicated that there were no statistically significant differences among the MMCI and the forces of two major paired trunk muscles, as well as the absolute values of the L4/L5 joint reaction forces. Based on these examinations, it seems that Hypothesis 2 could be rejected.

3.3 Hypothesis 3: The Distribution of Trunk Flexion Angles has Significant Impact on the Low Back Model

Trunk flexion angles were assumed to follow lognormal distribution in the original model. The researcher changed it to normal distribution and the comparison between those two indicated that there were no statistically significant differences among the model input and output values. This could suggest that Hypothesis 3 be rejected.

3.4 Hypothesis 4: The Ranges of Path Trunk Posture Categories Have Significant Impact on the Low Back Model

The comparison between those two ranges did not yield statistically significant differences on the model input and output values, except for the absolute values of the L4/L5 lateral shear force ($t = 4.264$, $p < 0.0001$). The forces of two major paired trunk muscles tended to be lower, although the differences were not statistically significant.

It seems that Hypothesis 4 could be rejected in general; however, further analysis might be needed to find out why the L4/L5 lateral shear forces were statistically different.

3.5 Hypothesis 5: The Distribution and Values of Euler Angles That are Used to Determine the "Shoulder Rhythm" Have Significant Impact on the Shoulder Model

In the original shoulder model, the means and standard deviations of the Euler angles were obtained independently from the ranges of such angles for three subjects in the motion studies conducted by Högfors et al. (1991). Through the review of a modified shoulder rhythm model by Makhsous (1999), the researcher was able to find the following equations describing the estimates for the Euler angles for the clavicle and scapula in accordance to the humerus.

$$\alpha_c = -35.15 + 11.15 \cos[0.75(\beta_h + 90)] (0.08\alpha_h) \tag{1}$$
$$\beta_c = 18\{1 - \cos[0.8(\beta_h + 90)]\} + 9 \tag{2}$$
$$\gamma_c = 30\{1 - cos[0.75(\beta_h + 90)]\} + 3 \tag{3}$$

$$\alpha_s = 200 + 20\, cos[0.75(\beta_h + 90)] \tag{4}$$
$$\beta_s = -87 + 42\, cos[-0.75\beta_h - 70](0.1\gamma_h/90 + 1) \tag{5}$$
$$\gamma_s = 82 + 8\, cos\{(\alpha_h + 10)\sin[0.75(\beta_h + 90)]\} \tag{6}$$

The new Euler angles seem to be different from the old ones, especially the values of $\beta_{Scapula}$. The comparison of the model output values indicated that the majority of muscle forces tended to be significantly bigger; whereas the coracohumeral ligament force was significantly smaller ($t = 8.738$, $p < 0.0001$). On the other hand, the glenohumeral and sternoclavicular joint reaction forces were larger but the increases were not statistically significant, compared to those yielded from the original model.

Based on these comparisons, it seems that Hypothesis 6 should not be rejected. As there is still a strong need to continue studying the "shoulder rhythm," the examination of Hypothesis 6 might indicate that Euler angles are indeed crucial in term of the understanding of the shoulder model.

4 Discussion

The present study validated an integrated biomechanical modeling approach that was previously developed by the researcher to conduct the ergonomic evaluation of drywall installation through a sensitivity analysis. The results indicated that both the distribution of work cycles for a typical 8-hour workday and the distribution and values of Euler angles that are used to determine the "shoulder rhythm" seemed to have the most significant impact on the modeling approach. Whereas other assumptions including the distribution of trunk postures did not appear to have significant impact on the model output values.

This study extracted information from PATH data and applied it to the simulation of a hypothetical subject. It was noteworthy that PATH observations were made on a crew of eight workers over two hours. As it is desired to determine the most efficient number of worker participating in the study relative to the number of repeated measurements for each of these workers (Van der Beek and Frings-Dresen, 1998), there might be other work cycles in reality besides the 12 that were analyzed. Yet, for a simplified simulation of a typical 8-hour workday, only these 12 work cycles were examined. Similarly, the activity sequences for the observed drywall installation work were able to be established to allow the generation of eight-hour-workday activity series. The acceptance of Hypothesis 1 in the present study suggested that these activity sequences eventually determine both the overall probabilities of the 12 work cycles and the low back model output values.

Because most construction work involves non-routine activities, it is not uncommon to see that there are certain patterns/sequences that construction workers usually follow in order to finish the work. For example, ironworkers would have to put the rebar in place before tying it. The method in this study can be used for the evaluation of those types of construction work. However, for some other types of construction work, the activity sequence may not be necessarily fixed: e.g., laborers will have to do many miscellaneous activities based on project schedule and needs. Also, it may be difficult to identify all possible activity series. Thus, comprehensive understanding and capturing of work are always required and it may also involve more reasonable assumptions in order for a realistic simulation of cumulative activities.

In order to generate random numbers from the observational data categories, many assumptions had to be made in terms of distribution type and pertinent parameters. Particularly, different distributional assumptions about body part postures were made, due to a lack of information on how body postures change over time even when repeating the same job activities (Tak et al., 2007). As Tak et al. (2007) has tested the validity of the simulation model as a whole, the sensitivity analysis of the impact of the trunk postures on the low back model in this study might have provided some useful information about the validation of the integrated modeling approach. The rejection of Hypotheses 2, 3, and 4 indicated that the different probabilities, types, and ranges of parameter distributions did not affect the results significantly.

On the other hand, it seems that there is lack of sufficient information regarding the shoulder model input values, particularly on the distributions of joint (shoulder, elbow and wrist) angles and the Euler angles that determine the "shoulder rhythm." Because of these limitations, the results of the shoulder model sensitivity analysis were less significant than those of the low back analysis; and thus, may need further evaluation and verification.

As construction work always involves a variety of activities that incur different biomechanical demands, it is imperative to determine the probabilistic representation of biomechanical stress in order to understand both acute and cumulative trauma risk (Mirka et al., 2000). Mirka et al. (2000) developed the Continuous Assessment of Back Stress (CABS) method by estimating the time-weighted distribution of biomechanical stress throughout the workday, therefore providing an important insight into some of the activities that would have been neglected using traditional task analysis methods. The present study explored similar idea by examining the continuous physical loads on the drywall installers' low back and shoulder. In contrast to Mirka et al. (2000), it considered activity sequences for the purpose of studying muscle fatigue characteristics (Yuan, 2006).

Overall, the present study attempted to integrate observational work-sampling, computer simulation, and biomechanical modeling for ergonomic exposure assessment in a typical construction drywall installation work, where it is infeasible to perform direct measurement in the field. The results of the sensitivity analysis implied that such integration might provide an applicable examination of exposure variability particularly reflected by the non-routine feature of the work.

Acknowledgments. The researcher thanks Dr. Bryan Buchholz of University of Massachusetts Lowell for providing guidance on the biomechanical modeling and Dr. Laura Welch of CPWR (Center for Construction Research and Training) for providing information on drywall installation tasks and activities. This study was supported by CPWR through NIOSH cooperative agreement OH009762. Its contents are solely the responsibility of the authors and do not necessarily represent the official views of CPWR or NIOSH.

References

Bean, J.C., Chaffin, D.B., Schultz, A.: Biomechanical model calculation of muscle contraction forces: a double linear programming method. Journal of Biomechanics 21(1), 59–66 (1988)

Buchholz, B., Paquet, V.L., Punnett, L., Lee, D., Moir, S.: PATH: A work sampling-based approach to ergonomic job analysis for construction and other non-repetitive work. Applied Ergonomics 27(3), 177–187 (1996)

Buchholz, B., Paquet, V.L., Wellman, H., Forde, M.: Quantification of ergonomic hazards for ironworkers performing concrete reinforcement tasks during heavy highway construction. American Industrial Hygiene Association Journal 64(2), 243–250 (2003)

Chang, Y.W., Hughes, R.E., Su, F.C., Itoi, E., An, K.: Prediction of muscle force involved in shoulder internal rotation. Journal of Shoulder and Elbow Surgery 9(3), 188–195 (2000)

Chiou, S.S., Pan, C.S., Keane, P.: Traumatic injury among drywall installers, 1992 to 1995. Journal of Occupational and Environmental Medicine 42(11), 1101–1108 (2000)

Dempster, W.T.: Space requirements of the seated operator. WADC-TR-55-159, Aerospace Medical Research Laboratories, Dayton, Ohio (1955)

Drillis, R., Contini, R.: Body segment parameters, BP174-945. Tech. Rep. No. 1166.03, School of Engineering and Science, New York University, New York (1966)

Earle-Richardson, G., Jenkins, P., Fulmer, S., Mason, C., Burdick, P., May, J.: An ergonomic intervention to reduce back strain among apple harvest workers in New York State. Applied Ergonomics 36(3), 327–334 (2005)

Forde, M., Buchholz, B.: Task content and physical ergonomic risk factors in construction ironwork. International Journal of Industrial Ergonomics 34(4), 319–333 (2004)

Gordon, C.C., Bradtmiller, B., Churchill, Y., Clauser, C.E., McConville, J.T., Tebbetts, I.O., Walker, R.A.: Anthropometric Survey of U.S. Army [data file]. Available from National Technical Information Service Website (1988), http://www.ntis.gov

Högfors, C., Peterson, B., Sigholm, G., Herberts, P.: Biomechanical model of the human shoulder joint – II. The shoulder rhythm. Journal of Biomechanics 24(8), 699–709 (1991)

Hsiao, H., Stanevich, R.: Injuries and ergonomic applications in construction. In: Bhattacharya, A., McGlothlin, J.D. (eds.) Occupational Ergonomics, Theory and Applications, pp. 545–568. Marcel Dekker, Inc., New York (1996)

Hughes, R.E., An, K.: Monte Carlo simulation of a planar shoulder model. Medical & Biological Engineering & Computing 35, 544–548 (1997)

Jung, K., Kwon, O., You, H.: Development of a digital human model generation method for ergonomic design in virtual environment. International Journal of Industrial Ergonomics 39(5), 744–748 (2009)

Lemasters, G.K., Atterbury, M.R., Booth-Jones, A.D., Bhattacharya, A., Ollila-Glenn, N., Forrester, C., et al.: Prevalence of work related musculoskeletal disorders in active union carpenters. Occupational and Environmental Medicine 55, 421–427 (1998)

Lipscomb, H.J., Dement, J.M., Loomis, D.P., Silverstein, B., Kalat, J.: Surveillance of work-related musculoskeletal injuries among union carpenters. American Journal of Industrial Medicine 32, 629–640 (1997)

Lipscomb, H.J., Dement, J.M., Gaal, J.S., Cameron, W., McDougall, V.: Work-related injuries in drywall installation. Applied Occupational and Environmental Hygiene 15(10), 794–802 (2000)

Makhsous, M.: Improvements, Validation and Adaptation of a Shoulder Model. Doctoral Dissertation, Chalmers University of Technology, Goteborg, Sweden (1999)

Marras, W.S., Jorgensen, M.J., Granata, K.P., Wiand, B.: Female and male trunk geometry: size and prediction of the spine loading trunk muscles derived from MRI. Clinical Biomechanics 16, 38–46 (2001)

Mirka, G.A., Marras, W.: A stochastic model of trunk muscle coactivation during trunk bending. Spine 18(11), 1396–1409 (1993)

Mirka, G.A., Kelaher, D.P., Nay, D.T., Lawrence, B.: Continuous Assessment of Back Stress (CABS): A new method to quantify low-back stress in jobs with variable biomechanical demands. Human Factors 42(2), 209–225 (2000)

Pan, C.S., Gardner, L.I., Landsittel, D.P., Hendricks, S.A., Chiou, S.S., Punnett, L.: Ergonomic exposure assessment: an application of the PATH systematic observation method to retail workers. International Journal of Occupational and Environmental Health 2, 79–87 (1999)

Pan, C.S., Chiou, S.: Analysis of biomechanical stresses during drywall lifting. International Journal of Industrial Ergonomics 23, 505–511 (1999)

Pan, C.S., Chiou, S.S., Hendricks, S.: The effect of drywall lifting method on workers' balance in a laboratory-based simulation. Occupational Ergonomics 3, 235–249 (2002/2003)

Paquet, V.L., Punnett, L., Buchholz, B.: An evaluation of manual materials handling in highway construction work. International Journal of Industrial Ergonomics 24, 431–444 (1999)

Paquet, V.L., Punnett, L., Buchholz, B.: Validity of fixed-interval observations for postural assessment in construction work. Applied Ergonomic 32, 215–224 (2001)

Paquet, V.L., Punnett, L., Woskie, S., Buchholz, B.: Reliable exposure assessment strategies for physical ergonomic stressors in construction and other non-routinized work. Ergonomics 48(9), 1200–1219 (2005)

Park, J.K., Boyer, J., Tessler, J., Casey, J., Schemm, L., Gore, R., Punnett, L.: Inter-rater reliability of PATH observations for assessment of ergonomic risk factors in hospital work. Ergonomics 52(7), 820–829 (2009)

Roebuck, J.A., Kroemer, K.H.E., Thomson, W.G.: Engineering anthropometry methods. Wiley-Interscience, New York (1975)

Rosenberg, B., Yuan, L., Fulmer, S.: Ergonomics of abrasive blasting: a comparison of high pressure water and steel shot. Applied Ergonomics 37, 659–667 (2006)

Tak, S., Punnett, L., Paquet, V., Woskie, S., Buchholz, B.: Estimation of compressive forces on lumbar spine from categorical posture data. Ergonomics 50(12), 2082–2094 (2007)

The University of Michigan, Center for Ergonomics. Three Dimensional Strength Prediction Program, v4.2: User's Manual (1999)

Van der Beek, A.J., Frings-Dresen, M.: Assessment of mechanical exposure in ergonomic epidemiology. Occupational and Environmental Medicine 55, 291–299 (1998)

Yuan, L.: Biomechanical analysis of the physical loads on the low back and shoulder during drywall installation. Doctoral Dissertation, University of Massachusetts Lowell, Lowell (2006)

Yuan, L., Buchholz, B., Punnett, L., Kriebel, D.: Estimation of muscle contraction forces and joint reaction forces at the low back and shoulder during drywall installation. In: Proceedings of the 51st Annual Meeting of Human Factors and Ergonomics Society, Baltimore, MD (2007)

Optimization for Lunar Mission Training Scheme Based on AnyBody Software

Jing Zhang[1], Rong Zhou[1], Jingwen Li[1], Li Ding[1,*], and Li Wang[2]

[1] School of Biological Science and Medical Engineering, Beihang University,
Beijing, China
{wysrxh,buaazhourong}@163.com, ljwz8901@be.buaa.edu.cn,
ding1971316@buaa.edu.cn
[2] National Key Laboratory of Human Factors Engineering,
China Astronaut Research and Training Center, China
hhlwang@sohu.com

Abstract. Since majority of the lunar missions are accomplished by the upper limbs according to literature analysis, it is necessary for us to focus on studying astronauts' upper limb movement. This paper aims at studying the training schemes for the lunar mission through computer simulation with AnyBody software. Knocking, one of the typical lunar missions was selected as the study subject. Based on the verification experiment of earth's gravity level, the model of AnyBody software can be used to simulate lunar missions. An optimization of knocking move were provided by our AnyBody model.

Keywords: simulation, lunar mission training, optimization.

1 Introduction

Lunar exploration is one of the most significant objects in the near future. Comprehending the characteristics of human movement under the lunar environment is necessary to the early training and the success of lunar missions. The method of simulating calculation used in the aerospace field provides details about astronauts' moves during exploration, and it enables to shorten training period and improve efficiency. Traditional method of training task selection not only involves too much experiment but also is strongly affected by researchers' perspective. Compared to traditional method, simulating calculation can provide much more reliable guideline about training program. So the method of simulating calculation has many advantages over traditional methods. Documents showed that models applied to astronaut activity simulation were mostly physical models[1-3],such as the stick model [4], the spherical space toroidal model [5], the entity split model [6], the surface model [7] and so on. However, these models do not consider astronauts' physiological features, and have many limitations in evaluating safety and comfort.

AnyBody is the software that can excellently simulate human ergonomics and analyze biomechanics, and it considers human skeletal muscle system well. By

---

* Corresponding author.

V.G. Duffy (Ed.): DHM/HCII 2013, Part II, LNCS 8026, pp. 169–178, 2013.
© Springer-Verlag Berlin Heidelberg 2013

importing integral human skeleton and muscles model and setting initial parameters, the software can automatically calculate each human bone and muscle's condition. Currently, this software is wildly applied in the field of ergonomics and biomechanics, such as analysis of a femoral-fracture fixation-plate implant [8], musculoskeletal computational analysis of the influence of car-seat design [9], ergonomic analysis of manual materials handling tasks [10], musculoskeletal model of the mandible [11] and so on.

Literature analysis results showed that during the lunar exploration, most tasks are related to upper limb [12]. This paper focuses on computer simulation that based on AnyBody. A typical move, knock, is chosen as our analysis object, because knock is one of the most frequent moves during lunar exploration. And later, an optimum training scheme is acquired according our simulation.

2   Knocking Modeling and Simulation

Musculoskeletal human-body model discussed in the study was built in the AnyBody Modeling System. A specific model environment was constructed by importing parameters including acceleration of gravity, initial posture and kinematics data. Then the model was driven to move as pre-set. The model was built under earthly environment. Setting the gravity of the model to be the earthly gravity ($g=-9.81m/s^2$). The initial posture is standing naturally. Keep the trunk straight, the left arm fall naturally and the right arm completing the knocking move. Initially, the right arm flexed 40° (Namely, the included angle of the right upper arm and vertical direction is 40°), and the fore arm flexed 110° on that basis(Namely, the included angle of the fore arm and the horizontal direction is 60°). A hammer weighs 0.64kg was grabbed by the right hand. The countertorque was added to the right wrist to imitate the state of wearing spacesuit. Then the kinematics parameters were imported into the model to motive the right arm to complete the knocking move. The right fore arm knocked down from initial posture to the horizontal direction with the upper arm nearly keeping still. The simulation model was used to calculate the following six schemes. Knocking movement was performed under the angular velocity of 60°/s and 80°/s separately with the right shoulder joint adducting 15°(Hereinafter referred to as Add 15°),adducting 0°(Add 0°)and abducting 15°(Abd 0°).

The simulation model under the lunar environment was set afterwards. Setting the gravity of the model to be the lunar gravity ($g=-1.622m/s^2$).The initial posture and knocking move were identical with the earth's model. Fifteen lunar schemes were calculated by the lunar model. Knocking movement was performed under the angular velocity of 60°/s, 70°/s and 80°/s with the right shoulder joint adducting 15°,10°(Hereinafter referred to as Add 10°),5°(Add 5°),0°and abducting 5°(Abd 5°).

The AnyBody software showed max muscle activity and muscle force when each scheme calculation was finished. The muscle force of deltoideus (Hereinafter referred to as Del), biceps brachii (Bi), triceps brachii (Tri) and trapezius (Tra) was selected to be analyzed among the large results. The study chose the average value of muscle force to be the analysis index.

3   Model Verification

3.1   Testing Program

To verify the validity of the results got by AnyBody software, verification experiment under the earthly environment was performed. The four muscles (Del, Tri, Bi, Tra) which were considered on the AnyBody software were selected to be the study objects. Surface electromyography (SEMG) and subjective assessment were the indices in the verification experiment.

Subjects. 10 young males that coincide with AnyBody model's body size such as height and weight were selected for the verification experiment on the premise of not informed anything about the simulation results. All the subjects were in good health, without muscle fatigue, taking no strenuous exercise 24hours before and getting used of the experimental requirement.

Sports Load, Signal Acquisition and Processing. Subjects adopted standing posture which the trunk remained straight. The angle between the right fore arm and horizontal direction was 60°, while the angle between the right upper arm and the vertical direction was 40°. The right hand which gripped hammer was tied on the countertorque producing equipment. The left arm falls naturally. Knocking at the position and the angular velocity as the schemes set in the earthly simulation model. Stable rap rhythm was provided by Cherub WSM330 mechanical metronome; countertorque was offered by BTE PRIMUSRS; SEMG was acquired by BIOPAC SYSTEM MP150 bioelectricity acquisition and processing system. Disposable AgCl electrode placed in the standard position of Del, Tri, Bi and Tra was used for acquiring SEMG. The sampling rate was 1000Hz. After experiment of each scheme, subjective assessment was given by the subjects. The subjective assessment refers to Borg Rating of Perceived Exertion Scale (RPE) [7], which is illustrated in Table. 1.

Table 1. Borg Rating of Perceived Exertion Scale(RPE)

Number	Level of Fatigue
6	No exertion at all
7	Extremely light
8	
9	Very light
10	
11	Light
12	
13	Somewhat hard
14	
15	Hard (heavy)
16	
17	Very hard
18	
19	Extremely hard
20	Maximal exertion

3.2   Model Verification Results

The average muscle force of Del, Tri, Bi and Tra, and the sum of the four muscles' forces were obtained after processing the 6 earth's schemes' results, which were shown in Figure 1 and Chart 2 separately.

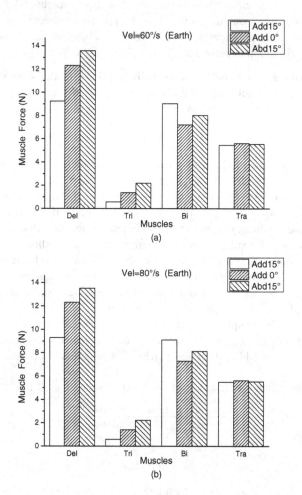

Fig. 1. The average muscle force of four muscles of the earthly simulation (a. Vel=60°/s; b. Vel=80°/s)

Table 2. Earthly simulation results of muscle force sum (N)

	Add 15°	Add 0°	Abd 15°
Vel=60°/s	24.347	26.565	29.384
Vel=80°/s	24.511	26.663	29.390

Figure 1 displays that the average muscle force of the Del and the Tri at the posture of Abb 15°are less than that at Abb 0 °and Abd 15°,which are on the increase along with the shoulder joint's states changing from adduction to abduction. The value of the Tra at the three positions are similar. While the value of the Bi get the minimum at Add 0°, and the value at Add 15°is slightly higher than that at Abd 15°. Accordingly, we can choose the specific scheme as the optimal one based on the specific requirement of a certain muscle. For example, if the Biceps brachii is asked to have the least effort, while no requirements are asserted on other three muscles, the scheme, knocking at Add 0°is the best choice. While considerating the four muscles to give a whole consideration, kocking at Add 15° is the optimum, as three muscles (Tri, Del, Tra) of four are minimal at the position. The sum of the four muscles shown in Chart.2 also supports the view point.

In addition, while knocking move was operated at different angular velocities at the same position,the average muscle force differences are subtle, shown in Chart.2. The value of sum totals of four muscles at the Vel of 80°/s is slightly greater than that at the Vel of 60°/s. While the influence of the knocking velocity is very slight, and it won't influence the distribution of average muscle force at the three positions.

To sum up, among the 6 schemes simulated under the earth's environment, the scheme of knocking at the velocity of 60°/s and at the position of Add 15°is the optimal one.

In the verification experiment, SEMG data were filtered by the 20~500Hz band pass filter and 50Hz band stop filter. To analyse the data, five obvious and consecutive waves were cut out from the whole EMG.

In this study, absolute waveform average was the analysis index. The absolute waveform average is the average of instantaneous EMG amplitude in a period of time, which can display the number, the types and the synchronization of active motion units when muscles acted, and which is also related to the central neural control function in different muscles under different loads. Considering the individual difference, absolute waveform average was normalized in the paper.(See Fig. 2.)

From Add15°, Add0° to Abd15°, as shown in Fig.2, the normalized data of Del, Bi, Tra increased while the Tri decreased slightly. The advantage of the add15° is obvious for the muscle force in that position is smaller to most muscles. In the matter of velocity, the value at 80°/s is always greater than that at 60°/s, but the trend to position stays the same. That is to say, the velocity has something to do with muscle force, but it doesn't influence the position trend. In conclusion, Add15°, Vel=60°/s is the best in the all six schemes.

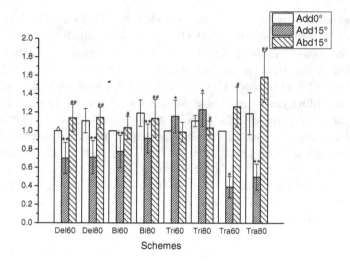

Fig. 2. The normalized results of absolute waveform (* means compared to Add 0°, the difference is significant（p<0.05）;# means compared to Add15°, the difference is significant（p<0.05）;^ means compared to Abd15°, the difference is significant (p<0.05）;##,** means extremely significant difference（p<0.01）)

The subjective assessment results are shown in Fig.3.

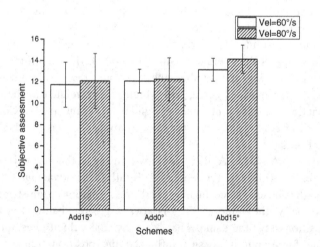

Fig. 3. The subjective assessment results

As in Fig.3, from adduction to abduction, the number of subjective assessment increased one by one, in other words, subjects think it's more and more difficult to knock. Seen from the data at 80°/s and 60°/s, the velocity has impact on subjective scores, while it doesn't affect the whole trend in different positions. Thus, the subjective assessment was well corresponding with the SEMG results. Add15°, Vel=60°/s is also the optimum scheme.

As a whole, the AnyBody software calculation results was coincide with the verification experiment results under the earth gravity. So, it is credible that the optimum scheme for different projects can be calculated through the AnyBody software. This has provided a way for us to study the schemes under the lunar gravity.

4   Selection of Moon Optimal Scheme

After dealing with the 15schemes calculation results under the lunar gravity by AnyBody software, the average muscle force and muscle force sum of Del, Tri, Bi and Tra were got.(See Table 3 and Fig.4).

Fig.4 shows the muscle force trend of different positions under 3 velocities. Considering protecting astronauts' Tri, Add15°is the optimum scheme. If only consider the muscle force of Del, Add0° may be the best.

Fig.5 illustrates the muscle force under different velocity in the position of Add15°. From the Fig.5, under 3 different velocities, the muscle force of Del, Tri, Tra change slightly, but the muscle force of Bi increases along with the velocity.

In order to get the most labor-saving knock scheme and ensure the comfort of most muscles, choosing the sum of 4 muscles (See Table 3)as the index [14], Add15°, Vel=60°/s is the best scheme.

Table 3. Lunar simulation results of muscle force sum (N)

	Add15°	Add10°	Add 5°	Add 0°	Abd 5°
Vel=60°/s	19.372	24.297	27.574	30.496	30.937
Vel=70°/s	21.957	24.343	27.684	30.467	33.218
Vel=80°/s	23.042	24.448	27.679	30.482	33.371

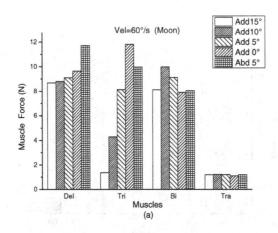

Fig. 4. The average muscle force of four muscles of the lunar simulation (a. Vel=60°/s, b. Vel=70°/s, c. Vel=80°/s)

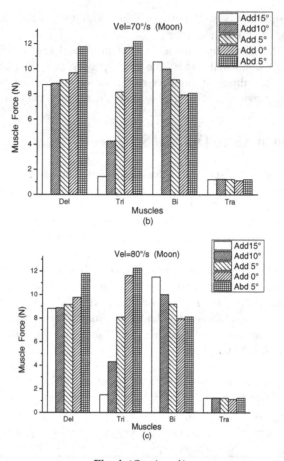

Fig. 4. (*Continued.*)

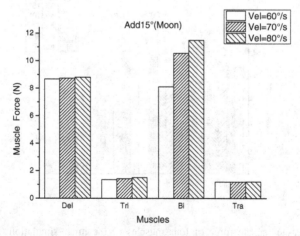

Fig. 5. The average muscle force of muscles under different velocity (Add15°)

5   Conclusion

Through the verification experiment, simulation by using AnyBody software is feasible.

In this paper, we set the knock project as an example, and provide a way to choose better training scheme for future lunar missions as well as other similar missions. This method can improve training efficiency greatly and reduce the workload in optimizing the training scheme.

The training schemes for astronauts are various and complicated especially the lunar mission, which add a lot of new tasks. Therefore, the aware of using simulation to optimize training scheme is indispensable and particularly important. This study laid the foundation of choosing more complex and changeable lunar training scheme for further.

Acknowledgements. This project is supported by National Science Foundation of China, the project number is 51175021.

References

1. Yang, F.: Computer Simulation of Astronaut Extravehicular Activity. Beihang University, Beijing (2003)
2. Wei, B., Yuan, X.: A Study on Three Dimensional Modeling of Human Body in Man-machine System Simulation. Space Medicine & Medical Engineering 10(6), 443–446 (1997)
3. Yang, L.-Q., Liu, X.-G., Qin, L.-B., Zhao, Y.-L.: Summarization of Human Body Molding Technology Development for Man-machine Engineering Field. Journal of Academy of Armored Force Engineering 20(2), 59–63 (2006)
4. Man, H.: Physical Models of Human Body Movements(Summary). Journal of Beijing University of Physical Education 21(1), 39–43 (1998)
5. Kexiang, G., Shuqiu, Z., Xianping, C., Xuyang, D., Lei, L.: Exploring the Method of Human Body 3D Modeling. Journal of Capital Normal University 24(4), 17–20 (2003)
6. Tianlu, M., Zhaoqi, W.: An Efficient Method for Customizing Individual 3D Virtual Human Body. Journal of Computer Aided Design & Computer Graphics 17(10), 2191–2195 (2005)
7. Wu, D., Jun, H., Ding, Y., Lu, B.: The Research of New Work Pattern and Technologies on the Rapid Development of Large Product with Complex Surface. China Mechanical Engineering 14, 1235–1237 (2002)
8. Grujicic, M., Arakere, G., Xie, X.: Design-optimization and material selection for a femoral-fracture fixation-plate implant. Materials and Design 31, 3463–3473 (2010)
9. Grujicic, M., Pandurangan, B., Xie, X.: Musculoskeletal computational analysis of the influence of car-seat design/adjustments on long-distance driving fatigue. International Journal of Industrial Ergonomics, 1–11 (2010)
10. David, W., Wagner, M.P.: Reed, John Rasmussen, Assessing the Importance of Mo-tion Dynamics for Ergonomic Analysis of Manual Materials Handling Tasks using the AnyBody Modeling System. SAE Technical Paper 2007-01-2504, SAE International, Warrendale, PA (2007)

11. de Zee, M., Dalstra, M., Cattaneo, P.M.: Validation of a musculo-skeletal model of the mandible and its application to mandibular distraction osteogenesis. Journal of Biomechanics 40, 1192–1201 (2007)
12. Zhang, N., Tian, Y., Xu, H.: DING Li.Classified Statistics and Analysis of AstronautsTypicalActions during Extravehicular Activity. Space Medicine & Medical Engineering 24(5), 366–368 (2011)
13. Borg, G.A.: Psychophysical bases of perceived exertion. Medicine and Science in Sports and Exercise 14(5), 377–381 (1982)
14. Wang, D., Yu, L., Zhou, X., Wang, C.: Study on the 3D Mathematical Mode of the Muscle Groups Applied to Human Mandible by a Linear Programming Method. Journal of Biomedical Engineering 21(1), 85–88 (2004)

Evaluation of Muscle Fatigue Based on Surface Electromyography and Subjective Assessment

Qian-Xiang Zhou[1], Zhong-Qi Liu[1,*], and Fang Xie[2]

[1] School of Biological Science and Medical Engineering,
Beihang University, Beijing 100191, China
[2] General Technology Department,
China North Vehicle Research Institute Beijing, 100072, China
zqxg@sjtu.edu.cn, liuzhongqi@buaa.edu.cn,
chrisie_xie@163.com

Abstract. In this paper, an assessment model for muscle fatigue was constructed with mean fatigue energy and subjective feeling of fatigue degree for the entire process of the experiment. The model which combined objective and subject data will be valuable for improving work efficiency and for monitoring muscle fatigue. To investigate the relationship between surface electromyography and subjective assessment of muscle fatigue, twenty young male volunteers participated in the experiment of pistol holding and aiming. sEMG of the anterior deltoid was recorded during the entire process, while fatigue assessments (Borg scale) were collected every 30s. We divided the signal into several parts and then octave band method was used to calculate mean energy of each part. An equation was derived based on the relationship between the mean energy of sEMG and Borg scale. The results demonstrated that a quadratic curve reflected the relationship between fatigue energy and fatigue sensation, which suggests that fatigue energy can be calculated to use to collect sEMG activity recordings, and that fatigue sensation can be determined using this evaluation model. This model therefore provides a suitable basis for developing fatigue-monitoring equipment based on sEMG activity, as well as providing a theoretical and design basis for monitoring the fatigue levels of operators, and designing and planning jobs to make them more ergonomic and intuitive.

Keywords: sEMG, subjective assessment, muscle fatigue, octave band, fatigue energy.

1 Introduction

Muscle contraction can drive body movement and it is easy to cause muscle fatigue, thus it reduce work efficiency and may cause serious injury to the muscle. Therefore, it is important to develop a method of assessing muscle fatigue during operation, which may produce valuable results in terms of designing controls, planning rational working systems and preventing occupational injuries.

---

* Corresponding author.

V.G. Duffy (Ed.): DHM/HCII 2013, Part II, LNCS 8026, pp. 179–185, 2013.
© Springer-Verlag Berlin Heidelberg 2013

In present, muscle fatigue assessment is mainly according to sEMG, ultrasound image, dynamic heart rate, biochemical testing, largest independent contraction force and subjective assessment[1-3]. Ultrasound and biochemical estimation methods may cause interference in the process of measurement, while maximal voluntary contraction   (MVC) force measurement of muscle fatigue requires frequent measurement of MVC and thus affect the work flow, meanwhile the subject will be exhausted by MVC testing. Although dynamic heart rate do not influence the subject, it is unsuitable for the evaluation of low-load local muscle fatigue.

sEMG measures the bioelectric phenomenon that occurs on the surface of skin in association with muscle activity. It contains a wealth of information about muscle contraction; the changes of sEMG to a large extent can reflect the muscle activity state. The measurement of sEMG will never bring any pain to the subject, and does not affect the completion of the action. Many studies have investigated muscle fatigue by means of average rectified value (ARV), root mean square (RMS), median frequency   (MDF), mean frequency(MNF)[4-6], fractal dimension, complexity and entropy[7][8] of sEMG. During muscle fatigue, the amplitude of sEMG increase, MDF, MNF, complexity and entropy decrease continuously, fractal dimension showed growing trend. All of them can be used to characterize the physiological indicators of muscle charge. The usefulness power of sEMG concentrated in the range of 50~150Hz, while the evaluation of muscle fatigue in the frequency domain covers the entire range of sEMG from 0 to 500Hz. Octave is a scale of frequency, and the range of frequency is divided into several sections, as to each section, there are upper frequency limit, lower frequency limit and centered frequency. Using octave method, sEMG can be divided into several parts in frequency domain. Zhou et al. used sEMG of the biceps barchii and the Borg scale to evaluate local muscle fatigue in the upper limb after isometric muscle action, then analyzed the sEMG by one-third band octave method, and got an equation to determine the degree of muscle fatigue [9]. In this paper, an assessment model for muscle fatigue was constructed using mean fatigue energy and subjective feeling of fatigue degree for the entire process of the experiment. The model which combined objective and subject data will be valuable for improving work efficiency and for monitoring muscle fatigue.

2   Method

2.1   Subjects

Twenty healthy young male volunteers (mean age (21.3±2.39) years, mean weight (62.94±5.63) Kg, mean height (169.09±4.25) cm) were involved in this study. All subjects voluntarily participated in the experiment and right handed, having no recent strenuous exercise and without upper limb muscle fatigue before the experiment.

2.2   Apparatus

sEMG acquisition and analysis system (JE-TB0810), disposable Ag/Agcl electrode and 75% alcohol were used to acquire sEMG.

2.3   Procedure

The main steps of the experiment were as follows:

Before the experiment, all subjects were trained to make a good understanding of the purpose, process, Borg scale scoring rules and regulation of this experiment by using experimental instruction for the purpose of eliminating the tension in subjects.

Make sure that electrodes were attached to the apophysis of the muscle belly of the anterior deltoid, the two electrodes separated by 2~3cm. Before placing the electrodes, the relevant areas of skin were shaved and cleaned.

Following the action tips to hold the pistol and using sEMG acquisition and analysis system to record the sEMG of the anterior deltoid, the sampling frequency was1000Hz.

All subjects were asked to describe the degree of muscle fatigue according to Borg scale (Table 1) every 30s until exhausted or the arm fell 10°.

Table 1. Borg scale

Score	Description
0	Nothing at all
0.5	Extremely weak
1	Very weak
2	Weak
3	Moderate
4	Slightly strong
5	Strong
6	Moderately strong
7	Fairly strong
8	Quite strong
9	Very strong
10	Extremely strong

3   Evaluation Model of Muscle Fatigue

According to the objective and subject data obtained in the experiment, establish the evaluation model of muscle fatigue as follows:

To avoid the effects of power frequency, mechanical vibrations and ECG noise, the sEMG data were initially subjected to finite impulse response band-pass filter and an adaptive notch filter. Band-pass filter can be achieved by using Kaiser window in Matlab.

During the experiment, record sEMG continuously and wrote down the subject' s fatigue assessment every 30s. Assuming there were N fatigue assessments, the sEMG can be divided into N parts (Table 2).

Table 2. Sequence number and its signal range

Sequence number	Signal range
1	(1*30-10)~ (1*30+10)s
2	(2*30-10)~ (2*30+10)s
i	(i*30-10)~ (i*30+10)s
n-1	((n-1)*30-10)~ ((n-1)*30+10)s
n	(n*30-20)~ (n*30)s

Calculate the Fourier transform of each signal and then using one-third band octave method to get the energy of each signal. The formula for calculating the energy E(fi) is

$$E(f_i) = \sum_{f=f_l}^{f_u} F(f) \tag{1}$$

In this formula, f is the frequency of sEMG activity switched by Fourier transformation; f_i is the centre frequency; f_l is the lower frequency limit; f_u is the upper frequency limit; $E(f_i)$ is the energy value of sEMG after Fourier transformation. One-third, one-sixth and one-twelveth band octave method are the commonly used method. In this paper, we use one-third band octave spectrum to analysis the sEMG, the center, lower and upper frequency limits of one-third band octave spectrum were shown in Table 3., where $\frac{f_u}{f_l} = 2^{\frac{1}{3}} \approx 1.2599$ and $f_i = \sqrt[2]{f_l f_u}$.

The maximum one-third band octave spectrum of 0~20s sEMG is divided by the octave spectrum during muscle fatigue to eliminate individual differences and the relevant octave spectrum $E'(f_i)$ is obtained.

Fatigue energy of sEMG is calculated according to the following formula:

$$E_f(j) = \sum_i B(f_i) E'(f_i) \tag{2}$$

In the formula, $E'(f_i)$ is the relative octave spectrum; f_i is the center frequency; $B(f_i)$ is the coefficient of frequency spectrum which is calculated using the Blackman window. The formula for obtaining $B(f_i)$ is

$$B(f_i) = \begin{cases} 0.42 + 0.5 \cos\left(\frac{\pi f_i}{f_0}\right) + 0.08 \cos\left(\frac{2\pi f_i}{f_0}\right) \\ \qquad\qquad (0 < f_i \le f_c) \\ \quad 0 \qquad\qquad (f_i \ge f_c) \end{cases} \tag{3}$$

In the formula, f_c is the virtual cut-off frequency $B(f_i)$. Because the frequency of sEMG ranges from 0 to 500Hz, when f_i=500Hz, f_u>500Hz, therefore f_c=400Hz.

Table 3. Center, lower and upper frequency limits of one-third band octave spectrum

Center frequency(Hz)	Lower frequency limit	Upper frequency limit
1	0.89	1.12
1.25	1.11	1.40
1.6	1.43	1.80
2	1.78	2.24
2.5	2.23	2.81
3.15	2.81	3.54
4	3.56	4.49
5	4.45	5.61
6.3	5.61	7.07
8	7.13	8.98
10	8.91	11.22
12.5	11.14	14.03
16	14.25	17.96
20	17.82	22.45
25	22.27	28.06
31.5	28.06	35.36
40	35.64	44.90
50	44.54	56.12
63	56.13	70.72
80	71.27	89.80
100	89.09	112.25
125	111.36	140.31
160	142.54	179.59
200	178.18	224.49
250	222.72	280.62
315	280.63	353.58
400	356.36	448.98
500	445.45	561.23

4   Results and Discussion

The sEMG and fatigue assessment were recorded until the subject exhausted or the arm fell over a certain level, so the length of each subject's sEMG are different, got the mean energy of sEMG which have the same Borg scale as shown in table 4.

Table 4. Borg scale and mean energy

Borg scale	Mean energy	Borg scale	Mean energy
0	5.895	5	6.248
0.5	6.223	6	6.513
1	6.022	7	6.989
2	5.967	8	7.103
3	6.062	9	7.105
4	6.284	10	8.256

Took mean energy $E_{mean}(j)$ as independent variables, while the Borg scale as dependent variables, two kinds of curves were tested to describe the relationship between $E_{mean}(j)$ and the Borg scale. They are quadratic, cubic, quartic and logarithmic curves.

The expression of quadratic curve:

$$y = -2.0914x^2 + 33.5872x - 124.7 \tag{4}$$

with a correlation coefficient R of 0.9427.

The expression of cubic curve:

$$y = 0.2619x^3 - 7.6347x^2 + 72.3782x - 214.5 \tag{5}$$

with a correlation coefficient R of 0.9429.

The expression of quartic curve:

$$y = -0.3512x^4 + 9.9533x^3 - 107.369x^2 + 526.2112x - 985.2267 \tag{6}$$

with a correlation coefficient R of 0.9429.

The expression of logarithmic curve:

$$y = 30.857 \, ln(x) - 53.25 \tag{7}$$

with a correlation coefficient R of 0.9036.

According to statistical theory, the result is considered to be better if the correlation coefficient R is larger, therefore, one-variable polynomials is better. The maximum value of quadratic and quartic curve are 10.08 and 10.25, they are beyond the scope of Borg scale. Thus cubic curve represents a reasonable and accurate muscle fatigue evaluation model based on sEMG and fatigue assessment.

During the experiments, several factors, such as individual volunteer, electromagnetic interference and recovery after fatigue, were accounted for and therefore did not influence the overall results. Consecutive measurements of sEMG activity can therefore be used as a relatively straightforward method of evaluating fatigue, after calculation with the proposed algorithm. This represents a more convenient and practical method than time domain analysis based on sEMG activity.

5   Conclusion

This study evaluates muscle fatigue of the anterior deltoid when holding a pistol and aiming. The evaluation of muscle fatigue based on sEMG and fatigue assessment. sEMG is objective signal in time domain while fatigue assessment is subjective which reflects the felling of subjects.

The results show that cubic curve of one-variable polynomials reflected the relationship between mean fatigue energy and Borg scale. According to the model, mean energy of sEMG can be calculated, so that Borg scale and corresponding fatigue assessment can be obtained. This model therefore provides a suitable basis for developing fatigue-monitoring equipment based on sEMG activity, as well as providing a theoretical and design basis for monitoring the fatigue levels of operators, and designing and planning jobs to make them more ergonomic and intuitive.

Acknowledgement. This work is supported by the Technology Foundation of National Science (A0920132003) and the Natural Science Foundation of China (31170895).

References

1. Zhou, Q.X., Wang, C.H.: Review on Body Assessment of Human Operation. Space Medicine and Medical Engineering 22(3), 226–230 (2009)
2. Jun, S., Yan, Z.Z., Lei, X., et al.: Evaluation of the muscle fatigue based on ultrasound images. In: Proceedings of the 6th World Congress on Intelligent Control and Automation, Dalian China, pp. 10332–10336 (2006)
3. Niu, Y.P.: Research the New Method of Detecting Muscle Fatigue by Using Ultrasound Imaging. Journal of Beijing Sport University 31(2), 205–207 (2008) (in Chinese)
4. Liu, H.T., Cao, Y.Z., Xie, X.B., et al.: Estimation of muscle fatigue degree using time-varying autoregressive model parameter estimation of surface electromyography. Chin. J. Biomed. Engineer. 26, 493–497 (2007)
5. Kang, H.G., Dingwell, J.B.: Dynamics and stability of muscle activations during walking in healthy young and older adults. Journal of Biomechanics 42(14), 2231–2237 (2009)
6. Mario, C., Vladimir, M., Stanko, T., et al.: Surface EMG based muscle fatigue evaluation in biomechanics. Clinical Biomechanics 24, 327–340 (2009)
7. Ye, W., Wang, J., Liu, J.H.: The sEMG signal complexity changes during and following local muscle fatigue induced by isometric loading. China Sport Sci. 24, 19–23 (2004)
8. Wang, D.M., Wang, J., Ge, L.Z.: sEMG Time-frequency Analysis Techniques for Evaluation of Muscle Fatigue and its Application in Ergonomic Studies. Space Medicine and Medicinal Engineering 16(5), 387–390 (2003) (in Chinese)
9. Zhou, Q.X., Chen, Y.H., Ma, C., et al.: Evaluation of upper limb muscle fatigue based on surface electromyography. Science China Biomechanics 54, 939–944 (2011)

Part II
Ergonomics of Work with Computers

The Effectiveness of Alternative Keyboards at Reducing Musculoskeletal Symptoms at Work: A Review

Nancy Baker

Department of Occupational Therapy
University of Pittsburgh
nab36@pitt.edu

Abstract. Alternatively configured keyboards have been extensively marketed as one method to reduce musculoskeletal symptoms and musculoskeletal disorders in computer operators. This paper reviews current evidence about the effectiveness of alternative keyboards at reducing risky postures and improving musculoskeletal symptoms. In general, the literature strongly supports the ability of alternative keyboards to reduce potentially risky postures, but is much more equivocal about their ability to reduce musculoskeletal symptoms in the workplace.

Keywords: Computer keyboards, ergonomics, musculoskeletal symptoms.

1   Introduction

Since 2000 there has been a proliferation of alternative keyboard designs purported to reduce risky postures associated with musculoskeletal disorders of the upper extremity (MSD-UE). There are over a dozen alternative keyboard designs, and alternative keyboards now outsell flat keyboards [1]. Despite this proliferation, there has been only limited research on the effectiveness of alternative keyboard designs in reducing MSD-UE and musculoskeletal symptoms (MSS) in the real world of the workplace.

2   Mechanisms of Alternative Keyboard Designs

Alternative keyboards were created based on the hypothesis that non-neutral postures of the forearm and wrists can affect musculoskeletal health by placing joints at greater mechanical and physiological disadvantage [2]. Studies have found associations between forearm supination, wrist flexion/extension, and wrist ulnar/radial deviation postures and MSS/MSD-UE [3], and several studies [4-7] have found that keyboard operators may assume these potentially risky postures during keyboard operation. Alternative keyboards have focused on reducing these postures by angling parts of the standard flat keyboard to reduce the amount of angle that the forearm or wrist must achieve to allow the fingers to interact with the keyboard. There are three areas of adaptations to standard keyboards that are thought to reduce these postures; roll angle

V.G. Duffy (Ed.): DHM/HCII 2013, Part II, LNCS 8026, pp. 189–195, 2013.

Fig. 1. Keyboard adaptations to reduce postures: a) roll angle (pronation/supination); b) pitch angle (wrist flexion/extension); c) yaw angle (wrist ulnar/radial deviation)

for pronation/supination, pitch angle for wrist flexion/extension, and yaw angle for ulnar/radial deviation (Nelson et al 2000) (Fig. 1). Each alternative keyboard configuration has varying degrees of changes in each of these angles.

3   Effectiveness of Alternative Keyboard Designs

3.1   Effectiveness of Alternative Keyboard Designs at Reducing Risky Postures

Early research examining alternative keyboard designs was cross-sectional, and examined if alternative keyboards improved these risky postures. These studies found that most alternative keyboard designs were very effective at reducing risky forearm and wrist postures [8]. However, these studies had limited generalizability to "real world" keyboard operators, since the studies took place in laboratories under ideal conditions. Most of these efficacy studies assumed that their subjects' kinematics performances were well adapted after a minimal acclimation time, 20 minutes or less. In addition most subjects' data collection were completed in one session with the keying on each keyboard ranging from 3 to 60 minutes [9-17]. Those studies that did provide a longer acclimation period, 5 consecutive days [18] and 20 hours prior to participating in the study [19], did not measure postural changes in depth or did not provide baseline information on the postures prior to the keyboard acclimation. The assumption that subjects' postures are stabilized very quickly on alternative keyboards may be false, as Hedge et al. [20] reported that alternative computer keyboard users took from between 4 to 6 weeks to adjust to the novelty of their new keyboard.

An additional concern for the validity of these efficacy studies is that MSS was rarely included as an outcome. Only five of these studies examined the effect of alternative keyboard on musculoskeletal pain. While the laboratory studies that have examined musculoskeletal pain while using alternative keyboards [10, 12, 13, 21, 22] generally reported that using an alternative keyboard decreased musculoskeletal pain, they had flaws in design or reporting which made this reduction difficult to attribute solely to the presence of the alternative keyboard. Overall, in the laboratory, alternative keyboard configurations appear to have only a slight effect on reducing immediate musculoskeletal pain.

Thus, while these studies indicate that alternative keyboards alter short-term postures, they do not confirm that alternative keyboards alter long term postures. Of more significance, these studies do not make the direct link between reductions in risky postures and reductions in MSS in the workplace over an extended period of time.

3.2   Effectiveness of Alternative Keyboard Designs at Reducing MSS.

There have been only seven studies that have examined alternative keyboard use in the workplace [20, 23-27], and only four were randomized clinical trials with standard keyboard control groups [20, 23, 26, 27]. The most frequently evaluated keyboard was a fixed split-angle keyboard which provides mild reductions in the roll angle and yaw angle. These trials only marginally support the use of alternative keyboards as an effective method to reduce MSS. While subjects in the alternative keyboard group demonstrated significant reductions in MSS over time, differences between groups were generally not significant [20, 23, 26], indicating that users of both keyboards, standard and alternative, improved, or there were only one or two significant results in multiple measures [26, 27], which could be an artifact of multiple statistical testing. Of these studies, only Tittiranonda and colleagues [26] examined workers with MSD-UE such as carpal tunnel syndrome and tendonitis. She found a significant difference in overall symptoms at 6 months in those using the split-angle keyboard in comparison to a standard board, but not in those using other, more angled designs.

Based on the literature, we designed a randomized, cross-over study to examine the effectiveness of one alternative keyboard design, a fixed split-angle keyboard, in reducing MSS in a real-world situation [23]. Our study, as with those cited earlier, did not strongly support the use of this alternative design for a population of symptomatic computer operators. Seventy-seven symptomatic computer operators (2 or greater pain level on a numerical rating scale from 0 to 10) were randomly assigned to receive either a fixed split-angle keyboard first or standard flat board first. After 5 months, subjects "crossed over" and received the other study keyboard for the remaining five months. Thus, all subjects used both keyboards, only the order in which they used them varied. Subjects completed weekly online discomfort surveys [28, 29], and rated the usability of each keyboard after use.

We analyzed the results as dichotomous outcomes (had MSS yes/no), as the data was not normally distributed, using generalized estimating equation (GEE) method for longitudinal data analysis. There were no significant differences between the two groups for MSS for any body part (neck, back, right and left upper extremity). Close to 100% of subjects reported MSS at the start of the study, but by 7 to 8 weeks this number had reduced to approximately one third (See Fig. 2). Even when subjects crossed over to the other study keyboard, this percentage remained essentially the same and remained level to the end. Thus, for this sample of computer operators, the fixed split-angle keyboard was no more effective at eliminating MSS than a standard flat keyboard.

We also examined subjects' perceptions of the ease of use of the fixed split-angle keyboard. We asked them to rate the usability of both keyboards on a likert scale with questions such as "This keyboard was awkward to use," "The keys on this keyboard were smooth and easy to use," and "I found it easy to adapt to this keyboard." For all usability parameters, subjects significantly preferred the standard keyboard at both baseline and follow-up. Many subjects reported that it took a month or more for them to become acclimated to the fixed split-angle design. Despite these perceptions, half the subjects indicated that, overall, they preferred the fixed split-angle keyboard to the standard keyboard [23].

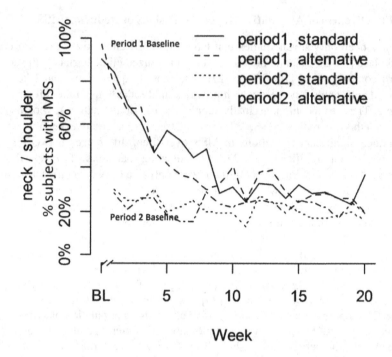

Fig. 2. Percent of subjects experiencing elimination of MSS at the neck/shoulder. Note that almost 100% of subjects started with MSS (Period 1 Baseline) and that regardless of keyboard assignment, approximately 2/3 no longer had MSS by week 7-8. This number remained essentially constant throughout the rest of the study, even with the introduction of the second keyboard (Period 2 Baseline).

We did have one intriguing outcome. There was a significant interaction effect for medication use. This interaction effect suggested that a significantly larger proportion of subjects used medication when they started with the fixed split-angle keyboard and switched to the standard keyboard (20% to 32% = 12%) than when they started with the standard keyboard and switched to the fixed split-angle keyboard (51% to 45% = 6%). Since medication use may be indicative of increased symptoms we inferred that severity of symptoms might be a moderator of the effect of the keyboards. To explore this, we completed post hoc exploratory analyses on the data of the first half of the study only. We examined if baseline symptom severity moderated the effect of type of keyboard on follow-up symptom severity. Our analyses suggested that the fixed split-angle keyboard was significantly more effective in reducing MSS for those with moderate to severe MSS at baseline than those who had none to mild MSS [30]. While these results are promising, they were only obtained on half the data, and should be interpreted with caution. More research is needed to determine if and how baseline severity affects the effectiveness of a fixed split-angle keyboard.

The results of our study exemplify the results of current research related to alternative keyboards. While laboratory studies support the ability of alternative keyboards to reduce risky postures, "real world" studies do not find an overwhelming significant benefit for alternative keyboard users. Our post hoc analyses may shed light onto why alternative keyboards are believed to be effective. For those with severe MSS, fixed split-angle keyboards may be more effective at reducing computer associated pain than standard keyboards. Thus, computer operators with significant pain, often those with actual disorders, may experience real and significant reductions of their symptoms due to an alternative keyboard. This supposition is supported by the results reported by Tittiranonda and colleagues [26], the only study that has been completed on people with actual MSD-UE.

4   Conclusions

These results offer tentative support to the adoption of alternative keyboards for those experiencing severe MSS. However, our research, and research done by others, does not really support the use of alternative keyboards for those with mild symptoms, or as a preventative measure. Given that the long acclimation period for the alternative keyboard, and that the perceived usability is less than that of the standard keyboard, clinicians should consider carefully before they prescribe an alternative keyboard as a prophylactic measure.   Further research which examines the effectiveness of alternative keyboards at reducing MSD-UE must be completed to understand under what circumstances alternative keyboards should be used. In addition, research on the effectiveness of other alternative keyboard designs in the workplace is almost non-existent. Studies examining designs that are more extreme in reducing postures or that are novel in some other way should be completed.

Acknowledgements. The author would like to acknowledge the National Institute for Occupational Safety and Health (NIOSH) (R01 OH008961) for providing funding for the alternative keyboard project reported in this paper.

References

1. Rempel, D.: The split keyboard: An ergonomic success story. Hum. Factors. 50, 385–392 (2008)
2. Kumar, S.: Theories of musculoskeletal injury causation. Ergonomics 44, 17–47 (2013)
3. Gerr, F., Monteilh, C., Marcus, M.: Keyboard use and musculoskeletal outcomes among computer users. J. Occup. Rehabil. 16, 265–277 (2006)
4. Simoneau, G., Marklin, R., Monroe, J.: Wrist and forearm postures of users of conventional computer keyboards. Hum. Factors 41, 413–424 (1999)
5. Baker, N.A., Cham, R., Cidboy, E., Cook, J., Redfern, M.: Kinematics of the fingers and hands during computer keyboard use. Clin. Biomech. 22, 34–43 (2007)
6. Sommerich, C.M., Marras, W.S., Parnianpour, M.: A quantitative description of typing biomechanics. J. Occup. Rehabil. 6, 33–55 (1996)
7. Baker, N.A., Redfern, M.: Potentially problematic postures during work site keyboard use. Am. J. Occup. Ther. 53, 386–397 (2009)

8. Baker, N.A., Cidboy, E.: The effect of three alternative keyboard designs on forearm pronation, wrist extension, and ulnar deviation: A Meta-Analysis. Am. J. Occup. Ther. 60, 40–49 (2006)

9. Baker, N.A., Cham, R., Cidboy, E., Cook, J., Redfern, M.: Digit kinematics during typing with standard and ergonomic keyboard configurations. Int. J. Ind. Ergonom. 37, 345–355 (2007)

10. Chen, C., Burastero, S., Tittiranonda, P., Hollerbach, K., Shih, M., Denhoy, R.: Quantitative evaluation of 4 computer keyboards: Wrist posture and typing performance. In: Proceedings of the Human Factors and Ergonomics Society 38th Annual Meeting. Human Factors and Ergonomics Society (1994)

11. Hedge, A., Powers, J.R.: Wrist postures while keyboarding: Effects of a negative slope keyboard system and full motion forearm supports. Ergonomics 38, 508–517 (1995)

12. Marklin, R.W., Simoneau, G.G.: Effect of setup configurations of split computer keyboards on wrist angle. Phys. Ther. 81, 1038–1048 (2001)

13. Nelson, J.E., Treaster, D.E., Marras, W.S.: Finger motion, wrist motion and tendon travel as a function of keyboard angles. Clin. Biomech. 15, 489–498 (2000)

14. Simoneau, G.G., Marklin, R.W.: Effect of computer keyboard slope and height on wrist extension angle. Hum. Factors 43, 287–298 (2001)

15. Szeto, G.P., Ng, J.: A comparison of wrist postures and forearm muscle activities while using an alternative keyboard and a standard keyboard. J. Occup. Rehabil. 10, 189–197 (2000)

16. Treaster, D.E., Marras, W.S.: An assessment of alternate keyboards using finger motion, wrist motion and tendon travel. Clin. Biomech. 15, 499–503 (2000)

17. Zecevic, A., Miller, D.I., Harburn, K.: An evaluation of the ergonomics of three computer keyboards. Ergonomics 43, 55–72 (2000)

18. Smith, M.J., Karsh, B.-T., Conway, F.T., Cohen, W.J., James, C.A., Morgan, J.J., et al.: Effects of a split keyboard design and wrist rest on performance, posture, and comfort. Hum. Factors 40, 324–336 (1998)

19. Marklin, R.W., Simoneau, G.G., Monroe, J.F.: Wrist and forearm posture from typing on split and vertically inclined computer keyboards. Hum. Factors 41, 559–569 (1999)

20. Hedge, A., Goldstein, M., Hettinger, L., Varner, C., Silva, D., Malafronte, J., et al.: Longitudinal study of the effects of an adjustable ergonomic keyboard on upper body musculoskeletal symptoms. In: Proceedings of the Human Factors and Ergonomics Society 46th Annual Meeting. Mira Digital Publishing, Baltimore (2002)

21. Nordstrom, D.L., Vierkant, R.A., Layde, P.M., Smith, M.J.: Comparison of self-reported and expert-observed physical activities at work in a general population. Am. J. Ind. Med. 34, 29–35 (1998)

22. Woods, M., Babski-Reeves, K.: Effects of negatively sloped keyboard wedges on risk factors for upper extremity work-related musculoskeletal disorders and user performance. Ergonomics 48, 1793–1808 (2005)

23. Baker, N.A., Moehling, K., Park, S.Y.: The effect of a fixed split-angle keyboard on musculoskeletal discomfort: A randomized cross-over trial. Work (submitted)

24. Ripat, J., Giesbrecht, E., Quanbury, A., Kelso, S.: Effectiveness of an ergonomic keyboard for typists with work related upper extremity disorders: A follow-up study. Work 37, 275–283 (2010)

25. Ripat, J., Scatliff, T., Giesbrecht, E., Quanbury, A., Friesen, M., Kelso, S.: The effect of alternative style keyboards on severity of symptoms and functional status of individuals with work-related upper extremity disorders. J. Occup. Rehabil. 16, 707–718 (2006)

26. Tittiranonda, P., Rempel, D.M., Armstrong, T., Burastero, S.: Effect of four computer keyboards in computer users with upper extremity musculoskeletal disorders. Am. J. Ind. Med. 35, 647–661 (1999)
27. Moore, J.S., Swanson, N.G.: The effect of alternative keyboards on musculoskeletal symptoms and disorders. In: Proceedings of the 10th International Conference on Human-Computer Interaction. Erlbaum, Mahwah (2003)
28. Gerr, F., Marcus, M., Monteilh, C., Hannan, L., Ortiz, D.J., Kleinbaum, D.: A randomised controlled trial of postural interventions for prevention of musculoskeletal symptoms among computer users. Occup. Environ. Med. 62, 478–487 (2005)
29. Rempel, D.M., Krause, N., Goldberg, R., Benner, D., Hudes, M., Goldner, G.U.: A randomised controlled trial evaluating the effects of two workstation interventions on upper body pain and incident musculoskeletal disorders among computer operators. Occup. Environ. Med. 63, 300–306 (2006)
30. Baker, N.A., Moehling, K.: The moderating effect of the severity of baseline musculoskeletal discomfort on the effect of an alternative keyboard: A 5-month randomized clinical trial. In: Human Factors and Ergonomics Society 56th Annual Meeting. Human Factors and Ergonomics Society, Boston (2012)

The Biomechanical and Physiological Effect of Two Dynamic Workstations

Juliane Botter[1], Eva-Maria Burford[1], Dianne Commissaris[2], Reinier Könemann[2], Suzanne Hiemstra-van Mastrigt[2], and Rolf Peter Ellegast[1]

[1] Institute for Occupational Safety and Health of the German Social Accident Insurance, Sankt Augustin, Germany
[2] TNO Work and Employment, Hoofddorp, The Netherlands
{juliane.botter,eva-maria.burford,rolf.ellegast}@dguv.de,
{dianne.commissaris,reinier.konemann,suzanne.hiemstra}@tno.nl

Abstract. The aim of this research paper was to investigate the effect, both biomechanically and physiologically, of two dynamic workstations currently available on the commercial market. The dynamic workstations tested, namely the Treadmill Desk by LifeSpan and the LifeBalance Station by RightAngle, were compared to the more conventional seated and standing workstations, through a randomized repeated measures design. Hypothesized was that the use of these dynamic workstations would have an effect on posture, physical activity, energy expenditure and muscular activity. Preliminary results suggest that the dynamic workstation increase physical activity and heart rate compared to the seated workstation.

Keywords: physical activity, computer work, dynamic workstations, joint angle, electromyography, energy expenditure, heart rate.

1 Introduction

As a result of numerous factors, both lifestyle and work-related, physical inactivity is becoming an increasing problem which results in an elevated risk of developing numerous health problems [1]. As a consequence of industrialization, physical workload is being reduced which results in even more of the workforce being affected by physical inactivity. The implications of this change in the nature of how work is performed, results in the traditional ergonomics paradigm of "less is better" as no longer being suitable for today's society [1].

As a result of physical inactivity, workers who maintain prolonged seated postures are at a greater risk of developing chronic diseases such as cardiovascular disorders and type II diabetes [2] as well as developing musculoskeletal disorders in the upper back and neck region [3]. The negative effects of inactivity as a result of a prolonged seated posture at work cannot be compensated by only increasing activity levels during leisure time [4]. In order to prevent the above mentioned health risks, it is necessary to find suitable means of introducing more activity into the workplace

V.G. Duffy (Ed.): DHM/HCII 2013, Part II, LNCS 8026, pp. 196–204, 2013.
© Springer-Verlag Berlin Heidelberg 2013

environment that goes beyond the extent of taking the stairs [5]. One of these potential solutions, which might increase long-term activity, is dynamic workstations which combine a computer workstation with physical activity [5].

There is only limited research-based information available on the effects that these machines can have on individuals. The effect of energy expenditure for obese office workers that a treadmill desk could have has been investigated [5]. Furthermore the effect that a walking station and a cycling workstation has on performance has been investigated by Straker et al. [6], but only limited physiological and physical measures were obtained in conjunction with the performance data.

2   Method

Through a randomized repeated measures design, the physiological and biomechanical effect of two different dynamic workstations was assessed in comparison to two more conventional workstations, namely a standing and a seated workstation. After an adaptation phase, each participant was required to complete a set of standardized tasks at each station. The order of the workstations and tasks was randomized for each participant.

The aim of this study was to determine the effect of the different workstations on physical activity, posture and muscle activation for the musculus trapezius p. descendens. The study was carried out in the laboratory under realistic VDU office conditions.

2.1   Participants

Twelve healthy participants, 6 males and 6 females, all who predominantly perform computer-based tasks as the main component of their work, volunteered. The participant group had a mean age of 38.7 years (SD 11.4 years), a mean height of 171.3 cm (SD 8.8 cm) and a mean weight of 75.0 kg (SD 15.4 kg). Participants with chronic diseases or any health problems were excluded. All procedures were explained and informed consent was obtained prior to testing.

For the EMG results, the participant group was reduced to 10 volunteers (5 males and 5 females). This sub-collective group had a mean age of 36.9 years (SD 11.0 years), a mean height of 170.4 cm (SD 9.3 cm) and a mean weight of 75.7 kg (SD 16.4 kg).

2.2   Workstations

Each dynamic workstation was assessed at two intensity levels. The Treadmill Desk TR1200-DT5 by LifeSpan was assessed at a speed of 0,6 km/h and 2,5 km/h and the

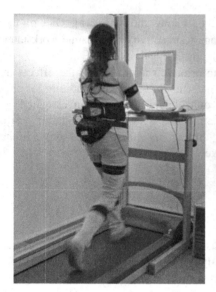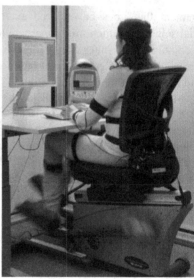

Fig. 1. The Treadmill Desk (left) and the LifeBalance Station (right) in the laboratory set-up with a participant wearing the data capturing equipment

LifeBalance Station by RightAngle was assessed at an intensity level of 4 (9 Watts) and 12 (17 Watts), both at 40 RPM. Figure 1 shows the dynamic workstations in the laboratory set-up with a participant wearing the CUELA [7] and EMG system.

2.3   Tasks

All participants performed a standardised set of five different office-based and computer tasks. The battery of tasks included a typing task, a reading task, a mouse dexterity task, a telephone task and a set of computer-based cognitive tasks. Participants were required to complete a habituation period for all tasks and workstations prior to the start of the testing phase.

2.4   Instrumentation and Measures Assessed

Physiological measures assessed included electromyography (EMG) of M. Trapezius, heart rate and indirectly-measured energy expenditure, calculated using heart rate and the formula by Strath et al. [9]. Bilaterally muscle activation for the musculus trapezius p. descendens was assessed by EMG measures using the Biomonitor ME6000 (Mega Electronics Ltd). Heart rate was recorded throughout testing using the Polar WearLink sensor and monitor model RS400.

Biomechanical measures assessed or determined included a comprehensive postural analysis and physical activity intensity index [8] for each station. The CUELA system [7] was used to determine body posture, joint angles and the acceleration of the individual body parts. The recorded values are presented as the difference to a predefined standing reference position. On the basis of the acceleration signals, the physical activity intensity index (PAI) was calculated [8] and can be considered as an indicator for body movement.

2.5   Analysis

The results were analysed using descriptive statistics and the mean, standard deviation and percentiles of the frequency distribution were calculated over all participants for each of the six stations. The results have been presented in the form of boxplots (5th, 25th, 50th, 75th and 95th percentile; the rhombus representing the mean).

The results of the posture analysis have been presented in degrees for the described joint or limb and the EMG data was normalised as the percentage of maximum voluntary contraction (%MVC). Due to the small values of the PAI, results have been presented as %g (100*absolute value). Significance testing and a more comprehensive statistical analysis are still outstanding and will be completed at a later stage.

3   Results

3.1   Muscle Activation

Figure 2 and 3 show the results of muscle activation of M. Trapezius left and right in the form of boxplots.

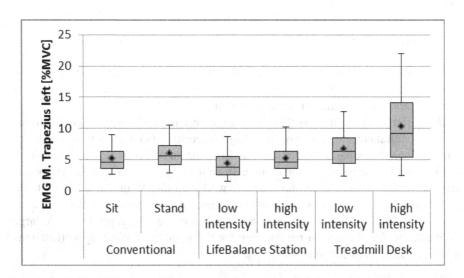

Fig. 2. Muscle activation of left Trapezius in %MVC (mean values represented by the rhombus)

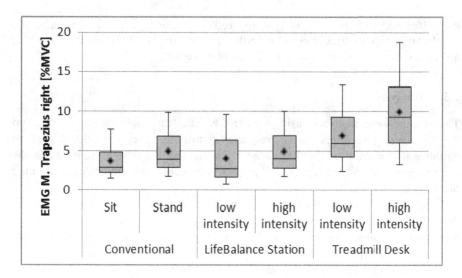

Fig. 3. Muscle activation of right Trapezius in %MVC (mean values represented by the rhombus)

The highest muscle activation was achieved on the Treadmill Desk for the high intensity condition. Figure 2 and 3 depict large differences between 5th and 95th as well as between 25th and 75th percentiles of the results. These differences are larger for both dynamic workstations and higher intensity levels when compared to conventional workstations.

3.2   Posture Analyse

Table 1 shows the 50th and 95th percentiles of the frequency distribution and the standard deviation for all workstations for the joint angles in degrees for cervical spine flexion, trunk inclination, trunk flexion and L5 inclination.

By differentiating the workstations into seated workstations (conventional sitting, LifeBalance Station low and high intensity) and standing workstations (conventional standing, Treadmill Desk low and high intensity), differences in posture can be analysed. Cervical spine flexion was predominantly lower for the standing workstations than for seated workstations. With regards to trunk inclination, a retroverted posture of the trunk in comparison to the reference position was measured for all stations except for the Treadmill Desk. A large difference in the above data can be seen for the seated and standing workstations with regards to trunk flexion.

Table 1. Joint angles (°) for cervical spine flexion, trunk inclination, trunk flexion and L5 inclination

	Conventional		LifeBalance Station		Treadmill Desk	
	Sitting	Standing	Low Intensity	High Intensity	Low Intensity	High Intensity
Cervical Spine Flexion (°)						
50%ile	8,7	5,6	9,6	10,5	8,3	8,0
	(12,4)	(6,9)	(6,9)	(6,7)	(6,9)	(4,2)
95%ile	11,5	9,6	12,0	12,7	13,8	11,6
	(12,6)	(9,6)	(6,7)	(6,5)	(8,0)	(5,3)
Trunk Inclination (°)						
50%ile	-10,1	-1,2	-11,5	-10,7	2,2	0,5
	(13,1)	(6,4)	(9,4)	(10,8)	(5,5)	(5,5)
95%ile	-7,8	1,6	-10,1	-9,2	6,2	3,2
	(13,3)	(7,8)	(9,3)	(10,7)	(6,3)	(5,9)
Trunk Flexion (°)						
50%ile	37,2	13,8	42,5	42,3	12,4	15,2
	(15,6)	(10,4)	(16,4)	(15,5)	(10,5)	(11,3)
95%ile	39,5	17,5	45,6	45,0	16,8	18,7
	(16,2)	(11,5)	(16,3)	(16,1)	(11,1)	(11,2)
L5 Inclination (°)						
50%ile	-28,4	-7,8	-32,7	-31,8	-3,9	-7,0
	(17,4)	(8,9)	(16,2)	(17,5)	(8,3)	(10,3)
95%ile	-26,2	-5,3	-31,3	-29,8	-0,3	-4,3
	(17,5)	(9,1)	(16,1)	(17,3)	(8,3)	(10,2)

3.3   Physical Activity Intensity

The results of the physical activity intensity indexes for the entire body are shown in boxplots in Figure 4.

The highest value for physical activity was, as expected, measured on the treadmill desk at the high intensity. The 50th percentile of the frequency distribution for the treadmill desk was over 12 times higher when compared to the conventional seated workstation. There was a slight increase for the LifeBalance Station compared to the conventional workstations.

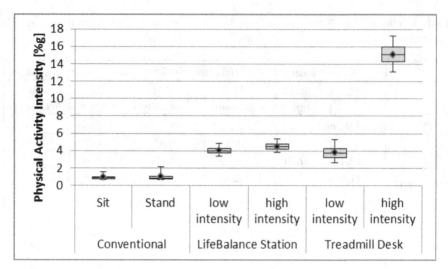

Fig. 4. Results of the physical activity intensity index for all stations in %g for the entire body (mean values represented by the rhombus)

3.4   Energy Expenditure

As shown in Figure 5, the lowest mean energy expenditure was recorded for the conventional seated workstation. For the dynamic workstations, the energy expenditure increased when compared to the seated workstations as well as for the higher intensities when compared to the lower intensities.

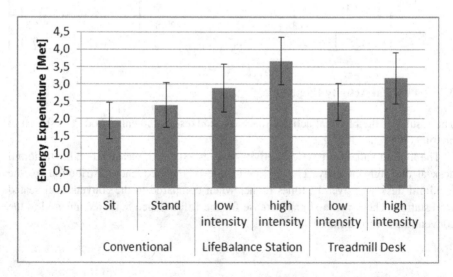

Fig. 5. Mean (and standard deviation) calculated energy expenditure for all stations in MET

4   Discussion

Significance testing and further statistical analysis has not yet been performed, therefore the following discussion will give a brief and superficial explanation for the above mentioned results.

The differences in posture with regards to trunk inclination, flexion and L5 inclination between the LifeBalance Station and the Treadmill Desk were expected. Similarly the posture resulting for both of the dynamic workstations, as expected, was comparable to the respective conventional workstations.

As reported in section 3.3 there was only a slight increase in physical activity from the lower to the higher intensity level of the LifeBalance Station. The results and differences for the PAI values for the two intensities on the LifeBalance Station were expected to be similar as to those recorded for the two intensities on the Treadmill Desk. As the physical activity was calculated on the basis of the acceleration signals and as there was no difference in RPM for the lower and higher intensity of the LifeBalance Station, the PAI only shows slight differences for this station. Despite this, there was still an increase in PAI on both dynamic workstations compared to conventional sitting. Both Thompson et al. [10] and Levine and Miller [5] have reported health benefits due to movement, even if it is only a small amount of physical activity. On the basis of the PAI results, these workstations may be able to bring more physical activity in daily office work.

As expected, the energy expenditure was greater for the dynamic workstations than for the conventional workstations. Even though the formula by Strath et al. [9] is known to overestimate energy expenditure for low strain tasks [11], it would appear, as expected, that the dynamic workstations have a higher energy expenditure than the conventional workstations. It may be possible that the presented results for the low intensities of the dynamic workstations were too high and therefore potentially the difference between the low intensity and high intensity conditions would be greater. Furthermore this would lead to a greater increase in energy expenditure for the higher intensities on the dynamic workstations in comparison to the conventional seated workstation. Due to these results, the dynamic workstations, especially the higher intensities, could be used to achieve a higher daily energy expenditure. The differences between the stations and intensity levels will be described at a later point in more detail after significance testing and more comprehensive statistical analyses have been performed.

References

1. Straker, L., Mathiassen, S.E.: Increased physical work-loads in modern work – a necessity for better health and performance? Ergonomics 52(10), 1215–1225 (2009)
2. U.S. Department of Health and Human Services: Physical Activity Guidelines for Americans (2008), http://www.health.gov/paguidelines/guidelines (last visited: October 10, 2012)

3. Sjøgaard, G., Jensen, B.R.: Low-level static exertions. In: Marras, W.S. (ed.) Fundamentals and Assessment Fools for Occupational Ergonomics, pp. 14/1-14/13. Taylor & Francis, CRC Press, Boca Raton (2006)
4. Ekblom-Bak, E., Hellénius, M.-L., Ekblom, B.: Are we facing a new paradigm of inactivity physiology? British Journal of Sports Medicine Online (February 4, 2010)
5. Levine, J.A., Miller, J.M.: The energy expenditure of using a "walk-and-work" desk for office workers with obesity. British Journal of Sports Medicine 41, 558–561 (2007)
6. Straker, L., Levine, J., Campbell, A.: The effects of walking and cycling computer workstations on keyboard and mouse performance. Human Factors: The Journal of the Human Factors and Ergonomics Society 51, 831–844 (2009)
7. Ellegast, R.P., Kraft, K., Groenesteijn, L., Kraus, F., Berger, H., Vink, P.: Comparison of four specific dynamic office chairs with a conventional office chair: impact upon muscle activation, physical activity and posture. Appl. Ergonomics 43(2), 296–307 (2012)
8. Weber, B.: Entwicklung und Evaluation eines Bewegungsmesssystems zur Analyse der physischen Aktivität (IFA-Report 2/2011). In: Dissertation, vol. 82, pp. 41–53. Deutsche Sporthochschule, Köln (2011)
9. Strath, S.J., Swartz, A.M., Bassett, D.R., O'Brien, W.L., King, G.A., Ainsworth, B.E.: Evaluation of heart rate as a method for assessing moderate intensity physical activity. Medicine & Science in Sports & Exercise 32(suppl. 9), 465–470 (2000)
10. Thompson, W.G., Foster, R.C., Eide, D.S., Levine, J.A.: Feasibility of a walking workstation to increase daily walking. British Journal of Sports Medicine 42(3), 225–228 (2008)
11. Freedson, P.S., Miller, K.: Objective monitoring of physical activity using motion sensors and heart rate. Research Quarterly for Exercise and Sport 71(suppl. 2), 21–29 (2000)

The Effect of Dynamic Workstations on the Performance of Various Computer and Office-Based Tasks

Eva-Maria Burford[1], Juliane Botter[1], Dianne Commissaris[2], Reinier Könemann[2], Suzanne Hiemstra-van Mastrigt[2], and Rolf Peter Ellegast[1]

[1] Institute for Occupational Safety and Health of the German Social Accident Insurance, Sankt Augustin, Germany
{eva-maria.burford,juliane.botter,rolf.ellegast}@dguv.de
[2] TNO Work and Employment, Hoofddorp, The Netherlands
{dianne.commissaris,reinier.konemann,suzanne.hiemstra}@tno.nl

Abstract. The effect of different workstations, conventional and dynamic, on different types of performance measures for several different office and computer based task was investigated in this research paper. The two dynamic workstations assessed were the Lifespan Treadmill Desk and the RightAngle LifeBalance Station, and the two conventional workstations assessed were a seated and a standing workstation. Through a randomized repeated measures design, the effect of these different workstations was assessed for a series of tasks consisting of a reading, typing, telephone, mouse dexterity task and a battery of computer-based cognitive tasks. Hypothesized was that the use of these dynamic workstations would have different effects on the performance measures for the different types of tasks.

Keywords: task performance, computer work, dynamic workstations, reaction time, accuracy.

1 Introduction

The importance and contribution of general physical activity to the maintenance of good health, both physically and cognitively, has become more prominent with the increased research into the negative consequences of physical inactivity [1]. Numerous lifestyle and work aspects can contribute to physical inactivity which can result in an increase in the risk of developing chronic diseases such as cardiovascular disorders and type II diabetes [1]. Additionally numerous negative effects have been associated with prolonged sitting and sedentary work, such as an increased risk of low back pain [2] and musculoskeletal disorders [3]. The negative effects of this inactivity cannot be compensated by only increasing activity levels during leisure time [4] and require alternative means of including more physical activity in daily life. A potential means of counteracting physical inactivity is that of dynamic workstations [5].

As dynamic workstations are recent additions to the commercial market, there is only limited research-based information available on the implications or effects that

V.G. Duffy (Ed.): DHM/HCII 2013, Part II, LNCS 8026, pp. 205–212, 2013.

these stations have on work performance. The spectrum of tasks where this has been investigated is limited [6-7]. As these workstations are being introduced as feasible alternatives to current workstations, the influences on performance needs to be comprehensively considered. This research paper aimed at investigating the effect on performance for various office and computer based tasks for two different dynamic workstations currently available on the commercial market. As a result of the different tasks requiring different skills and resources from the worker, it was hypothesized that the performance of different tasks would be differently affected as a result of these workstations.

2   Method

Using a randomized repeated measures design, the performance of five different basic computer and office tasks was assessed for six different workstation conditions in a laboratory under realistic VDU office settings. The six different workstation conditions consisted of two conventional workstations and two different dynamic workstations, with each dynamic workstation tested at two different intensities. The conventional workstations included seated and standing workstations, and the dynamic workstations included a treadmill station, the Treadmill Desk TR1200-DT5 by LifeSpan, and a semi-recumbent elliptical machine station, the LifeBalance Station by RightAngle. The walking workstation was assessed at a speed of 0.6km/h (WS1) and 2.5 km/h (WS2), and the semi-recumbent elliptical machine station was assessed at 40 RPM at an intensity level of 4 which resulted in 9 Watts resistance (LBS1) and an intensity level of 12 which resulted in 17 Watts resistance (LBS2). Each participant performed a randomized order of a set of standardized tasks at each station. Furthermore the order in which the workstations were assessed was randomized and each participant was required to complete a habituation phase for both the workstations and the tasks.

2.1   Tasks

The series of tasks selected for this research were aimed at simulating basic office tasks and included five different tasks, namely a typing task, a reading task, a telephone task, a mouse dexterity task and a battery of computer-based cognitive tasks. The content selected for the typing, reading and telephone tasks were set so that the difficulty level was approximately standardized and no content was repeated between the workstations for one participant. Each of these tasks had a set duration of five minutes. The reading task had on average every 100 words a character rotation, and the number of correctly identified errors and number of characters read were used as performance criteria. For the typing task, the participants were required to copy a text from a window in the top half of the computer screen to a word document situated in the bottom half of the screen and the task was assessed for both speed and accuracy. The telephone task was aimed at assessing the effect that the dynamic workstations would have on speech quality and participants were required to repeat a spoken text through a telephone. Performance was assessed by the number of words spoken and the number of errors made in the repetition. The subjective quality of the spoken text was rated with the MOS scale [8]. The mouse dexterity test, based on Fitts Law [9], consisted of two different tasks, namely one with a randomized stimulus ("Random Circles") and the second one with a predefined response pattern ("Multi-direction"). The battery of cognitive tasks consisted of a Go/No go association task [10], a subitizing task [11], an Eriksen Flanker Test [12], and a memory task. For the mouse dexterity task and each of the cognitive tasks, accuracy scores and reaction times were recorded.

2.2   Participants

Twelve volunteers, all who have VDU workstations and predominantly perform computer-based tasks as the main component of their work, agreed to participate in this study. The participant group consisted of 6 males (mean age: 39.2 SD: 10.1), with a mean height of 1,76m (± 7.3) and a mean weight of 85kg (± 11.1), and 6 females (mean age: 38.2 SD: 13.5), with a mean height of 1,66m (± 7.7) and a mean weight of 65kg (± 12.5). Participants with any health problems, acute or chronic, were excluded.

2.3   Analysis

The results have been preliminarily analysed using descriptive statistics. The mean and standard deviation were calculated over all participants for each of the six workstation conditions. A comprehensive inferential statistical analysis is still outstanding and will be completed at a later point. Consequently the results in this paper are only described and no explicit conclusions can be drawn.

3   Results

3.1   Reading Task

Reading was assessed by means of speed (the number of characters read) and accuracy (the number of correctly identified characters). Figure 1 depicts these results. The most characters read were at the workstation WS2 (7070 characters) and the least number of characters were read at workstation WS1 (6556 Characters). The most identified errors occurred at the workstation LBS2, followed by the conventional seated workstation with a 0.1% difference. The workstation WS1 had the worst score with the least percent of errors identified. For both workstations LBS1 and LBS2, similar sores and variations were obtained despite the differences in intensity levels.

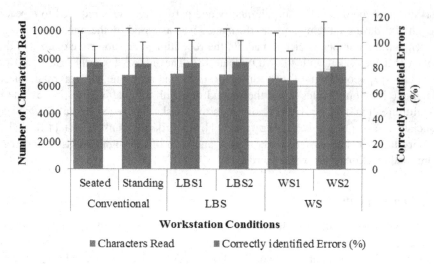

Fig. 1. The mean number of characters read and the percent of errors correctly identified for the reading task for each of the workstation conditions (Standard Deviation)

3.2   Typing Task

The performance results, in the form of characters typed, as seen in Figure 2, was best for the conventional standing workstation (908.2 characters) and worst for the workstation WS2 (815.8 characters). The mean characters typed at the seated and LBS 2 workstations only differed minimally (a difference of 1.3 characters type). With regards to accuracy, the best mean performance was for the conventional standing workstation (10.8 errors), followed by the conventional seated workstation (12.2 errors). The most errors were recorded for the workstation WS2 (18.8 errors).

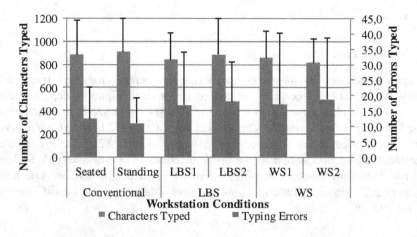

Fig. 2. The mean number of characters and errors typed for the typing task for each of the workstation conditions (Standard Deviation)

3.3 Telephone Task

From the results in Table 1, it is visible that with regards to the mean performance results, the workstation conditions did not strongly differ from one another. The mean percent of errors spoken for all the workstations did not show large differences, with all mean values being approximately 6% despite large standard deviations. The smallest mean percent of errors was obtained for the LBS2 workstation (6.0%) and the largest was for the LBS1 workstation (6.77%).

The results from the subjective evaluation of the speech quality using the MOS scale yielded scores for all the workstations between 4 and 5. At a rating of 4 the speech quality is defined as good with the level of distortion being perceptible but not annoying. A rating of 5 defines the speech quality as excellent and the level of distortion as imperceptible. For both of the high intensities of the dynamic workstations, the worst rating on the MOS scale for the workstations was obtained.

Table 1. The mean number of words that were spoken, the percent of errors that occurred in the spoken text and the MOS scale rating for each of the workstations (Standard deviation)

	Conventional		LBS		WS	
	Seated	Standing	LBS1	LBS2	WS1	WS2
Words	450.0	461.7	451.8	453.7	456.4	456.2
Spoken	(47.3)	(38.1)	(46.2)	(45.0)	(32.8)	(40.6)
Errors	6.2	6.5	6.8	6.0	6.3	6.7
(%)	(4.9)	(6.5)	(5.4)	(3.4)	(4.9)	(6.2)
MOS	4.8	4.9	4.7	4.3	4.8	4.6
Scale	(0.4)	(0.3)	(0.3)	(0.8)	(0.4)	(0.5)

3.4 Mouse Dexterity Task

The mean results for the reaction time and score obtained for the two mouse dexterity tasks for each workstation condition are depicted in Table 2.

Table 2. Mean reaction time (ms) and score for the two mouse dexterity tasks for each of the workstation conditions (Standard deviation)

Mouse Dexterity Task	Performance Criteria	Conventional		LBS		WS	
		Seated	Standing	LBS1	LBS2	WS1	WS2
Multi-direction	Reaction time	696.0	706.1	715.9	726.7	748.8	804.7
		(114.9)	(114.4)	(139.9)	(116.9)	(125.7)	(113.9)
	Score	1240.6	1243.8	1181.5	1175.5	1165.4	1034.3
		(158.3)	(75.0)	(72.8)	(98.4)	(94.6)	(88.9)
Random Circles	Reaction time	610.5	643.6	652.2	655.4	662.0	697.8
		(101.9)	(112.4)	(110.8)	(103.6)	(105.2)	(114.4)
	Score	1162.9	1147.3	1140.3	1119.4	1109.0	1074.7
		(67.6)	(76.3)	(87.3)	(64.3)	(79.4)	(70.9)

For both of the mouse dexterity tasks, the fastest mean reaction time was for the seated workstation, with 696.0 ms (±114.9) and 610.5 ms (±101.9) for the task "Multi-direction" and "Random Circles" respectively. The slowest mean reaction time was recorded for the workstation WS2, with 804.7 ms (±113.9) and 697.8 ms (±114.4) for the task "Multi-direction" and "Random Circles" respectively.

3.5   Cognitive Tasks

The mean results for reaction time and accurracy for each of the cognitive tasks for each workstation condition are depicted in Table 3. The mean reaction time for the Go/No-go task for each of the workstations was between 383.3 ms and 419.0 ms, with the quickest mean reaction time recorded for the standing workstation and the slowest for the workstation WS1. With regards to accurracy, the lowest score was obtained for the seated workstation and the highest was for the workstation LBS1. For the subitizing task, the mean reaction time was the slowest for the seated workstation (997.6 ms) and the quickest for the LBS2 workstation (929.8 ms). Both of the high intensity dynamic workstations obtained the highest percent of correct responses, namely 84.6% for the WS2 workstation and 82.5% for the LBS2 workstation.

Table 3. Mean reaction time (ms) and accuracy score (%) for all the cognitive tasks for.each of the workstation conditions. (Standard deviation)

Task	Performance Criteria	Conventional		LBS		WS	
		Seated	Standing	LBS1	LBS2	WS1	WS2
Go/No-Go	Reaction time	394.3 (55.1)	383.3 (79.1)	405.2 (46.3)	399.8 (56.0)	419.0 (57.3)	404.7 (40.0)
	Accurracy (%)	94.6 (5.4)	95.1 (5.6)	98.5 (2.9)	94.8 (3.1)	96.1 (4.7)	96.9 (3.0)
Subitizing Task	Reaction time	997.6 (83.5)	978.2 (124.5)	959.8 (132.6)	929.8 (96.1)	983.2 (84.2)	939.0 (100.7)
	Accurracy (%)	80.5 (8.2)	80.0 (11.5)	82.1 (9.8)	82.5 (8.7)	80.3 (11.7)	84.6 (8.7)
Eriksen Flanker	Reaction time: Congruent	494.6 (78.1)	470.9 (80.0)	497.0 (96.5)	472.3 (71.4)	487.4 (64.8)	474.6 (78.8)
	Reaction time: Incongruent	545.4 (86.8)	516.0 (84.1)	555.3 (136.8)	514.5 (63.1)	520.7 (58.5)	523.4 (92.8)
	Accurracy (%)	99.2 (1.9)	97.9 (2.5)	98.3 (2.4)	98.3 (2.4)	98.8 (2.2)	98.3 (2.4)
Working Memory	Reaction time	688.7 (107.5)	682.0 (131.0)	721.3 (102.2)	681.3 (109.8)	709.7 (108.5)	695.0 (130.5)
	Accurracy (%)	76.7 (11.2)	79.8 (16.5)	74.9 (8.1)	83.1 (9.5)	84.8 (9,4)	76.6 (11.1)

For the Erikson Flanker test, for all workstations the mean congruent reaction time was less than the mean incongruent reaction time. The quickest mean congruent reaction time was measured for the standing workstation (470.9 ms), with the slowest measured for the LBS1 workstation (497.0 ms). The quickest mean incongruent reaction time was measured for the LBS2 workstation (514.5 ms), with the slowest measured for the LBS1 workstation (555.3 ms). The highest percent of correct responses was obtained for the seated workstation (99.2%) and the lowest was for the standing workstation (97.9%). The accuracy for this task also had the smallest standard deviations for the workstations compared to the standard deviations for the accuracy of the other tasks. The quickest mean reaction time for the memory test was recorded for the LBS2 workstation (681.3 ms) and the slowest was for the LBS1 workstation (721.3 ms). The highest percent of correct responses was recorded for the WS1 workstation (84.8%), and the lowest was for the LBS1 workstation (74.9%).

Noticeable was that for all tasks, the mean reaction times were higher for the lower intensity than the higher intensity for both the LBS and the WS workstations with exception to the incongruent reaction time of the Erikson Flanker test at the WS workstations. With regards to percent of correct responses, each workstation condition except the workstation LBS2 and the standing workstation, had the highest accurracy for one of the cognitive tasks.

4   Discussion

In this research, a group of basic tasks which contribute to daily office work was assessed to determine the effect of the type of workstation they were performed at for several different performance characteristics. As the inferential statistical analysis has not yet been completed, the results can only be very briefly and generally discussed.

For reading, the workstation that yielded the least characters read and least number of correctly identified errors was the WS1 but the most characters read were for the workstation WS2 and the most identified errors was for the workstation LBS2.

The lowest mean performance results for both the typing and the mouse dexterity tasks of the workstation WS2 may be attributed to biomechanical factors. During walking, specifically at the higher speed when compared to the workstation WS1, the individual was less stable as a result of the small movements of the upper trunk produced during walking [13], and despite supporting the upper limbs on the treadmill desk, the upper limb fine motor movements were affected and consequently both speed and accuracy were impaired.

The mean performance values, for both of the mouse dexterity tasks, for the LBS workstations were not as low as for the WS stations, which may also be explained by biomechanical factors. Potentially as a result of the backrest and that the upper body may have moved less during cycling at the LBS workstations, and a more stable base may have been provided in the seated position than during walking [13].

The performance results, both objective and subjective, for the telephone task, did not show large differences between the workstations and these differences may even prove to be negligible with further statistical analysis.

Available literature provides contradicting information regarding the effect of moderate and acute exercise on basic cognitive processes [6-7]. The mean descriptive results from the cognitive tasks appear confounding as some tasks obtained a higher performance score with regards to accuracy or reaction time at the dynamic workstations and some at the conventional workstations. This may have been as a result of the different task demands between the cognitive tasks. For all of the above described results, more comprehensive statistical analyses are required before drawing substantial conclusions.

5   Conclusion

Numerous studies have shown that physical activity not only promotes physical health but may also be associated with a long term positive effect on cognitive ability. This further highlights the need to incorporate physical activity more in everyday life. Pending further statistical analysis, this research may have practical implications by contributing to the knowledge required for providing guidelines for implementing these types of workstations into the work environment and determining the most suitable type of work to perform at these types of workstations.

References

1. Straker, L., Mathiassen, S.E.: Increased physical work-loads in modern work – a necessity for better health and performance? Ergonomics 52(10), 1215–1225 (2009)
2. Todd, A.I., Bennett, A.I., Christie, C.J.: Physical implications of pronologed sitting in a confined posture – a literature review. Journal of the Ergonomics Society of South Africa 19(2), 7–21 (2007)
3. Carter, J.B., Banister, E.W.: Musculoskeletal problems at VDT work: A review. Ergonomics 37, 1623–1648 (1994)
4. Ekblom-Bak, E., Hellénius, M.-L., Ekblom, B.: Are we facing a new paradigm of inactivity physiology? British Journal of Sports Medicine Online (February 4, 2010)
5. Levine, J.A., Miller, J.M.: The energy expenditure of using a "walk-and-work" desk for office workers with obesity. British Journal of Sports Medicine 41, 558–561 (2007)
6. Straker, L., Levine, J., Campbell, A.: The effects of walking and cycling computer workstations on keyboard and mouse performance. Human Factors: The Journal of the Human Factors and Ergonomics Society 51, 831–844 (2009)
7. Tomporowski, P.D.: Effects of acute bouts of exercise on cognition. Acta Psychologica 112, 297–324 (2003)
8. Gu, L., Harris, J.G., Shrivatav, R., Sapienza, C.: Disordered speech assessment using automatic methods based on quantitative measures. EURASIP Journal on Applied Signal Processing 9, 1400–1409 (2005)
9. Fitts, P.M.: The information capacity of the human motor system in controlling the amplitude of movement. Journal of Experimental Psychology 47(6), 381–391 (1954)
10. Nosek, B.A., Banaji, M.R.: The go/no-go association task. Social Cognition 19(6), 625–666 (2001)
11. Simon, T., Cabrera, A., Kliegl, R.: A new approach to the study of subitizing as distinct enumeration. In: 15th Annual Conference of the Cognitive Science Society, June 18-21, pp. 929–934. Institute of Cognitive Science, Erlbaum (1993)
12. Eriksen, B.A., Eriksen, E.W.: Effects of noise letters upon the identification of a target letter in a nonsearch task. Perception & Psychophysics 16(1), 143–149 (1974)
13. Winter, D.A.: Human balance and posture control during standing and walking. Gait and Posture 3, 193–214 (1995)

Evaluating Comfort Levels of a Workstation with an Individually Controlled Heating and Lighting System

Elsbeth M. de Korte[1,2,*], Lottie F.M. Kuijt-Evers[1], Marleen Spiekman[1],
Linda Hoes-van Oeffelen[1], Bianca van der Zande[3], Gilles Vissenberg[3],
and Gerard Huiskes[4]

[1] TNO, Hoofddorp, The Netherlands
{elsbeth.dekorte,lottie.kuijt,marleen.spiekman,
linda.hoes}@tno.nl
[2] Delft University of Technology, Faculty Industrial Design Engineering, Delft,
The Netherlands
[3] Philips Research, Eindhoven, The Netherlands
{gilles.vissenberg,bianca.van.der.zande}@philips.com
[4] Koninklijke Ahrend, Sint Oedenrode, The Netherlands
ghuiskes@ahrend.com

Abstract. Comfort complaints, such as high or low temperatures, lack of privacy and concentration loss, are regularly reported in today's offices. Most comfort aspects, such as lighting, ventilation, decoration and climate are regulated on global level, while for optimal comfort experience customized settings on personal level is desired, which requires a more direct personal control. A method is described to evaluate comfort levels of a workstation with individually controlled radiant heating and lighting. The aim is to examine the band-width of peoples' comfort zone of radiant temperature and illumination when doing office work.

Keywords: Office, personal environmental control, workstation, heating, lighting, comfort, energy efficiency, intelligent building.

1 Introduction

Increasingly, workplaces must support rapid technology development and implementation and meet continuous changing work demands of the modern knowledge worker. Measures such as teleworking, open plan offices and working with shared work-stations have been positioned as providing at least partial solutions to many of these challenges (Lee & Brand, 2005; De Croon et al, 2005).

Comfort is rated as one of the most important factors at the office. Ambient features of the environment, like lighting, temperature, noise, presence of windows, have an important influence on attitude, behavior, satisfaction and performance of

---

* Corresponding author.

V.G. Duffy (Ed.): DHM/HCII 2013, Part II, LNCS 8026, pp. 213–222, 2013.

workers (Bauer et al., 2003; Lee & Brand, 2005; Hedge et al., 2009). However, many problems with open offices have been documented, such as noise, lack of privacy, thermal discomfort and concentration loss (Zhang et al, 2010; Lee & Brand, 2005). Apart from office chair, desk and computer settings, the current workplace fits badly with the personal needs and preferences. So far, research has been guided by the search for a universally applicable set of optimum comfort conditions in the working environment. (Cole & Brown, 2011). Most comfort aspects in the current environments, such as lighting, ventilation, decoration and climate are regulated on global level. However, for optimal comfort experience customized settings on a local, personal level is desired.

One of the focusses of 'Intelligent Building research' is using intelligence to provide occupant comfort, wherein a building explicitly enables its users to make appropriate adjustments in their local environmental conditions and at the same time providing and maintaining operational efficiencies in energy use. The challenge for designers and manufacturers is then to support these users with appropriate, ergonomic and understandable user interfaces (Cole & Brown, 2011). Increased personal control over the environment conditions can be realized by providing just acceptable environmental conditions on global level combined with personal fine-tuning on local workstation level. The essence is that on all the settings of light, climate, sound and atmosphere the greatest possible shift is pursued from averaged, spatial settings to individual, local settings. A first example of such a system with individual ventilation at workplace level based on research of Melikov (2004), is on the market.

The scientific literature gives evidence that providing personal control over the working environment (e.g., adjustment of lighting, temperature and air movement) has beneficial effects on comfort, job satisfaction and productivity (Lee and Brand 2005; Bauer ea, 2003; Hedge ea, 2009; Zhang et al., 2010; Veitch et al., 2008). However, in some studies no effects or negative effects are reported as well: e.g. Boyce et al. (2006) found no effects and Veitch & Gifford (1996) found that giving personal control over lighting conditions led to slower work and lower productivity. In this context, it is important to distinguish between real personal control (the availability and the ease of use of the aspects that one can modify in the physical environment) and the experienced control (the experienced personal influence, the importance of the impact and consequences of the use of this influence). The interaction with the environment is an essential part and various factors such as behavior, attitude, (intuitive) design and ease of use play a role in the actual use and proper use of individually controlled environments (Hedge, 2009).

Research on the effects of providing personal control of environmental conditions is in its infancy. Although literature suggest that personal control of environmental conditions is beneficial for productivity, comfort and health, up until now these are not investigated in detail. There is little information on the triggers for exercising personal control over the environmental conditions and on the behavior of personal control over time when office workers are provided with the freedom to adjust their local environmental conditions (Hedge, 2009). There is a need for clarity on aspects such as the values office workers choose and how it affects work performance and comfort experience.

The objectives of the study are to identify the potential of a local individually controlled environment to increase comfort experience and simultaneously maintain or decrease energy use, to study office workers response to the system and to identify design characteristics important for application in practice. This paper describes the method to evaluate comfort levels of a workstation with individually controlled radiant heating and lighting. The aim is to examine the band-width of peoples' preferred comfort zone of radiant temperature and illumination when doing office work. It is intended to find out whether the preferred radiant temperature and illumination differs for different initial values at local and global room level and whether personal fine-tuning affects comfort and task performance.

2   Methods

2.1   Experimental Setting

The experiment takes place in a climate room which looks like an ordinary office room. However, to assure a standard situation regarding lighting, the windows are blinded. The base air temperature is kept on 18°C and the room is lit by indirect lighting. A prototype of a workstation with individually controllable local radiant heating and lighting (Figure 1) is positioned in the middle of the room, in such a way that the participants face the door (Figure 2).

The heating system consists of radiant panels which are fixed in front of the participant under the desk and at trunk height. The lighting system is mounted above the desk (2 meters above floor) and consists of dimmable TL lights, which provides direct light on the desktop. The participants are able to adjust the radiant temperature and the illumination level of the local system by pushing a "plus" or "minus" button in a computer screen, without knowing the current radiant temperature or illumination level or contrast level. The color of the desk surface is: RAL 9010. The color temperature of the light (direct and indirect) is 3000K.

2.2   Experimental Design

Radiant Heating

The basic air temperature (T_{air} [°C]) in the experimental room is 18°C, which is lower than comfortable for a sitting person, but reasonable when walking around. The participant, who performs standardized tasks sitting, has the possibility to tune the temperature at his work space by means of local radiant heating panels. The radiant temperature (T_{rad} [°C]) and the air temperature (T_{air} [°C]) at the work space together result in the operational temperature (T_{op} [°C]) at the work space.

In the experimental design of the radiant heating there is one independent parameter: the initial value of the operational temperature ($T_{op;ini}$ [°C]) at the work space. In the experiment two initial values were tested, a low and a high initial value, respectively 18°C and 23°C (Table 1).

Table 1. Initial operational temperature $T_{op;ini}$ at global workspace level, dependent on the air temperature T_{air} and initial radiation temperature $T_{rad;ini}$ due to the radiant panels

$T_{op;ini}$ [°C]		T_{air} [°C]
		18
$T_{rad;ini}$ [°C]	Low (off)	18
	High	23

There are 3 dependent variables:

- The preferred operational temperature ($T_{op;pref}$ [°C]) at the work space; this is the temperature which was tuned by the participant by turning the local radiant heater up or down.
- The difference between the comfort level before and after tuning.
- The difference between performance level before and after tuning.

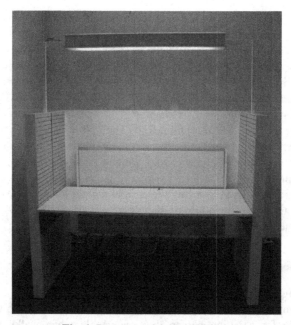

Fig. 1. Prototype of the workstation

Illuminance

The experiment room is lit by indirect light with a relative low basic illuminance level (E_{indir} [Lux]), that is too low for working comfortably. The participant is able to increase the illuminance level at his desk via direct light (E_{dir} [Lux]). The indirect illuminance (E_{indir} [Lux]) and the direct illuminance (E_{dir} [Lux]) at the work space together result in the operational illuminance level (E_{op} [Lux]) at the work space.

In the experimental design of the illuminance experiment there were two independent (2X2) parameters (Table 2):

- The indirect illuminance level (E_{indir} [Lux]), which were 150 lux and 300 lux respectively,
- And the initial value of the direct luminance level (E_{dir} [Lux]) at the work space, of which the latter is expressed in the resulting operational illuminance level ($E_{op;ini}$ [Lux]) at the work space, which were 150 or 300 Lux at the low level (depending on the indirect component) and 3000 Lux at the high level.

Table 2. Initial operational illuminance $E_{op;ini}$ at work space, dependent on the indirect illuminance level E_{indi} and initial direct illuminance level $E_{dir;ini}$ due to the direct light

$E_{op;ini}$ [Lux]		E_{indir}[Lux]	
		Low: 150	High: 300
$E_{dir;ini}$	Low (off)	150	300
[Lux]	High	3000	3000

There are 3 dependent variables:

- The preferred operational illuminance level ($E_{op;pref}$ [Lux]) at the work space; this is the illuminance level which was tuned by the participant by turning the direct lighting up or down.
- The difference between the comfort level before and after tuning.
- The difference between performance level before and after tuning.

2.3   Subjects

Twenty subjects will participate in the study. They are aged between the 35-45 years. The subjects wear a jeans, a cotton long sleeve or blouse, socks and shoes.

2.4   Task

The subjects perform a dual visual memory task as described by Capa et al. (2008). During 3 seconds a letters is shown on the computer screen. The participants have to compare this letter with four letters in a recognition set, which is on the screen for 3 seconds. The goal is to indicate if the letter in the memory set is in the recognition set by pressing the "yes" key or -if the letters is not in the recognition set- by pushing the "no" key with the right and left index finger respectively. The "yes" and "no" key are the ctrl keys at the right and the left of the space bar of a computer keyboard. The keys are indicated with a green (along with the written text "yes") and red label (along with the written text "no") respectively. The participants also have 3 seconds to answer. The recognition set changes every time and the probability that a letter appears in the recognition set or not is equal. At the end of each trial, participants receive feedback on their reaction time, which concerns the response speed and the type of error. To increase the difficulty of the task, a counting task is added. The recognition set is presented in either red or green color. Participants are asked to count the number of red recognition sets while carrying out the visual memory search task.

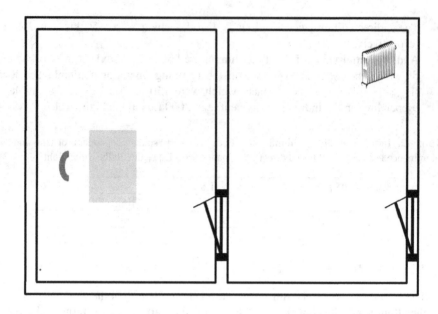

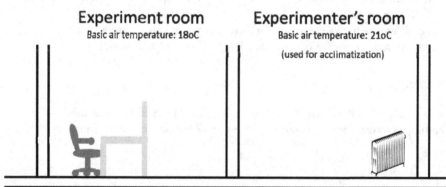

Experiment room
Basic air temperature: 18oC

Experimenter's room
Basic air temperature: 21oC

(used for acclimatization)

Fig. 2. Experimental setup

One condition consists of 64 trials. Each condition has a fixed number of red recognition sets. Participants are instructed to react as quickly as possible without making errors. Simultaneously, they have to count the number of red recognition sets. At the end of each block of 64 trials, the participants have to indicate the number of red recognition sets. After that, they receive feedback on their performance for both the visual memory search task (average reaction speed and number of errors) as well as the counting task (correct number of red recognition sets).

2.5   Hypotheses

The hypotheses are formulated for radiant temperature (RT), illuminance (I) or both (RT&I) and are divided in three categories:

Hypotheses on the Differences in Preferred Tuning Levels:

H1. There will be intra-subjective differences among the preferred level of tuning (RT&I)

H2. Inter-subjective differences will be larger than intra-subjective differences (RT&I)

H3. The preferred level of tuning of the radiant temperature by the participant is dependent on the initial value of the radiant temperature (RT)

H4. The preferred level of tuning of the direct local illuminance level by the participant is dependent on the initial value of the direct local illuminance level (I)

H5. The preferred level of tuning of the direct local illuminance level by the participant is dependent on the initial value of the indirect room illuminance level. (I)

Hypotheses on the Differences in Perceived level of Comfort:

H6. Measured comfort level is higher after fine-tuning than before. (RT&I)

H7. The comfort level after fine-tuning isn't dependent of the initial value of the radiant temperature. (RT)

H8. The comfort level after fine-tuning isn't dependent of the initial value of the direct local illuminance level. (I)

H9. The comfort level after fine-tuning is dependent of the initial value of the indirect room illuminance level. (I)

Hypotheses on the Differences in Task Performance

H10. Task performance is higher after fine-tuning than before. (RT&I)

H11. Task performance after fine-tuning isn't dependent of the initial value of the radiant temperature. (RT)

H12. Task performance after fine-tuning isn't dependent of the initial value of the direct local illuminance level. (I)

H13. Task performance after fine-tuning isn't dependent of the initial value of the indirect room illuminance level (I)

2.6 Measurements

Temperature

Three types of temperatures are relevant in the experiment: the air temperature T_{air}, the radiant temperature T_{rad} and the operational temperature T_{op}. During the experiment the air temperature is measured continuously in the middle of the room and under the desk, using a shielded air thermometer. The radiant temperature is measured continuously near the participant, using a black-globe thermometer. The total radiant panel power (P_{rad} [W]) is calculated on the basis of a pre-established calibration curve.

The initial and preferred operational temperature $T_{op;ini}$ and $T_{op;pref}$ are a function of the total radiant panel power (P_{rad} [W]). The relation between the total radiant panel power and the operational temperature is calibrated before the experiment. The operational temperature is calculated as the average between the air temperature and the radiant temperature. To produce the calibration curve, the air and radiant temperature are measured at the participant's empty seat.

Illuminance

Using a Hagner lux meter, the operational illuminance (E_{op} [Lux]) is measured at the desk and in the room, using a Hagner lux meter. Also the total direct lighting power (P_{light} [W]) is measured. These parameters are calculated on the basis of a pre-established calibration curve.

The initial and preferred operational illuminance levels $E_{op;ini}$ and $E_{op;pref}$ are a function of total direct lighting power (P_{light} [W]). The relation between the total direct lighting power and the operational illuminance levels at the desk are calibrated before the experiment for the two indirect illuminance levels that are used in the experiment (150 respectively 300 Lux, also measured at the desk). Also the consequence of the ratio of direct and indirect illuminance on the luminance differences in the room are recorded before the experiment, using a photo camera.

Comfort

Subjective measurements of thermal and visual comfort are performed using questionnaires. Thermal sensation is measured in general and for separate body parts (head, neck, trunk, upper arms, lower arms, hands, upper legs, lower legs, feet), using a VAS scale with verbal anchors on both sides, ranging from too cold to too warm. Thermal comfort is measured using a 4 point scale, ranging from very uncomfortable to comfortable. Visual comfort is measured using questions concerning various aspects of visual perception, also using VAS scales. Comfort is measured before and after tuning of the temperature and illuminance by the participants.

Task Performance

The task performance is indicated by the output of the dual visual memory task (Capa, 2008). The average response time and the number of errors, as well as the correct number of red recognition sets is used as indication for task performance.

2.7   Measurement Protocol

The participant is welcomed in the research lab. During 20 minutes he acclimatizes in a room with a temperature of 21°. During this period, the participant is informed about the study and general participant information is collected. Furthermore, he gets acquainted with the dual visual memory task to avoid learning effects. After the acclimatization, the participant goes in the experimental room and takes place at the workstation (the initial values of the radiation temperature and local illumination are set by the experimenter just before the participant enters the room). The seat and desk are adjusted to the participants anthropometry. Then, the participant sits behind the desk performing a standard reading task. After 15 minutes, the dual visual memory task is performed and the comfort questionnaire is filled in. After 30 minutes, the participant is allowed to adjust the radiation temperature and local illumination according to his preference, while sitting behind the desk and performing a standard reading task. After 45 minutes, the dual visual memory task is performed again followed by the comfort questionnaires. This is repeated three more times for different initial values for radiation temperature and indirect and direct illumination. The different initial conditions are counterbalanced over the participants.

2.8   Data Analysis

GLM repeated measures is carried out using SPSS in order to test the hypotheses.

3   Conclusion

This article merely proposed a method to evaluate comfort levels of a workstation with an individually controlled heating and lighting system. When the applied principles of personal environmental control indeed increases comfort levels, such a work station concept may yield significant progress on personal environmental wellbeing of office workers. Results on the interdependency between preferred and initial values of radiant temperature and illumination give input for the design of individually controlled systems for heating and lighting. Results will be presented at the conference.

Acknowledgments. This publication was supported by the Dutch Ministry of Economic Affairs, Koninklijke Ahrend and Philips.

References

1. Lee, S.Y., Brand, J.L.: Effects of control over office workspace on perceptions of the work environment and work outcomes. Journal of Environmental Psychology 25, 323–333 (2005)
2. de Croon, E., Sluiter, J., Kuijer, P.P., Frings-Dresen, M.: The effect of office concepts on worker health and performance: a systematic review of the literature. Ergonomics 48(2), 119–134 (2005)
3. Bauer, W., Lozano-Ehlers, I., Greisle, A., Hube, G., Keiter, J., Rieck, A.: Office 21–Push for the future better performance in innovative working environments. Fraunhofer, Cologne/Stuttgart (2003)
4. Hedge, A., Khalifa, E., Zhang, J.: On the control of environmental conditions using personal ventilation systems. In: Proceedings of the Human Factors and Ergonomics and Ergonomics Society (2009)
5. Zhang, H., Arens, E., Kim, D., Buchberger, E., Bauman, F., Huizenga, C.: Comfort, perceived air quality, and work performance in a low-power task-ambient conditioning system. Building and Environment 45, 29–39 (2010)
6. Cole, R.J., Brown, Z.: Reconciling human and automated intelligence in the provision of occupant comfort. Intelligent Buildings International 1(1), 39–55 (2009)
7. Melikov, A.K.: Personalized ventilation. Indoor Air 14, 157–167 (2004)

8. Veitch, J.A., Newsham, G.R., Boyce, P.R., Jones, C.C.: Lighting appraisal, well-being and performance in open-plan offices: A linked mechanisms approach. Lighting Res. Technol. 40, 133–151 (2008)
9. Boyce, P.R., Veitch, J.A., Newsham, G.R., Jones, C.C., Heerwagen, J., Myer, M., Hunter, C.M.: Lighting quality and office work: Two field simulation experiments. Lighting Research & Technology 38, 191–223 (2006)
10. Veitch, J.A., Gifford, R.: Choice, perceived control, and performance decrements in the physical environment. Journal of Environmental Psychology 16, 269–276 (1996)
11. Capa, R.L., Audiffren, M., Ragot, S.: The interactive effect of achievement motivation and task difficulty on mental effort. Int. J. Psychophysiol. 70(2), 144–150 (2008)

Assessment of Body Surface Potential Mapping in VDT-Operators

Anna Janocha[1], Marcin Grabowski[1], Witold Pilecki[2], Robert Skalik[1],
Krystyna Laszki-Szczączhor[2], Ewa Janocha[3], Piotr Frąszczak[4],
and Małgorzata Sobieszczańska[2]

[1] Department of Physiology
Department of Pathophysiology
Medical University of Wroclaw, Poland
[2] The Czerniakowski Hospital, Warsaw, Poland
[3] Central Clinical Hospital of the Ministry of Interior, Warsaw, Poland
anna.janocha@umed.wroc.pl

Abstract. Computer is a genius invention that has made human work more efficient. In spite of undeniable benefits, everyday long-term contact with computer screens is an occupational risk, which induces various undesirable health consequences. Exposure of the VDT-operators to the harmful occupational factors may lead to functional disorders like arrhythmia. BSPM is a diagnostic method enabling global and precise sampling the heart potentials all over the thoracic surface owing to the large number of recording electrodes. Data collected from 87 ECG waveforms is graphically presented as the body surface maps of various formats. Non-dipolar distribution of QRST isointegral maps reflects a heterogeneity of the refractory periods of the ventricles, which is supposed to account for creating a substrate for malignant and life-threatening arrhythmias. This method can be a specific indicator of the increased risk of severe ventricular arrhythmias occurring prior to abnormalities detectable on the standard 12-lead ECG recordings.

Keywords: VDT-operators, BSPM, QRST maps, ventricular arrhythmias.

1 Introduction

Computer and Internet are genius inventions that attracted millions of people from all over the world and made human work more efficient. In spite of undeniable benefits, computer revolution is assumed to endanger human health. Sight exposure to electromagnetic irradiation is the most frequently mentioned negative factor. However, it is often forgotten that there is a whole gamut of negative computer-related factors, like forced slouching position in front of the computer screen and the others, which may lead to functional disorders within the cardiac conductive system resulting in cardiac symptoms like arrhythmia (Janocha et al, 2003).

Body surface potential mapping (BSPM) is a diagnostic method which enables global and precise sampling the heart potentials all over the thoracic surface owing to the large number of the recording electrodes. The results of BSPM examinations are

V.G. Duffy (Ed.): DHM/HCII 2013, Part II, LNCS 8026, pp. 223–231, 2013.

displayed graphically in the form of so-called "heart maps" which comprise three different types: isopotential, isointegral and isochrones maps. The first kind of map shows a distribution of the instant heart potential over the thorax, the second one depicts resultant potential fluctuations occurring within the given time intervals of the cardiac cycle (area under the ECG curve) and the third type reflects the propagation of the heart depolarization over the thoracic surfaces in time. In the present study, we used isointegral maps. BSPM is of advantage over the conventional ECG in relation to a selective assessment of the individual portions of the heart and enables a detection of local electrical events unavailable with the standard precordial leads (Sobieszczańska, 2005). The BSPM method, holding its unique spatial sensitivity to the regional cardiac events, which is caused by the large number of the exploring electrodes, could be used as a complementary procedure for detecting local electrical events. In particular, a sequence of activation and repolarization of the heart in the entire cardiac cycle, which is presented in the maps as a migration of the positive and negative potential areas of specific distribution over the entire thorax, seems to be of great importance while a significant increase in incidence of malignant ventricular arrhythmias in the population of VDT-operators is observed. Non-dipolar distribution of QRST isointegral maps can be a specific indicator of the increased risk of severe ventricular arrhythmias in this population (Abildskov, 1987).

The aim of the present study was to investigate possible intraventricular conduction disturbances in VDT-operators using QRST isointegral maps.

2   Methodology

2.1   Material

The investigations were performed in the total number of 80 subjects enrolled after taking the informed consent to the following study groups: group I was constituted by the 40 persons (age range: 20-25 years; 12 females ad 28 males) working with computer from 5 to 8 hours every day (VDT-operators), in whom a feeling of heart

Table 1. Characteristics of group I and group II

Parameters	Group I	Group II	P
Mean age [years]	24.3 ± 1.71	23.8 ± 1.57	NS
M/F [%]	70/30	70/30	NS
BP_S [mm Hg]	123.5 ± 17.51	122.8 ± 15.19	NS
BP_D [mm Hg]	78.4 ± 8.63	75.6 ± 7.94	NS
Conventional ECG	No abnormalities	No abnormalities	–
Somatic symptoms	Heart palpitations	Free from symptoms	–

N – number of subject; M – male; F – female; BP_S – systolic blood pressure; BP_D – diastolic blood pressure; NS – not significant; p – probability.

palpitations was common somatic symptom. The group II, serving as a control one, comprised 40 persons (age range: 20-25 years; 12 females and 28 males) who worked with computer occasionally, and were age- and sex-matched. Characteristics of these subgroups are compiled in Table 1.

2.2   Method

In the all study persons, the recordings of BSPM were performed using a specialized HPM-7100 Fukuda Denshi system (Japan) composed of the central unit, microprocessor HP-710, 16-inch screen and preamplifier IB-300. The system performs the simultaneous registrations from the 87 specific mapping leads. A frequency of the ECG signals sampling was 1000 samples/s for each of the used channels (Fukuda Denshi, 1990). The electrode standardized array was applied using one-use electrodes placed on 13 adhesive strips mounted in rows on the anterior and posterior thoracic surfaces (designated on the maps the letters A to M), as displayed in Figure 1.

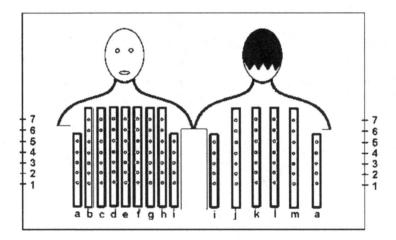

Fig. 1. Scheme of electrodes placement on the thoracic surfaces

Data collected from the 87 ECG waveforms were graphically presented as the body surface maps of various formats. The isointegral maps (Int-QRST) represent a summation of the all instant heart potentials and contain a global characteristics of the cardioelectric field within the assigned time interval of the cardiac cycle. This sort of maps reduces significantly an abundant load of the ECG information provided by the isopotential maps.

The investigation protocol was approved by the local Bioethics Committee.

Statistical Analysis

Standard statistical Student t-test was applied for comparison of the two variables. The values are presented as the mean ± SD, and a level of statistical significance was set at p<0.05. Non-parametric data was given as the absolute numbers or percentages.

3   Results

The long-term investigations carried out in the Department of Pathophysiology of Wroclaw Medical University were aimed at establishing the patterns of the isopotential maps for 95 healthy subjects. Next, the isointegral maps for the whole

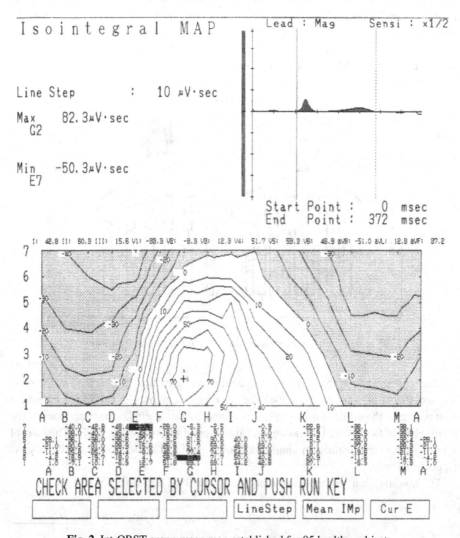

Fig. 2. Int-QRST group-mean map established for 95 healthy subjects

cardiac cycle (Int-QRST) averaged for these subjects were elaborated. In the group-mean (pattern) Int-QRST map established for this group, bipolar distribution was observed (Fig. 2).

The subsequent figures show the example of Int-QRST maps obtained in group I (Fig. 3) and group II (Fig. 4).

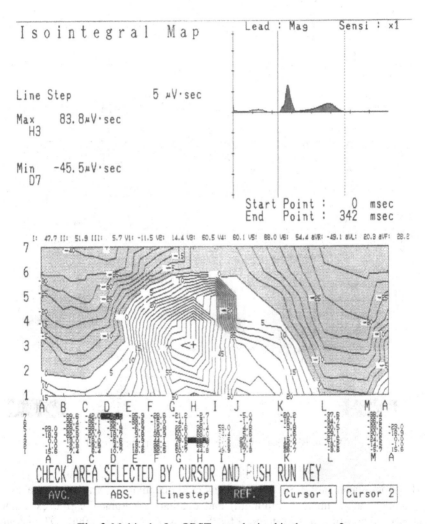

Fig. 3. Multipolar Int-QRST map obtained in the group I

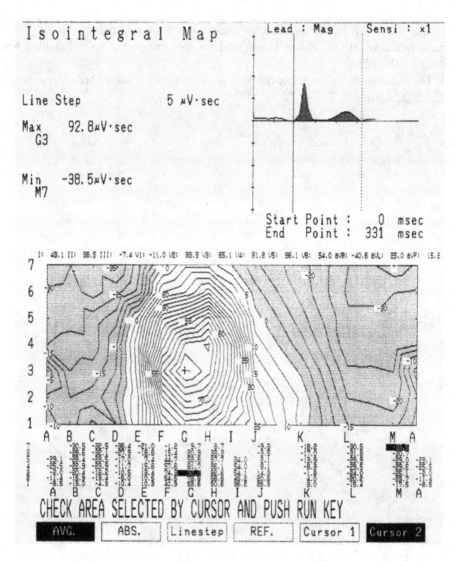

Fig. 4. Bipolar Int-QRST map obtained in the group II

The group-mean Int-QRST map contains both quantitative parameters (the values of potential maximum and minimum) and qualitative parameters (the extremums location) and constituted the reference for the maps obtained from the VDT-operators (group I) and persons from group II working with computer occasionally. Comparison of the mentioned parameters presented on those maps with the pattern map are compiled in Table 2.

Table 2. Quantitative and gualitative parameters of Int-QRST maps obtained in group I, group II and pattern map

Parameters	Group I	Group II	Pattern map
Mean numbers of extremums	3.53 ± 1.14 (2-8)	2.05 ± 0.22 (2-3)	2.03 ± 0.23 (2-4)
Potential max:			
mean value	83.8 µV·sec	92.8 µV·sec	82.3 µV·sec
location	H3	G3	G2
Potential min:			
mean value	-45.5 µV·sec	-38.5 µV·sec	-50.3 µV·sec
location	D7	M7	E7

The percentage of normal and abnormal Int-QRST maps in the group I, group II and the pattern group are presented in Figure 5.

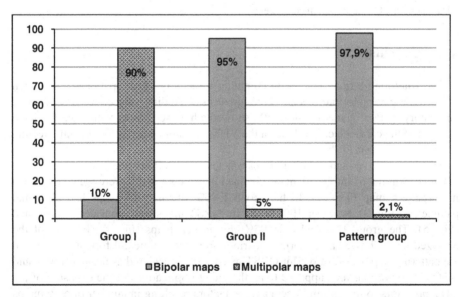

Fig. 5. Percentage of bipolar and multipolar maps in groups I and II and in the pattern group

Mean number of extremums showed a clear tendency to increase gradually with time of dialogue with computer. This relationship is presented in Figure 6.

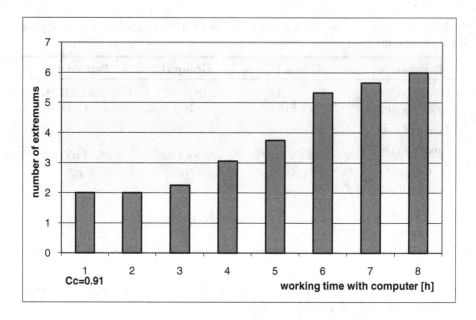

Fig. 6. Correlation between number of extremums and working time with computer in the VDT-operators. Cc – correlation coefficient

4   Conclusions

Everyday long-term contact with computer screens is an occupational risk, which induces various undesirable health consequences, including subjective complaints of circulatory system. A method of BSPM showed a high sensitivity with regard to local changes of the cardioelectrical field in the VDT-operators who suffered from a feeling of heart palpitations (Tab. 1).

The quantitative and qualitative parameters as well as the mean number of potential extrema of Int-QRST maps obtained in groups I and II were compared to the mean-pattern map (Tab. 2). In the group I 90% of analyzed maps had abnormal parameters (Fig. 3), however 10% of the Int-QRST maps were considered as normal (Fig. 5). The group II revealed in 95% the normal maps (Fig. 4), but 5% of the analyzed maps showed an abnormal distribution in the isointegral format, whereas in the pattern group 97,9% of the Int-QRST maps were considered as normal (Fig. 2 and 5). Our observations are supposed to be the direct implications of the exposure of the VDT-operators to the harmful occupational factors resulting in number of extremums (Fig. 6).

The results obtained in group I are considered as a reflection of the local ventricular repolarization dispersion (undetectable on the standard 12-lead ECGs), which indicates an increased risk of serious ventricular arrhythmias.

In the group II, the number of potential extrema were significantly lower (p<0.001) than in the group I and near the number of potential extrema on the reference map (Tab. 2). In the persons from group II, without concomitant conditions, QRST isointegral maps presented a normal bipolar nature (two extrema), although, as compared with the pattern map, the statistically significant differences were found concerning the values of extrema (maxima and minima), which also suggested slightly increased arrhythmogeneity in this group.

The BSPM method could be considered as an additional tool for detecting local electrical events. In particular, a sequence of activation and repolarization of the heart in the entire cardiac cycle, which is presented in the maps as a migration of the positive and negative potential areas of specific distribution over the entire thorax seems to be of great importance while a significant increase in incidence of malignant ventricular arrhythmias in the population of VDT-operators is observed. Non-dipolar distribution of QRST isointegral maps can be a specific indicator of the increased risk of severe ventricular arrhythmias occurring prior to abnormalities detectable on the standard 12-lead ECG recordings, which is of great importance especially in prevention of life-threatening arrhythmias (Sobieszczańska, 2005; Abildskov, 1987).

References

1. Janocha, A., Salomon, E., Borodulin-Nadzieja, L., Skalik, R., Sobieszczańska, M.: Symptoms of depression in the VDT – operators. In: Stephanidis, C., Jacko, J. (eds.) Human - Computer Interaction: Theory and Practice. Proceedings of HCI International 2003, vol. 2, pp. 1366–1370. Lawrence Erlbaum Associates, Publishers, Mahwah (2003)
2. Sobieszczańska, M.: Body surface potential mapping. Introduction to the method. Górnicki Medical Publishers, Wrocław (2005)
3. Abildskov, J.A., Greek, L.S.: The recognition of arrhythmia vulnerability by body surface electrocardiographic mapping. Circulation 75(suppl. III), III79-III83 (1987)
4. Fukuda Denshi Co. Ltd. Heart potential mapping system. Fukuda Denshi Co. LTD Bulletin, Tokyo (1990)

Hand and Arm Support for Computer Workstation

Ghi-Hwei Kao and T.K. Philip Hwang

National Taipei University of Technology
No.1, Sec. 3, Zhongxiao E. Rd., Da'an Dist., Taipei City 10608, Taiwan
ghi.box@gmail.com, phwang@ntut.edu.tw

Abstract. Individuals who spend long hours leaning on the desk in tasks like writing, typing or operating a mouse often suffer from Cumulative Repetitive Stress such as Tendonitis, Carpal Tunnel Syndromes and general tissue pain. Increased instance of excessive mechanical stress in the shoulders can also be a product of improper wrist and forearm support. This study use Rapid Upper limb Assessment to examine user's working action and posture on writing, typing and mouse operation. Proposed wrist support and palm inclined plane were attached at the table edge for improving desk support structure. Users test was carried out to validate the usability of wrist support design with positive result.

Keywords: arm support, occupational musculoskeletal symptoms, working area.

1   Introduction

Improper posture is generally referred to a fixed or restricted limb position, as well as the following poor conditions:

- The over-uploaded muscles and tendons,
- The asymmetric force of Joint,
- Sustained isometric strength.

Squire (1956) pointed out that when the elbow moving on the desk for working, it should consider the whole arm interactions which include hand, upper and lower arm. When using a keyboard, the user generally adjusts his/her upper and lower arm to adapt the fingertips to the keyboard. To avoid twisted and asymmetrical positions, employed rules of normal and maximum working area were employed to define the horizontal working area that includes:

- supporting area, upper body and arm support,
- working area: visual work and data inputting work, and
- Storage area.

When working at computer workstation, the user employs his/her forearms for keyboard and mouse operation that causes the arms to be held in a support-less

V.G. Duffy (Ed.): DHM/HCII 2013, Part II, LNCS 8026, pp. 232–238, 2013.

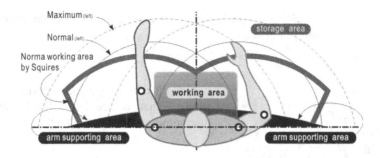

Fig. 1.

position. A lack of support leads to stress on the shoulder muscles, and an extra circulatory burden on the heart (Pheasant, 1998).Therefore, there are two areas; supporting and working areas; the body is using for computer work like typing, writing and using mouse. When using a mouse, the forearm is always resting on the desk surface. If the forearm couldn't rest on the table edge, the user's arm must move vertically and horizontally, it will be supported by the movement of the 3rd lever from the shoulder, it will make user feel pain from the shoulder stress.(Kunz, 2006).

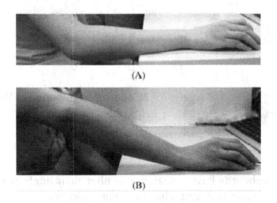

Fig. 2.

Heretofore, a lot of Ergonomics focuses on people's back and proper seating when working, people also potentially stressing or injuring on neck, shoulders and wrists. Actually, whether people are using a mouse or a keyboard, a proper wrist support is important. It not just for the wrists and helping to prevent Repetitive Strain Injury and Carpal Tunnel, but also for the shoulders, which hold a lot of tension from the awkward position. Many studies (Harvey & Peper, 1997) point out that the wrist should keep in a nature angle when typing.

Following are the gel wrist support from the market displaces pressure points and provides comfort while computing.

Gel filled wrist support. Flexible gel filling helps reduce wrist strain and discomfort whilst working on the PC.[i]

Hypoallergenic memory foam molds to the body's contours to provide maximum support and help relieve wrist discomfort.[ii]

Keeps wrist in ergonomically correct position. Platform can bridge desk corners and help extend desk edge.

Compact and portable Wrist Support helps prevent and alleviate mouse arm.

Many market keyboards have the ability to alter their angle with the little legs on the bottom. A wrist rest can also be found and they make them both for keyboard and on mousepads. Arm and wrist support apparatus have been designed to accommodate either the arm or the wrist, even both. Some devices are fixed on chair as an arm. Following are the resting wrists on desktop when working on the keyboard or mouse causing awkward wrist postures.

---

[i] Wrist Support with Gel, retrieve from:
   http://www.durable-uk.com/gb/products/detail/5749/
   wrist-support-with-gel.html
[ii] Memory Foam Wrist Pillow Platform l, retrieve from:
   http://www.cleansweepsupply.com/pages/item-kmw62819.html

Positive slope of keyboard tray causes awkward wrist postures.

Position keyboard tray flat or slightly negative.

2   Design Solution

Fig 3 shows the 3 forearm positions on the desk: wrist on the edge of the desk (A), half of the forearm on the desk (B), and whole forearm on the desk (C)[iii].

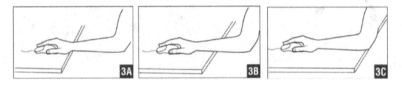

Fig. 3. Forearm positions on the desk

According to somatoscope, the limb is an open chain composed by the rotation joints which surround shoulder joint, the mechanical of limbs are the third class lever. A lever system includes a fulcrum (F), a load (R) which can be due to mass and/or resistance due to friction, and a force generating system (E) which in our case is skeletal muscle contraction. Most muscles in body are involved in Third Class Lever systems.

The way to improve the 3rd class lever force structure is to offer a support between wrist and elbow, that's the reason why people always lean their body on the table edge.

[iii] Contact Pressure in the Wrist During Computer Mouse Work 1, retrieve from:
< http://www.healio.com/orthopedics/journals/ortho/
%7B191a0519-bc3e-4e2b-8193- 396ee88d0437%7D/
contact-pressure-in-the-wrist-during-computer-mouse-work >

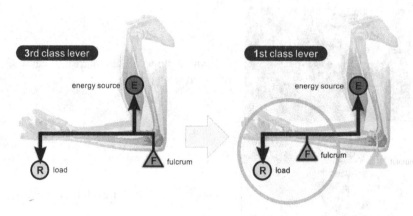

Fig. 4.

Although table edge provide forearm a support which might reduce the stress from the shoulder, but it cannot keep the arm and wrist in a nature position, because the wrist would bent up to provide the space for fingers to move, and it might cause to the Carpal Tunnel Syndromes.

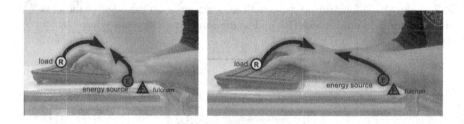

Fig. 5.

After the study, proposes a solution for this situation, the design features are as fig 6:

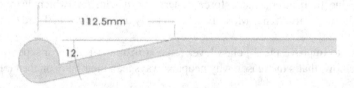

Fig. 6.

- The wrist support design provide wrist with a proper support and shift the 3rd class lever movement into the 1st class lever movement which is a better mechanical structure for user to work on table.
- A 10cm in12 degree inclined plane for palm to rest in. It enables palm to accommodate as another support point which is closer to operating fingers than that of forearm support from table edge in traditional design. Short lever support can effectively reduce the stress from arm and shoulder.
- The positive 12 degree slope can easily adjust the hand, wrist and arm into a nature and proper way in force.

This desk edge include the flat surface for fingers tasks, a 12∘inclined plane for palm rest and 2 cm cylindrical curved edges for wrist to reduce over-stretching.

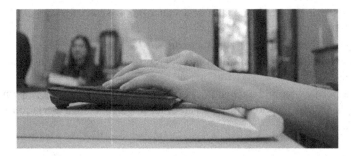

Fig. 7.

In addition to using the keyboard, and also for the use of the mouse or writing.

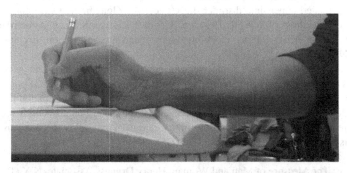

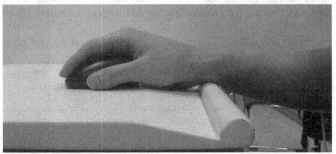

The advantages of this design are:

- Share the forearm lord from the supporting.
- Ability to avoid unnatural upper limb.
- Reduce energy consumption.
- Better fingers typing activities.

3   Conclusion

This study aiming to provide the computer user with design of nature carpal angle and carpal posture. The findings as follows:

- A 12 degree inclined plane palm rest can offer a space for carpal flexion and extension;
- the wrists can stay nearly horizontal condition;
- carpal flexion and extension affect the degree of ulnar deviation as well as radial deviation;
- When carpal flexion and extension takes places, muscles gain more pain because they might increase the load of flexor in order to balance ulnar deviation and radial deviation.

References

1. Amstrong, T.T., Martin, B.J., Franzblau, A., Rempel, D.M., Johnson, P.W.: Mouse input and work related upper limb disorder. In: Grieco, A., Molteni, G., Occhipinti, E., Piccoli, B. (eds.) Proceedings of WWDU 1994, pp. 375–380. Elsevier Science, Amsterdam (1995)
2. Harvey, R., Peper, E.: Surface electromyography and mouse position. Ergonimics 40(8), 781–789 (1997)
3. Das, B., Grady, R.M.: The normal working area in the horizontal plane A comparative analysis between Farley's and Squires' concepts. Ergonomics 26(5) (1983)
4. Kunz, B., Kunz, K.: Hand Reflexology. Dorling Kingderley Limited, London (2006)
5. Albertsson, P., Falkmer, T.: Is there a pattern in European bus and coach incidents? A literature analysis with special focus on injury causation and injury mechanisms. Accident Analysis and Prevention 37(2), 225–233 (2005)
6. Tanner, J.: Better Back. Dorling Kindersley Book, N.Y (2003)
7. Tilley, A.: The Measure of Man and Woman. Henry Dryness Associate, N.Y (1993)
8. Sanders, M.S., McCormic, E.J.: Human Factors in Engineer & Design, 7th edn. Mcgraw-Hill Inc., N.Y (1992)
9. Pheasant, S.: Body space. In: Anthropometry, Ergonomics and the Design of Work, 2nd edn. Taylor & Francis, London (1998) ISBN 0748403264
10. http://www.completerehabsolutions.com/blog/ergonomics-the-science-of-sitting-part-ii/ (retrieved)

The Effects of Touch Screen Virtual Keyboard Key Sizes on Typing Performance, Typing Biomechanics and Muscle Activity

Jeong Ho Kim[1], Lovenoor S. Aulck[2], Ornwipa Thamsuwan[3], Michael C. Bartha[4], Christy A. Harper[5], and Peter W. Johnson[1,3]

[1] Department of Environmental and Occupational Health Sciences, University of Washington, Seattle, USA
{jhkim01,petej}@u.washington.edu
[2] Department of Bioeingeering, University of Washington, Seattle, USA
laulck@u.washington.edu
[3] Department of Industrial and Systems Engineering, University of Washington, Seattle, WA
ot7@u.washington.edu
[4] Ergonomics Research and Development Program, Hewlett-Packard, Houston, USA
Michael.Bartha@hp.com
[5] Personal Systems Group, Hewlett-Packard, Houston, USA
christy.harper@hp.com

Abstract. The goal of the present study was to determine whether different touch screen virtual keyboard key sizes affected typing productivity, typing forces, and muscle activity. In a repeated-measures laboratory experiment with 21 subjects, typing speed, accuracy, muscle activity, and typing forces were measured and compared between four different key sizes: 13x13, 16x16, 19x19, and 22x22 mm. The results showed that 13 mm keyboard had a 15% slower typing speed ($p < 0.0001$) and slightly higher static (10th %tile) shoulder muscle activity (2%, $p = 0.01$) as compared to the other keyboards with larger keys. The slower typing speed and slightly higher shoulder muscle activity indicated that 13 mm keyboard may be less optimal for touch typing compared to the larger key sizes.

Keywords: Virtual interface, typing forces, electromyography, typing speed, accuracy.

1 Introduction

As smart phones and tablet PCs have become increasingly prevalent, the touchscreen virtual keyboard has become a mainstream interface. From an ergonomics standpoint, touch screen virtual keyboards have a potential advantage in that key size and spacing between keys could be controlled by the device software and adjusted according to users' anthropometry. However, as tablet PCs gravitate towards smaller sizes for better portability, the key sizes on a virtual keyboard are often forced to be smaller than the existing standards for keyboard design [1-2].

V.G. Duffy (Ed.): DHM/HCII 2013, Part II, LNCS 8026, pp. 239–244, 2013.

13 X 13 mm

16 X 16 mm

19 X 19 mm

21 X 21 mm

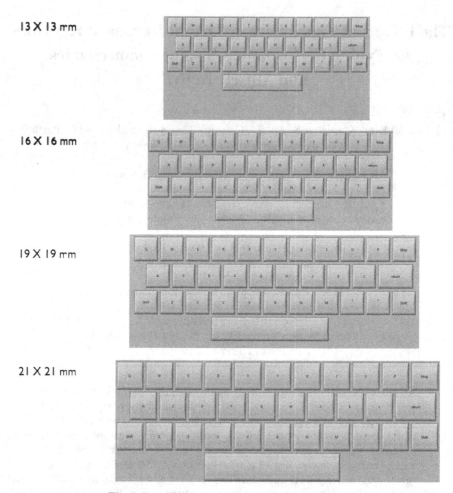

Fig. 1. Four different key sizes tested in the study

Virtual keyboard key sizes may affect typing performance and alter physical risk factors associated with computer-related musculoskeletal disorders (MSDs). Accordingly, an inappropriate key size may adversely affect typing productivity and cause awkward finger and/or wrist postures which can increase typing forces and/or muscle activity, which are well-known risk factors for MSDs [3-4]. Unfortunately, despite a few existing guidelines [1-2], no consistent recommendations for key sizes on touch screen virtual keyboards are available [5]. Therefore, it is important to understand how virtual keyboard key size may affect typing performance and physical exposures.

2   Methods

2.1   Subjects

A total of 21 subjects (12 male and 9 female) with an average age of 24.5 years (range 18-49 years) were recruited to participate in the study through e-mail solicitations. All subjects were experienced touch typists with no history of upper extremity musculoskeletal disorders and 19 subjects were right hand dominant. The experimental protocol was approved by the University's Human Subjects Committee and all subjects gave their written consent prior to their participation in the study.

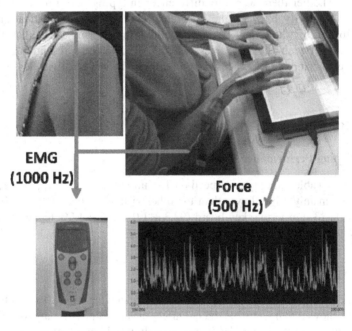

Fig. 2. Study set up

2.2   Experimental Design

In the repeated-measures laboratory experiment, subjects typed for two five-minute sessions on a touch screen virtual keyboard with the four following key sizes (shown in Fig. 1): 13×13 mm, 16×16 mm, 19×19 mm, and 22×22 mm (Width × Height mm). The gutter size surrounding the keys was kept at fixed size of 2.0 mm. The presentation of the key sizes was randomized to minimize potential confounding effects with order. During the typing sessions, typing productivity including typing speed (words per minute) and accuracy (% key correctly typed) were recorded. Using Electromyography (EMG), muscle activity was also recorded from the right extensor digitorum communis (EDC), flexor digitorum superficialis (FDS), and the right trapezius (TRAP) at a sample rate of 1000 Hz (Fig. 2). Lastly, typing forces were measured at 500 Hz by placing the devices on a 36 cm x 18 cm x 0.64 cm force platform mounted to a six-degree of freedom force/torque load cell (Mini40E, ATI Inc., USA).

2.3   Data Analysis

Statistical analysis was conducted in JMP (Version 9; SAS Institute Inc., USA). A *mixed model* with *restricted maximum likelihood estimation* (REML) was used to determine whether there were any differences in typing performance, typing force, and muscle activity between the different key sizes. Any statistical significance was followed by the *Tukey-Kramer* method to determine whether there were differences between the key sizes tested. All data are presented as mean and standard error; and significance was noted when Type I error was less than 0.10 or 0.05.

3   Results

3.1   Typing Performance

As shown in Table 1, net typing speed on 13 mm virtual keyboard (23.3 ± 1.0 WPM) was approximately 15% slower than the other virtual keyboards (p < 0.0001) while accuracy on 13 mm virtual key-board (92.3 ± 1.0 %) was 4.5% higher than the other virtual keyboards (p = 0.004).

3.2   Typing Forces

Due to technical difficulties, typing forces were calculated from 20 subjects (Table 1). The result showed that key sizes did not affect mean and peak typing forces; however, mean typing forces on 13 mm keyboard were slightly higher than the other keyboards (p = 0.13).

3.3   Muscle Activity

Due to technical difficulties, muscle activity data were recorded from 19 subjects. Static (10th %tile), median (50th %tile), and peak (90th %tile) muscle activity were compared between the different key sizes (Table 1). The results indicated that virtual key size had little effect on EDC and FDS muscle activity whereas static (10th %tile) TRAP muscle activity on 13 mm virtual keyboard was 2.5% higher as compared to 19 and 22 mm virtual keyboards (p = 0.06 and 0.06, respectively).

Table 1. Mean (SE) typing performance [n=21], typing forces [n=20], and muscle activity [n=19]. Rows with different superscripts indicate key sizes which are significantly different

			Keyboard				
			13 mm	16 mm	19 mm	22 mm	p-value
Performance		Typing speed (WPM)	23.3 (1.0)[a]	27.0 (1.0)[b]	27.0 (1.0)[b]	27.5 (1.0)[b]	< 0.0001
		Accuracy (%)	92.3 (1.0)[a]	90.3 (1.0)[b]	88.7 (1.0)[b]	88.9 (1.0)[b]	0.004
Typing force (N)		Mean	1.06 (0.06)	0.97 (0.06)	0.96 (0.06)	0.97 (0.06)	0.13
		Peak	2.12 (0.13)	2.11 (0.13)	2.18 (0.13)	2.20 (0.13)	0.69
Muscle activity (%MVC)	EDC	10th %tile	6.9 (0.5)	6.6 (0.5)	6.6 (0.5)	6.5 (0.5)	0.26
		50th %tile	11.0 (0.9)	11.0 (0.9)	11.0 (0.9)	10.9 (0.9)	0.99
		90th %tile	18.8 (2.4)	19.0 (2.2)	19.2 (2.2)	19.1 (2.1)	0.81
	FDS	10th %tile	2.3 (0.3)	2.2 (0.2)	2.3 (0.3)	2.3 (0.3)	0.57
		50th %tile	4.0 (0.4)	3.8 (0.3)	4.0 (0.4)	4.1 (0.5)	0.71
		90th %tile	13.4 (1.7)	13.7 (1.6)	15.3 (2.2)	14.9 (2.1)	0.19
	TRAP	10th %tile	12.6 (2.5)[a]	11.3 (2.2)[a,b]	9.9 (2.0)[b]	10.3 (2.1)[b]	0.01
		50th %tile	16.7 (3.2)	15.7 (2.9)	14.7 (2.6)	14.4 (2.8)	0.06
		90th %tile	21.9 (4.0)	21.6 (3.7)	21.1 (3.5)	19.7 (3.7)	0.16

4   Conclusion

The present study was conducted to determine whether different key sizes on a touch screen virtual keyboard affected typing productivity, typing biomechanics and muscle activity. The study findings suggested that 13 mm keyboard may be less optimal fir touch typing compared to the larger key sizes given slower typing speed and higher shoulder muscle activity. The slower typing speed with the 13 mm keyboard was somewhat counterbalanced with an increase in typing accuracy indicating there may be a speed and accuracy tradeoff starting somewhere around a virtual key size of 13 to 16 mm.

This study found that 13 mm keyboard had a slower typing speed as compared to the larger key sizes whereas there were no differences between the other keyboards. This finding was in-line with a previous study [6], which showed significant decrease in typing speed when key sizes of a conventional physical keyboard are smaller than 16 mm. Insufficient clearance between fingers due to smaller key sizes may have resulted in the decreased typing speed.

The results also found that static (10th %tile) shoulder muscle activity was slightly higher on 13 mm keyboard compared to the other larger key sizes. The smaller key sizes may have increased visual demand to locate keys on the virtual keyboard and consequently, resulted in higher shoulder muscle activity.

To sum up, the slower typing speed and slightly higher shoulder muscle activity indicated that 13 mm key size for virtual keyboard interface may be less preferable for touch typing compared to the larger key sizes.

References

1. ANSI/HFES 100-2007, Human Factors Engineering of Computer Workstations. Human Factors and Ergonomics Society. Santa Monica, CA, USA (2007)
2. ISO/TS 9241-411, Ergonomics of human-system interaction - Part 411: Evaluation methods for the design of physical input devices. International Organization for Standardization, Geneva, Switzerland (2012)
3. Armstrong, T.J., Foulke, J.A., Martin, B.J., Gerson, J., Rempel, D.M.: Investigation of applied forces in alphanumeric keyboard work. American Industrial Hygiene Association Journal 55(1), 30–35 (1994)
4. Rempel, D., Serina, E., Klinenberg, E., Martin, B.J., Armstrong, T.J., Foulke, J.A., et al.: The effect of keyboard keyswitch make force on applied force and finger flexor muscle activity. Ergonomics 40(8), 800–808 (1997)
5. Sesto, M.E., Irwin, C.B., Chen, K.B., Chourasia, A.O., Wiegmann, D.A.: Effect of Touch Screen Button Size and Spacing on Touch Characteristics of Users With and Without Disabilities. Human Factors 54(3), 425–436 (2012)
6. Yoshitake, R.: Relationship between key space and user performance on reduced keyboards. Applied Human Sciences 14(6), 287–292 (1995)

Model Reconstruction of Human Buttocks and the Shape Clustering

Lijing Wang and Xueli He

Fundamental Science on Ergonomics and Environment Control Laboratory
School of Aeronautic Science and Engineering
Beihang University, Beijing, China, 100191
Wanglijing505@163.com

Abstract. The purpose of this study is to reconstruct the buttock model of Chinese young men, and categorize the buttock model by k-means clustering algorithm. Thirty men participated in our anthropometric study. The buttocks of subjects were pasted with the mark-points: coccyx (upper margin), trochanters (both sides of the margin), and the middle points on separation line between hip and thigh (lower margin) as the points of the boundary mark-points; ischial tuberosities, anus, as the function mark-points. Three-dimensional (3D) points cloud data, obtained by scanner, was imported into reverse engineering software for the reconstruction of buttock surface model. Then surface models were imported into CATIA software. The horizontal width, the vertical width, and the thickness of the buttocks were measured in 3D shape model. The k-means clustering algorithm was used to individually cluster the dimensions of horizontal width, the vertical width, and the thickness into two groups. The 3D buttock model was successfully reconstructed by 3D scan technology. The models of buttock can be categorized into eight types: long - wide - thick, long - wide - thin, long - narrow - thick, long - narrow - thin, short - wide - thick, short - wide - thin, short - narrow - thick, short - narrow - thin.

Keywords: Reconstruction, anthropometric, k-means clustering algorithm, three-dimensional (3D), buttock model.

1 Introduction

Anthropometry data is one of the most important fundamental tools in the design and ergonomic evaluation of a product; it is the design basis of products related to human dimension, which will improve the comfort of products by human-match-product reasonably [1]. The traditional anthropometric measurement tools including tape measure, calipers, gauges and special measuring instrument for human data acquisition, which leave out the spatial relationships between those measured item. When products need to be adapted to the parts of the human body, the traditional anthropometric data is insufficient to guide the design of the product, for lack of such shape information and spatial relationship information. However, the emergence of non-contact three-dimension(3D) measurement instrument greatly improve the

V.G. Duffy (Ed.): DHM/HCII 2013, Part II, LNCS 8026, pp. 245–251, 2013.

suitability between product and human body, making the tailor-made and personalized products, such as apparel, shoes, hats, helmets, become a reality. The three-dimensional anthropometric undoubtedly provide richer information for ergonomic design and safety assessment of the product [2].

Many researchers have established three-dimensional surface model of different body part, and they were applied to product design and evaluation related to human body, such as helmets [3, 4], shoes [5, 6, 7,], cushion [8], apparel [9] and so on.

With continuous improvement of people's life quality, customers require more accurate size system to help them buy more suitable products. Hence, good product design has never been more closely related with correct anthropometric measurements data. Typically, buttock model meets with extensive needs in producing comfortable cushion and good pants type. First, for seat shape, it is designed to be symmetrical simulating the shape of the buttocks, to assure hip part gets enough support, and also its contact area with the surface of chair shall increase, thereby to reduce the pressure, and to relieve the buttocks extrusion fatigue caused by obstruction of blood circulation [10]. Second, when it comes to pants designs, designers often encounter fundamental problems like waist-hip differential, waist-hip loose amount and upper crotch area movement deformation. To solve these issues, it is necessary to refer to the size of the hips, such as hip circumference, hip thickness [11]. Therefore, another cloth type: skirt shape, similar to pants, relates to human waist and hips form [12]. Thus to conclude, effective hip shape model has important significance for product design.

Currently, China's national size standard defines adult female's breast and waist circumference as two basic components characterizing clothes size, chest-waist differential and waist-hip differential are used to categorize human body type into 4 classes: Y, A, B, C. However, studies indicate that this method of classification does not well reflect the female body shape variance, the features of female body are not correctly classed and represented, and also suggest that body shape classification should be processed separately: by different body part such as chest, waist and buttock independently[13]. According to youth women pants size research, 57% of female pants do not fit, in which major problems are with waist-buttocks ratio unfitness, tight crotch etc[14]. In traditional pants production process, templates are built based on standard body type by region. These templates meet with general need of normal people, but have many limitations. People with flat or prominent bottom wearing these pants may come across different kinds of problems: prominent type finds the back crotch curve line too short, and their bottom strained. Flat type is troubled with a fat bottom appearance and has loose crotch [15]. Traditionally, people construct a structure diagram of trousers and then deal with these issues qualitatively, by means of lengthening or shortening side seam or back crotch curve [16]. Flat/prominent body type crotch structure has been studied quantitatively, but no researchers consider solving this problem by reclassify the bottom sizing system [17].

There is no research in the establishing of 3D buttock model and sizing system. When establishing the buttock model, the size with width and length, and thickness need to consider. So the purpose of this study was to establish human buttock 3D model, and cluster analysis the samples using the k-means algorithm.

2   Materials and Method

2.1   Materials

3D scanner with raster display technology (3D CaMega, China, accuracy up to 0.02mm), the black mark- point pieces, white underwear.

2.2   Subjects

Thirty undergraduate men, height range: 160-183cm, weight range: 47-90kg. All subjects were volunteers and were paid for their participation.

2.3   Scan and Reconstruction of Buttock Model

Mark- Points. Boundary mark- points: coccyx (upper margin), trochanters (left and right margin), the middle points on separation line between buttock and thigh (under margin).

Function mark- points: ischial tuberosities, anus.

The mark-points are shown as in Fig. 1.

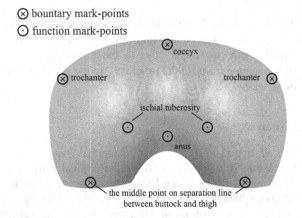

Fig. 1. Mark-points on buttock surface

Measurement Posture. Subjects need to keep bending posture, upper body being perpendicular to the thigh, while ensuring that the plane of buttock being parallel to the camera lens plane.

Design of Coordinate System. The design of coordinate system is based on space analytic method, that the buttock plane (a plane parallel to the camera lens plane) is set as XY plane, the vertical direction through the surface is set as the Z-axis (i.e., space or Z coordinates), and pointing posteriorly; the XZ plane is parallel to the horizontal plane, and Y-axis is the perpendicular through the plane, and pointing cranially; frontal plane through the anus point is set YZ plane, through which plane perpendicular is the X-axis, and pointing to the right is positive direction.

2.4   Reverse Reconstruction of Buttock 3d Model

The result of the 3D scan was a set of spatial points with their corresponding 3D coordinates named the point cloud. Several steps were employed to model the acquisition process. Firstly, the point cloud was entered into the Geomagic Studio (Geomagic,USA), a reverse engineering software. The point-cloud model was then packaged into a polygon model by filling the holes, by processing the edges to form a basic continuous polygonal patch. Secondly, the model was converted to Nurbs surface in order for being able to be imported into the industrial modeling software. Then, the point-cloud model became a surface model by establishing a curved path in Geomagic Studio. The special mark-points were marked on the surface model. The final surface model and the feature points were output as Nurbs model. Thirdly, Catia (Dassault Systemes S.A., Franch) directly imported the Nurbs model created from Geomagic with the feature points and characteristics of surface points for 3D surface reconstruction of buttock.

2.5   Measure the Dimensions

The buttock model, reconstructed in Gemagic,was imported into CATIA (Dassault Systemes S.A., Franch). The horizontal width (the left edge to the right edge of the buttocks), the vertical width (the upper edge to the lower edge), and the buttocks thickness (the veticle distance from ischial tuberosity to the plane of trochanters) were measured in 3D shape model.

2.6   Statistical Analysis

The *1*-st, *5*-th, *50*-th, *95*-th and *99*-th percentile, mean and standard error values of all three measured dimensions (the horizontal width, the vertical width, and the buttocks thickness) were determined using standard statistical procedures by using the SPSS 18.0 (IBM Corporation, Chicago, USA). The k-means clustering algorithm was used to individually cluster the dimensions of horizontal width, the vertical width, the buttocks thickness into two groups.

3   Results

3.1   Reconstruction of Buttock Model Based on 3d Scan

To eliminate errors produced from model reconstruction and body shaking during the scan process in a certain extent; all subjects need to be scanned twice. The average values across these two trials were reported. During the data processing, the twice scan data of one subject was averaged firstly, and then performed the group data processing. The reconstruction buttock model is shown in Fig. 2.

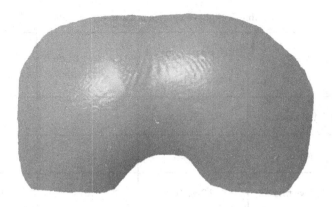

Fig. 2. The reconstruction buttock model

3.2   Percentile Statistics

Three measurement dimension values were measured from three-dimensional buttock model of thirty subjects, the horizontal width, the vertical width, and the buttocks thickness. *1*-st, *5*-th, *50*-th, *95*-th, *99*-th values were obtained through data processing, as shown in Table 1.

Table 1. The *1*-st, *5*-th, *50*-th, *95*-th, *99*-th values of measurement dimensions

	The horizontal width(mm)	The vertical width(mm)	The thicness(mm)
1-st	94.60	163.58	14.37
5-th	96.49	185.52	17.84
50-th	133.96	239.23	50.20
95-th	186.62	309.62	80.87
99-th	192.88	319.12	83.05

3.3   Clustering Analysis

The horizontal width, the vertical width, and the thickness of buttock model are individually divided into two groups by *k*-means clustering algorithm bottom. And then based on the value of the three measurement project classification, permutations

Table 2. Eight categories of clustering results

	The horizontal width(mm)	The vertical width(mm)	The thickness(mm)
Long-wide-thick	159.85	262	63.31
long-wide-thin	159.85	262	27.12
long-narrow-thick	126.06	262	63.31
long-narrow-thin	126.06	262	27.12
short-wide-thick	159.85	234	63.31
short-wide-thin	159.85	234	27.12
short-narrow-thick	126.06	234	63.31
short-narrow-thin	126.06	234	27.12

and combinations of the eight categories of the buttocks model: long - width - thickness, long - wide - thin, long - narrow - thick, long - narrow - thin, short - wide - thick, short - wide - thin, short - narrow - thick, short - narrow - thin.

4   Conclusion

In this study, the three-dimensional model of the human buttock was successfully reconstructed by three-dimensional scanning technology. The buttock models included the points of boundary points, anus, ischial tuberosities. Eight categories of the buttock models were formed by the cluster analysis of the horizontal width, the vertical width, and the buttocks thickness.

5   Discussion

We didn't find a principle for the categorization of buttock model, and so far, the buttock model haven't been used to the design and evaluation the product relative to buttock. So the rationality of the categorization of buttock model can't be verified and analyzed.

References

1. Sanders, M.S., McCormick, E.J.: Human Factors in Engineering and Design. McGraw-Hill Science (1993)
2. Niu, J.: Multi-resolution Shape Description and Clustering of 3D Anthropometric Data for Population Fitting Design. Tsinghua University. Engineering PhD thesis, pp. 1–4 (2009)
3. Zeigen, R.S.: A head circumference sizing system for helmet design. WADD Technical Report, 60-631 (1960)
4. Hong, L., Li, Z., Li, Z.: Rapid preliminary helmet shell design based on three-dimensional anthropometric head data. Journal of Engineering Design 19(1), 45–54 (2008)
5. Chung-Shing, W.: An analysis and evaluation of fitness for shoe lasts and human feet. Computers in Industry 61, 532–540 (2010)
6. Jia, Y., Cheung, J.T.-M., Fan, Y., Zhang, Y., Leung, A.K.-L., Zhang, M.: Development of a finite element model of female foot for high-heeled shoe design. Clinical Biomechanics 23, S31–S38 (2008)
7. Emma, J., Pratt, M.L., Reeves, J.M., van der Meulen, B.W., Heller, T.R.: The development, preliminary validation and clinical utility of a shoe model to quantify foot and footwear kinematics in 3-D. Gait & Posture 36, 434–438 (2012)
8. Sonenblum, S.E., Sprigle, S.H.: 3-dimensional Phantom Buttocks Tissue Deformation across Cushions
9. Loker, S., Ashdown, S., Schoenfelder, K.: Size-specific Analysis of Body Scan Data to Improve Apparel Fit. Journal of Textile and Apparel, Technology and Management 4(3) (spring 2005)
10. Juan, L., Hui, L., Wang, X.: The design of passenger's seat on urban bus. China Western Technology 9(11), 32–34 (2010)
11. Lihua, Z.: Study the relationship between the construction and comfort of pants. Beijing Texile 26(2), 50–53 (2005)
12. Jian, L., Rong, Z., Ni, G., Duan, X.: Relationship between the skirt shape and the waist hip shape of human body. Journal of Beijing Institute of Clothing Technology 25(4), 1–8 (2005)
13. Lin, G., Xin, Z.: Curve form and classification method of youth female based on three dimension. Journal of Beijing Institute of Clothing Technology 28(1), 22–25 (2008)
14. Chen, X., Hu, L., Chen, Z.: Study on the constitution of young women's pants specifications. Shanghai Textile Science & Technology 37(5), 4–6 (2009)
15. Ronggeng, Z., Xiong, S.: Specially designed clothes cut out skills, pp. 30–32. Jindun Press, Peking (1991)
16. Hu, X.: Dealing skills in structure design of special body type clothes. China and Foreign Clothes (3), 22–23 (1997)
17. Rui, Z., Hong, D.: Research on the seat structure of trousers on prominent hip and scooped hip. Journal of Xi'an University of Engineering Science and Technology 19(1), 41–45 (2005)

Visualizing Design Problems and Solutions of Workstations on Ships

Monica Lundh[1], Mikael Blomé[2], Steven Mallam[1], and Joanna Paraïso[1]

[1] Maritime Human Factors, Department of Shipping and Marine Technology, Chalmers University of Technology, SE-412 96 Gothenburg, Sweden
{monica.lundh,steven.mallam,joanna.paraiso}@chalmers.se
[2] Ergonomics and Aerosol Technology, Department of Design Sciences, Faculty of Engineering, Lund University, P.O. Box 118, SE-221 00 Lund, Sweden
mikael.blome@design.lth.se

Abstract. The prevailing knowledge of ergonomics is not always taken into consideration while designing ships or introduced too late for it to be effective. Studies have shown that improvements of the working environment can be done with small efforts. Dissemination of research results is not always straight forward or effective due to failure to present research findings in appropriate and accessible forms for different audiences Research suggests that an interactive and explorative learning experience should be supported by technology like web resources. To reach the end users involved in the design of ships, the aim of the current study was to design and evaluate a prototype of an interactive multimedia module. The results showed good scores considering the usability aspects learning, understanding and meaningfulness. A Multimedia module like this can serve two purposes; create a learning situation and be used as a channel through which research results can be disseminated.

Keywords: case study, ergonomics, education, maritime design, multimedia, working environment.

1   Introduction

The expanding possibilities of new technology during the last decades have led to changes and development in the design of ships [1]. This has impacted the working environment and how working tasks are performed [2]. Traditional tasks involving heavy lifts and awkward postures is still a reality for crew members [3] and technical development has led to changes in performance requirements and new working tasks [4-6]. However, the design process seems to fail in meeting the consequences of technological changes in order to successfully design a working environment that supports the working tasks on board [3]. Ergonomics has a long tradition of research with extensive publications in literature and standards [7-10]. In addition, there are national and international regulations in ship design considering maritime safety and the design of working environments [8, 11, 12].

V.G. Duffy (Ed.): DHM/HCII 2013, Part II, LNCS 8026, pp. 252–260, 2013.
© Springer-Verlag Berlin Heidelberg 2013

The prevailing knowledge of ergonomics is not always taken into consideration while designing the control centers on ships, or is introduced too late in the design process for it to be effective [2]. A design which does not support operational procedures and task performance risk inducing inappropriate behavior among the crew members as they are compelled to find alternative ways to complete their tasks [2]. Any changes made in the design of the ship is costly and time consuming once the ship is built and in operation. Thus, it is important to use a multi-disciplinary team approach for new ship design and involve naval architects, ergonomists and crew members in the planning of a new ship in order to utilize knowledge and resources from diverse perspectives.

Studies have shown that considerable improvements of the working environment can be done with rather small efforts [3]. However, in general, the dissemination of research results to the industry is not straight forward or effective. Furthermore, research results and the knowledge within the area of ergonomics needs to be applied early in the design process in order to be cost effective and maximize design capabilities. Today, the research-practice gap is increasingly expanding [13, 14]. Often research does not reach beyond academic borders [15] and this can often be attributed to the failure to present research findings in appropriate and accessible forms for different audiences [16, 17]. Laurillard [18] suggests that an interactive and explorative learning experience should be supported by technology through CD and web resources. The learning experience should involve students in discussions which have a communicative media form supported by traditional seminar methods. Our research focuses on the development of appropriate educational material, derived from research results, that enhances students learning process and also takes into account today's technology to support and facilitate the learning process. An example of a typical interactive media form is a web-based platform used in online distance courses. Students can gain control of the learning experience by freely pursuing information based on individual learning strategies and curiosity. In additional, traditional classroom teaching provides possibilities to apply different seminar methods in order to communicate and interact with a group of students.

1.1   Aim of Paper

Therefore, the aim of the current study was to design and evaluate a prototype of an interactive multimedia module. The module aims at being suitable for individuals, as well as collective exploration and education about specific design problems found in recent research in the engine department. Different design solutions related to working environment in the engine department on merchant ships is also addressed.

2   Material and Methods

The development of a suitable interactive prototype should emerge from the understanding of the learning problem and the users' needs. Such a prototype should be developed by a multi-disciplinary team using a participatory design process involving researchers and potential users.

This, and other important aspects were met by applying Huang's [19] recommended five-phased process for designing high-quality interactive multimedia learning modules: (1) understand the learning problem and the users' needs; (2) design the content to harness the enabling technologies; (3) build multimedia materials with web style standards and human factors principles; (4) user testing of the module; and (5) evaluate and improve design. The application of the five phases in the current research is described in the following sections.

Phase 1 – The Learning Problem
The learning problem in the current research was to present different ergonomic challenges affecting the work environment in the engine department correspondent to the users' needs. The concept was presented by using examples of different tasks which are performed by the engine crew. The ergonomic inaccuracies and its effects in the situation was highlighted and supported by speech and text.

The challenge was to present this information in such a way that it would support the collective learning process among students and teachers. When presenting the information in the prototype, efforts were made to adjust and apply a simpler and more understandable vocabulary that suited a novice user group.

Phase 2 – Content Design
The second phase dealt with the problem of finding a didactic approach with supporting technology to present the information to stimulate and strengthen the students' learning process. Since the research on ergonomical requirements often is based on task performance, it was rather easy to find illustrating examples from the working life in the engine department on board that could support the learners' associations to their own experiences and thereby support their learning.

Phase 3 – Build with Standards and Principles
In this phase, the design ideas of the pedagogical concept were realized as an interactive prototype that met the users' learning and needs: an interface with high usability.

Nielsen [20] presents a list of ten important heuristics to evaluate interaction usability: visibility of system status; match between system and the real world; user control and freedom; consistency and standards; error prevention; recognition rather than recall; flexibility and efficiency of use; aesthetic and minimalist design; help users recognize, diagnose and recover from errors; help and documentation. In the current research, some of these heuristics were fulfilled by following established design standards from websites, such as symbols for navigation control and interaction with animations. The 'error prevention' and 'help and documentation' heuristics were easily fulfilled since the interface was a viewer where the users explored information by navigating and viewing, and not by making changes or adding information.

Considering this research, the most interesting and challenging of these heuristics was 'aesthetic and minimalist design'. Sharp et al. [21] recommend a design as simple as possible for users to accomplish tasks by removing unnecessary functionality, process steps and visual clutter, but also an aesthetically pleasing and pleasurable experience. Jordan [22] also highlights the importance of pleasure of use that not only gives functional benefits but emotional ones. This position is clearly apparent among commercial multimedia products that strive for usage based on curiosity and attention.

The scenarios in this study were animated as 2D cartoon characters showing obvious expressions of either happiness or disappointment, and the environments were generated with a minimum level of details. The prototype was built with a mix of commercial software.

Phases 4 and 5 – Test and Improvements
These phases include user testing and evaluations of the pedagogical concept and the interactive prototype to improve the design and evaluate the research study. During the earlier development phases of the prototype, testing, evaluation and improvements of the interactive module were made iteratively between the authors (who had expert knowledge about interface design, ergonomical requirements and the work environment in the engine department).

2.1   Design and Performance of Testing Procedure and Evaluations

Sharp et al. [21] present a general framework to evaluate usability according to six usability goals: effectiveness, efficiency, safety, utility, learnability, and memorability. But they stress the importance of also considering them together with user experience goals (e.g. to be aesthetically pleasing). User experiences are defined by the standard ISO9241-210 [23] as, 'A person's perceptions and responses that result from the use or anticipated use of a product, system or service'. Considering this study, the aspects of interest were:

Usability

- Effectiveness – is the content relevant and meaningful?
- Efficiency and utility of the prototype – interactive and communicative media such as web material used in a classroom/seminar setting.
- Learnability – understanding of how to explore the content of the prototype.

User Experience

- This was explored to clarify the participants´ impressions and attitudes of the interactive prototype.

The data was collected by a questionnaire.

3   Tests and Evaluations with Students

The educational material was tested and evaluated in a class of 11 upper-secondary marine engineer students. The students had a mean age of 28 years ranging from 22 to 45 years, only male.

3.1   The Prototype

The information and knowledge of ergonomical requirement were visualized with scenarios of life on board, illustrations, photos, speech and animations (Figure 1). The starting page introduced and generally defined ergonomical requirements. The prototype was implemented into PowerPoint and visualized in the form of a slide show. The user navigated through the up and down keys on the key board and by clicking with the cursor on different headlines. The prototype was compiled of six slides.

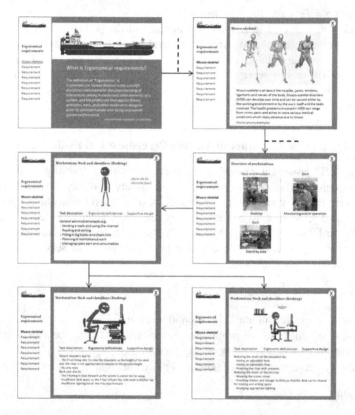

Fig. 1. Six screenshots of the interactive prototype showing paths to specific design examples

The test leader first gave a demonstration of the prototype using a computer and slide projector. The participants did then get the opportunity to try the prototype. After the demonstration and trial the participants filled in a questionnaire.

3.2   Questionnaire

A questionnaire embracing 10 questions were used were the students were asked about the usability and user experience. Questions like "What do you think about this way of learning?" were asked but also questions like "How would you like to have this kind of information presented?" where the participant were asked to choose among different given alternatives.

4   Results

The usability and user experience aspects represented in the questionnaire are summarized in Table 1.

Table 1. Results from the questionnaire

Questions	Answers
What do you think about this way of learning?	Good (100%)
What do you think about the design of the interface?	Good (100%)
How would you like the information presented?	Web page (37%) Application for smart-phones or tablets (26%) Large screen (37%)
Is the subject meaningful?	Yes (100%)
Did you understand the content of the prototype?	Yes (100%)
Would sound improve the presentation?	Yes (100%)
What type of sound?	Sound effects (15%) Speech (46%) Music (8%) Recorded interviews (31%)
What do you prefer, real photos or drawings?	Photos (50%) Drawings (50%)

5   Discussion

This paper reports on the development and evaluation of an interactive prototype presenting research findings about the design problems on board and suggesting alterations which could improve the work environment in the engine department. Early changes in the design process are cost effective [2, 3]. A supportive design with focus on how tasks are being performed reduces the need for the crew having to adapt to less optimal design solutions and thus mitigating unnecessary risk taking [2].

However, previous research gives evidence that ergonomic knowledge is sparsely used in the design process and if used introduced to late in the design process to be effective [2]. There is also evidence of an increasing gap between researchers and practice [13, 14]. Making research results easy accessible for end users within the shipping domain could enhance the awareness of ergonomic matters and bring research-practice closer together. This can in turn have a positive effect on the design process through increased knowledge of ergonomics among the end-users involved in the design of ships. Not being able to reach beyond the academic border when disseminating research results is said to be attributed to failure to present result in an appropriate and accessible form [16, 17]. Thus, this approach to visualize research findings in combination with relevant knowledge as a multimedia tool could aid the strive to adapt the presentation of research results to the target group [18].

This evaluation showed that the multimedia prototype had good scores considering the usability aspects learning, understanding and meaningfulness. The design was also considered good. However, the users preferred photos equally to drawings and would like to increase and add different kinds of sound to the prototype. The results also indicate that a development of the prototype into a full functioning module should present the information with different kinds of visualizations and multimedia effects. These findings are in part contradictory to previous findings were a design as simple as possible is recommended [21]. Sharp et.al. [21] recommend a removal of process steps and visual clutter. The results from this study indicating an equal preference of photos and for adding of sounds could be attributed the high recognition of the different situations as they are directly derived from common tasks executed on board by the crew members.

This study also indicates that adjustments and presentation of new and further specific information should be done with a participative and iterative approach as in this study. The users also had different preferences to how the information should be presented; web-page, application for smartphones and tablets or via a large screen as was the case in this study. It would therefore be preferable and a challenge to design the information suitable to all three distribution channels.

6   Conclusions

A Multimedia module, as suggested in this study, can serve two purposes; it can create a learning situation for student but also to be used as a channel through which research results can be disseminated and presented. The module can not only be used for students. By using different channels of presenting the information e.g. web page and applications for smart phones and tablets the module can be made easily available for other end-users like crew members and shipping companies.

Future work will include further development of the module and tests of the learning objectives. However, the shipping business is a highly international and thus the module need to be tested in a multi-cultural context to ensure that the learning objectives are being fulfilled.

References

1. Olofsson, M.: The Work Situation for Seamen on Merchant Ships in a Swedish Environmnet. In: Department of Transportation and Logistics 1995. Chalmers University of Technology, Gothenburg (1995)
2. Lundh, M., et al.: Working Conditions in the Engine Department - A qualitative study among engine room personnel onboard Swedish merchant ships. Applied Ergonomics 42, 384–390 (2011)
3. Lundh, M.: A Life On the Ocean Wave - Exploring the interaction between the crew and their adaption to the development of the work situation on board Swedish merchant ships. In: Department of Shipping and Marine Technology 2010. Chalmers University of Technology, Gothenburg (2010)
4. Hansson, K.-Å.: Fartyget och fartygsorganisationen som en komplex arbetsmiljö - om kvalitetsstyrning och säkerhet (The Ship and the Organization of the Ship as a Complex Work Environment - About Quality management and Safety). In: Institutionen för Arbetsvetenskap1996. Tekniska högskolan i Luleå, Luleå (1996)
5. Mårtensson, M.: Sjöfarten som ett socialt system - Om handelssjöfart, risk och säkerhet (The Shipping Industry as a Social System - About the Merchant Navy, Risk and Safety). In: Institutionen för Arbetsvetenskap 2006. Luleå tekniska universitet, Luleå (2006)
6. Wagner, E., Lundh, M., Grundevik, P.: Engine Control Rooms - Human Factors Fieldstudies. MSI Design, Chalmers University of Technology. SSPA Sweden, Göteborg (2008)
7. Bridger, R.S., et al.: Occupational Stress and Strain in the Royal Navy 2007. Occupational Medicine 58, 534–539 (2008)
8. IMO, MSC/Circ.834 Guidelines for Engine- Room Layout, Design and Arrangement, ed. M.S. Commitee1998, London: International Maritime Organization, IMO.
9. IMO, MSC-MEP.7/Circ.3 Framework for Consideration of Ergonomics and Work Environmnet, ed. M.S. Committee2006b, London: International Maritime Organisation
10. Ivergård, T., Hunt, B.: Handbook of Control Room Design and Ergonomics, 2nd edn. CRC Press (2009)
11. IMO, SOLAS The International Convention for the Safety of Life at Sea2001. International Maritime Organisation, London
12. IMO, MSC 82/15/4 Role of the Human Element, ed. M.S. Committee2006a, London: International Maritime Organization, IMO
13. Bruneel, J., D'Este, P., Salter, A.: Investigating the factors that diminish the barriers to university–industry collaboration. Research Policy 39(7), 858–868 (2010)
14. Chung, A.Z.Q., Shorrock, S.T.: The research-practice relationship in ergonomics and human factors - surveying and bridging the gap. Ergonomics of Hybrid Automated Systems 54(5), 413–429 (2011)
15. Sobell, L.C.: Bridging the gap between scientists and practitioners: The challenge before us. Behavior Therapy 27(3), 297–320 (1996)
16. Dowie, J.: The research-practice gap and the role of decision analysis in closing it. Health Care Analysis 4(1), 5–18 (1996)
17. Moffatt, S., et al.: "Impact? What impact?" Epidemiological research findings in the public domain: a case study from north-east England. Social Science & Medicine 51(12), 1755–1769 (2000)
18. Laurillard, D.: Rethinking university teaching: a conversational framework for the effective use of learning technologies, 2nd edn. RoutledgeFalmer, London (2002)

19. Huang, C.: Designing high-quality interactive multimedia learning modules. Computerized Medical Imaging and Graphics (29), 223–233 (2005)
20. Nielsen, J.: Designing Web Usability: The practice of simplicity. New Riders Publishing, Indianapolis (2000)
21. Sharp, H., Rogers, Y., Preece, J.: Interaction design: beyond human-computer interaction, 3rd edn. Wiley, Chichester (2011)
22. Jordan, P.W.: Designing pleasurable products: an introduction to the new human factors. Taylor and Francis, London and New York (2000)
23. ISO9241-210, Human-Centered Design Process for Interactive Systems2010: European Committee for Standardization

Chair Based Measurements of Sitting Behavior a Field Study of Sitting Postures and Sitting Time in Office Work

Matthijs P. Netten[1], L.H.M. van der Doelen[1,2], and Richard H.M. Goossens[1,3]

[1] Delft University of Technology, Faculty of Industrial Design Engineering, Section Applied Ergonomics and Design, Delft, The Netherlands
{m.p.netten,R.H.M.Goossens}@tudelft.nl
[2] BMA Ergonomics, Zwolle, The Netherlands
B.van.der.doelen@bma-ergonomics.com
[3] Erasmus University Rotterdam, Department of Neuroscience, The Netherlands

Abstract. In order to understand the relation between prolonged sitting and the relation to health outcome, the behavior while being seated must be studied.

A total of 41 office workers participated in a study whilst performing their regular work for eight weeks, whilst sitting on a measuring office chair (Smart Chair). The first two (control) weeks they were not aware of the measuring abilities of the chair. After this, two groups were made to distinguish between the effects of chair instruction and smart feedback on sitting postures (Van der Doelen et al. 2011).

In this paper the data has been analyzed in another way. The aim of this paper is to explore the characteristics of sedentary behavior for 41 subjects during their regular office work over eight weeks by measuring the events of sitting and absence from their office chair.

Results showed that the office workers in this study on average have very long sitting events, that exceed general recommendations. Results showed that the office workers in this study on average have very long sitting events, that exceed general recommendations. Recommendations for 5 minute breaks every hour are met by 85% of the participants. However recommendations on sitting les than 20 minutes were met by 5% of the participants. None of the participants met the recommendations on all of their days during the field study.

The sedentary behavior shown in this study underlines the importance to monitor and influence sedentary behavior while considering the individual sedentary patterns. Further knowledge on analyzing sedentary patterns is needed.

Keywords: device-based measures, sedentary behavior.

1   Introduction

The amount of time spent in sedentary situations has increased since the introduction of new communication technologies, like the computer. Some studies report that prolonged sitting can have adverse effects on health outcomes [1]. For some people the workplace covers an important part of the sedentary life of people and it is

V.G. Duffy (Ed.): DHM/HCII 2013, Part II, LNCS 8026, pp. 261–268, 2013.

suggested that for those workers it is the key setting for health promotion interventions [2]. Therefore, in order to understand the relation between prolonged sitting and the relation to health outcome, the behavior while being seated at the office must be studied.

Self-reported measures for sedentary behavior are used [3] or device-based measures [2,4,5]. Although research suggests that self-reported measures are a valid method to assess sedentary behavior [6],it is also noted that this method cannot uncover the more detailed patterns of sitting during the day [6]. Device-based measures overcome this problem. Most device-based measures use accelerometer technology [2,4,5]. Sedentary behavior can be studied in more detail and has shown e.g. that workdays are associated with more sitting and less walking/standing time than leisure days [2].

Another approach is to place sensors in the office chair that can measure presence or even postures [7,8,9,10]. The current research utilized such a device-based measuring tool that is not noticeable to the respondent. The office chair in our study, has integrated sensors that can both measure time spent sitting as well as calculate sitting postures. The chair can give feedback to the end-user by means of a tactile signal and a label attached to the chair. This, so called Smart Chair has been developed and launched by the Dutch company BMA Ergonomics.

The aim of this paper is to explore the characteristics of sedentary behavior for 41 subjects during their regular office work over eight weeks by measuring the events of sitting and absence from their office chair.

2   Method

A field study using office chairs with measuring technology was conducted from October to December 2010. Subjects were employees of a large financial institute in Brussels, Belgium. They could be included in the study if they worked at least 3 days a week and reported working with a computer more than 4 hours per day. They were not included if there was a history of musculoskeletal problems in the last 6 months.

2.1   Subjects

Participants were 41 volunteers (19 females, 22 males) that worked at four different departments. The participants were divided into two research groups, each consisting of two occupational groups; 'Administrative' and 'IT'. The participants should perform their regular office tasks while using a measuring chair.

Female participants had a mean age of 42.4 yrs (sd 8.6). They had a mean height of 166.1 cm (sd 5.9) and a mean body weight of 70.0 kg (sd 12.2). Male participants had a mean age of 46.3 yrs (sd 9.9), a mean height of 179.0 cm (sd 6.2) and a mean weight of 84.2 kg (sd 11.3).

2.2   Measuring (Office) Chair: Smart Chair

The chair calculates postures based on pressure values of sensors in the seat surface and back of the seat. Postures are calculated at 1 Hz and logged by the chair. The measuring system is fully integrated in the chair cushioning. Figure 1 shows the different postures that the Smart Chair can distinguish. In this paper we only report the time that participants were sitting on the chair in any posture versus the time that the participant was absent from the chair.

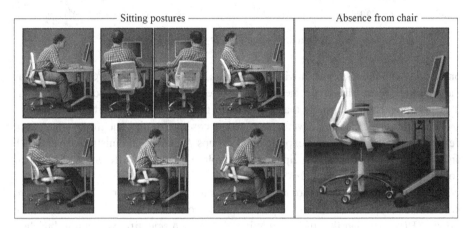

Fig. 1. Postures by the Smart Chair

2.3   Experimental Set-up

Subjects used the chairs during 8 weeks. The first two weeks were considered a control condition to measure regular sitting behavior. During these first two weeks the subjects received a Smart Chair that measured their posture, but no instruction or feedback was given during that time.

At the start of the intervention condition all participants received the same training instruction about chair settings and ergonomic workplace settings (e.g monitor height, desk height). Part of them (n=22) also got extra feedback from the chair about sitting behavior [10].

The researchers collected the data from the chairs at times that the users were absent.

2.4   Data Analysis

Duration of sitting events, duration of absence events, number of sitting events per workday , number of absence events per workday and the total time of the workday were calculated from the data for each subject. Figure 2 illustrates these measures. The length of a workday is defined as the time between the first contact with the chair

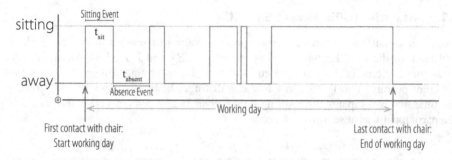

Fig. 2. Outcome measurements in Sitting pattern

on that day and the last contact with the chair on that day. A sitting event is defined as the interval where the chair measures postures (presence). As soon as the chair measures no postures for more than 60 seconds, the absence event starts.

The calculated measures were averaged according to the subgroups that were defined in the original study (experimental groups A and B, administrative versus IT and male versus female participants), to explore potential differences. Statistical comparisons were not made.

Adherence to sitting recommendations was assessed using three different boundaries. Ryan et al (2011) reported these from general recommendations by experts. He concluded that these guidelines still lack a scientific validation, but they deliver do insights in how the different recommendations are met.

The recommendations used were a maximum sitting time of 20 min ; a maximum sitting time of 30 min and a 5-min break every hour , which was operationalized as a maximum sitting time of 55 min.

3   Results

For the 41 subjects a total of 964 working days were collected that met the criteria. The study was performed with a Smart Chair prototype that was still in development. Some data was lost due to technical issues. This led to a loss of 134 working days.

3.1   Typical Data

Lengths of the sitting events and absence events were used to depict (figure 3) sitting patterns from three randomly selected participants.

Participant 2 remains sedentary (84,8% of the working day with 6 sitting events of 74 ± 46 min) longer than participant 1 (18 sitting events of 16,1 ± 21,3 min) or participant 3(22 sitting events of 18,8 ± 18,5 min).

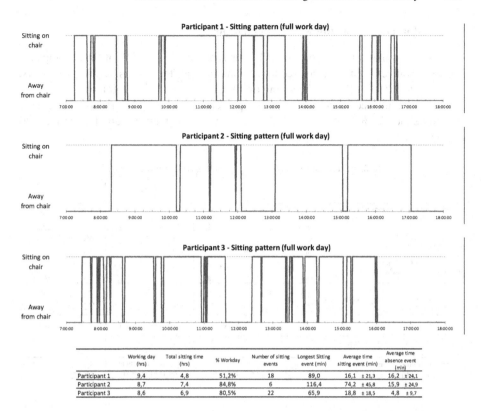

	Working day (hrs)	Total sitting time (hrs)	% Workday	Number of sitting events	Longest Sitting event (min)	Average time sitting event (min)	Average time absence event (min)
Participant 1	9,4	4,8	51,2%	18	89,0	16,1 ± 21,3	16,2 ± 24,1
Participant 2	8,7	7,4	84,8%	6	116,4	74,2 ± 45,8	15,9 ± 24,9
Participant 3	8,6	6,9	80,5%	22	65,9	18,8 ± 18,5	4,8 ± 9,7

Fig. 3. Typical data for three randomly chosen participants

3.2   Sitting versus Absence

Table 1. Sitting and absence events and their outcome divided in three different subgroups

Subgroup Research Phase	Working day total time Average (hrs)	sd (hrs)	Sitting time on working days Average (hrs)	% of workday	Absence Eventes Average (min)	sd (min)	Max (min)	avg. events / workday	Sitting Events Average (min)	sd (min)	Max (min)	avg. events / workday
A												
Control condition	8,04	1,44	5,22	64,8%	14,1	24,9	253,8	12,1	24,0	25,6	181,7	13,1
Test condition	7,98	1,23	5,08	63,6%	13,4	26,7	388,3	13,0	21,7	24,1	208,7	14,0
B												
Control condition	8,00	1,11	5,72	71,5%	13,6	25,5	257,1	10,1	31,0	31,4	206,1	11,1
Test condition	7,76	1,60	5,42	69,8%	13,4	25,5	284,7	10,5	28,3	29,2	200,4	11,5
Admin												
Control condition	7,77	1,51	5,55	71,4%	12,1	24,7	257,1	11,0	27,7	29,4	206,1	12,0
Test condition	7,72	1,56	5,20	67,3%	12,2	25,0	297,9	12,4	23,2	25,2	200,4	13,4
ICT												
Control condition	8,19	1,00	5,51	67,2%	15,0	25,6	234,3	10,7	28,1	29,2	181,7	11,7
Test condition	7,96	1,35	5,33	67,0%	14,5	27,0	388,3	10,9	26,9	28,6	208,7	11,9
Female												
Control condition	8,12	1,12	5,70	70,2%	14,1	25,4	207,2	10,3	30,3	32,1	181,7	11,3
Test condition	7,96	1,37	5,52	69,4%	13,2	25,0	257,1	11,0	27,6	29,8	206,1	12,0
Male												
Control condition	7,92	1,36	5,36	67,6%	13,5	25,1	388,3	11,4	26,0	26,5	208,7	12,4
Test condition	7,77	1,52	5,05	65,1%	13,5	26,9	339,2	12,1	23,2	24,5	193,9	13,1

3.3   Adherence to Sitting Recommendations

Table 2 shows that 5 minute breaks in 1 hour is attainable for 85% of the participants. However none of them met this recommendation on all their measured working days. 21 ± 15% to 23% ± 18% of the sitting events are longer than 55 minutes.

The 20 minute recommendation shows percentages of 5% of participant that meet this guideline. 53% ± 20% to 49 ± 20% of the sitting events are longer than 20 minutes.

Table 2. Adherence to sedentary guidelines for both test conditions

		20 min			30 min			55 min		
		avg	sd	range	avg	sd	range	avg	sd	range
Average number of events longer than recommendation (number/working day)	Control condition	5,7	1,8	1 - 9	4,2	1,6	0 - 8	1,8	1,2	0 - 6
	Test condition	5,5	1,9	0 - 11	3,9	1,7	0 - 9	1,6	1,2	0 - 5
Average number of sitting events longer than recommendations (%)	Control condition	53%	20%		41%	21%		23%	18%	
	Test condition	49%	20%		37%	20%		21%	15%	
Cumulative time of sitting events longer than recommended (hrs/working day)	Control condition	4,8	1,6	0,4 - 8,3	4,2	1,7	0,5 - 7,6	3,0	1,6	0,9 - 7,2
	Test condition	4,4	1,6	0,4 - 8,4	3,8	1,7	0,5 - 8,4	2,8	1,5	0,9 - 6,9
Percentage cumulative time of sitting events longer than recommended relative to total sitting time (%)	Control condition	85%	12%		73%	18%		50%	21%	
	Test condition	82%	14%		69%	20%		48%	21%	
1 working day longer than recommended (number)		11 (of 16 total events)			9 (of 12 total events)			6 (of 12 total events)		
Participants meeting recommendations every day (number)		0			0			0		
Participants meeting recommendations on any day (number)		2 (5% of population) on total of 3 days			9 (22% of population) on total of 17 days			2 (85% of population) on total of 177 days		

4   Discussion

The smart chair is used as an unobtrusive instrument to monitor behavior close to the workplace. This means it is not able to monitor individual sitting time on other chairs, e.g. during meetings or (lunch)breaks. Long absence events in chair data during lunch or meetings can be sedentary after all. However these breaks do count to interrupt sitting time. A workday in this study was defined as the time between first contact and last contact with the chair by the test user. Activities before or after this timeframe could be missing in the presented data. Total sitting time during workdays in this study can thus be underestimated, although this is expected to be a minor difference considering the average time of the observed working days that remains within a range of 7,7 – 8,2 hrs in subgroups.

McRady & Levine (2009) reported total sitting times during workin days of 9,95 ± 2 hr using person bound accelerometers. Ryan (2011) found similar sitting times and absence times as found in this study.

The adherence to sedentary guidelines also showed similar findings. Although the participants of this study show even less adherence to the 20 minute guideline. Of the sitting events 49% ± 20% - 53% ± 20% are longer than 20 minutes. These sitting times accumulate to 85% ± 12% - 82% ± 14% of total sitting time.

This study does show that the 5 minute break per hour seems attainable for most people. Although this study didn't show any participants that met recommendations during every day during the field study.

Participants were selected on their type of work (desk work, working minimum 4 hrs behind computer screen) which can partly explain the high total sitting time compared to other studies. The culture of work within the company that we visited can also be of influence.

Nonetheless the participants of this study show that many hours at work are spend sedentary. It must be noted that the individual differences can be large, as can be seen in figure 3. A measuring chair could therefor be a good solution to monitor and influence people in their sedentary behavior while considering these large individual differences.

All participants had a fixed personal workspace (desk and chair). Data was analyzed when it corresponded to their working schedules. All other data that was collected (coincidentally) by the chair was ignored for analysis.

The Smart Chairs that were used still were at a developing stage. Some technical problems were encountered. It did however result in missing data. It is assumed that the loss of data was a random event and not related to the outcome of sitting patterns per individual.

The study that was done, was not designed to explore sedentary behavior. The hypothesis underlying this data was whether the Smart Chair is able to influence sitting postures through feedback about sitting behavior .

Next step that are currently explored are about constructing a measure that can relate break regime (number of moments and timing) to sedentary events. The Smart Chair itself could be used to give feedback on exceeding sitting time recommendations directly on occurring of the event. At this point the system is mainly focussed on improving sitting postures.

Following the exploration of this data further analysis / research is wanted to gain more insights in the sitting patterns of office workers. With intensive office-base deskwork, measurements of sedentary times and times of absence with a measuring chair a good solution. This chair can deal with individual differences based on their sedentary patterns. Important aspects that need further study:

- Can longer sitting events be related with longer absence as compensation? Frequency distribution of these patterns can be considered to construct a risk index for sedentariness. Long sitting times with few moments to interrupt seem more high risk than similar total sitting time divided over more events. Discern the test subjects in degree of calmness. Calm versus restless sitter. And above this, can this be related to the amount and lengths of breaks/sitting time?
- Quality of sitting postures vs sitting patterns. Does number and length of brakes relate to the quality of postures during sitting bouts?

5   Conclusion

Results showed that the office workers in this study on average have very long sitting events, that exceed general recommendations. Recommendations for 5 minute breaks every hour are met by 85% of the participants. However recommendations on sitting les than 20 minutes were met by 5% of the participants. None of the participants met the recommendations on all of their days during the field study.

The sedentary behaviour shown in this study underlines the importance to monitor and influence sedentary behaviour while considering the individual sedentary patterns. Further knowledge on analyzing sedentary patterns is needed.

Acknowledgement. The researchers would like to thank the Belgian financial institute that enabled us to do field research on such a scale. The support and efforts during this research were and still are greatly appreciated.

Also, the support from the consortium member BMA Ergonomics (also the Belgian Subsidiary) and Salland Electronics during the research is greatly appreciated.

References

1. Thorp, A.A., Owen, N., Neuhaus, M., Dunstan, D.W.: Sedentary Behaviors and Subsequent Health Outcomes in Adults: A Systematic Review of Longitudinal Studies, 1996–2011. American Journal of Preventive Medicine 41(2), 207–215 (2011)
2. McCrady, S.K., Levine, J.A.: Sedentariness at work: How much do we really sit. Obesity 17(11), 2103–2105 (2009)
3. Jans, M.P., Proper, K.I., Hildebrandt, V.H.: Sedentary Behavior in Dutch Workers. Differences Between Occupations and Business Sectors. American Journal of Preventive Medicine 33(6), 450–454 (2007)
4. Chastin, S.F.M., Granat, M.H.: Methods for objective measure, quantification and analysis of sedentary behaviour and inactivity. Gait and Posture 31(1), 82–86 (2010)
5. Matthews, C.E., Chen, K.Y., Freedson, P.S., Buchowski, M.S., Beech, B.M., Pate, R.R., Troiano, R.P.: Amount of time spent in sedentary behaviors in the United States, 2003-2004. American Journal of Epidemiology 167(7), 875–881 (2008)
6. Clark, B.K., Thorp, A.A., Winkler, E.A.H., Gardiner, P.A., Healy, G.N., Owen, N., Dunstan, D.W.: Validity of self-reported measures of workplace sitting time and breaks in sitting time. Medicine and Science in Sports and Exercise 43(10), 1907–1912 (2011)
7. Tan, H.Z., Slivovsky, L.A., Pentland, A.P.: A Sensing Chair Using Pressure Distribution Sensors. IEEE/ASME Trans. Mechatronics 6(3), 261–268 (2001)
8. Mutlu, B., Krause, A., Forlizzi, J., Guestrin, C., Hodgins, J.K.: Robust, Low-Cost, Non-Intrusive Recognition of Seated Postures. In: Proceedings of 20th ACM Symposium on User Interface Software and Technology (UIST 2007), Newport, RI (2007)
9. Zheng, Y., Morrell, J.B.: Avibrotactile feedback approach to posture guidance. In: 2010 IEEE Haptics Symposium, Waltham, Massachusetts, USA (Boston Area), pp. 351–358 (2010)
10. Van der Doelen, L.H.M., Netten, M.P., Goossens, R.H.M.: &NES University of Oulu, Finnish Institute of Occupational Health, the Oulu University of Applied Sciences, University of Eastern Finland, and University of Lapland, E. R. Y, Tactile feedback to influence sitting behaviour during office work. In: äyrynen, S.V. (Ed.), NES - Wellbeing and Innovation Through Ergonomics, pp. 380–385. Oulu, Finland (2011)
11. Ryan, C.G., Grant, P.M., Dall, P.M., Granat, M.H.: Sitting patterns at work: Objective measurement of adherence to current recommendations. Ergonomics 54(6), 531–538 (2011)

Temporal Dependence of Trapezius Muscle Activation during Sustained Eye-Lens Accommodation at Near

Hans O. Richter[1], Camilla Zetterberg [1], and Mikael Forsman[1,2]

[1] Centre for Musculoskeletal Research, University of Gävle, Sweden
{Hans.Richter,Camilla.Zetterberg}@hig.se
[2] Occupational Medicine, IMM Institute of Environmental Medicine,
Karolinska Institut, Stockholm, Sweden
Mikael.Forsman@ki.se

Abstract. In this experimental study different levels of oculomotor load were induced via optical trial lenses. The aim was to investigate the temporal dependence of a moderate visual load on trapezius muscle activity. Trapezius muscle activity was measured with bipolar surface electromyography (EMG). Sixty-six subjects with a median age of 36 (range 19–47, std 8) viewed a black and white Gabor grating (5 c/deg) through 0 D, and -3.5 D lenses, in periods of 7-min. An auto refractor was used to continuously sample data on eye-lens accommodation during the vision tasks. Response-diopters were used as a dichotomous high/low accommodation grouping variable. For these groups EMG amplitudes during minutes 1-7 per each lens trial were studied separately with Generalized Estimating Equations (GEE). The analysis results showed significant increases in trapezius muscle activity over time for both viewing conditions. For the binocular -3.5 D condition response-diopters gave a significant positive contribution to the EMG amplitude. The results indicate that sustained eye-lens accommodation at near, during ergonomically unfavorable viewing conditions, may increase the risk for trapezius muscle myalgia.

Keywords: Visual ergonomics, Gaze stabilization, Electromyography, Eye-lens accommodation, Computer work, Neck.

1   Introduction

Disorders of the visual and musculoskeletal systems are major public health problems affecting substantial proportions of the general population in their work, daily living and social life. National Institute for Occupational Safety and Health (NIOSH) reports that over 80% of those who work with computers suffer from eye and/or musculoskeletal complaints. Despite the fact that many causes have been identified which is responsible for neck and upper extremity pain, the underlying mechanisms are still poorly understood. The point of departure for the present research is the notion that accommodative/vergence eye movements are intrinsically integrated with head and scapular area muscle functionality and that the coupling between these effectors lay the foundation for visually mediated musculoskeletal mechanisms.

V.G. Duffy (Ed.): DHM/HCII 2013, Part II, LNCS 8026, pp. 269–275, 2013.

In order to perceive small details in the surround, e.g. an alphanumerical character displayed on an electronic screen, the light has to be appropriately refracted. The process of adjusting the curvature of the crystalline eye lens, which brings images into sharp focus in the plane of the retina, is called accommodation. The accommodative response consists of a tightly coupled triad of eye movements: dioptric (D) adjustment of the crystalline eye lens; convergence/divergence of both eyes toward the locus of fixation; and pupillary constriction/dilatation. The accommodative system of the eye adjusts the curvature of the lens, thereby changing its refractive power, allowing the formation of a clear retinal image of an object located at a different distances than the present. This reaction is controlled by the ciliary muscle which changes the curvature of the lens.

Accommodation and vergence mechanisms in the visual system in all likelihood form one biologically plausible pathway by which augmentation of eye-muscle activity cause an increase in neck/shoulder muscle activity; over time, this could develop into discomfort, pain or ache. A sufficient description of the mediating sensorimotor events may be part of an answer to the question about why some types of neck pain occur. Hence, such mechanisms, if properly understood, have the potential to explain how and why augmented eye muscle activity leads to increased neck/shoulder muscle activity.

Recent work on trapezius muscle activation, as measured with surface EMG, has shown that brief and extended periods of large amplitudes of ocular accommodation, when the ciliary muscle is highly contracted, are coupled to an increase in static trapezius muscle activity level [1, 2]. The previous results showed, more specifically, that increasing the tone of the ciliary muscle, by placing an optical minus lens in front of both eyes and at the same time seeing to that the lack of focus incurred is compensated for by binocularly increasing eye-lens accommodation, was significantly coupled to a bilateral increase in trapezius muscle activity.

These and other results together suggest that sustained eye-lens accommodation has the ability to trigger a postural stabilization response. The exact mechanism(s) linking eye-neck/scapular muscle activity with one another however remains elusive. So far the temporal aspects of exposure to deficient visual ergonomics have not been addressed. The relationships between ciliary muscle load and trapezius muscle activation levels, previously observed on a group level [1, 2], could be related to time. However, the dimension of time was discarded from the results communicated in Richter et al. [1, 2]. Against this background, the purpose of the present study is to investigate temporal dependence of trapezius muscle activity during sustained eye-lens accommodation at near.

The first hypothesis stated that trapezius muscle activation levels, as measured by surface EMG, increase over time during visually demanding near work (hypothesis 1). An increase in EMG is hypothesized to result from the visually demanding near work, since they invoke sustained mental attention to the task [3, 4], and sustained eye-lens accommodation. Excess effort to achieve required accommodation may be triggered by mental/physical task demands [5, 6] and carry over to the musculoskeletal system. The temporal unfolding of trapezius muscle EMG activity, as a result of experimentally controlled intensive near work, is generally unknown at present.

The second hypothesis stated that trapezius muscle activation levels are modulated by response-diopters, such that more eye-lens accommodation than what is called for relative an ergonomically appropriate work condition, leads to more EMG and vice versa (hypothesis 2). Response-diopters, an indirect measure of ciliary-muscle load, may be assumed to represent an idiosyncratic characteristic which, if high in a relative sense (e.g. due to uncorrected hypermetropia, inappropriately close working distance to visual display, etc), could cause an increase in trapezius muscle activation [1, 2].

2   Methods

2.1   Participants

Sixty-six participants (median age 38, range 19-47, 54 females and 12 males) were recruited, 33 with neck pain and 33 healthy controls. To exclude participants with eye diseases, the participants were examined by a licensed optometrist. No one was excluded due to eye diseases. All participants were recruited through advertisement. Informed consent was obtained from each participant. The study was approved by the Uppsala University Medical Ethical Review Board, Uppsala, Sweden (2006:027).

2.2   Visual Task

The vision task consisted of 7-min of accommodation/convergence on a contrast varying Gabor grating displayed on a computer screen (Sony F520 CRT monitor and a VSG video board. Cambridge Research System Ltd, Rochester, UK). The contrast threshold of the grating was determined using the von Békésy tracking method. The target consisted of a fixation cross on a black- and white sine wave Gabor grating. The contrast of the Gabor grating varied throughout the task (Contrast=(Lmax-Lmin)÷(Lmax+Lmin), L = luminance). Distance to screen was 0.65 m (1.5 D) and the centre of the grating was placed in the midline of the eyes, with the gaze angle approximately 15° downwards. For maximal stimulation of accommodation, the spatial frequency of the Gabor grating was set to 5 c/deg. Before the vision task started, the contrast of the Gabor grating was zero and only the fixation cross was visible. To start the vision task, the volunteers pushed a hand-held, low-force button and the contrast of the grating increased (speed 0.8 percent/s.). When the volunteers perceived the grating, he/she pushed the button and the contrast froze for a short period. After a pause of random length (1.5-3.5 s.), the contrast of the grating decreased. When the grating became invisible to the participant, he/she pushed the button. This was repeated for seven minutes. With each response, the subjects caused a reversal of the contrast course and the computer recorded each level of contrast at which this occurred. A standardized task instruction was used: "Look at the fixation-cross and the black-and-white Gabor grating. Carefully focus on the fixation cross so that it is maximally sharp and clear at all times". Accommodation stimuli in each of the two trial-lens conditions were fixed and determined by the sum of the spherical power of the trial-lens(es) and the distance to the screen (expressed in D). The accommodation response varied and was assessed with an auto refractor (Power

Refractor R03, Plusoptix, Nürnberg, Germany). Accommodation stimuli were 5.0 D in the minus-lens condition and 1.5 D in the neutral-lens condition. To overcome the experimentally induced blur in the minus-lens condition and obtain a maximally sharp image of the Gabor grating, the participant had to sustain ciliary contraction corresponding to a 5 D change of optical power in the eye-lens.

2.3   Electromyography and Electrocardiography

EMG and ECG were recorded during rests and during vision tasks. EMG and ECG signals were amplified, band-pass filtered (EMG: 10-500 Hz, ECG 0.05-35 Hz), and sampled at 2000 Hz (EMG100C, BIOPAC Systems, Inc., Santa Barbara, CA, USA). ECG was used to decrease disturbances from heart signals on raw EMG. The ECG disturbances were assumed to be stable over the heartbeats in each condition. The timing of the R-peaks in the ECG signals was estimated, and the ECG contributions around the R-peaks ($\pm$ 0.2 s) in the EMG signals were averaged from the rest measurements. The estimated contributions were next subtracted from the EMG signals. To identify the timings of the QRS peaks in the ECG, the signal was down-sampled to 1000 Hz and high-pass filtered by a third-order Butterworth filter with a cut-off frequency of 4 Hz. The signal was subsequently divided into 2-s windows and the lowest, maximum value from these periods was identified: the threshold value for identifying R-peaks was set at 0.78 of this maximum value.

The EMG recordings were root-mean-square (RMS) converted in 0.1 s windows, quadratically adjusted for noise (the lowest 0.4 s moving RMS value of the recordings during rest), and normalized to submaximal reference contractions. The mean RMS value of the middle 10 s of three 15 s submaximal contractions was used to normalize and express the measurement data in %RVE (reference voluntary electrical activity). The 50th percentile of the normalized RMS-values for each minute was chosen as the parameter of the muscular activity level. For the rest period, minutes one, two and three were first used in order to assess the stability of the EMG activity. In the main analysis the average rest period EMG across min 1-3 was thereafter used. For the vision tasks minutes one through seven (min 1-7) was used. Hereafter, these 50th percentiles from rest and vision task will be referred to as EMG_{rest} (average of min 1-3) and EMG_{task} (min 1-7), respectively. A logarithmic transform was applied on EMG_{rest} and EMG_{task} prior to the statistical analysis in order to correct for a tilt in the distribution of data which was skewed with most participants exhibiting very low or low activation levels with a tail in the right direction.

ECG was also used to assess the heart rate variability (HRV) as markers of autonomic reactivity (e.g. as due to arousal) during the experiments. Analyses of the variation of intervals between consecutive heartbeats have been shown to quantify the autonomic heart regulation and the balance between sympathetic and parasympathetic activation (Task Force, 1996). Because of the very short periods as basis for the HRV calculation, standard deviation of the times between the R-peaks, the NN intervals (SDNN, standard deviation of RR intervals) was the chosen variable. SDNN is simple to calculate and should, in comparison to the frequency band variables, make use of the one-minute data in a more efficient way.

2.4   Statistical Analysis

General Estimating Equation (GEE) was used to analyze the EMG data. GEE provides a general framework for analysis of polychotomous continuous data and relaxes several key assumptions of traditional regression models [7, 8, 9].

The original data consisted of 66 subjects x 7 minutes thus 462 data points. After outlier removal (<5%) residuals from the different factor in the model were in acceptable agreement with the normal distribution (i.e., with the great majority of logEMG-values within ±1.96 std). The requirement of homogeneity of variance was satisfactorily met.

All statistical tests on EMG were run on a mean of left and right trapezius using the 50th percentile %RVE. Statistical analyses were performed with PASW 18.0 for Windows (SPSS Inc., Chicago, IL, USA).

Rest-Period. To examine if time (min 1-3) was a mediating cause behind progressively increased trapezius muscle activation levels across time, two Generalized Estimating Equations (GEE) models were tested, one for each rest period immediately preceding the visual tasks. The purpose was to ascertain that the trapezius muscle was relaxed and that the EMG activity did not exhibit an increase in activity that could be due to biomechanical effects (which then would be a confounding variable when the effect of the vision task was analyzed).

Visual Task. To examine if oculomotor load was a mediating cause behind progressively increased trapezius muscle activation levels across time, two Generalized Estimating Equations (GEE) analytic approaches were utilized, one for each experimental lens condition (±0 D, and -3.5 D). A dichotomous variable, $RD_{low/high}$, in each experimental lens condition was set to 'low' for those whose average response diopter was below the mean level for that lens, and to 'high' for those above the mean level. This indirect measure of oculomotor load was analyzed together with trapezius muscle EMG over minutes 1-7 together with several additional independent variables. In the initial analytic step GEE tested the effect of the following independent variables on $logEMG_{task}$: $logEMG_{rest}$, SDNN, time, and $RD_{low/high}$. In the final analytic step the two GEE models was restricted to include only those independent variables which passed the threshold for significance ($p<0.05$). The variance contribution from $logEMG_{rest}$ on $logEMG_{task}$ was included in the models in order to render the dependent variable less biased by musculoskeletal activity unrelated to the experimental treatment. The effect of SDNN was assessed in order to control for autonomic nervous system activation which could be a potential confounding variable. The measures of time included minutes (minutes 1-7) within trial-lens condition.

3   Results

3.1   EMG Activity during Rest (min 1-3)

No effect of time (min 1-3) or trend thereof on logEMG activity was evident in any of the rest periods preceding the two vision tasks ($p>0.05$).

3.2   EMG Activity during Vision Task (min 1-7)

The activation levels of trapezius muscle activity ($logEMG_{task}$) was related to baseline activity ($logEMG_{rest}$) in both lens conditions ($p<0.001$). Time impacted on $logEMG_{task}$ in both lens conditions ($p<0.001$). Response diopters ($RD_{low/high}$) raised muskuloskeletal activation ($logEMG_{task}$) in only the binocular minus lens condition ($p<0.05$). See Table 1.

Table 1. Model Summary[1]

Viewing condition	Independent variable	Slope (β)	p-value	Goodness of Fit (QIC)
Lens blur (-3.5 D)	$LogEMG_{rest}$	0.505	<0.001	
	Time	0.026	0.001	
	$RD_{Low/High}$	0.187	0.016	
				64.5
Neutral reference (±0 D)	$LogEMG_{rest}$	0.478	<0.001	
	Time	0.027	0.001	
				76.4

[1]Dependent variable: $logEMG_{task}$.

4   Discussion

There were no trends in the data indicating that EMG activity increased during rest period (baseline). During the rest period subjects sat in the same chair, assumed the same posture, and were not allowed to move during 3 minutes. Since EMG (across min 1-3) was stable over time, biomechanical effects of the sitting posture on EMG_{task} may be ruled out.

The results from the present GEE analyses gave support for hypothesis one, which stated that EMG would increase over minute 1-7 due to the mental/physical task demands. Sympathetic arousal (e.g. caused by mental stress) can be ruled out as a cause behind the observed increase in trapezius muscle activity because no sign of this was apparent in the ECG recordings and analysis of heart-rate variability.

Hypothesis two, which stated that sustained periods of static accommodation/vergence load have a significant effect on muscle activity in the trapezius muscle, with more ciliary muscle load leading to more trapezius muscle EMG activity, was confirmed in the minus lens viewing condition. The neutral reference condition (±0 D) did not induce trapezius muscle EMG activation that was significantly associated with contraction of the ciliary muscle. In the minus lens viewing condition (-3.5 D) a statistically significant relationship between response diopters, and trapezius muscle EMG activation was found.

During the minus lens viewing condition accommodation/convergence was not optimally postured onto the target, resulting in blur and/or double vision in the retinal image. For those participants that compensated for the induced blur by increasing the ciliary muscle tonus and the dioptric power of the crystalline eye-lens, averaged trapezius muscle EMG activity was significantly larger in magnitude. When triggered by strenuous near work, central nervous system efferentation targeted to the oculomotor system may cross over to motor tracts and drive and posture the visual-musculoskeletal effectors in a synergistic fashion. The end result of this synergy may be "too much" gaze stabilization. Notably, oculomotor load of the type studied here may arise due to numerous other causes than by minus blur, e.g. be triggered by an uncorrected hyperopia, exophoria or general fatigue of eye-lens accommodation, etc.

The present results confirm and extend previous research [1, 2] and suggest that sustained eye-lens accommodation at near, during ergonomically unfavorable viewing conditions, may increase the risk for trapezius muscle myalgia.

Acknowledgments. This study was supported by grants from the Swedish Council for Working Life, Social Research Grant 2005-0488 and 2009-1761.We thank our volunteers for their generosity and patience. Research engineer Nils-Göran Larson is acknowledged for excellent engineering assistance. Ph.D. Hans Högberg is acknowledged for expert statistical advice.

References

1. Richter, H.O., Bänziger, T., Abdi, S., Forsman, M.: Stabilization of gaze: a relationship between ciliary muscle contraction and trapezius muscle activity. Vis. Res. 23, 2559–2569 (2010)
2. Richter, H.O., Bänziger, T., Forsman, M.: Experimental oculomotor load and static trapezius muscle activity. EJAP 111, 29–36 (2011)
3. Iwanaga, K., Saito, S., Shimomura, Y., Harada, H., Katsuura, T.: The effect of mental loads on muscle tension, blood pressure and blink rate. J. Physiol. Anthropol. Appl. Human Sci. 19, 135–141 (2000)
4. Mehta, R.K., Agnew, M.J.: Effects of concurrent physical and mental demands for a short duration static task. International Journal of Industrial Ergonomics 41, 488–493 (2011)
5. Malmstrom, F.V., Randle, R.: Effect of a concurrent counting task on dynamic visual accommodation. Am. J. Optom. Physiol. Opt. 61, 590–594 (1984)
6. Birnbaum, M.H.: Nearpoint visual stress: a physiological model. J. Am. Optom. Assoc. 55, 825–835 (1984)
7. Ballinger, G.: Using Generalized Estimating Equations for Longitudinal Data Analysis. Organizational Research Methods 7, 127–150 (2004)
8. Ghisletta, P., Spini, D.: An Introduction to Generalized Estimating Equations and an Application to Assess Selectivity Effects in a Longitudinal Study on Very Old Individuals. Journal of Educational and Behavioral Statistics 29, 421–437 (2004)
9. Hanley, J.A., Negassa, A., Edwardes, M.D., Forrester, J.E.: Statistical analysis of correlated data using generalized estimating equations: an orientation. Am. J. Epidemiol. 157, 364–375 (2003)

Setting That Mouse for Tracking Tasks

Ransalu Senanayake and Ravindra S. Goonetilleke

Human Performance Laboratory,
Department of Industrial Engineering and Logistics Management
Hong Kong University of Science and Technology
Clear Water Bay, Hong Kong
{rsenanayake,ravindra}@ust.hk

Abstract. A pointing device plays an important role in human-computer inte-raction. The computer mouse is a convenient device for both pointing and steer-ing. The literature related to the effect of mouse gain on steering tasks is scarce. An experiment was conducted with 10 participants and each participant was asked to traverse a constrained path using a computer mouse. There were three levels of gain approximately equal to 2.3, 10, and 15. The experiment had 11 levels of difficulty (D/P) based on path width (P) and path length (D) and three trials for each combination of D and P. Performance was evaluated using movement time taken to traverse the path. The results showed that movement time is minimized, in feedback-controlled steering tasks, at a gain of around nine.

Keywords: Pointing devices, Mouse, Gain, Drury's Law, Steering Law.

1   Introduction

1.1   Mouse as an Input Device

The computer mouse [1, 2] is a popular pointing device even today for different types of human-computer interaction tasks. Without a pointing device such as a mouse, the computer would have not been a device that would have been easy to use.   The major functionality of the mouse is mapping human hand movements on a 2D plane to a computer screen. In modern graphical user interfaces, the more common mouse re-lated tasks are pointing the cursor or moving the cursor through a constrained path. Human performance in pointing tasks has been studied by Fitts [3] and his results have been applied in many human-computer interaction related settings [4, 5].

1.2   Movements in Constrained Paths

The model (equation 1) for movements in constrained paths was proposed by Drury [6] and it has been widely known as the steering law [7-10].

$$\text{Movement Time} = a \times (\text{Index of Difficulty}) + b \qquad (1)$$

V.G. Duffy (Ed.): DHM/HCII 2013, Part II, LNCS 8026, pp. 276–281, 2013.

where a and b are constants and the Index of Difficulty is defined with respect to path length (D) and path width (P),

$$\text{Index of Difficulty (ID)} = \frac{D}{P} \qquad (2)$$

Equation (1) only holds for large ID values where visually controlled hand movement is required [11]. If the path width is relatively large, then the task can be completed in an open-loop manner where smooth pursuit eye movements are not required. Thibbotuwawa et al. [8, 9] showed that movements are ballistic when the ID is less than 8 to 10. Furthermore, for ballistic tasks, the model of movement time changes to that given in equation (3).

$$\text{Movement Time} = a' \times \sqrt{D} + b' \qquad (3)$$

where a' and b' are constants.

1.3   Mouse Gain

Gibbs [12] determined that the gain (G) of a joystick, defined as the ratio between displacement of display pointer to movement affects movement time as follows:

$$\text{Movement Time} = 0.91 - 0.02 \times \frac{1}{G} \qquad (4)$$

However, Buck [13] and Arnaut et al. [14] showed that device gain does not have any effect on movement time. Jellinek and Card [15] observed a U-shaped variation for movement time with mouse gain in pointing tasks. However, they claimed that movement time should not have any effect on input device gain explaining that mouse resolution and the small space available contributed to the U-shaped curve. In 2001 Accot and Zhai [16] reported that Index of Performance (IP) given by equation (5) has an inverted U-shape curve with gain, and IP is a maximum when gain is between two to four.

$$\text{Index of Performance (IP)} = \frac{1}{\text{Gradient of equation (1)}} \qquad (5)$$

However, they have used a graphics tablet and therefore the optimum gain value may not be applicable for an optical mouse. This experiment is an attempt to determine the gain for a mouse that minimizes movement time in steering tasks.

2   Method

2.1   Participants

Five right-handed males and five right-handed females were participants in the experiment. They were undergraduate and graduate students of the Hong Kong University of Science and Technology. On average, participants used a computer mouse 4.1 hours per day. They did not have any disabilities or defects in their hands or vision that might affect performance. Participants were paid HKD 50 for their time.

2.2   Equipment

The task was to move the mouse cursor through a constrained path. The tracking software was developed using C++. The software also recorded all mouse clicking events and cursor positions with a software timer. A Logitech G9X high precision optical mouse on a gaming mouse pad and an Acer T232HL LED display with a screen resolution of 1920×1080 was used. The display was positioned at a 60^0 upward angle from the horizontal plane.

2.3   Experimental Design

The experiment was a within-subject design with mouse Gain and ID as independent variables. The experiment was run for eleven IDs, four of which were ballistic tasks, and the other seven were visually controlled tasks based on the Thibbotuwawa et al. [8, 9] classification. Each Index of Difficulty had two combinations of Path Length (D) and Path Width (P) ratios. Therefore, there were twenty-two experimental conditions. Each participant completed a practice trial of forty-eight conditions followed by three experimental trials with each trial having twenty-two random conditions. These conditions were performed for mouse gains of 2.3, 10, 15 in a random order for each participant.

2.4   Procedure

Prior to the experiment, participants were asked to adjust the monitor brightness and chair position to a comfortable level. A rectangular path with a black circle on the left-hand side was presented to the participant (Fig. 1) and he/she was instructed to click on the black circle to initiate and steer through the path towards the end as fast as possible. If the cursor touched the border of the path, it was considered as an error and that condition was repeated at the end of the twenty-two conditions. The participant had no time pressure in any condition. Participants were given a 10-minute break when changing from one mouse gain to another.

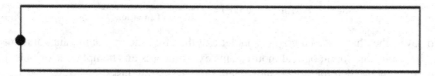

Fig. 1. A sample path

3   Results and Analysis

A repeated measure ANOVA was performed, separately, for the ballistic and visual control task. For visually controlled tasks, Gain and (D/P) were significant (Greenhouse-Geisser probability, $F(1.586, 14.277) = 11.505$, $p < 0.005$; $F(1.110, 9.9987) = 40.041$, $p < 0.001$). For Ballistic tasks, Gain and $\sqrt{D}$ were significant (Greenhouse-Geisser probability, $F(1.273, 11.456) = 14.697$, $p < 0.005$; $F(1.088, 9.791) = 36.187$, $p < 0.001$).

The data for ballistic tasks and visually controlled tasks were regressed separately (Fig. 2 and Fig. 3).

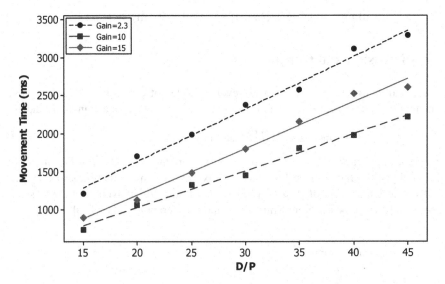

Fig. 2. MT vs (D/P) relationship for visual control tasks

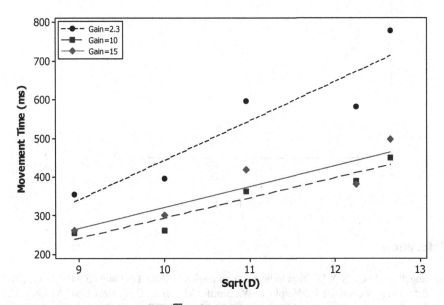

Fig. 3. MT vs $\sqrt{D}$ relationship for visual control tasks

The Gradient of each line in the visually controlled tasks was plotted against mouse gain as shown in Fig. 4. The fitted quadratic curve is given in equation (6). The minimum of the curve was calculated, and it is at a gain of 9.4.

$$\text{Gradient} = 0.416 \times (\text{Gain})^2 - 7.788 \times (\text{Gain}) + 84.623 \tag{6}$$

4   Discussion and Conclusions

It was found that movement time for all levels of Index of Difficulty varies depending on the mouse gain (equation 7). The minimum movement time is at a gain of around 10.

$$(\text{MT})_{\text{Gain}=2.3} \geq (\text{MT})_{\text{Gain}=15} \geq (\text{MT})_{\text{Gain}=10} \tag{7}$$

The results support the idea of a U-shaped curve for steering tasks. Further, it can be concluded that the Index of Performance is maximum when the mouse gain is around 9.4. This particular level of gain of a mouse that minimizes movement time in steering tasks appears to be different from that found for a graphics tablet [16].

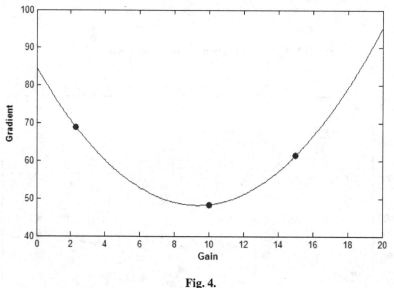

Fig. 4.

References

1. Engelbart, D.C.: X-Y Position indicator for a display system. US Patent 3,541,541 (1967)
2. Johnson, J., Roberts, T.L., Verplank, W., Smith, D.C., Irby, C.H., Beard, M., Mackey, K.: The Xerox Star: a retrospective. Computer 22, 11–26 (1989)
3. Fitts, P.M.: The information capacity of the human motor system in controlling the amplitude of movement. Journal of Experimental Psychology 47, 381–391 (1954)

4. Soukoreff, R.W., MacKenzie, I.S.: Towards a standard for pointing device evaluation, perspectives on 27 years of Fitts' law research in HCI 61, 751–789 (2004)
5. MacKenzie, I.S.: Fitts' law as a research and design tool in human-computer interaction. Journal of Human-Computer Interaction 7, 91–139 (1992)
6. Drury, C.G.: Movements with lateral constraint. Ergonomics 14, 293–305 (1971)
7. Accot, J., Zhai, S., Belin, A.E.: Beyond Fitts' law: models for trajectory-based HCI tasks. In: Proceedings of the SIGCHI Conference on Human Factors in Computing Systems, pp. 295–302. ACM, New York (1997)
8. Thibbotuwawa, N., Goonetilleke, R.S., Hoffmann, E.R.: Constrained path tracking at varying angles in a mouse tracking task. Human Factors 54, 138–150 (2012)
9. Thibbotuwawa, N., Hoffmann, E.R., Goonetilleke, R.S.: Open-loop and feedback-controlled mouse cursor movements in linear paths. Ergonomics 55, 476–488 (2012)
10. Hoffmann, E.R.: Review of models for restricted-path movements. International Journal of Industrial Ergonomics 39, 578–589 (2009)
11. Drury, C.G., Daniels, E.B.: Performance limitations in laterally constrained movements. Ergonomics 18, 389–395 (1975)
12. Gibbs, C.B.: Controller design: Interactions of controlling limbs, time-lags, and gains in positional and velocity systems. Ergonomics 5, 385–402 (1962)
13. Buck, L.: Motor performance in relation to control-display gain and target width. Ergonomics 23, 579–589 (1980)
14. Arnaut, L.Y., Greenstein, J.S.: Is display/control gain a useful metric for optimizing an interface? Human Factors 32, 651–663 (1990)
15. Jellinek, H.D., Card, S.K.: Powermice and user performance. In: CHI 1990 Proceedings of the SIGCHI Conference on Human Factors in Computing Systems, pp. 213–220. ACM, New York (1990)
16. Accot, J., Zhai, S.: Scale Effects in Steering Law Tasks. In: Proceedings of the SIGCHI Conference on Human Factors in Computing Systems, pp. 1–8. ACM, New York (2001)

Considering Ergonomic Aspects of Head-Mounted Displays for Applications in Industrial Manufacturing

Sabine Theis[1], Thomas Alexander[1], Marcel ph. Mayer[2], and Matthias Wille[3]

[1] Fraunhofer FKIE, Wachtberg, Germany
{sabine.theis,thomas.alexander}@fkie.fraunhofer.de
[2] Institut für Arbeitswissenschaft, RWTH Aachen University, Germany
m.mayer@iaw.rwth-aachen.de
[3] Bundesanstalt für Arbeitsschutz und Arbeitsmedizin, Dortmund, Germany
wille.matthias@baua.bund.de

Abstract. In this paper, we apply a comprehensive approach to evaluate and analyze potential physiological and subjective workload effects of the application of head-mounted displays (HMDs) during a typical 3.5 hrs assembly operation. The approach refers to physical as well as cognitive workload associated with HMDs. The methods for capturing and determining physiological workload include an analysis of visual acuity, of visual field, electromyography (EMG), and general posture analysis (OWAS). Subjective ratings for overall workload (BLV, RSME) and simulator sickness (SSQ) are considered and analyzed in order to complete the analysis. Their feasibility and practical implementations are discussed based on the results of a pre-test with a smaller sample size in order to give recommendations for their practical use during on-going experiments and for future industrial applications.

Keywords: Head-mounted displays, ergonomics, physiological measures, strain, electromyography, visual field, BLV, SSQ.

1 Introduction

A rapidly advancing technological evolution of novel, small and bright displays has led to novel head-mounted displays (HMDs). In addition to specialized futuristic applications, present HMDs have become increasingly applicable for multiple industrial applications. They facilitate a context-specific integration of relevant instructional information within the primary field-of-view while the user is able to continue the primary task of manufacturing. This reduces the need for an active, spatial and thus disturbing shift between a manufacturing task on the one hand and work instructions on supplementary media (paper/screen) on the other. In addition to this, both hands are available for ambidextrous work and employees are not required to interact with supplementary paper or computer media. As a consequence, critical postures resulting in additional physiological workload, reduced performance and occupational diseases may also be reduced. Moreover, assembly or manufacturing personnel, for example, can be substantially relieved during their work.

V.G. Duffy (Ed.): DHM/HCII 2013, Part II, LNCS 8026, pp. 282–291, 2013.

On the other hand, certain HMDs come along with negative side effects, which may result in poor task performance. They include technical design issues (e.g. peripheral obstructed view and muscle tension caused by inconvenient weight distribution) as well as perceptive/cognitive aspects of information representation on HMDs (e.g. information overload caused by comprehensive additional information). Several empirical studies have already investigated aspects for typical navigation and orientation tasks. In order to address practical aspects of HMD usage in a manufacturing context by giving recommendations which aim at a secure and strain optimal usage, it is required to investigate the interplay of measures which are able to capture substantial strain dimensions.

1.1   Head-Mounted Displays

Head-mounted displays generally consist of one or two displays and an optical module positioned in front of the eye(s) by a special head support or a helmet. By providing one screen per eye, binocular HMDs, as opposed to monocular HMDs, enable a stereoscopic, three-dimensional view. The optical modules shift the focus of the virtual image several meters in front of the users' eye. Hence, the virtual surface size increases [1]. HMDs can be classified by their transparency (See-through/Lookaround   [2], [3]). A See-through HMD projects the image via a semitransparent mirror into the user's field of view, while a closed or Lookaround HMD excludes the real background. In some cases transparent HMDs are equipped with an opaque slider to close the semitransparent mirror in order to hide too bright or disturbing backgrounds.

In most cases the HMD reduces the natural human field of view to 20-40°. This is especially important for closed HMDs [4], [5]. Furthermore, display electronics of See-through HMDs are often fixed at the side, which likewise obstructs the field of view. Another restriction of See-Through HMDs consists in visual information that overlaps relevant real world objects [6], [7]. For the practical use limited luminosity (for white: max. 1.800 cd/m²) and low contrast (contrast: 300:1) of the screens, complicates outdoor (ca. 8.000 cd/m² overcast sky) usage of HMDs.

1.2   An Ergonomic Viewpoint

A comprehensive analysis of workload starts by defining the concept of stress and strain. Both are different from each other with respect to their relation to the human operator [8]. Strain is usually defined as objective, neutral dimension acting from the outside on the human. Stress describes the effect of this dimension on the human operator and can be observed at different levels: the physiological, verbal-subjective, and action level. [9] point out that several indicators for the different dimensions of strain are required. [10] e.g. suggest the following terms as ergonomic evaluation criteria for HMDs: human performance, strain, fatigue, and the occurrence symptoms of simulator sickness. Simulator sickness itself is often observed with closed HMDs [11]. Impairments of the visual system and headache during or after exposure were additionally observed for 92% of the examined sample. Further studies investigating physiological effects of HMD usage particularly focused on the visual system. Different types of perceptual disorders like i.e. wrong depth perception, defective estimations of height and inclination as well as incorrect movement perception were also observed. Similar deficits were found for helicopter pilots using HMDs [12]. These results were also supported by [13] when using binocular HMDs. Other implications of HMD usages are accommodation errors by accommodative spasms and current, instrument induced myopia [14]. It is unclear how these effects change during long-term use. Differences between a binocular HMD and conventional displays could not be identified by [15], the symptoms only appeared with monocular HMD. [16] considered the interplay of the eyes, the visual overlay, focus depth, position of the eyes as well as eye movement and dominance, related to the use of a monocular HMD. The interaction of both eyes (mono-/binocular) and visual overlay (dynamic / static background) affected task time to a greater extent. Transparent HMDs are consequently not suitable for dynamic and complex environments where visual attention is particularly important. [17] showed that navigation and orientation tasks conducted with HMDs produced higher values for the symptoms of the simulation sickness than with a handheld display, while the performance measured through task time was better. Similar experiments comparing a conventional display with a head-mounted display could not verify differences between displays, but also showed higher values for simulator sickness symptoms. Furthermore the subscales fatigue and strain of the BLV (Belastungsverlaufstest, test for temporal change of workload) increased if performed with an HMD [18]. Negative side effects of an HMD on strain, fatigue and simulator sickness were confirmed by [19]. Furthermore, they found that sight might be restricted by the HMDs display box and hence, stimuli within the peripheral field of view could easily be overlooked, so that the peripheral awareness decreases.

An application of HMDs for industrial manufacturing has only become possible for the last few years. Previously HMDs were predominantly utilized for futuristic applications in augmented or virtual reality implementations. Contemporary usage increasingly incorporates areas like assembly, maintenance, picking or system surveillance [20]. As a consequence users are wearing the HMD longer and more frequent and as part of demographic change a higher percentage of elderly becomes part of the user group [21]. Ergonomic approaches have to take this into account.

2   Method

The present work refers to a pretest analyzing the interrelationship between different physiological and subjective methods for determining workload. They are applied to test the occurrence of long-term effects of different types of HMD (See-through [HMD-ST] and Look Around [HMD-LA]) and a conventional flat screen during an experimental 3.5 hour manufacturing scenario (independent variable). The methods include measures and analysis of variables like task time, subjective workload, posture, symptoms of simulator sickness, muscle activity, visual acuity and perimetry (dependent variables).

In total, two female and four male subjects aged 22-54 years (M = 32 years, SD = 11.5) took part in the preliminary test. All of them had normal or corrected to normal sight. According to the Ishihara test [22] none of them suffered from dyschromatopsia, as well as none of them had any experience with HMDs.

Participants indicated their previous experience with assembly work on a 5-point scale (1 = no experience, 5 = long experience) with 2.33 (s = 1.21) on average, which is a medium experience level.

The experimental task consists of four working segments with duration of 48 minutes each during which the participants perform different maintenance tasks. After finishing each maintenance task segment they rate their mental effort and rest for 10 minutes. Tasks include assembly operations at an Opel Omega B X20SE engine, carburetor, starter and alternator. Instructions are sequentially displayed and illustrated by means of a virtual 3D engine model and photos. In addition textual guidance is given. The engine is mounted on a height-adjustable lifting table. Tools were handed to the participant to minimize distractions and reduce unwanted side effects.

3   Results

The results of the pre-test were used for a first evaluation and test of the experimental setup. It needs to be emphasized that they must be put into perspective of the small sample size.

3.1   Visual Acuity

Visual acuity did not change after performing the experimental task conducted with distinct display types. There were no differences found for the conventional screen (left eye: Mw = 1, right eye: Mw = 1), the HMD-ST (left eye: Mw = 0.8, right eye: Mw = 0.8) or the HMD-LA (left eye Mw = 1; right eye Mw = 1).

3.2   Visual Field

The mean defect on both eyes increases with the conventional screen and decreases with the HMD (see: fig. 1). Independent of exposure, the changes (positive as well as negative) appear to be stronger on the right than on the left eye. This might be explained by the order of examination or by the small sample size. The defect of the participant with the HMD-ST (left eye: -2.2 dB, right eye: -5.3) also increases stronger than the one with the HMD-LA (left eye: - 0.1 dB, right eye: - 0.5 dB).

Table 1. Mean value of the Mean Defect (MD) [dB] of the left and the right eye before and after the task depending on display type

Condition	MD (dB) left eye (Mw)		MD (dB) right eye (Mw)	
	before	after	before	after
S (n = 2)	2,6	3,3	1,5	4,7
HMD-ST (n = 1)	4,7	2,5	8,3	3
HMD-LA (n = 3)	2,7	2,7	2,6	2
Total (n = 6)	3	2,9	3,1	3

3.3   Performance

Apart from working segment two, where the participants with the conventional screen (S) completed the task faster than the other groups, the participant with the HMD-ST was the fastest.

Table 2. Mean value of task time (min.) depending on display type within working segments

Segment		n	mean
WS 1	S	2	34,74
	HMD-ST	1	31,93
	HMD-LA	2	35,12
	Total	5	34,33
WS 2	S	2	34,52
	HMD-ST	1	45,96
	HMD-LA	2	43,10
	Total	5	40,24
WS 3	S	2	19,45
	HMD-ST	1	19,15
	HMD-LA	2	21,26
	Total	5	20,11
WS 4	S	2	36,15
	HMD-ST	1	26,55
	HMD-LA	2	34,69
	Total	5	33,64

3.4   Posture Analysis

The items "head tilted to one side" and "head tilted back" did not occur during the video based posture analysis OWAS (Ovako Working Posture Analysis System). HMD a slightly smaller proportion (Mw = 70.5%) of all head positions is classified as "free" than with the screen (Mw = 72.5%). A slightly larger proportion of the head of the group with HMD (Mw = 28.75%) falls into the category "tilted forward". The results follow a presumed track that unfavorable head positions may happen during HMD use. If this is a relevant effect will be shown by the analysis of a larger sample in the course of the main study.

3.5   Muscle Activity

Fig. 1 shows the normalized, bilateral muscle activity (%MVE, %RVE) of the neck muscles M. Trapezius pars descendens (LTRAP [left], RTRAP [right]), M. Sternocleidomastoideus (LSCM, RSCM) and M. splenius capitis (LSPLN, RSPLN), depending on display type and working segments. At the M. splenius capitis the highest

Table 3. Data sets (n) per muscle within working segments depending on display type

Muscle	RSPLN				LSPLN				RTRAP				LTRAP				RSCM				LSCM			
Segment	1	2	3	4	1	2	3	4	1	2	3	4	1	2	3	4	1	2	3	4	1	2	3	4
HMD	4	4	3	3	4	4	3	3	4	4	4	4	4	4	4	4	4	4	3	3	4	4	3	3
Screen	2	2	2	1	2	2	2	1	2	2	2	1	2	2	2	1	2	2	2	1	2	2	2	1
Sum	6	6	5	4	6	6	5	4	6	6	6	5	6	6	6	5	6	6	5	4	6	6	5	4

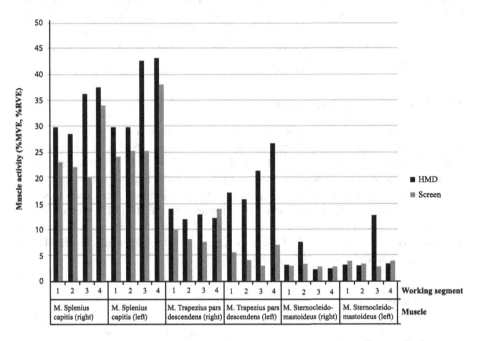

Fig. 1. Muscle activity (%MVE, %RVE) within working segments depending on display type

muscle activity is observed independent from display and working segment. The biggest difference between HMD and screen can be observed at the left side of the M. Trapezius pars descendens and on both sides of the M. splenius capitis. Muscle activity of the LSPN, RSPLN and LTRAP considerably goes up towards the end of the entire experimental task passed with the HMD.

3.6   Mental Effort

The RSME value describes subjective perceived mental effort on a scale from 0 to 150. It was surveyed as a starting point before the experimental task and during the individual working segments. As a result there are five evaluation points for all display types, which show an increase from the initial value to the second one. This demonstrates that the RSME is sensitive towards the stress. During all remaining four segments no interpretable trend or further increase revealed. The striking difference between HMD-LA and the other conditions are likely due to individual rating differences, since they also occur at the beginning.

3.7   Simulator Sickness

Comparing the simulator sickness scores measured before and after the task, interesting tendencies show up. Nausea values increase for all display types but slightly more under HMD-ST exposure (n=1; BS: 0 to 9,54; HMD-ST 0 to 19,08; HMD-LA 9,54 auf 28,62). Values of the oculomotor and disorientation scale go up within the HMD group while the ones of the screen group go down, so the results indicate the expected direction, even if to a limited extend. Further interpretation is not appropriate given the small sample size.

3.8   Subjective Perceived Strain

The BLV scores appear to be controversial and difficult to interpret. In general, all scores are on a low level. Achievement motivation values before (1,67) and after (2,67) the task only increased for the HMD-LA, which could be interpreted as a decrease in motivation caused by the experimental task. Fatigue shows across all groups a slight increase, while the rating of the performance item increases less intense with conventional screen and HMD-ST than with the HMD-LA (screen: 2,0 to 2,5; HMD-ST: 1 to 1,5; HMD-LA: 1,67 to 3,83). Mental strain shows a decrease in the screen condition at the end of the experiment (1.5 to 1.0), while the HMD-LA emerges a moderate increase (1.0 to 1.83).

4   Discussion

Conducted pre-tests were aimed at evaluating the interplay and applicability of a set of subjective and objective methods towards a comprehensive view of industrial long-term usage of HMDs. During a 3.5 h manufacturing task different physiological methods were applied. Questionnaires examined simulator sickness and workload. They all were, as expected, sensitive towards capturing workload parameters. The results provide a first impression of what might be expected from the main experiment data. Yet, results have to be evaluated in view of the fact that in total n=6 took part in the experiments, which lead to a group size of n=1 for the HMD See-through group, n=3 for the HMD Lookaround and n=2 for the conventional screen group. Certainly we are not interpreting the data to derive conclusions about strain caused by HMD usage; instead we want to learn which measures are worthwhile for further considerations or which need improvement for their application.

The experimental task consisting of 3.5 hours manufacturing assignments was easily conducted by manufacturing experts and novices. Some minor changes in the 3D engine model had to be implemented in order to prevent misunderstandings. Few textual instructions had to be formulated more precisely and subtasks had to be shortened so as to avoid mental underload.

Subjective and objective methods plus experimental task smoothly pooled into the entire experimental procedure, even if the sum of all inquiries prolongs the total test time. Some participants reported dwindling motivation during the tests and it cannot be precluded that this does not influence results; so before further experiments, load caused by the experiment itself needs to be minimized.

With respect to objective strain measures, visual acuity, mean defect of the visual field, task time and head-posture were analyzed. Alterations of visual acuity were not found. However, the measurement is based on law requirements for capturing visual acuity to determine whether a person is able to operate machinery or vehicles. It might be possible that very small changes cannot be detected in this way, but it is questionable how relevant these changes would be for a practitioner. This research focuses on a practically relevant approach.

The muscle activity was captured by electromyographic data acquisition of the M. Trapezius pars descendens, M. Sternocleidomastoideus und M. Splenius capitis on the left and right side. Until now, little was known about which muscles are strongly affected or causing headache by HMD usage during manufacturing work. Since muscle activity highly depends on hardware and work task, initially all neck muscles accessible by surface electromyography were measured in order to determine a focus based on pre-test results. Neck muscles are characterized by superposition of individual muscle layers. Usually muscle activities in those areas are gathered by fine wire electrodes to enhance signal quality, but in order to relieve participants and due to ethical reasons, this approach was disregarded. Results suggest that the M. Trapezius pars descendens and M. Splenius capitis are relevant to consider. Their activity increases towards the end of the task and increasing muscle activity might indicate muscular fatigue. Additionally a clear difference between the HMD group and the conventional display group showed up. One explanation for this could be the M. Splenius capitis' attempt to antagonize the main weight on the front part of the head (HMD). Unfortunately EMG measurements require high compliance of the participants and require some additional steps for preparation. The need to shave the neck could discourage participants to take part in the experiments. In addition EMG requires controlled temperature conditions and adequate clothing to prevent transpiration, because it makes electrodes break loose from the skin. The results concerning the visual field of the participants are also relevant. While the mean defect (dB) increases within the conventional screen group, it increases within the HMD-group. The fact that even very young participants show a defect prior to the experimental task, suggests that the method and its execution (cooperation/concentrativeness of the participant) have a strong influence on the data. It is well worth considering if the method can be categorized as an objective one.

All methods proved to be suitable for this specific application of long-term strain evaluation during the use of HMDs. In terms of total experiment time and the participants motivation during the tests one can advise against the inflationary use of tests before and after the experimental task. It is deeply interesting if findings of ongoing main experiments are going to reflect pre-test results, and how they compare to similar experiments about workload during long-term HMD usage [23].

References

1. Alexander, T.: Virtuelle Umgebungen. In: Schmidtke (ed.) Handbuch der Ergonomie, ch. A-12.1. BundesamtfürWehrtechnik und Beschaffung, Koblenz (2007)
2. Bowman, D.A., Kruijff, E., LaViola, J.J., Poupyrev, I.: 3D User Interfaces. Theory and Practice. Addison-Wesley, Wokingham (2004)
3. Velger, M.: Helmet-Mounted Displays and Sights. Artec House, Inc., Norwood (1998)
4. Renkewitz, H., Alexander, T.: Perceptual issues of Virtual & Augmented Realities. In: Alexander, T., Goldberg, S. (eds.) Virtual Environments for Intuitive Human-System Interaction – Human Factors Consideration in the Design, Use, and Evaluation of AMVE Technology. RTO-TR-HFM-121-Part-II. Neuilly-sur-Seine: NATO RTO (2007)
5. Stereo3d. Stereoscopic 3D Virtual Reality Homepage - Complete Market Surveys of 3D-Glasses VR-Helmets 3D-Software (2012), http://www.stereo3d.com (retrieved October 2012)
6. Meehan, J.: Advanced Display Technologies: What have we lost?, vol. XII(3). Human Systems IAC Gateway, Wright-Patterson AFB, OH (2001)
7. Pfendler, C., Thun, J.: Geografische Orientierung mit egozentrischen und geozentrischen Karten auf einem Head-Mounted Display und einem Personal Digital Assistant. Fraunhofer FKIE Bericht Nr. 192, Wachtberg (2010)
8. Rohmert, W., Rutenfranz, J.: Arbeitswissenschaftliche Beurteilung der Belastung und Beanspruchung an unterschiedlichen industriellen Arbeitsplätzen. In: BundesministerfürArbeit, Sozialordnung (eds.), ReferatÖffentlichkeitsarbeit, Bonn (1975)
9. Wallbott, H.G., Scherer, K.R.: Person x Reaktion x Situation. ZurVersuchsplanung in der Stressforschung. PsychologischeRundschau, 143–152 (1985)
10. Leger, A., Jennings, S., Roumes, C., Gidel, E., Thorndykraft, D., Hecker, P., Kolletzki, D., Pfendler, C., Kooi, F., Bailley, R., Pinkus, A.R., Rash, C.E.: Common Methodological Basis for Evaluation and Testing of Visionic Devices. RTO-TR-HFM-091. AC/323 (HFM-091) TP/76. RTO (NATO), BP 25, F-92201, Neuilly-sur-Seine Cedex, France (2008)
11. Kennedy, R.S., Berbaum, K.S., Lilienthal, M.G.: Simulator Sickness Questionnaire: An Enhanced Method for Quantifying Simulator Sickness. The International Journal of Aviation Psychology 3(3), 203–220 (1993)
12. Rash, C.E., Suggs, C.L., Mora, J.C., Van De Pool, C., Reynolds, B.S., Crowley, J.S.: Visual Issue Survey of AH-64 Apache Aviators, USAARL Report No. 2002-02. U.S. Army Aeromedical Research Laboratory. Fort Rucker, Alabama (2002)
13. Howart, P.A., Costello, P.J.: The Nauseogenicity of Using a Head-Mounted Display, Configured as a Personal Viewing System, for an Hour. In: Proceedings of the Second FIVE International Conference Palazzo dei Congressi, Pisa, Italy (1996)
14. Peli, E.: The visual effects of head-mounted display (HMD) are not distinguishable from those of desk-top computer display. Vision research 38(13), 2053–2066 (1998), http://www.ncbi.nlm.nih.gov/pubmed/9797951 (retrieved September 2012)
15. Sheedy, J., Bergstrom, N.: Performance and comfort on near-eye computer displays. Optometry and Vision Science: Official Publication of the American Academy of Optometry 79(5), 306–312 (2002), http://www.ncbi.nlm.nih.gov/pubmed/12035988 (retrieved March 2013)
16. Laramee, R.S., Ware, C.: Rivalry and interference with a head-mounted display. ACM Transactions on Computer-Human Interaction 9(3), 238–251 (2002), doi:10.1145/568513.568516
17. Pfendler, C.: Bewertung mobiler Displays zur Darstellung von Karten für geografische Orientierungsaufgaben. Z. Arb. Wiss. 4, 235–244 (2007)

18. Pfendler, C., Widdel, H.: Psychological Effects of Work with a Helmet-Mounted Display. In: Schmidt, L., Schlick, C., Grosche, J. (eds.) Ergonomie und Mensch-Maschine–Systeme, Springer, Heidelberg (2008)
19. Pfendler, C., Thun, J.: Geografische Orientierung mit egozentrischen und geozentrischen Karten auf einem Head-Mounted Display und einem Personal Digital Assistant. Fraunhofer FKIE Bericht Nr. 192, Wachtberg (2010)
20. Völker, K., Adolph, L., Pacharra, M., Windel, A.: Datenbrillen – Aktueller Stand von Forschung und Umsetzung sowie zukünftige Entwicklungsrichtungen. In: Neue Arbeits- und Lebenswelten. Bericht zum 56. Arbeitswissenschaftlichen Kongress vom 24. – 26. März 2010 at the Technischen Universität Darmstadt (S.61-65), pp. 61–65. GfA-Press, Dortmund (2010)
21. Wille, M., Grauel, B., Adolph, L.: Head-Mounted Displays – Bedingungen des sicheren und beanspruchungsoptimalen Einsatzes. Bundesanstalt für Arbeitsschutz und Arbeitsmedizi (eds.): Datenbrillen – Aktueller Stand von Forschung und Umsetzung sowie zukünftiger Entwicklungsrichtungen. In: Workshop on 20th June 2011 in Dortmund (2012), http://www.baua.de/de/Publikationen/Fachbeitraege/Gd63.html (retrieved)
22. Ishihara, S.: Tests for Colour Blindness. Kanehara, Shuppan, Tokyo (1974)
23. Wille, M., Grauel, B., Adolph, L.: Head Mounted Displays Beanspruchung im Langzeiteinsatz. Bericht zum 59. Arbeitswissenschaftlichen Kongress vom 27. Februar – 01. März 2013 at the Hochschule Niederrhein. GfA-Press, Krefeld (2012)

Extraction of Light Stripe Centerline
Based on Self-adaptive Thresholding
and Contour Polygonal Representation

Qingguo Tian[1,2], Yujie Yang[1,2], Xiangyu Zhang[1,2], and Baozhen Ge[1,2]

[1] College of Precision Instrument and Opto-electronics Engineering,
Tianjin University, Tianjin 300072, China
[2] Key Laboratory of Opto-electronics Information Technology of the Ministry of Education,
Tianjin 300072, China
Tianqingguo@tju.edu.cn

Abstract. Extracting light stripe centerline is the key step in the line-structure light scanning visual measuring system. It directly determines the quality of three-dimensional point clouds obtained from images. Due to the reflectivity and/or color of object surface, illumination condition change and other factors, gray value and curvature of light stripe in image will vary greatly that makes it very difficulty to completely and precisely extract sub-pixel centerline. This paper presents a novel method for light stripe centerline extraction efficiently. It combines the integral image thresholding method, polygon representation of light stripe contour and adaptive center of mass method together. It firstly locates light stripe region and produces binary image no matter how change gray values of light stripe against background. Then the contour of light stripe is extracted and approximately represented by polygon. Based on the local orthogonal relationship between directions of light stripe cross-section and corresponding polygon segment, the direction of light stripe cross-section is calculated quickly. Along this direction, sub-pixel centerline coordinates are calculated using adaptive center of mass method. 3D scanning experiments with human model dressed colorful swimsuit on a self-designed line laser 3D scanning system are implemented. Some comparisons such as light stripe segmentation using 3 thresholding methods, the time used and the smoothness are given and the results show that the proposed method can acquire satisfying data. The mean time used for one image is not beyond 5 ms and the completeness and smoothness of point clouds acquired by presented methods are better than those of other two methods. This demonstrates the effectiveness and practicability of the proposed method.

Keywords: centerline extraction, light stripe, integral image thresholding, polygon representation, adaptive center of mass.

1   Introduction

Extraction of light stripe centerline is a key technique in the line-structure light scanning visual measuring system [1]. It directly determines the quality of three-dimensional (3D)

V.G. Duffy (Ed.): DHM/HCII 2013, Part II, LNCS 8026, pp. 292–301, 2013.

world coordinate points obtained from images. Light stripe gray image records distorted light stripe information which is modulated and scattered by the measured object surface and captured by CCD detector. On one hand due to the reflectivity and color of object surface and illumination conditions, the gray value of light stripe in image will be uneven. On the other hand due to change of object surface curvature and tilt angle of object surface to the light plane the curvature and width of light stripe in image may be vary largely. So it's very difficult to precisely and fast extract light stripe centerline.

In order to efficiently extracting light stripe centerline, three steps must be tackled carefully. First is to locate the light stripe region in virtue of the gray difference between light stripe (foreground) and background. When gray value has bimodal distribution in image series, one can use global single thresholding method (GSTM) to segment light stripe region [2, 3]. If reflectivity of the object surface under test is uneven and/or illumination condition changes greatly, the gray distribution is uneven too, so the GSTM will lose some useful light stripe segments whose gray values are not remarkably larger than background's, and eventually result in losing some 3D point clouds. WU Qing-yang, et al. [4] and Zhang Lei, et al. [5] apply OTSU method [6] to adaptive compute optimal threshold for segmentation. Second step is to calculate center coordinate. Most common methods include maximum value method, thresholding method, Gaussian approximation, center of mass, linear approximation, Blais and Rioux detector, and parabolic estimator. Although first two methods have faster speed, they can only provide pixel precision. Ref. [7] provides a systematic comparison of latter five methods and concludes that all of them display performance within the same sub-pixel precision range. Ref. [8] indicates that center of mass has characteristics of fast speed and high precision. Third step is to calculate the direction of light stripe cross-section. Because only along this direction, the center coordinate calculated by center of mass method has more accurate. Forest, et al. [9] scan each image column to calculate the center coordinate, which can have a right result only when light stripe is approximately horizontal. If the curvature of object surface changes greatly, the curvature of light stripe will change greatly too, column scanning method will result in losing some useful data. There are many references researching how to calculate the direction of light stripe. Steger, et al. [10] present Hessian matrix method to calculate the direction of light stripe, HU Kun, et al. [11] apply tremendous template Gaussian convolution to compute Hessian matrix so that speed up the calculation of direction of light stripe. WU Qing-yang, et al. [4] defines several alterable direction templates to calculate direction of light stripe. BAZEN, et al. [12] combine gray gradient and principal component analysis method to calculate direction of light stripe. JIA Qian-qian, et al. [13] applies light stripe contour gray gradient approximation to calculate its direction. The existing light stripe direction calculating algorithms have some drawbacks, such as calculating complicatedly, time-consuming, etc. They can hardly meet the real time requirement for light stripe centerline extraction.

This paper presents a fast and efficient light stripe centerline sub-pixel extraction method which is especially suitable for object surface with changeable reflectivity and/or color. The rest of this paper is organized as follows: The proposed algorithm is developed in Section 2, its experimental results and quantitative and qualitative comparisons with other methods are discussed in Section 3, and finally, conclusions are presented in Section 4.

2   The Proposed Method for Centerline Extraction

The proposed method for light stripe centerline extraction includes 3 main steps: localization of light stripe region; computation of light stripe cross-section direction and calculation of sub-pixel center coordinates.

2.1   Apply Integral Image Thresholding Method to Locate Light Stripe Region

As discussed above, if the reflectivity and/or color of tested object surface change greatly, gray values of light stripe will become uneven greatly too. Fig. 4(a) is a real light stripe image captured by CCD camera from a colorful swimsuit model. The gray values of light stripe within dash line rectangle are obviously larger than those within dash line ellipse. In order to solve this problem and locate whole light stripe region, this paper adopts the method in Ref. [14] to segment gray image and produce corresponding binary image.

Let II be an integral image having same size with the original gray image $I_{m\times n}$ where m is the number of rows and n is the number of columns. Let $I(x, y)$ be gray value of pixel (x, y) in $I_{m\times n}$, so the function value $f(x, y)$ in II can be calculated using formula (1)

$$f(x, y) = I(x, y) + f(x, y-1) + f(x-1, y) - f(x-1, y-1) \tag{1}$$

The sum function $s(x, y)$ within local square window with center (x, y) and window size $2l+1$ in image I can be fast calculated by formula (2). Providing left-up coordinate of window is (x_1, y_1), right-down coordinate is (x_2, y_2) and $x_2 - x_1 = y_2 - y_1 = 2l+1$, so

$$s(x, y) = \sum_{i=x-l}^{x+l} \sum_{j=y-l}^{y+l} I(x_i, y_j)$$
$$= f(x_2, y_2) + f(x_1, y_1) - f(x_2, y_1) - f(x_1, y_2) \tag{2}$$

Finally, through formula (3) one can judge whether a pixel (x, y) belongs to light stripe region or belongs to background.

$$bw(x, y) = \begin{cases} 0, count \times I(x, y) < T(x, y) = ratio \times s(x, y) \\ 1, count \times I(x, y) >= T(x, y) = ratio \times s(x, y) \end{cases} \tag{3}$$

Where count is sum of pixels in window, *ratio* is a predefined coefficient and *ratio* < 1. By formula (1) to (3) one can extract light stripe completely and produce a corresponding binary image.

2.2   Calculation of Local Light Stripe Cross-Section Direction

Referring to Fig. 1, the direction $\mathbf{n}$ of light stripe cross-section is perpendicular to the direction of light stripe contour $\overline{pq}$ in a small region. So we can quickly calculate direction of local light stripe cross-section through calculating the direction of local light stripe contour. The detail calculation process is presented in our previous paper [15], here only give brief steps.

Firstly, the contour C of light stripe is tracked in binary image using method based on Ref. [16]. The contour C has 3 characteristics: a) contour is enclosed and corresponds to a light stripe segment, b) it can recognize light stripe with holes automatically, and c) points on C are anticlockwise sorted.

Secondly, using polygon P_i to represent contour C_i satisfying that distance from any pixel on contour C_i to polygon P_i is less than a preliminary distance threshold d_{th}.

Thirdly, for an edge $\overline{pq}$ in polygon P_i as illustrated in Fig. 1, providing the coordinate of p and q is (x_p, y_p) and (x_q, y_q) respectively. The direction vector $\mathbf{v}_{\overline{pq}}$ can be easy computed as $(x_q - x_p, y_q - y_p)$.

Fourthly, due to direction $\mathbf{n}_{cross}$ of cross-section of light stripe between point p and q are orthogonal to $\mathbf{v}_{\overline{pq}}$, it can be calculated as $-\dfrac{1}{\mathbf{v}_{\overline{pq}}}$.

2.3   Calculation Sub-pixel Center Coordinates Using Adaptive Center of Mass

As illustrated in Fig. 1, let s_b be a start point, s_e be corresponding end point, and $\mathbf{n}$ be direction vector, a scanning line l_{scan} can be defined. The sub-pixel center coordinate can be computed using formula (4) and (5).

$$x_{cen} = \frac{\displaystyle\sum_{s_j \in l_{scan} \,\&\, s_j \in Inner(C)} x_{s_j} \times I(s_j)}{\displaystyle\sum_{s_j \in l_{scan} \,\&\, s_j \in Inner(C)} I(s_j)} \tag{4}$$

$$x_{cen} = \frac{\displaystyle\sum_{s_j \in l_{scan} \,\&\, s_j \in Inner(C)} y_{s_j} \times I(s_j)}{\displaystyle\sum_{s_j \in l_{scan} \,\&\, s_j \in Inner(C)} I(s_j)} \tag{5}$$

where s_j is on scanning line l_{scan}, $s_j \in Inner(C)$ represents that s_j is inside contour C. From Fig. 1 one can see that the cross-section's width is changeable. Using formula (4) and (5) to compute center coordinate can not only acquire sub-pixel precision, but be adaptive to the width change of cross section.

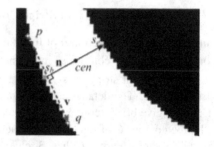

Fig. 1. The relationship between directions of local contour and cross-section

3   Experiments and Result Analyses

3D scanning experiments with human upper body model dressed colorful swimsuit on a self-designed line laser 3D scanning system [17] are implemented. The experimental setup is shown in Fig. 2. The light source is line-structure red laser source. Four pillars make a square, and a scanning head consisting of an upper scanning unit and a lower scanning unit moves up and down along each pillar driven by servo motor with micrometer accuracy, so the scanning system includes 8 scanning units. The measurement volume is a cylinder of diameter 1000mm by height 2000mm, and the width and depth resolution is 1mm and 2mm respectively. The photos from 4 views of tested human upper body model dressed colorful swimsuit are shown in Fig. 3.

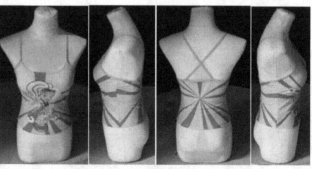

Fig. 2. The experimental setup

Fig. 3. Photos of colorful swimsuit human model

3.1   The Light Stripe Localization Results

Firstly we compare light stripe localization results using different thresholding methods. Fig. 4(a) is one original light stripe image. Due to the color of swimsuit, gray values of light stripe are very uneven. Fig. 4(b) is the light stripe localization result using OTSU. For this image, the calculated threshold value is 45. The useful light stripe region has been localized, but the cross section width varies at different position because of uneven gray change. Fig. 4(c) and (d) are results using GSTM. Fig. 4(c) adopts threshold value 40; the shape of light stripe region is similar to that using OTSU. Fig. 4(d) adopts threshold value 70, light stripe has been broken. This inevitably results in losing some 3D point data. Fig. 4(e) and (f) are light stripe localization results using IITM with parameters window size = 7, *ratio* = 0.86 and window size = 5, *ratio* = 0.75 respectively. The shapes of two results are very similar and cross section width changes not very obvious. All these demonstrate that the IITM is not sensitive to parameters and can obtain good light stripe localization result.

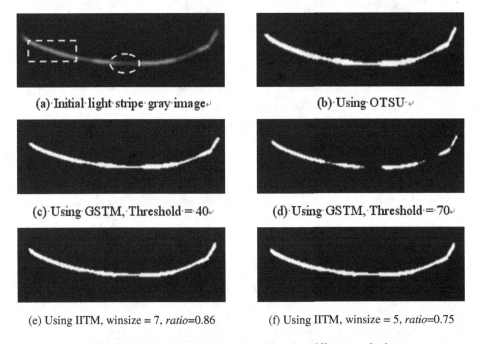

(a) Initial light stripe gray image

(b) Using OTSU

(c) Using GSTM, Threshold = 40

(d) Using GSTM, Threshold = 70

(e) Using IITM, winsize = 7, *ratio*=0.86

(f) Using IITM, winsize = 5, *ratio*=0.75

Fig. 4. Light stripe segmentation results using different methods

3.2   3D Point Cloud Model Integrality Analysis

We indirectly evaluate light stripe centerline extraction results, such as completeness, time used and smoothness using 3D point clouds obtained from light stripe images. Because we can acquire whole 3D point clouds of colorful model shown in Fig. 3 utilizing upper 4 scanning units, subsequent analysis is based on point clouds obtained by upper 4 scanning units and labeled with (1), (2), (3), (4). With distance threshold value for polygon representation d_{th} equals 3.0, 3D point clouds after deleting outlier noises are displayed in Fig. 5. Fig. 5(a) shows results using GSTM and threshold value for all images is 40. Due to surface color change, ambient light change and CCD camera's performance difference, there is a lack of points in point clouds, especially in dash-line ellipse regions of point clouds labeled with (1) and (4). This indicates that GSTM with threshold = 40 can't extract all light stripe region. Fig. 5(b) shows point clouds using OTSU. The threshold calculated by OTSU for any image may be different. Similar to Fig. 5(a), some points have not been calculated. Fig. 5(c) shows point clouds using IITM with parameters window size = 5 and *ratio* = 0.85. Every pixel's threshold may be different when using IITM to localize light stripe. The fact that there has no lack of points in Fig. 5(c) demonstrates that using IITM can localize all light stripes.

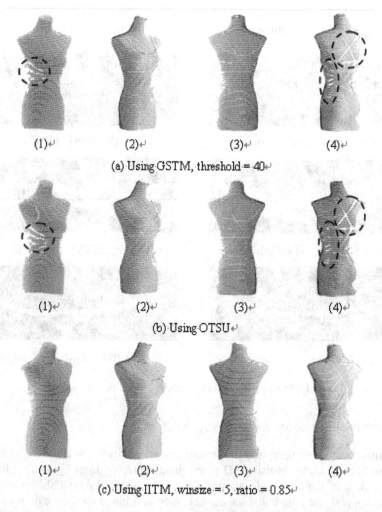

(1)   (2)   (3)   (4)

(a) Using GSTM, threshold = 40

(1)   (2)   (3)   (4)

(b) Using OTSU

(1)   (2)   (3)   (4)

(c) Using IITM, winsize = 5, ratio = 0.85

Fig. 5. Point clouds obtained by scanning units using different thresholding method

3.3   Time Analysis

The algorithm was coded in C++ and compiled for 32 bits using the Visual C++ compiler under Windows XP SP3 and the computer used has 2.8G dual core CPU and 4G memory. Tab. 1 is the statistics of time and number of processed images. The numbers of processed images are not equal to each other for 3 methods because we assume that an image is valid only if the light stripe was extracted from it. The number of processed images using OTSU is 1696 that is more than that using other 2 methods. Contrast to point clouds in Fig. 5, this implies again that method using OTSU process more useless images, produce more noises, but lose many useful light stripe information. The mean time used with GSTM, OTSU and IITM is 3.495ms, 3.831 and 4.347ms respectively. The standard deviation of time using three thresholding methods is 1.493ms, 1.668ms and 1.585ms. Total time is 4987.434ms, 6497.944ms and 5885.799ms respectively. From these results, one can see that although the time used for one image with IITM is a little larger than those with other 2 methods, due to the number of processed images is minimal, the total time used is not maximum.

Table 1. The time statistics for different light stripe centerline extraction methods

Items Methods	Frames of Processed images	Min time (ms)	Max time (ms)	Mean time (ms)	Std (ms)	Total time (ms)
GSTM threshold=40	1427	1.683	14.222	3.495	1.493	4987.434
OTSU	1696	2.785	19.076	3.831	1.668	6497.944
IITM winsize=5, ratio=0.85	1354	3.177	14.551	4.347	1.585	5885.799

3.4   Smooth Contrast of Light Stripe Centerlines

We reconstruct mesh models [18] from point clouds shown in left column of Fig. 5, and apply the smooth characteristics of mesh model to contrast the smoothness of light stripe centerline extracted. Fig. 6 shows the reconstructed mesh model results. The smoothness of mesh model in Fig. 6(b) is better than mesh model in Fig. 6(a), and the smoothness of mesh model in Fig. 6(c) is best. These results show that in the process of light stripe localization, method using IITM has minimal influence on smoothness of light stripe centerline, at the same time the smoothness of light stripe centerline extracted by method using GSTM is worst. These are consistent with results shown in Fig. 4.

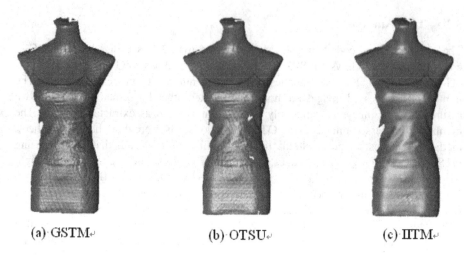

(a) GSTM   (b) OTSU   (c) IITM

Fig. 6. The mesh model of point clouds obtained using different thresholding method

4   Conclusions

For 3D digitising of object surface with large reflectivity and/or color change using line-structure laser scanning vision measuring system, extracting light stripe sub-pixel centerline is key and hard problem, but must be resolved firstly. The method proposed in this paper combines the integral image thresholding image segmentation method, polygon representation of light stripe contour and self-adaptive center of mass together. From time statistics one can conclude that the proposed method can probably extract light stripe centerline in real time if we deeply optimize the program to improve its run efficiency. From the 3D point clouds and corresponding mesh models it is obvious that the proposed method can acquire whole and smooth 3D data that is better than those obtained by other 2 methods. Our further work is focus on research of 3D color modeling of object surface.

Acknowledgements. The paper is supported by National natural science foundation of China (No. 61027012, No. 61177002).

References

1. Gao, S., Zhao, M., Zhang, L., et al.: Dual-Beam Structured Light Vision System for 3D Coordinates Measurement. In: Proceedings of the 7th World Congress on Intelligent Control and Automation, pp. 3687–3691. Chongqing (2008)
2. Yang, S., Cho, M., Lee, H., Cho, T.: Weld line detection and process control for welding automation. Meas. Sci. Technol. 18(3), 819–826 (2007)
3. Liu, W., Jia, Z., Wang, F., et al.: An improved online dimensional measurement method of large hot cylindrical forging. Measurement 45, 2041–2051 (2012)

4. Wu, Q.-Y., Su, X.-Y., Li, J.-Z., et al.: A New Method for Extracting the Centre-line of Line Structure L ight-stripe. Journal of Sichuan University (Engineering Science Edition) 39(4), 151–155 (2007) (in Chinese)
5. Zhang, L., Xu, Y., Wu, C.: Features Extraction for Structured Light Stripe Image Based On OTSU Threshold. In: Proceedings 4th International Symposium on Knowledge Acquisition and Modeling, KAM, pp. 92–95 (2011)
6. Otsu, N.: A Threshold Selection Method from Gray level Histogram. IEEE Transactions on SMC (9), 62–67 (1979)
7. Fisher, R.B., Naidu, D.K.: A comparison of algorithms for subpixel peak detection. Image Technology: Advances in Image Processing, Multimedia and Machine Vision (1996)
8. Haug, K., Pritschow, G.: Robust laser-stripe sensor for automated weld-seam-tracking in the shipbuilding industry. In: IECON Proc. Ind. Electron. Conf., vol. 2, pp. 1236–1241 (1998)
9. Forest, J., Salvi, J., et al.: Laser stripe peak detector for 3D scanners. A FIR filter approach. In: Proceedings of the 17th International Conference on Pattern Recognition (ICPR 2004), vol. 3, pp. 646–649 (2004)
10. Steger, C.: An unbiased detector of curvilinear structures. IEEE Transactions on Pattern Analysis and Machine Intelligence 20(2), 113–125 (1998)
11. Hu, K., Zhou, F., Zhang, G.: Fast extrication method for sub-pixel center of structured light stripe. Chinese Journal of Scientific Instrument 27(10), 1326–1329 (2006) (in Chinese)
12. Bazen, A.M., Gerez, S.H.: Systematic methods for the computation of the directional fields and singular points of fingerprints. IEEE Transactions on Pattern Analysis and Machine Intelligence 24(7), 905–918 (2002)
13. Jia, Q.-Q., Wang, B.-X., Luo, X.-Z.: Extraction of central positions of light stripe in sub-pixel in 3D surface measurement based on light sectioning method. Optics and Precision Engineering 18(2), 390–396 (2010) (in Chinese)
14. Bradley, D., Roth, G.: Adaptive Thresholding Using the Integral Image. Journal of Graphics 12(2), 13–21 (2007)
15. Tian, Q.-G., Ge, B.-Z., Li, Y.-P., et al.: Real-time extraction of light stripe central line based on contour polygonal representation. Optics and Precision Engineering 18(2), 1357–1362 (2010) (in Chinese)
16. Haig, T.D., Attikiouzel, Y., et al.: Border following: new definition gives improved borders. IEEE Proceedings-I 139(2), 206–211 (1992)
17. Ge, B.-Z., Tian, Q.-G., Young, K.D., Sun, Y.-C.: Color 3D digital human modeling and its applications to animation and anthropometry. In: Duffy, V.G. (ed.) HCII 2007 and DHM 2007. LNCS, vol. 4561, pp. 82–91. Springer, Heidelberg (2007)
18. Tian, Q.-G., Ge, B.-Z., Yu, D.-Y., et al.: An Incremental Projection-based Surface Reconstruction Algorithm from Scattered Data. Journal of Image and Graphics 11(10), 1409–1413 (2006) (in Chinese)

Part III

Anthropometry, Posture and Motion Modeling

Artificial Neural Network-Based Prediction of Human Posture

Mohammad Bataineh, Timothy Marler, and Karim Abdel-Malek

Virtual Soldier Research Program–Center for Computer-Aided Design
The University of Iowa
Iowa City, IA 52242, USA
mohammad-bataineh@uiowa.edu,
{tmarler,amalek}@engineering.uiowa.edu

Abstract. The use of an artificial neural network (ANN) in many practical complicated problems encourages its implementation in the digital human modeling (DHM) world. DHM problems are complicated and need powerful tools like ANN to provide acceptable solutions. Human posture prediction is a DHM field that has been studied thoroughly in recent years. This work focuses on using a general regression neural network (GRNN) for human posture prediction. This type of ANN has advantages over others when incorporated in DHM problems like posture prediction. A new heuristic approach is also presented in this study to determine the GRNN parameters that lead to the best performance and prediction capability. The results are promising: a high success rate is obtained for predicting 41 outputs, which represent the upper-body degrees of freedom of a human model. This work initiates future focus on embedding GRNN to generalize human posture prediction in a task-based manner.

Keywords: Digital human modeling and simulation, artificial neural network, posture prediction.

1 Introduction

Digital human modeling (DHM) is a human representation on computer software or a computer model used to perform analyses and evaluations related to human performance. DHM studies have developed and facilitated the study of many human-related fields. As one of these fields, human posture prediction is incorporated in studying and analyzing many ergonomic studies, human-machine workplaces, vehicle designs, etc. Hence, studying posture prediction is critical for understanding human performance when a powerful method or approach is needed to predict accurate and reliable postures. This reliability can be provided by incorporating prediction tools like an artificial neural network (ANN). ANN is a mathematical model for predicting system performance (i.e., system output) inspired by the structure and function of human biological neural networks. ANNs have been studied extensively and applied in various problems [1] and [2]. Their benefits have not yet been fully realized in the

V.G. Duffy (Ed.): DHM/HCII 2013, Part II, LNCS 8026, pp. 305–313, 2013.

context of human-posture models because there are many variations of ANNs, and selecting the appropriate form and associated parameters for a particular application can often be more of an art than a science.

The applications of solving human posture prediction problems are not new; various approaches, including some types of ANN, have been used to address these problems. A simulation of in-vehicle seated reaching movements was presented with a seven-degree-of-freedom (7-DOF) linkage structure depending on an inverse kinematics approach [3]. Then, an efficient numerical formulation was developed for the prediction of real postures [4]. Moreover, ANN has been used to predict the next steps or postures for many types of postures [5], [6]. This paper presents the use of the general regression neural network (GRNN) type of ANN to predict human posture for the following reasons: 1) to investigate potential issues when using GRNN to simulate tasks that involve contact constraints or other conditions involving Cartesian locations, 2) to provide initial work in posture prediction to discover the limitations of using GRNN in this DHM problem, and 3) to demonstrate the feasibility of predicting a large number of outputs using GRNN.

In general, the current state of the art does not demonstrate the use of ANNs for direct manipulation of joint angles in the context of a complete human model with a large number of DOFs. Most of the applied work was done using traditional ANN types like the feed-forward neural network, which has memory and training limitations when predicting a large number of outputs. Moreover, human posture prediction needs to be studied in a task-based manner like touching a point, box lifting, sitting/standing, etc. Thus, we propose not only exploring the use of ANNs for predicting upper-body posture but doing so in the context of a complete 41-DOF DHM. Furthermore, we demonstrate the determination of the appropriate ANN and ANN parameters for application to human posture prediction. Thus, the following contributions are achieved in this paper: 1) task-based posture predictions for a 41-DOF human model using ANN, 2) the first use of GRNN in task-based posture prediction with highly reasonable results, 3) prediction of a relatively large number of outputs (41) for a 41-DOF human model, and 4) introduction of a new fully automatic strategy for determining the Gaussian width (GW) parameter for optimal network performance.

2   Background

2.1   Human Model

The underlying human model used with this work is Santos [7], which is built on a biomechanically accurate musculoskeletal model with 55 DOFs. Santos's anthropometry can be altered on the fly as can the range of motion (ROM) for each joint. Human posture prediction on Santos is done using an optimization-based approach; conceptually, the joint angles (one for each DOF) provide design variables. The objective function(s) is one or more human performance measures, such as energy, discomfort, joint displacement, etc.

2.2   Neural Networks

ANN involves many neurons arranged in multiple interconnected layers. In much the same way that one learns, ANNs essentially provide a high-dimension surface (representing system output) fit to variables that control system behavior. The process of fitting the hyper surface to data points is called training, and the data points are called grid points. A single grid point represents a set of input parameters used to train the ANN. The term "off-grid points" refers to input parameters that were not actually used in a training case. This study uses GRNN, which is a type of radial-based neural network (RBNN) [8], [9]. The use of GRNN has advantages, including fast training, smooth prediction, and the ability to handle a relatively large number of inputs and outputs.

In the GRNN architecture, $x = [x_1, x_2, \dots, x_R]$ (R is the number of inputs) provides the input for each neuron in the hidden layer. The hidden layer has Q neurons $[1, 2, \dots, Q]$ (Q is the number of training cases). Inside each hidden neuron, there is a radial transfer function that produces output depending on the provided input, so the final output depends on the radial distance of the input from the basis function's center [8]. The Gaussian function is the most popular type of radial function [8], so it is used in this study. The hidden neuron's output enters all neurons in the output layer. Each neuron in the output layer essentially combines the received lines (the outputs of all hidden neurons) in a weighted sum to provide the final network outputs. The output layer has N number of neurons, which is the number of outputs $[y_1, y_2, \dots, y_N]$.

Figure 1 shows a flow chart for the mathematical steps that are calculated inside each neuron in both the hidden and output layers. Once the neuron receives the input $\mathbf{x}$, the sum of the absolute values between $\mathbf{x}$ and the components of the vector W_i^I (Equation 1) is calculated in the "Distance Function" to produce A_i, as in Equation 2. The dimension of the input weight matrix W^I, as shown in Equation 3, is QxR. Each row of W^I is referred to as an input weight vector associated with a corresponding hidden neuron. Then, the value A_i is multiplied by the bias constant B in the "scaling function" to provide a_i (Equation 4), which is called the radial distance. The bias B is responsible for the network sensitivity, which is directly calculated from a network parameter (GW). More detail about those two terms will be provided in the method section. The last step is to calculate the radial function outputs $h_i(a_i)$ to provide the neuron's output h_i (Equation 5), which represents the hidden neuron output. $h = [h_1, h_2, h_3, h_Q]$ represents the output from Q hidden neurons, which are provided to each neuron in the output layer. The figure shows the kth output neuron, which provides the kth output y_k (Equation 6). This output is calculated by calculating the sum of the dot product between the provided h and the output weight vector W_k^O (Equation 7) and divided by the sum of h components. In the output weight matrix W^O (Equation 8), W_k^O refers to the kth weight vector associated with a corresponding output neuron.

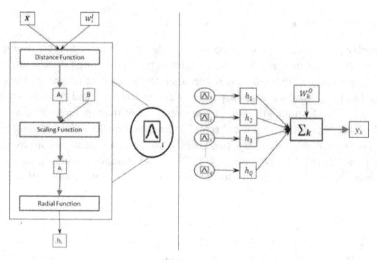

Fig. 1. The ith neuron at the hidden layer (at left), and the neuron at the output layer (at right)

$$W_i^I = [w_{i1}^I \; w_{i2}^I \; .... \, w_{iR}^I \;] \tag{1}$$

$$A_i = \sum_{j=1}^{R} |w_{ij}^I - x_j| \tag{2}$$

$$W^I = \begin{bmatrix} w_{11}^I w_{12}^I \; ... \; w_{1R}^I \\ w_{21}^I w_{22}^I \; ... \; w_{2R}^I \\ ... \; ... \; ... \; ... \; ... \; ... \\ w_{Q1}^I w_{Q2}^I \; ... \; w_{QR}^I \end{bmatrix} \tag{3}$$

$$a_i = A_i * B \tag{4}$$

$$h_i = rad(a_i) \tag{5}$$

$$y_k = \frac{\sum_{q=1}^{Q} h_q . w_{kq}^O}{\sum_{q=1}^{Q} h_q} \tag{6}$$

$$W_k^O = [w_{k1}^O \; w_{k2}^O \; .... \, w_{kQ}^O \;] \tag{7}$$

$$W^O = \begin{bmatrix} w_{11}^o w_{12}^o \; ... \; w_{1Q}^o \\ w_{21}^o w_{22}^o \; ... \; w_{2Q}^o \\ ... \; ... \; ... \; ... \; ... \; ... \\ w_{N1}^o w_{N2}^o \; ... \; w_{NQ}^o \end{bmatrix} \tag{8}$$

The training process is done simply in two steps. First, define the GW, which is the width of the Gaussian transfer function. Second, set the values of W^I and W^O to be the inputs and outputs, respectively, of the training cases. Each training case consists of a set of input x and output y. For the nth training case, the nth row of W^I takes the input vector x, while the nth column of W^O takes the output vector y. The remaining question in constructing and training the GRNN is how to define the GW for such a network.

3   Method

The network parameter (GW) is heuristically and automatically determined at any application. GW has a significant effect on the predicted results of the GRNN. The mathematical importance of the GW is that when the distance A_i equals GW, then the radial function's output (h_i in Equation 5) equals 0.5. A larger GW results in a wider radial function and vice versa. Given the application-dependent nature of ANNs, it is impossible to calculate the optimal GW [10]. Having large GW decreases the accuracy of the output. While small GW provides accurate results for the training grid points, it provides poor results when evaluating off-grid points. Thus, selecting the most appropriate GW is a tradeoff between covering all space between training cases and getting accurate results. GW also determines the bias (B) in the first hidden layer, shown in Equation 9. The factor of 0.833 is provided in the literature [8].

$$B = 0.833/GW \qquad\qquad (9)$$

The heuristic strategy for finding the best GW is incorporated in the training and construction of the network. The collected training cases are split into two parts, testing cases and true training cases, where the true training cases have all training cases except three cases (testing cases) that are used to test the network performance and never participate in the training. Then, 40 GRNNs are created or built, one for each of 40 different GWs. The GW values range from 0.05 to 2 in increments of 0.05, where this range represents all possible GW values within the inputs range. This range of GW values is chosen because the inputs are all normalized between -1 and 1, so the maximum difference is 2. The selected increment is small enough to exactly follow and specify the most accurate GW. Larger increments might pass the proper GW, while lower increments are useless because they are too small to have a notable effect on the produced network. The GW should also be positive. Next, for each network, R-square values are calculated between the predicted results from the network and the exact postures for the three selected testing cases and three other randomly selected on-grid (training) cases. Then, average R-square value is calculated for all six cases. The final step is choosing the maximum value in the vector, which corresponds to the best GW. By the end of this step, the training and testing steps are finished, and the best GW value for proper network performance has been identified.

Now, the proposed network along with the approach of finding its GW is applied on human posture prediction. The task is to touch a target point in front of the body with the right hand. The GRNN is used to predict 41 DOFs, which represent the upper body of the 55-DOF human model (Santos), to reach the fed target position. Figure 2 shows the 31 collected true training cases, which are randomly collected from the whole reachable zone on the front side of the body. For this task, the network has 3 inputs (target position in three dimensions) and 41 outputs (41 DOF). The optimal GW equals 0.25. The work of collecting the training cases and training the network was done on a Windows 7 computer with an Intel® Core™ 2 processor and 8 GB of RAM; the training and testing was done in a fraction of a second.

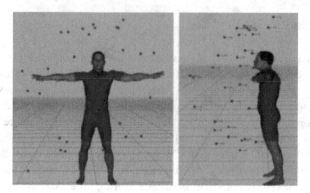

Fig. 2. Santos with the points that are used in the training cases shown in red; the figure has a front view (shown on left) and a side view (shown on right)

4   Results

Three off-grid cases are tested. On-grid points are not presented because testing the prediction of off-grid points reflects the general network prediction ability for any point in the training grid. Thus, if the GRNN predicts the off-grid points well, the general prediction ability for the network will be good. In addition, the network predicts on-grid points more accurately than off-grid points. The testing cases are selected randomly within the limits of training space (shown in Figure 2) and evaluated visually as well as statistically. Regarding the statistical results, adjusted R-squares are plotted for the three off-grid cases in Figure 3. These plots are for joint angles resulting from the network and actual Santos posture prediction outputs. The R-square values for all cases are above 0.97, which is highly acceptable from a statistical standpoint. Although these cases were not trained on the network, the results showed matching between predicted and actual values. These plots indicated that the network was able to interpolate all body joint angles properly to get acceptable accuracy. These results are statistically promising; the network is able to predict all joint angles quickly and accurately.

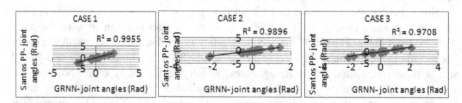

Fig. 3. Adjusted R-square values for the results of GRNN versus Santos PP for 41 DOFs of three off-grid testing cases

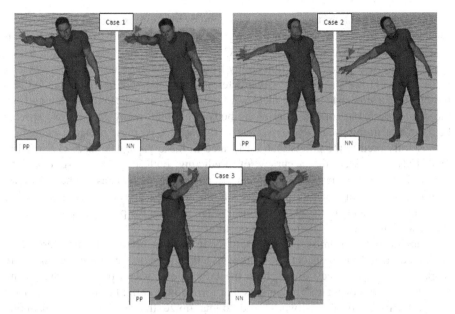

Fig. 4. Three off-grid postures in the task of touching a point for Santos posture prediction (PP) and GRNN

Visual comparisons for the three off-grid postures between posture prediction (exact posture) and predicted GRNN results are shown in Figure 4. In the figure, the red arrows refer to the target point locations. Note that there are some small errors in GRNN prediction for the joint angles, which lead the hand away from the required exact point location. The error was because the network is a general regression type, which interpolates between training cases, and it was not trained to predict the input target point with 100% accuracy. In all cases, Santos's hand moves toward the proper direction and close to the target point but with a small error. In general, the results show that the predicted joint angles, including the head and neck, were all tuned with the body corresponding to the target point position. The error in predicting the joint angles was minor, but still has a clear effect on touching the target point.

5   Discussion

A study of posture prediction for touching a point using GRNN showed that there is a potential use of the GRNN type of ANN for quick prediction of realistic postures. This prediction could be also generalized in a task-based manner and by training the network using various sources like motion capture. The results from this study were statistically promising since the network was able to predict 41 DOFs quickly and accurately, but with small error that prevents touching the target points exactly. Note that these small errors in GRNN prediction for the joint angles can manifest themselves as significant errors in the space (x, y, and z space). In all cases, Santos's hand moves toward the proper direction and close to the target point but with a small error.

The contact problem (touching an exact point or location) in this study was serious. Santos failed in exactly touching the target point for most of the tested cases. This problem occurred because the network GW value was relatively large for a task requiring highly accurate prediction ability from the network, touching a point exactly in the space. However, the GW value determined by the new heuristic method was reasonable for this task, because there were only 31 points collected for training from the whole reachable zone in front of the body, which left many gaps (empty spaces) between the training cases. Consequently, the used GW must be large enough to successfully predict the points that are located in these gaps. The large GW used in this study decreased the accuracy of predicting both on- and off-grid points. Generally, to solve the contact problem in posture-prediction tasks, there are two options: 1) collecting many training cases to decrease the gaps in the training grid or 2) adding constraints to the network construction to force the predicted postures from the network to be exactly in the proper position.

Along with the promising use of GRNN in posture prediction, there are some challenges and limitations in its current use that need to be addressed in future work. First, the accuracy of touching the target point was a problem when using GRNN. The type of inputs and outputs that form a task could be studied to improve the performance of the network used to maximize the accuracy. For example, training the network to predict joint center locations instead of joint angles has prospective success in producing more accurate results in posture prediction tasks. Second, the proper number of training cases to be chosen for such a task needs to be addressed.

Acknowledgement. This work is supported by the Office of Naval Research. The authors would also like to acknowledge the teamwork of the Virtual Soldier Research group at The University of Iowa.

References

1. Collobert, R., Weston, J.: A Unified Architecture for Natural Language Processing: Deep Neural Networks with Multitask Learning. In: Proceedings of the 25th International Conference on Machine Learning, pp. 160–167. ACM (2008)
2. Zha, X.: Soft Computing Framework for Intelligent Human-Machine System Design, Simulation and Optimization. Soft Computing 7(3), 184–198 (2003)
3. Zhang, X., Chaffin, D.: A Three-Dimensional Dynamic Posture Prediction Model for Simulating In-Vehicle Seated Reaching Movements: Development and Validation. Ergonomics 43(9), 1314–1330 (2000)
4. Abdel-Malek, K., Yu, W., Jaber, M.: Realistic Posture Prediction. SAE Digital Human Modeling and Simulation (2001)
5. Rezzoug, N., Gorce, P.: Prediction of Fingers Posture Using Artificial Neural Networks. Journal of Biomechanics 41(12), 2743–2749 (2008)
6. Zhang, B., Horváth, I., Molenbroek, J.F.M., Snijders, C.: Using Artificial Neural Networks forHuman Body Posture Prediction. International Journal of Industrial Ergonomics 40(4), 414–424 (2010)

7. Abdel-Malek, K., Yang, J., Kim, J., Marler, T., Beck, S., Swan, C.: Development of the Virtual Human Santos^{TM}. Digital Human Modeling 4561, 490–499 (2007)
8. Wasserman, P.D.: Advanced Methods in Neural Computing. Van Nostrand Reinhold, New York (1993)
9. Buhmann, M.D.: Radial Basis Functions: Theory and Implementations. Cambridge University Press, Cambridge (2003)
10. Specht, D.F.: A General Regression Neural Network. IEEE Trans. Neural Network 2(6), 568–576 (1991)

Markerless Motion Capture Integrated with Human Modeling for Virtual Ergonomics

Giorgio Colombo[1], Daniele Regazzoni[2], and Caterina Rizzi[2]

[1] Department of Mechanical Engineering, Polytechnic of Milan, Milan, Italy
giorgio.colombo@polimi.it
[2] Department of Engineering, University of Bergamo (BG), Dalmine, Italy
{daniele.regazzoni,caterina.rizzi}@unibg.it

Abstract. This paper refers to the context of virtual ergonomics and specifically addresses a case study of the commercial refrigeration industry. The aim is to develop a computer-aided platform to analyse end-users' postures and movements and ergonomically validate the design of device a man or woman may deal with. This paper describes the integrated use of human modeling and motion capture (Mocap) systems to perform ergonomic analysis relying exactly on real movements. Two optical Mocap systems, both low cost and markerless, have been considered: one based on six Sony Eye webcams and another one on two Microsoft Kinect sensors. Analogously, two human modeling tools have been adopted: Jack, specifically targeted for ergonomics and integrated with Microsoft Kinect, and LifeMod, a biomechanical simulation package. The proposed virtual ergonomics solutions have been experimented considering the case study of vertical refrigerator display units.

Keywords: Virtual ergonomics, Mocap, Digital human modeling, commercial refrigeration.

1 Introduction

Human factors are involved in several steps of product life (design, manufacture, maintenance, use, etc.) and keeping them into account since the early stages of the development process can be a key issue for a successful product. Several aspects, such as handling capability, physical condition and risk prevention, have to be considered as well as that human beings with different needs will interact with the product. This requires the development of products centered on human beings and suitable to the widest range of population characterized by different sizes, genders, ages, preferences and abilities [1] and the adoption of strategies and tools that permit to consider ergonomics aspects since the conceptual design stage.

In such a context, virtual ergonomics is the discipline that permits engineers to create and manipulate virtual humans to investigate the interactions between the users and the product. For example human factors, such as positioning, visibility, reaching, grasping and lifting of weights can all be evaluated by using virtual humans, providing a feedback to designers without the need for physical prototyping.

V.G. Duffy (Ed.): DHM/HCII 2013, Part II, LNCS 8026, pp. 314–323, 2013.

This paper provides an insight on this topic with particular attention to commercial refrigeration industry specialized in display units. It describes the use of virtual ergonomics techniques in the design process of display units used in supermarkets.

In this work we consider the integrated use of human modeling [1, 2] and motion capture (Mocap) [3] systems to perform ergonomic analysis relying exactly on real movements executed by operators in everyday activities and provide designer with guidelines to improve workers' environment and users' interaction. Actually, such an approach should avoid any potential approximation or mistake due to standardization of movements. The aim of the research is to develop a computer-aided platform to analyze workers' postures and movements and ergonomically validate the design of device a man or woman may deal with.

Regarding Mocap systems, we decided to use low cost techniques, developed for video games and entertainment, to verify their usability and performance in industrial context. Such technologies benefit from a huge investment on research that leads to a rapid evolution, but on the same time they keep affordable prices because of the target market they refer to.

The paper, after a description of the case study, presents the technical solutions adopted. The application to the case study and preliminary results of the experimentation are finally presented and discussed.

2   The Case Study and Users' Categories

As mentioned, we consider the design process of display units. The case study concerns the family of vertical refrigerator display units with or without doors, which are installed in groceries or supermarkets. Such machinery should accommodate the full range of users during its life cycle. At least we can distinguish three main groups of users that interact with the refrigerated display unit: customers picking up goods, workers in charge of checking exposed products and filling out shelves with new ones, and maintenance technicians who need to access to some specific components (Fig. 1). For each category some ergonomic aspects are more relevant than others: i.e., visibility and reachability of goods for customers, reachability of some display components for technicians and, the most important, posture and stress for operators who repeat the same task for hours and may occur in musculoskeletal disorders.

We mainly focus the attention on costumers and workers with the main goal of determining goods reachability for the first ones and suitability of working conditions for the latter. In fact, the task of loading the shelves may generate health disorders due to repeated actions, holding and lifting loads, uncomfortable postures, among the others. A preliminary study, based on interviews and direct observations, has been conducted to determine how the operators really behave and main operations to be reproduced during the tests in the lab to verify the feasibility of our approach. We also identified some occasional postures that permit to improve reachability but unacceptable because of dangerous postures or hygienic reasons (e.g., stepping on the first shelf).

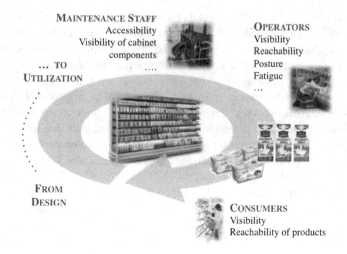

Fig. 1. Vertical display unit and main users' groups

3   Virtual Ergonomics Solutions

Our main goal has been to experiment the integration of low-cost Mocap systems with human modeling tools for virtual ergonomics of refrigerated display unit.

Figure 2 shows the virtual ergonomics solutions considered.

Regarding Mocap system, several solutions are available for different contexts such as military, entertainment, sports, and medical applications. According to the working principle four main categories can be identified [3]: optical, mechanical, inertial, and magnetic that can be used for testing and validation also in a combined way [4]. We considered two systems, both optical and markerless: the former based on Sony Eye webcams and the latter on Microsoft Kinect [5]. Initially, the Microsoft Kinect has been developed for game environment but it is attracting more and more attention from different contexts [6,7]. It is a markerless system bases on structured light that can track body motion with a depth sensor.

We have been using them to acquire the real movements and postures of operators so that the following simulation can be based on real data. They are not expensive and can be easily moved and, with some precautions, used also outside the lab in potentially any work environment we want to acquire.

Both systems foresee the adoption of iPi Motion Capture™ software [8], a non-real time markerless system developed to work with Sony Eyes webcams and recently with Microsoft Kinect. Its main features are:

- Possibility to use from 3 to 6 webcams and 1 or 2 Kinect sensors.
- A maximum acquisition area of 7 m x 7 m.
- Non real-time tracking.
- Input file format: MPEG.

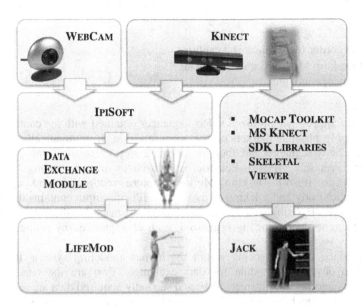

Fig. 2. Virtual ergonomics solutions

Concerning human modeling, we can find various tools of different complexity depending on the target application. They can be grouped in [1,9]: virtual human/actors for entertainment, mannequins for clothing [10], virtual manikin for ergonomic analysis [11, 12], and, finally, detailed biomechanical models [13].

We decided to use Siemens Jack [14, 15] and LifeMod [16]. Jack, a well-known human modeling system, has been chosen since it specifically targeted for ergonomics and is integrated with Microsoft Kinect. It permits to define complex scenes with virtual manikins and objects, simulate many tasks and evaluate posture and ergonomics factors also using analysis tools such as RULA (Rapid Upper Limb Analysis) to investigate work-related upper limb disorders, NIOSH (U.S. National Institute for Occupational Safety and Health) lifting equations to evaluate lifting and carrying tasks, and OWAS (Owako Working Posture Analysis System) to analyze postures during work. The second system, LifeMod, is a biomechanical simulation software that permits to generate a complete biomechanical model of the human body. It is a plug-in of ADAMS software, a multi-body analysis system. The creation of a model normally starts with the generation of a basic set of connected human segments based on the dimension contained in an anthropometric database; then, the joints, the muscles and the tendons are created and contact force with objects are defined.

3.1   Webcam-Based Solution

This solution comprises:
Hardware

- Six/four Sony Eye webcams with a resolution of 640x480 pixels at 60 Hz mounted on photographic tripods with semicircle disposition.
- Portable workstation Dell Precision M6500.

Software

- iPisoft Recorder (calibration and capture).
- iPisoft Desktop Motion Capture (tracking).
- Data Exchange module.
- LifeMod.

The system acquires synchronized video sequences obtained with the camera without having to apply physical markers on the operator's skin. It automatically recognizes the different body segments and, then for each time step, calculates joints position and orientation. Precisely, iPisoft Recorder synchronizes images recorded from the webcams while iPisoft Desktop Motion Capture recognizes and applies the segmentation of body and tracking of movement. iPisoft output contains the recorded movement in BVH (Biovision Hierarchical Data) format. iPisoft adopts a skeleton made of 27 joints hierarchically organized, each characterized by proper d.o.f. and constraints.

To reproduce the movements within the human modeling system, it has been necessary to develop a module for data exchange. Two are the reasons: firstly LifeMod uses another data format (SLF) and secondly acquired data are related to the real position of the human being's joints while the biomechanical software uses external markers placed on the skin surface. Therefore, we developed an ad-hoc algorithm in Matlab, which translates the information relative to the joint hierarchy and to the motion contained in the BVH file to a SLF one and a CMD script that relocates the markers accordingly to LifeMod representation.

Once the model is defined, simulation phase can begin. To obtain accurate simulations with the muscles and the articulations it's necessary to execute a first inverse dynamic simulation to drive the body with motion agents describing the movements to execute. Once that the movements are stored a direct dynamic simulation is run to calculate the forces created by the muscles and the stresses the body is subjected to. The outcome provided by the system consists of forces and momenta acting on each joint in each time step of the analysis.

3.2   Kinect-Based Solution

Kinect has been integrated both with LifeMod and Jack. Therefore, this solution comprises:

Hardware

- Two Microsoft Kinect sensors with a resolution of 640x480 pixels at 30 fps mounted on photographic tripod and connected via USB cable.
- Portable workstation Dell XPS.

Software

- iPi soft Recorder (calibration and capture).
- iPisoft Desktop Motion Capture (tracking).
- LifeMod and the Data Exchange module.

or

- Siemens Jack with Mocap Toolkit, a module specifically developed by Siemens for Kinect sensor, MS Kinect SDK v 1.0 libraries and SkeletalViewer to transfer data streaming acquired with Kinect sensor to Jack.

If we use LifeMod, as in the previous case iPi Recorder manages the recording of images and depth videos coming from Kinect, while the iPi Studio performs environment calibration and video analysis.

While using Jack, iPiSoft is not necessary. First, using Jack the virtual scene composed by the 3D model of the refrigerated unit and the operator avatar is created; then, the Kinect plug-in and the SkeletalViewer software are launched and the acquisition session can start. The skeleton used in the transition from Mocap to Jack is made of 21 joints whose positions and movements are tracked and there is not a hierarchy among them. This skeleton is less complex than Jack's one and some details cannot be taken into account (i.e., head rotation, fingers).

4   Experimentation

The solutions have been experimented with two vertical units: one with six shelves and doors for frozen goods and another one with 5 shelves and without doors for fresh goods. We used a simplified version of the real display units because some elements of the complete units (e.g., lateral walls) may interfere with the operator during motion capture.

We involved testers of both genders and different heights to evaluate if the motion capture system is affected by any problem. The pick and place operation of a bottle on each shelf has been considered and tasks performed by the testers have been acquired simultaneously with proposed solutions.

First we performed the calibration of the webcam-based solution that initializes the system and permits to correctly locate each camera in space. A semicircle disposition of the webcams at different heights around the operator is the best choice. Instead, the Kinect sensors were placed laterally to the actor. Figure 3 shows the lab setup/layout for the webcam and Kinect solution.

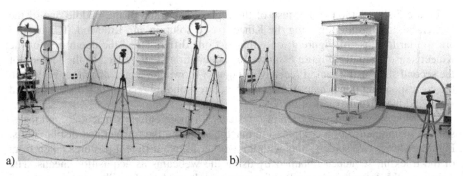

Fig. 3. Acquisition scenarios: a) Webcam-based; b) Kinect-based

Then, we validated the data exchange module as well as different ways of automatically changing the position of joints depending on height and structure of subjects. Once, preliminarily tested the technical solutions we started the real campaign.

Ten actors were asked to perform as much as possible as if they were in the real environment and to follow a precise routine to produce comparable results with operators characterized by different anthropometric measures. The routine defines the initial and final position of each movement to be performed.

Figures 4, 5 and 6 portray some examples of acquisition related to loading task for the vertical units. Figure 4 shows an example of acquisition carried out for the vertical unit with doors. One can see the representation of data related to the loading of the fourth shelf during the three main steps with the webcam-based solution. The first one refers to the environment where the webcam images are captured and elaborated for each time step to gather joints positions shown in the second image. The third representation comes from LifeMod where data have been converted, corrected and integrated with anthropometric databases.

Webcam view   Joints Positions   LifeMod

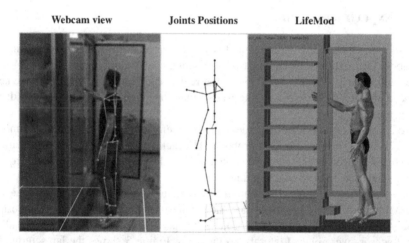

Fig. 4. Vertical unit with doors, Webcam+LifeMod: Loading the fourth shelf

Figure 5 shows the loading task of the highest shelf and of the middle one of the vertical unit without door using the Kinect-based solution and LifeMod. The images are similar to those of Figure 4; only the first one differs being the depth map of the Kinect sensor. Finally, Figure 6 shows the acquisition steps related to the loading of the second shelf using Jack. Precisely, Figure 6a shows the image acquired, Figure 6b the corresponding depth map, Figure 6c the corresponding reconstructed skeleton and Figure 6d the virtual avatar of the tester.

The Mocap systems have been also tested with more complex machines and tasks, such as maintenance of a compression machine feeding the refrigerated display units. Figure 7 shows two screen shots with the worker in two different postures taken from of the tracking sequence obtained by using the webcams as acquisition means. The image on the left shows the iPisoft avatar overlapped to the silhouette of the real worker, while the image on the right shows the skeleton obtained calculating the position of the key joints.

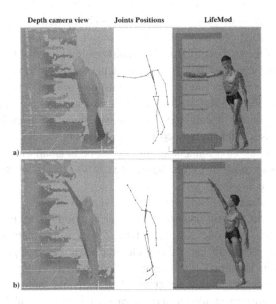

Fig. 5. Vertical unit without doors, Kinect+LifeMod: a) Loading highest shelf; b) loading the middle shelf

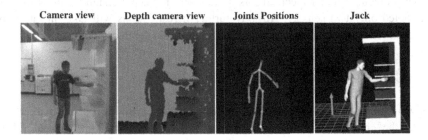

Fig. 6. Vertical unit without doors, Kinect+Jack: a) Loading the second shelf

Fig. 7. Frames of Mocap process with worker in two different postures

Results have been considered satisfying for both markerless optical systems and performances are adequate for work related analysis and interesting for research activity. Complex scenes benefit from redundant points of view (webcam solution), while simple environments allow easier depth camera acquisition (Kinect solution).

Webcam-based solution requires a calibration routine and is sensitive to environment light and contrast with actor. Besides, Kinect-based solution does not require complex routine to calibrate sensors and, thus, the overall setup is much shorter and it is less sensible to light conditions. This contributes to a better portability in almost any working environment where the scene is small enough to be seen by both sensors. In fact, only two (iPisoft) or one (Jack) sensors are supported and the area of acquisition is smaller.

Regarding the human modeling system, the main advantages of Jack are the direct integration with Kinect sensor and real time determination of ergonomics parameters; however it supports only one Kinect and there are some limitations affecting its performance when used with Jack. The skeleton does not always perfectly match the subject posture, this is particularly true when body's area overlap but improvements are under development and a new version will be available soon. LifeMod permits to create more detailed human model and an easy extrapolation of data for joint and segments but on the other hand there is the need for data exchange module and marker relocation and ergonomics parameters are not automatically calculated. Known problems about Kinect sensors mutual interference are significant as long as we adopted only two sensors. Anyway further investigations will take into account also scenarios with more sensors and, thus, solutions do depth camera interference.

5   Conclusions

This work aimed at exploiting low-cost motion capture solutions (optical-markerless) outside the entertainment domain together with a detailed biomechanical DHM solution and verifying their applicability in industrial domain.

The results reached so far are promising and valuable for several industrial applications since the accuracy of the Mocap system is good enough to assess ergonomics of potentially any workplace. In case of a product being directly used by customers, as the display unit we tested, the ability to simulate the interaction of real people brings important and unpredictable feedbacks to designers. The high portability of the Mocap systems allows using it also outside the lab so that real workers' motion can be captured and further developments comprehend an acquisition campaign in a supermarket. Actually, starting from real operators performing in the real workplace allows not only to be more precise but also to consider unknown postures or movements, either correct or wrong, performed by operators in their everyday activities.

References

1. Sundin, A., Ortengren, R.: Digital Human modelling for CAE applications. In: Salvendy, G. (ed.) Handbook of Human Factors and Ergonomics, 3rd edn., John (2006)
2. Duffy, V.G. (ed.): HCII 2007 and DHM 2007. LNCS, vol. 4561. Springer, Heidelberg (2007)
3. Furniss, M.: Motion capture. MIT Communications Forum, http://web.mit.edu/commforum/papers/furniss.html (accessed March 2013)
4. Schepers, H.M.: Ambulatory Assessment of Human Body Kinematics and Kinetics. PhD Thesis, Universiteit Twente, The Netherlands (2009), http://www.xsens.com/images/stories/PDF/ThesisSchepers.pdf
5. Microsft Kinect, http://www.xbox.com/en-US/kinect (accessed February 2013)
6. Stowers, J., Hay, M., Bainbridge-Smith, A.: Altitude control of a quadrotor helicopter using depth map from Microsoft Kinect sensor. In: Proceedings of the IEEE International Conference on Mechatronics, Istanbul, Turkey, April 13-15, pp. 358–362 (2011)
7. Raptis, M., Kirovski, D., Hoppe, H.: Real-time classification of dance gesture from skeleton animation. In: Proceedings of 10th Annual ACM SIGGRAPH/Eurographics Symposium on Computer Animation, Vancouver, BC, Canada, August 5-7, pp. 147–156 (2011)
8. http://www.ipisoft.com (accessed March 2013)
9. Rizzi, C.: Digital Human Models within product development process. In: Innovation in Product Design, pp. 143–166. Springer (2011)
10. Volino, P., Luible, C., Magnenat-Thalmann, N.: Virtual clothing. John Wiley and Son Ltd. (2008)
11. Green, R.F., Hudson, J.A.: A Method for Positioning Digital Human Models in Airplane Passenger Seats. In: Advances in Applied Digital Human Modeling. CRC Press (2011)
12. Colombo, G., Regazzoni, D., Rizzi, C.: Ergonomic design through virtual Humans. Computer-Aided Design and Applications 10(5), 745-755 (2013)
13. Colombo, G., Facoetti, G., Rizzi, C.: Virtual testing laboratory for lower limb prosthesis design. Computer Aided Design and Applications 10(4), 671–683 (2013)
14. Badler, N., Phillips, C.B., Webber, B.L.: Simulating Humans: computer graphics animation and control. Oxford University Press, Oxford (1993)
15. http://www.plm.automation.siemens.com/en_us/products/tecnomatix/assembly_planning/jack/ (accessed February 2013)
16. http://www.lifemodeler.com (accessed March 2013)

Automatic 3D Reconstruction of Transfemoral Residual Limb from MRI Images

Giorgio Colombo[1], Giancarlo Facoetti[2], Caterina Rizzi[2,3],
Andrea Vitali[3], and Alessandro Zanello[4]

[1] Department of Mechanical Engineering, Polytechnic of Milan, Milan, Italy
giorgio.colombo@polimi.it
[2] COGES Centre, University of Bergamo (BG), Dalmine, Italy
giancarlo.facoetti@unibg.it
[3] Department of Engineering, University of Bergamo (BG), Dalmine, Italy
{caterina.rizzi,andrea.vitali1}@unibg.it
[4] Humanitas Gavazzeni Clinic, Bergamo, Italy
alessandro.zanello@gavazzeni.it

Abstract. This work is part a new design platform for lower limb prosthesis centered on the patient's digital model and based on the integrated use of virtual prototyping tools. In particular, 3D detailed model of residual limb, that includes not only the external skin but also bones and soft tissues, is needed for socket design and finite element analysis to study the socket-residual limb interaction. In this paper, we present a procedure for 3D automatic reconstruction of the residual starting from MRI images. The output is a 3D geometric model, in a neutral format (IGES), which permits CAD information exchange among the modules composing the design platform. The reconstruction procedure consists of three different phases: image pre-processing, voxel segmentation, 3D models generation. Results have been considered promising and future activities to enhance the algorithm performance have been planned.

Keywords: Lower limb prosthesis design, MRI, 3D automatic reconstruction, segmentation.

1 Introduction

Nowadays, lower limb prosthesis design is carried out mostly following a hand-made procedure, and the final result heavily depends on the prosthetics' skills. In this context, we propose a new design platform for lower limb prosthesis design [1] whose main goal is to replace the traditional process with a virtual environment. The platform exploits several ICT tools such as 3D CAD and FEA (Finite Element Analysis) systems as well as biomechanical human models.

The platform comprehends two environments: the Prosthesis Modelling Lab and the Virtual Testing Lab. The first one allows the configuration and generation of the 3D prosthesis model, while the second permits to virtually set up the artificial leg and simulate patient's postures and gait.

V.G. Duffy (Ed.): DHM/HCII 2013, Part II, LNCS 8026, pp. 324–332, 2013.

The core of the new framework is the digital amputee around which the prosthesis is designed and tested. The amputee digital model is built using LifeMOD™, a biomechanical simulation package based on MSC ADAMS solver. Starting from a reference avatar, it is realized in two steps: the first concerns avatar's dimensioning and the latter residual limb linking. In this paper we focus the attention on the second step that requires the creation of a detailed model of the residual limb as well as some steps of the new design process. An example is the design of the prosthetic socket, the most important and critical component to ensure high quality prosthesis. It has to be realized in a custom way, according to the residual limb shape and patient's characteristics. To this end we have developed a virtual lab, named Virtual Socket Laboratory, which permits the prosthetics to design the socket around the digital model of the residual limb and to validate the 3D socket model by Finite Element Analysis (FEA) evaluating the interaction between the stump and the socket.

This means that a detailed digital model of the residual limb (i.e. including soft tissues and bones) is required and suitable for CAD and FEA environment. In fact, a detailed 3D model of the residual limb is fundamental to create an FE model, which allows the pressure distribution over the limb surface to be computed. The pressure is the commonly accepted that meaningful parameter to evaluate socket functionality is the contact pressure between the residual limb and socket during gait [2]. However, the final users (i.e., the prosthetics) of the platform usually have no specific skills in computer aided tools (e.g. those for medical image processing); therefore, we decided to implement a software module that automatically reconstructs, without human intervention, the 3D model of the stump.

In the following we first describe the procedure for the residual limb automatic reconstruction and adopted algorithms then, the preliminary experimentation with a case study. Finally, discussion of achieved results is reported.

2   Residual Limb Reconstruction

The detailed model of the residual limb, including external and internal (soft tissues and bones) parts is built from medical images acquired using MRI technique. Reconstruction from MRI scans is more challenging than from other medical imaging techniques [3], but we choose MRI since it is the less invasive for the patient and commonly used in considered field [4-7].

The reconstruction procedure is composed by three different phases: image pre-processing, voxel segmentation, 3D models generation. In the first one, the MRI images are pre-processed in order to reduce noise and digital artifacts. Initially, we tested a classic Gaussian smoothing but, in our case, this kind of filter did not preserve edge very well, so we decides to implement noise reduction with a 3D anisotropic diffusion filter [8]. This kind of noise reduction fits very well our purpose since it can also work in three dimensions and we can apply the filter to the whole 3D matrix of voxels. The second phase consists in segmenting the voxels belonging to the bone and those belonging to the external surface and in discarding the other voxels. The final output of this phase consists in two clusters of voxels that represent the geometry of bone and of the external surface from which we can derive the soft tissue. In the thirds phase, the procedure, starting from the voxels cluster of bones and soft tissues, creates the 3D geometric models. This operation is carried out using NURBS surfaces. The control points of the NURBS are placed on the external perimeter of the cluster, in order to define the correct shape. Then, the module can export a standard IGES or an STL file after triangulating the NURBS surface. In the following we illustrate the reconstruction of the soft tissue and of the bone, considering as reference a set of MRI images acquired from a transfemoral amputee (i.e., patient with amputation above knee). The automatic procedure has been implement using C++ languages, NURBS++ library, VTK library for polygonal conversion, and OpenCascade library for IGES exporting.

2.1   External Shape

The external surface of the residual limb is segmented in the following way. After having highly increased the contrast, edge detection by a canny filter is performed (the threshold value is 0.01) and small edges (segments with less than 50 pixels) are discarded (Figure 1). This operation is carried out slice by slice along both axial and coronal axes. The final result is a set of voxels that composes exactly the external surface of soft tissue (Figure 2).

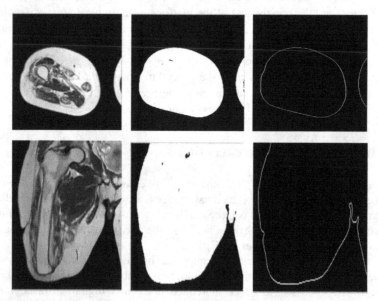

Fig. 1. External profiles detection: Axial and coronal slice (left), high contrast image (center), canny edge detection (right)

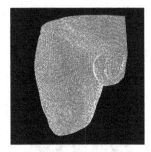

Fig. 2. Automatic segmentation of residual limb

2.2   Bone

Inner bone detection from a MRI scan is challenging because we have not a unique intensity level for every kind of tissue. Moreover, since we have to reconstruct the amputee bone, varying in size and shape, we cannot use an approach that exploits a-priori knowledge, such as ATLAS based segmentation or deformable models [9].

The MRI images can be considered as a 3D matrix of voxels, in which every single slice is part of a vertical stack. We decided to use a graph approach as proposed in [10], adapting the algorithm to a three dimensional matrix.

Initially, each voxel of the MRI volume belongs to a different cluster that has intensity mean corresponding to the voxel intensity. For performance reason, voxels with value equal to zero (intensity equal to zero means empty space) are discarded.

Then, we create a 3D graph where nodes correspond to clusters and edges (connecting clusters) have weight calculated as difference of the intensity between the two connected clusters. We use a 26 neighbors structure (all the neighbors voxels surrounding a voxel). The 3D graph is then segmented as described by the following pseudo code: (code is written in C++ language):

```
Sort edge by weights (from the lowest to the highest)
For every edge i...
   Get clusters A e B connected by edge i
   If (mean intensity difference between clusters A e B<
threshold K)
     Merge clusters A e B in a new cluster C
     Calculate features of cluster C (mean intensity)
   End
End
Final clusters analysis, discard clusters with size and
width/height ratio that doesn't fit bone shape
```

Figure 3 shows an example of the segmented cluster corresponding to the bone of the residual limb for the transfemoral amputee.

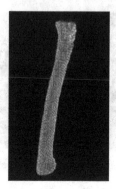

Fig. 3. Automatic segmentation of the bone

2.3   Geometric Models Generation

This phase consists in generating the 3D geometrical model of soft tissues and bone using NURBS surfaces and starting from the clustered voxels. Assuming the z-axis as the vertical axis of the clusters, we initially create a set of x-y planes intersecting the clusters from bottom to the top and with a regular step. For each plane, we create a NURBS circumference whose centre corresponds to the centre of the voxels belonging the plane. The radius of the circumference is set in such a way that the circle surrounds all the voxel belonging to the plane. Then, a convex hull operation is performed on the voxels belonging to the plane in order to obtain a closed perimeter and include any missing voxels. Afterward, for each NURBS circumference, each control point is moved toward the centre of the circumference itself until the point intersects the first voxel, which lies on the external surface of the voxel volume. Figure 4 shows the procedure.

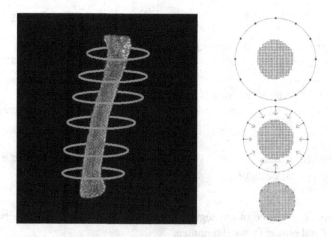

Fig. 4. NURBS perimeter voxels fitting

At this point each circumference has the shape of the external perimeter of the voxels group that the circumference surrounds. Finally the NURBS surface is generated by a lofting operation applied to the circumferences.

The NURBS surfaces can be exported in IGES format to the socket CAD system named SMA-Socket Modelling Assistant [11], specifically developed to design the prosthetic socket. It can be also easily converted by triangulation into a tessellated model and exported in STL format.

Figure 5 shows the NURBS and tessellated model of external surface while Figure 6 of the bone.

The more *U* and *V* NURBS parameters are higher, the more the NURBS surface matches the external voxels position; we figure out that U=20 and V=12 lead to a reasonable level of precision.

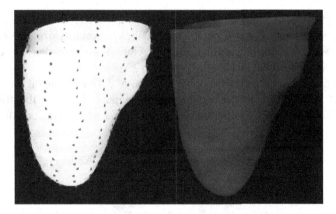

Fig. 5. NURBS (left) and tessellated (right) model of the external surface

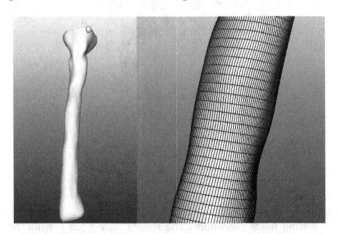

Fig. 6. NURBS (left) and tessellated (right) model of the bone

3   Preliminary Experimentation and Results

We experimented the automatic procedure with a test case of a transfemoral amputee.

We tested the algorithm on different sets of MRI scans of the same patient. External stump surface reconstruction is well performed with every set of MRI; obviously the final model accuracy depends on the resolution of the MRI images. Bone reconstruction, as previously said is more challenging. We found that the best settings of MRI scan for our purpose are the following:

- T2 weighted MRI.
- Slice thickness 2.0 mm.
- Pixel spacing 0.729 mm.
- Resolution 288x288.

In this case, the dimension of the matrix was 288 x 288 x 150 (resolution and number of slices). Based on the scanning parameters, a single voxel had size of 0.729 x 0.729 x 2.0 mm. We performed a normalization operation, so that every voxel had an intensity value between 0.0 and 1.0.

The models obtained have been used to both define a digital model of the transfemoral patient and to design the socket. Figure 7 shows the transfemoral patient's avatar with the reconstructed stump model and wearing the prosthesis.

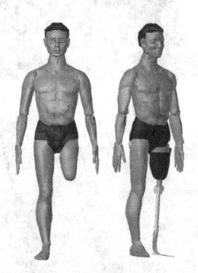

Fig. 7. Digital patient without (left) and with the prosthesis (right)

We compared the results with models reconstructed using a commercial package and following a hand-made procedure. The results have been considered promising, even if the model of the bone is less accurate. Anyway, it meets the requirements of the new prosthesis design framework consisting in an automatic reconstruction without human intervention, and geometrical models suitable for socket design and finite element analysis.

On the basis comparison, we have planned to improve the reconstruction of the bone. The segmentation graph algorithm loses some voxels belonging to the bone, due to high difference of voxel intensity. New features, such as texture characteristics [13], will be introduced during clustering. Furthermore, a shape analysis of the temporary cluster created during the segmentation will be performed to drive the segmentation toward the correct final clusters shape. In fact, a bone has a shape with a high ratio between height and width, and this information could be embedded into the algorithm to make it more effective and fast.

4   Conclusions

This paper proposes a software module that permits to reconstruct the 3D digital model of a transfemoral residual limb acquired with MRI without any human intervention. The implemented procedure runs completely in an automatic way and provides geometric models suitable for CAD and FEM phases of our new prosthesis design framework, in neutral format such as IGES files or STL.

The results compared with those obtained with a manual procedure have been considered promising and further enhancements have been planned to improve accuracy, especially of the reconstructed bone. We have also planned to extend and generalize the algorithm, firstly to transtibial residual limbs, and then to other type of applications, such as aortic aneurysm diagnosis.

Acknowledgements. The authors want to thank Fondazione Cariplo (Intesa Bank, Italy), which co-funded this research project. The authors want also to thank Nino Mansi for his precious collaboration and great availability to provide us with all necessary information.

References

1. Colombo, G., Facoetti, G., Rizzi, C.: A digital patient for computer-aided prosthesis design. Interface Focus 3(2) (2013)
2. Lee, W.C., Zhang, M., Mak, A.F.: Regional differences in pain threshold and tolerance of the transtibial residual limb: Including the effects of age and interface material. Archives of Physical Medicine and Rehabilitation 86(4), 641–649 (2005)
3. Zheng, Y.P., Mak, A.F.T., Leung, A.K.L.: State-of-the-art methods for geometric and biomechanical assessments of residual limbs: A review. Journal of Rehabilitation Research and Development 38(5), 487–504 (2001)
4. Faustini, M.C., Neptune, R.R., Crawford, R.H.: The quasi-static response of compliant prosthetic sockets for transtibial amputees using finite element methods. Medical Engineering & Physics 28(2), 114–121 (2006)
5. Zhang, M., Zheng, Y.P., Mak, A.F.T.: Estimating the effective Young's modulus of soft tissues from indentation tests - nonlinear finite element analysis of effects of friction and large deformation. Medical Engineering & Physics 19(6), 512–517 (1997)

6. Colombo, G., Filippi, S., Rizzi, C., Rotini, F.: A new design paradigm for the development of custom-fit soft sockets for lower limb prostheses. Computers in Industry 61(6), 513–523 (2010)
7. Lee, W.C.C., Zhang, M., Jia, X.H., Cheung, J.T.M.: Finite element modeling of the contact interface between trans-tibial residual limb and prosthetic socket. Medical Engineering & Physics 26(8), 655–662 (2004)
8. Perona, P., Malik, J.: Scale-Space and Edge Detection Using Anisotropic Diffusion. IEEE Transactions on Pattern Analysis and Machine Intelligence 12(7), 629–639 (1990)
9. Schmid, J., Magnenat-Thalmann, N.: MRI Bone Segmentation Using Deformable Models and Shape Priors. In: Metaxas, D., Axel, L., Fichtinger, G., Székely, G. (eds.) MICCAI 2008, Part I. LNCS, vol. 5241, pp. 119–126. Springer, Heidelberg (2008)
10. Felzenszwalb, P., Huttenlocher, D.: Efficient Graph-Based Image Segmentation. International Journal of Computer Vision 59(2), 167–181 (2004)
11. Facoetti, G., Gabbiadini, S., Colombo, G., Rizzi, C.: Knowledge-based system for guided modeling of sockets for lower limb prostheses. Computer-Aided Design and Applications 7(5), 723–737 (2010)
12. Bui, A.A.T., Taira, R.K.: Medical imaging informatics. Springer (2009)
13. Wu, J., Poehlman, S., Noseworthy, M.D., Kamath, M.V.: Texture Feature based Automated Seeded Region Growing in Abdominal MRI Segmentation. BioMedical Engineering and Informatics 2, 263–267 (2008)

Human Pose Estimation from Depth Image Using Visibility Estimation and Key Points

Sungjin Huh and Gyeonghwan Kim

Department of Electronic Engineering, Sogang University
CPO BOX 1142, Seoul 100-611, Rep. of Korea
{seungjin,gkim}@sogang.ac.kr

Abstract. In this paper, we propose the upper body pose estimation algorithm using 3-dimensional model and depth image. The conventional ICP algorithm is modified by adding visibility estimation and key points - extreme points and elbow locations. The visibility estimation keeps occluded points from participating in pose estimation to alleviate the affection of self-occlusion problem. Introduction of extreme points and elbow locations, which are extracted using geodesic distance map and particle filter, improves the accuracy of pose estimation result. The optimal parameters of the model are obtained from nonlinear mathematical optimization solver. The experimental results show that the proposed method accurately estimates the various human poses with self-occlusion.

Keywords: human pose estimation, 3D model based, modified ICP, self-occlusion, key points, geodesic distance.

1   Introduction

In Human Computer Interaction (HCI), introduction of gesture recognition provides more intuitive and convenient user interfaces than what traditional input devices do such as keyboards and mouses, etc. Since the recognition task is based on human poses, accurate estimation of the pose is an important prerequisite. Many research efforts have been made can be classified into two categories: marker-based methods and vision-based methods using RGB image sensor. The marker-based pose estimation methods which have been used in mainly film industry need burdensome suits or markers. Although estimation of pose using RGB image sensor is always preferred due to its convenience of data acquisition, loss of depth information during projection onto 2D image plane is a major hurdle for the pose estimation. Recently, pose estimation using depth image has been popularized by the Kinect sensor. Depth sensors are robust to variations of visual appearances such as illumination, texture, etc. The advantage of depth sensors and easy access of depth sensors lead vivid research on human pose estimation.

Shotton et al.[1] proposed a method of pose estimation using random forest[2] to segment an observed depth image into distinct body parts. Hemandez-Vela et al.[3] augmented graph-cut optimization to the method of Shotton et al.[1] to

V.G. Duffy (Ed.): DHM/HCII 2013, Part II, LNCS 8026, pp. 333–342, 2013.

improve the segmentation performance. The learning based approaches require large amount of database to cover the variety of human poses, and also have potential dependency on the database. The method proposed by Grest et al.[4] is based on the ICP(iterative closest point) algorithm to fit a body model to the depth image. Plagemann et al.[5] and Schwarz et al.[6] extracted anatomic key points from the depth images. However, depth cues, extensively used by Grest et al.[4] and the sparse key points[5][6] are prone to getting stuck into local minima in depth image and self-occlusion that are common in human pose.

In this paper, we define a 3-dimensional human upper body model and propose a pose estimation scheme by finding the optimal parameters, in order to alleviate the disadvantages of learning-based methods. To keep model parameters from deterioration due to the self-occlusion, visibility of a body part is continuously evaluated. Also, the local minima problem is effectively handled by inclusion of key points – extreme points and elbow joints - into the objective function. The optimal parameters are obtained by solving the mathematical optimization problem, similarly to the conventional ICP[7].

2   Human Pose Estimation Method

Given a sequence of depth images, a scheme of model based human pose estimation is described in this section. The articulated 3D body model is defined and nonlinear optimization is applied to the problem using a modified ICP algorithm. Unlike the conventional ICP algorithm, the modified version contains the visibility term and additional key points. Detailed description on the optimization method of the modified ICP algorithm and estimation of the key points are presented in the following sections.

2.1   Human Upper Body Model

In this paper, human upper body is prototypically modeled as concatenation of head, torso, and left/right arms as in Figure 1. To represent curvature of human body parts, the models of head and torso take on an elliptic cylinder and a cone, respectively. The arm model takes on a folding line to represent the flection of the elbow. The entire upper body model has 17 DOF: the translations of head, torso, and the angles of torso, shoulders and the elbow flection $(\mathbf{t}_{head}, \mathbf{t}_{torso}, \boldsymbol{\theta}_{torso}, \boldsymbol{\theta}_{arm}, \theta_{elbow})$. The sample points of each model of body parts are arranged in a regular grid and exploited to estimate the pose.

The pose of the articulated 3D model is assumed to be described by similarity transformation $S(\boldsymbol{\theta}, \mathbf{t})$, which contains rotation and translation. Figure 2 shows the conceptual projection process of the torso from 3D space onto 2D depth image plane $d(x, y)$, performed by a depth sensor. Since intrinsic and extrinsic parameters of the depth sensor are fixed, the pose is solely determined by $\boldsymbol{\theta}$ and $\mathbf{t}$.

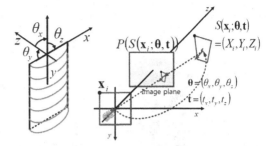

Fig. 1. The proposed 3-dimensional human body model

Fig. 2. Conceptual projection process of torso model with similarity transform and projection matrix

2.2 Modified ICP Algorithm

In our implementation, we made modification of the ICP algorithm which has shown successful results in human pose estimation[4][8][9][10][11]. The modified ICP algorithm is to find $\boldsymbol{\theta}^*$ and $\mathbf{t}^*$ which minimize the squared distance between the transformed model points $S(\mathbf{x}_1; \boldsymbol{\theta}, \mathbf{t})$ and the corresponding depth measurement $d_i = d(P(S(\mathbf{x}_i; \boldsymbol{\theta}, \mathbf{t})))$. The resulting objective function to be minimized has a form of

$$J_{ICP} = \sum_{i=1}^{N} g_i \cdot |d_i - Z_i|^2 \tag{1}$$

where $N, \mathbf{x}_i, Z_i$ and g_i represent the number of model points, i-th model point, depth of the transformed model point of $\mathbf{x}_i$ and the corresponding visibility function, respectively.

Self-occlusion occurred in human body pose estimation can be detected by comparing Z_i with the corresponding depth measurement d_i. The visibility function g_i is determined as (2),

$$g_i = \begin{cases} 0, & |d_i - Z_i| < c \\ 1, & \text{otherwise} \end{cases} \tag{2}$$

where c is a criterion for division. If the model point is occluded by another body part, the similarity transformed model point $S(\mathbf{x}_i; \boldsymbol{\theta}, \mathbf{t})$ is farther than the threshold c compared to the corresponding depth value d_i, and the g_i is set to be zero. In case self-occlusion occurs, the occluded model point needs to ge ignored in estimating $\boldsymbol{\theta}$ and $\mathbf{t}$. When self-occlusion is not considered, estimation of the parameters is seriously affected by wrong measurement, d_i. Figure 3 shows the role of visibility estimation. In Fig. 3(a), the torso model is heavily affected by self-occlusion and this makes the arm pose not to be estimated properly. Figure 3(b) shows that the problem of self-occlusion can be handled by the visibility estimation. In Fig. 3(b), the sample points on torso model that are occluded by the arm are eliminated from calculating the optimal parameters. Consequently, the pose is estimated properly without occluded points.

(a) Torso pose estimation without visibility estimation:the torso model is affected by self-occlusion and is not estimated properly

(b) Torso pose estimation with visibility estimation:the torso model is estimated properly with visibility estimation

Fig. 3. Role of the visibility estimation

2.3 Key Points from Geodesic Distance Map and Using Particle Filter

The parameter estimation by the conventional ICP tends to be trapped in a local minimum, as shown in Fig. 3(a). For more stable and reliable pose estimation, addition of extra key points[5][6] has been taken into account. In [5][6], they extracted key points based on the geodesic distance from the center of mass of the body. However, if the path from the center of the mass to an extreme point is cut off because of self-occlusion, the position of the extreme point cannot be determined properly. Based on the fact that torso parameters are relatively reliable than the others, locations of shoulders are easily determined. Unlike the method of [5][6], We are able to measure the geodesic distance from shoulders to extreme points even if the path from the center of mass to extreme points are occluded.

Euclidean distance between adjacent pixels u and v in 3D space is given by

$$d_e(u, v) = \left\| \frac{u}{d(u)} - \frac{v}{d(v)} \right\|, \tag{3}$$

and the geodesic distance between two point s, t is then

$$d_g(s, t) = \sum_{(u,v) \subset P_{s,t}} d_e(u, v) \tag{4}$$

where $P_{s,t}$ is the shortest path between s and t. Considering the initial direction of the path, the extreme points are distinguished from each other. Reducing the distance between the estimated position of extreme point and the tip of the arm model participates in objective function as (5). Figure 4 shows the position of estimated extreme points. The geodesic distance from shoulder is displayed in left column of Fig. 4. By considering the direction of geodesic distance to the extreme point and using non-maximal suppression, left/right extreme points are extracted as shown in right column of Fig. 4.

Besides the extreme points, the location of elbows takes significant role in estimating arm model parameters. Generally, the arm model is easier to lose the actual arm pose and stuck in local minimum than the torso and the head models because of its relatively large degree of movement of arm.

Therefore, estimating elbow location takes large advantage of improving accuracy. The particle filter is well known as a means for tracking nonlinearly fast moving objects due to its stochastic nature[12]. Kim and Kim[10] proposed a method of tracking limbs using the ICP and the particle filter. In this paper, the elbow location is estimated by particle filter based on distance from shoulder in geodesic distance map.

Particle filter estimates the unknown state e_t, which is the location of a particle on the image plane, from the observation $l_{1:t} = \{l_1, \ldots, l_t\}$ of which each element refers the distance from shoulders to the particle. Then the posterior density $p(e_t|l_{1:t})$ are approximated with a sum of N_p weighted particles $\left\{ e_t^{(i)}, w_t^{(i)} \right\}_{i=1}^{N_p}$ with $\sum_{i=1}^{N_p} w_t^{(i)} = 1$. The general procedure of the particle filter is followed: resampling, prediction, and update steps. Since the elbow location can move arbitrary, the particles are drawn and regenerated by uniform state transition model in prediction step. In update step, the weight of each particle is updated based on the observation likelihood as $w_t^{(i)} \propto p(l_t|e_t^{(i)})$. Figure 5 shows that the elbow location estimation encourages the model to escape local minimum.

The objective function to be minimized is defined as combination of conditions mentioned in the previous sections.

$$
\begin{aligned}
J &= J_{ICP} + J_{extreme} + J_{elbow} \\
&= \sum_{i=1}^{N} g_i \cdot |d_i - Z_i|^2 + \sum_{j=1}^{2} \left\{ p_{extreme,j} - S(x_{extreme,j}; \theta, t) \right\}^2 \\
&\quad + \sum_{j=1}^{2} \left\{ p_{elbow,j} - S(x_{elbow,j}; \theta, t) \right\}^2
\end{aligned}
\tag{5}
$$

where $p_{extreme}$ and p_{elbow} are estimated position of extreme point and elbow location in 3D space, respectively. Letting $\Theta = [\theta^T, t^T]^T$, the optimal solution Θ^* can be obtained by finding the parameters minimizes J as (6).

$$
\Theta^* = \arg\min_{\Theta} J
\tag{6}
$$

2.4   Nonlinear Optimization

Since the objective function given in (5) is highly nonlinear due to the nature of human pose and the visibility function g_i, optimization of the objective function is performed in an iterative manner. Though the simplest and straightforward method of optimization is gradient descent[13], i.e. $\Theta \leftarrow \Theta - \eta \nabla J(\Theta)$, excessive number of evaluating the gradient $\nabla J(\Theta)$ results in slow convergence. Moreover, difficulties in specifying the value of η is another reason to step aside from the gradient descent method.

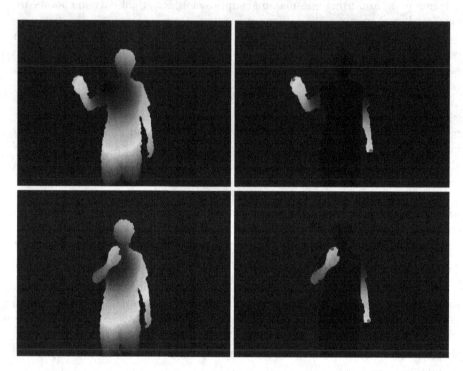

Fig. 4. Estimated extreme points based on the geodesic distance from shoulders: by considering the initial direction, the right hand is distinguished from the left hand

(a) Arm pose without elbow location estimation:the arm model stuck in a local minimum

(b) Arm pose with elbow location estimation:with assistance of elbow location, the arm model escaped a local minimum

Fig. 5. Role of elbow location estimation

Therefore, we employed Gauss-Newton method[13] for the optimization. Gauss-Newton method is one of variations of Newton's method and is widely used for data-fitting problems as (5). For brevity of description, (5) is rewritten in a least square form,

$$J(\Theta) = \mathbf{r}^T \mathbf{r}, \quad \mathbf{r} = [r_1, \ldots, r_M](M = N + 4) \tag{7}$$

where the residual $\mathbf{r}$ is a column vector containing the scalar components of J_{ICP}, $J_{extreme}$ and J_{elbow}. As given the objective function, the gradient $\nabla J(\Theta)$ and the Hessian matrix $\mathbf{H}$ of $J(\Theta)$ can be represented as,

$$\nabla J(\Theta) = 2(\mathbf{J}(\Theta))^T \mathbf{r}(\Theta) \tag{8}$$

$$\mathbf{H} = 2(\mathbf{J}(\Theta)^T \mathbf{J}(\Theta) + \mathbf{S}(\Theta)) \tag{9}$$

where $\mathbf{J}(\Theta)$ refers the Jacobian matrix and $\mathbf{S}(\Theta)$ refers the matrix whose (k, j)th component is

$$\sum_{i=1}^{M} r_i(\Theta) \frac{\partial^2 r_i}{\partial \theta_k \partial \theta_j}(\mathbf{x}). \tag{10}$$

Unlike the Newton's method, $\mathbf{r}$ is assumed to be linear in the Gauss-Newton method, i.e. $\partial^2 r / \partial \theta_k \theta_j = 0$. Then, the second derivatives in the Hessian matrix of $J(\Theta)$ vanishes and the Hessian matrix is approximated by

$$\tilde{\mathbf{H}} = 2\mathbf{J}(\Theta)^T \mathbf{J}(\Theta). \tag{11}$$

The approximation of Hessian matrix in (11) effectively eliminates the well-known instability problem of the Newton's method. At each Gauss-Newton iteration, update of Θ is calculated by

$$\Theta^{(k+1)} = \Theta^{(k)} - \tilde{\mathbf{H}}^{-1} \nabla J(\Theta). \tag{12}$$

In spite of the Gauss-Newton method, occasional divergences of solution are observed in our experiments. Therefore further relaxation of iterative optimization is used by employing ω-Jacobi method[14]. Solving (12) by the classic Jacobi method, the approximated Hessian matrix $\tilde{\mathbf{H}}$ is decomposed into a diagonal matrix $\mathbf{D}$ and the off-diagonal matrix $\mathbf{O}$,

$$\tilde{\mathbf{H}} = \mathbf{D} + \mathbf{O}. \tag{13}$$

Difference between the Jacobi method and the ω-Jacobi method is the introduction of an additional relaxation factor ω which controls contribution of a new solution to the previous solution. The ω-Jacobi method is described as

$$\Theta^{(k+1)} = (1 - \omega)\mathbf{D}^{-1} \nabla J(\Theta) - \omega \mathbf{D}^{-1} \mathbf{O} \Theta^{(k)}. \tag{14}$$

Since $\mathbf{D}^{-1}$ is a diagonal matrix, multiplication of $\mathbf{D}^{-1}$ and vectors in (14) are simply computed by component-wise division.

In the ω-Jacobi method, trade-off between the convergence speed and the stability of iterative solution is largely dependent on the relaxation factor ω. When $\omega > 1$, convergence becomes faster than the standard Jacobi method but suffers from instability, and vice versa. In our implementation, we took $\omega < 1$ to prevent the divergence in the iterative optimization.

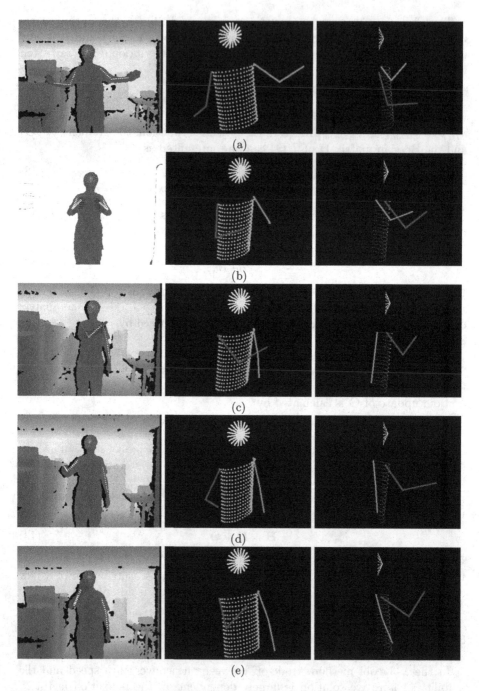

Fig. 6. Human pose estimation results:left column shows the result of pose estimation on depth image. Middle and right columns present the 3D pose corresponding to the left column.

3   Experimental Results

The proposed algorithm is evaluated in various human poses including self-occlusion and the estimation results are described in this section. The microsoft Kinect device was used to take depth images with a resolution of 640x480 pixels. As preprocess procedures, a modified mean filter and a Gaussian filter are applied to depth image for removing noise and smoothing.

Figure 6 shows the pose estimation results on depth images. In the left column, the estimated upper body model is displayed in 2D depth image. Occluded body and arm model points are marked blue and cyan respectively. 3D views of each pose are displayed in center and right columns, respectively. Figure 6(a) presents the accuracy of pose estimation. The model is estimated accurately not only the pose of arm but also the the angle of body. Figure 6(b) and 6(c) shows that the visibility estimation prevents torso model to be affected by occlusion. As stated in the previous section, the torso model points that is occluded by the arm are rejected in estimation of torso model for accuracy. Figure 6(d) and 6(e) illustrate the pose estimation results overcoming the situation that the upper arm is occluded by the lower arm. Not only the visibility function but also well estimated elbow locations and extreme points, the arm pose is estimated properly in spite of occlusion.

4   Conclusion

This paper has proposed a method for estimating human pose from sequences of depth images. We define a 3-dimensional human upper body model and estimate the parameters of the human pose using the modified ICP algorithm with visibility estimation and key points. Our model based algorithm does not require any training data and can estimate arbitrary pose for gesture-based HCI application. Because of visibility estimation, the model based pose estimation overcomes the self occlusion problem by neglecting occluded sample points. Key points obtained from geodesic distance map improve accuracy of arm pose estimation. The experimental results show that our method estimates various upper body poses in accuracy, including self-occlusion.

Acknowledgement. This research was partially supported by the Sogang University Research Grant (SRF-201214005).

References

1. Shotton, J., Girshick, R., Fitzgibbon, A., Sharp, T., Cook, M., Finocchio, M., Moore, R., Kohli, P., Criminisi, A., Kipman, A., Blake, A.: Efficient human pose estimation from single depth images. IEEE Transactions on Pattern Analysis and Machine Intelligence PP(99), 1 (2012)
2. Breiman, L.: Random forests. Machine Learning 45(1), 5–32 (2001)

3. Hernandez-Vela, A., Zlateva, N., Marinov, A., Reyes, M., Radeva, P., Dimov, D., Escalera, S.: Graph cuts optimization for multi-limb human segmentation in depth maps. In: IEEE Conference onComputer Vision and Pattern Recognition, pp. 726–732 (2012)

4. Grest, D., Woetzel, J., Koch, R.: Nonlinear body pose estimation from depth images. In: Kropatsch, W.G., Sablatnig, R., Hanbury, A. (eds.) DAGM 2005. LNCS, vol. 3663, pp. 285–292. Springer, Heidelberg (2005)

5. Plagemann, C., Ganapathi, V., Koller, D., Thrun, S.: Real-time identification and localization of body parts from depth images. In: IEEE International Conference on Robotics and Automation, pp. 3108–3113 (2010)

6. Schwarz, L.A., Mkhitaryan, A., Mateus, D., Navab, N.: Human skeleton tracking from depth data using geodesic distances and optical flow. Image and Vision Computing 30(3), 217–226 (2012)

7. Besl, P.J., McKay, H.D.: A method for registration of 3-D shapes. IEEE Transactions on Pattern Analysis and Machine Intelligence 14(2), 239–256 (1992)

8. Siddiqui, M.: Human pose estimation from a single view point. PhD thesis, University of Southern California, Adviser - Gerard Medioni (2009)

9. Knoop, S., Vacek, S., Dillmann, R.: Modeling joint constraints for an articulated 3D human body model with artificial correspondences in ICP. In: IEEE-RAS International Conference on Humanoid Robots, pp. 74–79 (2005)

10. Kim, D., Kim, D.: A novel fitting algorithm using the ICP and the particle filters for robust 3D human body motion tracking (2008)

11. Droeschel, D., Behnke, S.: 3D body pose estimation using an adaptive person model for articulated ICP. In: Jeschke, S., Liu, H., Schilberg, D. (eds.) ICIRA 2011, Part II. LNCS, vol. 7102, pp. 157–167. Springer, Heidelberg (2011)

12. Haug, A.: A tutorial on bayesian estimation and tracking techniques applicable to nonlinear and non-gaussian processes. MITRE Corporation, McLean (2005)

13. Chong, E.K., Zak, S.H.: An introduction to optimization. Wiley-interscience (2004)

14. Trottenberg, U., Oosterlee, C.W., Schüller, A.: Multigrid. Academic Pr. (2001)

Using Methods-Time Measurement to Connect Digital Humans and Motion Databases

Ali Keyvani[1,3,4], Dan Lämkull[2], Gunnar Bolmsjö[3], and Roland Örtengren[1]

[1] Department of Product and Production Development,
Chalmers University of Technology, Gothenburg, Sweden
{Ali.Keyvani,Roland.Ortengren}@Chalmers.se
[2] Virtual Methods & IT, Volvo Car Corporation, Gothenburg, Sweden
Dan.Lamkull@volvocars.com
[3] Department of Engineering Science, University West, Trollhättan, Sweden
Gunnar.Bolmsjo@hv.se
[4] Innovatum AB, Trollhättan, Sweden

Abstract. To simulate human motions in DHM tools, using techniques which are based on real human data is one promising solution. We have presented a solution in this study to connect motion databases with DHM tools. We have showed that using a motion database with MTM-based annotations is a promising way in order to synthesize natural looking motions. A platform consists of a Motion Database, a Motion Generator, and a DHM tool was introduced and tested. The results showed successful application of the presented platform in the designed test case.

Keywords: Digital Human Modeling, Motion Databases, Human Motion Simulation.

1 Introduction

Digital Human Modeling (DHM) tools are getting more applicable in the simulation of production lines. However, there are still major challenges to generate natural looking motions of daily tasks when using existing commercial software packages [1]. In spite of the availability of various techniques for the modeling of human motion, the functionality of DHM tools is still limited in practice [2]. Based on success stories in the game and film industries, generating motion using techniques which are based on real human data is one promising solution [3, 4]. Several challenges exist for using such data-driven techniques. There is a need for an extensive and properly structured motion database. Also, in order to compose a new motion based on the previously existing data, motions shall be suitably annotated in the database to be correctly searched and retrieved [5]. Finally, a connection between the DHM tool and Motion Database shall be established in a way that a requested scenario and retrieved motion can be communicated.

This study deals with these issues by using a motion database and Methods-Time Measurement (MTM) coding standard [6] to annotate a motion database. MTM is a

V.G. Duffy (Ed.): DHM/HCII 2013, Part II, LNCS 8026, pp. 343–352, 2013.

recognized standard and was originally focused on analyzing and measuring methods for performing manual works and setting standard times in which the worker should complete a task. Besides for the regular application of MTM, there are a number of studies which have utilized MTM in generating/analyzing human-like motions. For example, the MTM system has been used to generate motions for humanoid robots [7], to analyze ergonomic workload [8, 9], to simulate manual assembly sequence planning [10], and to generate motions for digital human models [11, 12].

Following these research works, this study highlights the feasibility to connect commercially available DHM tools to Motion Databases in a practical way. The objective of this work is to facilitate generation of natural looking motions. This is done by use of MTM vocabulary in the annotation of a Motion Database which is filled with captured human motions. In addition, a motion synthesizer module is developed. This module uses MTM vocabulary along with other information as communication objects between the user, Motion Database, and DHM tool in order to generate, search, and synthesize requested motion scenarios.

2   Method

Three main parts are involved in the motion generation process: Motion Database, Motion Generator, and DHM tool. These parts are interacting with each other in order to obtain desirable results. The Motion Database used in this study is a motion capture database presented by Keyvani *et al.* [13] and consists of several tables storing motions in a structured manner. The motion capture database supports different motion formats, multi skeleton configurations, and customized body zones (body zone is an optional collection of several joints recognized by a unique name e.g. right hand, upper body, etc.). Based on each skeleton configuration, these body zones are automatically matched with a reference joint table, and associated joints are then chosen. The Motion Database was filled with human motions which were gathered from different sources including Michigan Humosim laboratory [14], CMU Graphics Lab Motion Capture Database [15] , and an in-house motion capture laboratory. A new set of annotation category based on MTM vocabulary is introduced to the database, and motions are annotated based on the new category. The Motion Database is expandable during time, and can be counted as an independent module as long as it uses the same annotating conventions and communicates by a standard language (SQL in this case).

One purpose of this study is providing the capability to support available DHM tools with solutions taken from real human motion. Therefore, generally any DHM tool which can import and export required data should work fine with this system. Most of the commercially available DHMs, such as Jack [16], support a scripting language which can provide a connection to the tool for data extraction. Finally, the motion generator part consists of number of modules including Task Builder user interface, Query Manager, Motion Synthesizer, Inverse Kinematic engine, and Internal Visualizer, which are presented in more detail in this section.

2.1   Annotating of Motion Database

A new tagging category named MTM-Coding is introduced to the database schema. This category describes motions using a vocabulary based on the MTM-1 standard. The category consists of 20 main verbs (e.g. Reach, Move ...) and several sub-classes (called cases) defining the details of each basic motion. In the next step, the motions in the database are analyzed and annotated using the MTM coding. To do so, numbers of functions are implemented using Matlab to automatically detect the basic motions such as Reach, Move, and Turn. Manual adjustments were also needed in order to correct some of the wrong interpretations. For example, in a sample recorded motion, if the subject is transporting an object from one place to another, because no information is recorded in the motion files regarding the object, the system categorizes the motions as a 'Reach' instead of a 'Move', which has to be manually corrected. As a result, each motion in the database was divided into several motion segments, which were identified by different MTM codes. In general, three levels of tagging have been designed in the schema. Level I tags are the most general and apply to the whole motion (Table 1-Example 1). Level II tags are used to limit the scope of the tag spatially (Table 1-Example 2) or temporally, and level III tags are used to bound the tag domain both spatially and temporally (Table 1-Example 3). The MTM-Coding tags are mostly of a level III tag type, which means they bound the time (frame) range of the performed motion and also specify which joints are involved in each task. A number of advantages are gained by using the MTM system to categorize motions in the database:

- The MTM standard is well developed and provides a good level of detail.
- Multiple tags in parallel can be applied to a specific motion part.
- The assembly sheet instructions can be converted to the Task Builder format and vice versa, and the assembly sheet can be automatically generated after completion of the simulation.
- The process time can be calculated using the MTM standard.

Table 1. Structure of annotation table and examples of contents in the Motion Database

Field Name	Tag Type	Tag Value	Parent Category	Motion ID	BodyZone	Start Frame	End Frame
Field Type	String	String	Field	Integer	Field	Integer	Integer
Example 1	Gender	Male	General	2343	-	-	-
Example 2	Experiment Type	Seated	Posture	212	Upper Body	-	-
Example 3	Reach	R_B	MTM	212	Right Arm	100	147

2.2   Workflow

The workflow of a sample process is shown in Fig. 1. First, the user creates a task-sequence by using MTM codes in the Task Builder user interface (1). Meanwhile, the Task Builder module receives necessary information, such as manikin current posture, objects positions and subject anthropometry (2). Next, this information is processed by the Query Manager (3) and resultant queries based on the required task and geometrical properties of the task (e.g. start point, end point, and joint constraints) are generated (4). Next, the Motion Database is searched and matching results are sent back to the Query Manager (5). Consequently, the motion Synthesizer module uses the resultant data from the Motion Database (6), along with the Inverse Kinematic Engine module (7), to synthesize a new motion which is tailored for the requested task-sequence. The user has the option to preview the result in the internal visualizer and fine tune it if necessary (8). Finally, the result is sent back to the DHM tool to be visualized and further analyzed (9).

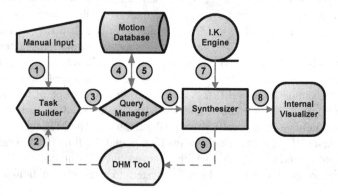

Fig. 1. Task-based motion generation workflow

2.3   Query Manager

A query manager is designed in the motion generator part to establish the communication between the database and the DHM tool. Required motions from the DHM tool are formulated using a sequence of MTM codes, along with motion specification (start point coordinates, end point coordinates, grip points, etc.) and subject anthropometry (stature, hand length, shoulder width, gender, etc.). The query manager searches the database for the closest matches, retrieves the results, and sends them to the motion synthesizer for any further necessary modifications. The query manager used in this study utilizes SQL language and a Matlab database toolbox to communicate with the Motion Database.

2.4   Motion Synthesizer

The motion synthesizer module consists of a set of functions implemented in Matlab, and enables the synthesis of a new motion based on segments of previously existing data in the database. Examples of these functions are cut, join, stretch, mix, blend, reposition, warp, etc.

It is likely that in many cases, an exact match would not be found among the existing motions stored in database. In such cases, the closest match is chosen and then a 'motion warping' technique similar to what is used by Witkin [17] is employed to reposition the end effector's positions. First, the new start/end point is resolved using an IK engine, and new joint angle values are determined. Then, obtained motion curves from the closest match are warped in order to match new start/end values. Eq.1 shows how the new values are calculated for each data point. For each data point $\theta(t)$ in time t between control points i and $i + 1$:

$$\dot{\theta}(t) = \theta(t) + \left(1 - \frac{t-t_i}{t_{i+1}-t_i}\right)^n (\theta_i - \theta(t)) + \left(\frac{t-t_i}{t_{i+1}-t_i}\right)^n (\theta_{i+1} - \theta(t)) \qquad (1)$$

When $t_i < t < t_{i+1}$

Where $\theta(t)$ is representing a new value for each data point in time t. θ_i and θ_{i+1} are values for control points and n is a custom weighting factor ($n=3$ is used).

3   Validation

A sample test case was designed and evaluated in order to validate the performance of the suggested solution. In this test case, we considered a scenario where a manikin (i) walks towards a table, (ii) squeezes between chair and table, (iii) sits on the chair, (iv) takes a part (bush) from a tray by right hand, (v) takes a part (pin) from a rack with left hand, (vi) inserts the pin in the bush's hole, and (vii) leaves the part on the table. Table 2 shows the MTM table of the test case while Table 3 shows the equivalent input generated by the user in the Task Builder. The current position of objects, grasp points, current posture, and subject's anthropometry were extracted from the external DHM tool. Generated query was sent to the Motion Database and the results were received back into Query Manager. To widen the search space and to consider solutions which can possibly fit after scaling the manikin, a relative measure of position over stature was used as search criteria. This means that for a subject with stature L, instead of searching for wrist position of X, a measure of X/L was searched and the matching result was scaled up/down if necessary. Also, for each specific task, different criteria were considered to sort the results for the closest match. As an example, for 'Reach' task, minimum deviation from requested start/end position was considered, or for 'Side_Step' task, closest stride length was considered. No 'Grasp' and 'Release' motions were available in the Motion Database, and therefore, no results were returned for those tasks. Simple grasp and release motions were manually generated and added to the database. In future developments, a hybrid method will be utilized to compensate these issues by mixing Database Motions with DHM generated motions to fill in the blanks. The 'Position' task is also simulated as 'Move'. In the next step, the final solution was tailored using motion synthesizer functions. Table 4 shows a summary of functions which are applied to different parts of the motion. Fig. 2. shows the layout of the designed test scenario and numbers of snapshots from the generated simulation. Roman numbers on each snapshot represent corresponding stage described at the beginning of this section.

Table 2. MTM table of the test case is shown. LH and RH column represents left hand and right hand motions respectively, which are determined by MTM codes. The thick line around cells shows combined motions and they are executed together. The MTM codes which are used are as follows: W_F: walk forward, SS_C2: side step, SIT: stand to sit, R_B: reach by itself, G_1A: select grasp, M_B: move broad, T_S: turn, R_C: reach crowded, G_4B: grasp, M_C: move control, G_2: Regrasp, P3SE: position, RL1: release, R_E: reach ease

Description	LH	Body	RH	Description
Walk to table front beside chair		W_F		
Squeeze between table and chair		SS_C2		
On chair		SIT		
			R_B	To bush in tray A
			G_1A	
			M_B	To position X
			T_S	Reorient the bush to keep hole horizontal
To pin in shelf B	R_C			
	G_4B			
To position Y	M_C			
Orient the pin horizontally	G_2			
Pin inside the bush hole	P3SE			
	RL1		RL1	
	R_E		R_E	

Table 3. Task Builder table created by the user. The values for parameters are automatically decided by the DHM tool and transferred to the task builder module. BodyZones and Order are determined by the user. Equal numbers in order column mean simultaneous execution of tasks. Right/left hand means wrist joint in addition to finger joints. Right/left arm means shoulder joints in addition to elbow and wrist joints. Right/left chain means all joints starting from the base of body, spine, thorax, and right/left arm.

MTM Task	Type	Order	BodyZone	Par1	Par2
Walk	W_F	1	LowerBody	Loc1	Loc2
Side Step	SS_C2	2	LowerBody	Loc2	Loc3
SIT	SIT	3	FullBody		
Reach	R_B	4	RightChain	RWrist Current Loc	Loc4
Grasp	G_1A	5	RightHand		
Move	M_B	6	RightHand	Loc4	Loc5
Turn	T_S	6	RightHand	CurrentValue	Coord1
Reach	R_C	7	LeftChain	LWrist Current Loc	Loc6
Grasp	G_4B	8	LeftHand		
Move	M_C	9	LeftChain	Loc6	Loc7
Grasp	G_2	9	LeftHand	Coord2	
Position	P3SE	10	LeftArm	Path1	
Release	RL1	11	RightHand		
Release	RL1	·11	LeftHand		
Reach	R_E	12	RightChain	Loc5	
Reach	R_E	12	LeftChain	Loc7	

Table 4. Summary of functions which are used during motion synthesis

Applied Function	Description	Example Task
Reposition	To shift a motion in order to match start position	Side Step (S.S)
Join	To join motion pieces together	Walk+S.S.
Warp	To change start end point of a motion	Reach
Blend	To smooth transition	Walk+S.S.+SIT
Reconfigure	To match different skeletons	-
Cut	To match start/end point	Move
Stretch	To scale the time of a process	Turn

4   Discussion

We have presented a solution in this study to connect motion databases with DHM tools. We have showed that using a motion database with MTM-based annotations is a promising way in order to synthesize natural looking motions. A platform consists of a Motion Database, a Motion Generator, and a DHM tool was introduced and tested. The results showed successful application of the presented platform in the designed test case.

We have noticed that when tailoring a new motion scenario there is a need to integrate data-driven methods, like what is presented in this study, with inverse kinematic techniques. This is especially important when a sufficiently close match in the database is missing, or when a complicated path needs to be followed. Moreover, using more smart methods to formulate the motion patterns and to extrapolate existing data for similar cases (re-targeting, re-subjecting) are desirable for such integration in the future.

At the moment, the user needs to define the tasks in a low-level language and assign the corresponding BodyZones manually to each task. In future work, a rule-based system will be substituted, which provides the capability to define tasks in a high-level language form. The low-level tasks and corresponding BodyZones are then inferred and assigned automatically.

We have observed that blending of motions pieces together and warping of motion-curves can increase the smoothness of the final motion, and therefore, the realistic look of it. A simple linear method has been used in this study just for evaluation purposes, while more sophisticated techniques which have been studied by other researchers such as Kovar [18], Ménardais [19], and Park [20] can improve the functionality of the system in the future.

In general when using motion capture a limited amount of persons is captured, thus it is often not tenable to claim that the motion behavior is valid for a larger group of people. To try to find a solution of this problem, several DHM-tool providers have developed scaling functions, thus it is possible to use a subject of any stature and scale the subject, such that it appears to match the anthropometry that is desired for testing. Currently, there is no data to support the assumption that this practice produces the same results as would be obtained using a subject who is actually of the desired size [21, 22].

The performance of a task is often limited by the ability to maintain balance [23]. According to Lockett *et al.* [24], body balance control is one feature that is required to properly and realistically simulate human activity. We have assumed that motions which are stored in the database have maintained balance in the timed of recording. However, one limitation to this assumption is that we have neglected the changes in balancing when mixing segments of motions from different parts of the body.

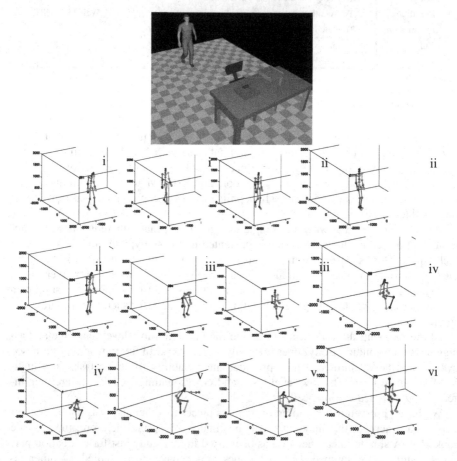

Fig. 2. Up: Layout of the test scenario, Down: Snapshots from the resulted simulation

Acknowledgment. Part of the data used in this project was obtained from mocap.cs.cmu.edu. This data was created with funding from NSF EIA-0196217. Another part of the data was received from Humosim laboratory at the University of Michigan. Access to these data provided valuable insight for the progress of this project, and usage of them in this study is acknowledged by the authors.

References

1. Lämkull, D., Hanson, L., Örtengren, R.: A comparative study of digital human modelling simulation results and their outcomes in reality: A case study within manual assembly of automobiles. Int. J. Ind. Ergonom. 39, 428–441 (2009)
2. Chaffin, D.B.: Improving digital human modelling for proactive ergonomics in design. Ergonomics 48, 478–491 (2005)
3. Zordan, V.B., Hodgins, J.K.: Motion capture-driven simulations that hit and react. In: Proceedings of the 2002 ACM SIGGRAPH/Eurographics Symposium on Computer Animation, pp. 89–96, 545276. ACM (2002)
4. Yamane, K., Kuffner, J.J., Hodgins, J.K.: Synthesizing animations of human manipulation tasks. ACM Trans. Graph. 23, 532–539 (2004)
5. Barbi, J., Safonova, A., Pan, J.-Y., Faloutsos, C., Hodgins, J.K., Pollard, N.S.: Segmenting motion capture data into distinct behaviors. In: Proceedings of Graphics Interface 2004, pp. 185–194. Canadian Human-Computer Communications Society, London (2004)
6. Karger, D.W., Bayha, F.H.: Engineered work measurement: the principles, techniques, and data of methods-time measurement background. Industrial Press, New York (1987)
7. Drumwright, E., Ng-Thow-Hing, V., Mataric, M.: Toward a vocabulary of primitive task programs for humanoid robots. In: International Conference on Development and Learning, ICDL (2006)
8. Laring, J., Forsman, M., Kadefors, R., Örtengren, R.: MTM-based ergonomic workload analysis. Int. J. Ind. Ergonom. 30, 135–148 (2002)
9. Christmansson, M., Falck, A.C., Amprazis, J., Forsman, M., Rasmusson, L., Kadefors, R.: Modified method time measurements for ergonomic planning of production systems in the manufacturing industry. Int. J. Prod. Res. 38, 4051–4059 (2000)
10. Kanai, S., Takahashi, H., Makino, H.: ASPEN: computer-aided assembly sequence planning and evaluation system based on predetermined time standard. CIRP Annals-Manufacturing Technology 45, 35–39 (1996)
11. Kuo, C.F., Wang, M.J.: Motion generation from MTM semantics. Comput. Ind. 60, 339–348 (2009)
12. Kuo, C.-F., Wang, M.-J.J.: Motion generation and virtual simulation in a digital environment. Int. J. Prod. Res. 50, 6519–6529 (2012)
13. Keyvani, A., Johansson, H., Ericsson, M., Lämkull, D., Örtengren, R.: Schema for Motion Capture Data Management. In: Duffy, V.G. (ed.) ICDHM 2011. LNCS, vol. 6777, pp. 99–108. Springer, Heidelberg (2011)
14. Reed, M.P., Faraway, J., Chaffin, D.B., Martin, B.J.: The HUMOSIM Ergonomics Framework: A new approach to digital human simulation for ergonomic analysis. SAE Technical Paper 01-2365 (2006)
15. Carnegie Mellon University's Graphics Lab, http://mocap.cs.cmu.edu
16. Siemens Product Lifecycle Management Software Inc., http://www.plm.automation.siemens.com/en_us/products/tecnomatix/assembly_planning/jack/index.shtml
17. Witkin, A., Popovic, Z.: Motion warping. In: Proceedings of the 22nd Annual Conference on Computer Graphics and Interactive Techniques, pp. 105–108. ACM (1995)
18. Kovar, L., Gleicher, M.: Flexible automatic motion blending with registration curves. In: Proceedings of the 2003 ACM SIGGRAPH/Eurographics Symposium on Computer Animation, pp. 214–224. Eurographics Association, San Diego (2003)

19. Ménardais, S., Multon, F., Kulpa, R., Arnaldi, B.: Motion blending for real-time animation while accounting for the environment. In: Proceedings of Computer Graphics International, pp. 156–159. IEEE (2004)
20. Park, S.I., Shin, H.J., Kim, T.H., Shin, S.Y.: On-line motion blending for real-time locomotion generation. Comput. Animat/. Virt. W. 15, 125–138 (2004)
21. Godin, C., Chiang, J., Stephens, A., Potvin, J.: Assessing the accuracy of ergonomic analyses when human anthropometry is scaled in a virtual environment. SAE Technical Paper 01-2319 (2006)
22. Johansson, I., Larsson, M.: Evaluation of the manikin building function in eM-RAMSIS when using Motion Capture. Department of Human Work Sciences. Luleå University of Technology (2007)
23. Parkinson, M.B., Reed, M.P.: Considering driver balance capability in truck shifter design. SAE Technical Paper 01-2360 (2006)
24. Lockett, J.F., Assmann, E., Green, R., Reed, M.P., Raschke, U., Verriest, J.-P.: Digital human modeling research and development user needs panel. SAE Transactions 114, 886–890 (2005)

Grip Force and CR-10 Ratings for Youth Females

Kai Way Li and Yu C. Lin

Department of Industrial Management
Chung Hua University, Hsin-Chu, Taiwan
kai@chu.edu.tw

Abstract. In this study, an experiment was conducted to measure the grip force for teenaged females at four pre-determined exertion levels on the CR-10 scale. The exertion levels of 2, 5, 7, and 10 corresponded to the 20%, 50%, 70%, and 100% of the maximum voluntary contraction (MVC). The subjects were required to grip a dynamometer using both dominant and non-dominant hand. The posture of the elbow was either straight down or at 90 degree flexion. Eight one females participated in the study. The analysis of variance (ANOVA) results indicated that the exertion level, elbow posture, handedness were all significant factors affecting the grip force. The Duncan's multiple range test results indicated that the grip force at exertion level 10 (208.95 N) was significantly ($p<0.05$) higher than those of the levels 7 (164.66 N), 5 (128.08 N), and 2 (56.65 N). The grip force at exertion level 7 was significantly ($p<0.05$) higher than those of the levels 5 and 2. The grip force at exertion level 5 was significantly ($p<0.05$) higher than that of level 2. The Duncan's multiple range test results indicated that the grip force at 180 degree elbow posture (142.26 N) was significantly ($p<0.05$) higher than that of the 90 degree posture (136.91 N). The interaction effects of the exertion level and hand used were also significant ($p=0.0035$). The overall Pearson's correlation coefficient between the CR-10 ratings and the grip forces was 0.84 ($p<0.0001$).

Keywords: hand exertion, power grip, subjective rating, CR-10.

1   Introduction

Applying grip force is very common not only on workplaces but also in our daily activities. Grip force is required when operating hand tools, carrying containers, or even standing and holding the rail on a bus or a subway train for balance purpose. Forceful hand exertion has been recognized as one of the major risk factors for hand/wrist musculoskeletal disorders [1-5]. Measurement of hand force has been conducted not only to assess the risk of upper extremity work-related musculoskeletal disorders but also for proper hand-object interface design [5-6]. Power grip is one of the hand functions that involves forceful hand exertions frequently and has been one of the most frequently assessed hand activities. The hand force or muscular strength when performing hand grip function may be measured using dynamometers or force gauges [7-10]. Grip force assessments and factors affecting the grip force have been discussed in the literature. But most of the studies in the literature are about adult data [11-13]. Assessments of grip force on youth females are not common.

V.G. Duffy (Ed.): DHM/HCII 2013, Part II, LNCS 8026, pp. 353–358, 2013.
© Springer-Verlag Berlin Heidelberg 2013

The purpose of the study is to determine the relationship of perceived exertion level and actual force applied for youth females and to discuss the relationship between grip force applied and subjective ratings of hand force exertion.

2   Methods

A laboratory study was conducted. This study was performed using the similar protocol as those in the literature [14].

2.1   Subjects

Eighty one females from a middle school in Changhwa, Taiwan were recruited as human subjects. All the subjects were healthy and were free from musculoskeletal injuries. Their age, stature, and body weight were 13.23 (±0.43) yrs, 153.4 (±12.6) cm, and 48.6 (±10.6) kg, respectively. Both the subjects and their parents signed informed consent for their participations in the study. All the subjects were right handlers. They were requested to refrain from physical activities at least one hour before participated in the experiment.

2.2   Apparatus

The grip force was measured using a TAKEI® 5001 hand dynamometer. This dynamometer was calibrated by the supplier before the experiment. A Borg CR-10 scale [15-17] was used for subjective rating.

2.3   Hand/posture Conditions

The hand exertions were measured under two handedness conditions and two elbow posture conditions. The elbow postures included 90° and 180° at the elbow. For

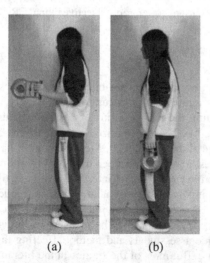

(a)   (b)

Fig. 1. 90 (a) and 180 (b) degree elbow postures

the 180° posture, the arm was straight down by the side. For the 90° posture, the upper arm was straight down by the side. The lower arm was flexed 90° and was horizontal (see Fig. 1). The wrist posture was natural for all testing conditions. There was no pronation or supination of the arm during the test. Both dominant hand and non-dominant hand were tested. This comprised four hand used and elbow posture conditions.

2.4   Grip Force Measurement

The nature and use of the CR-10 scales were communicated to all the subjects verbally before the experiment. The grip-to-scale procedure in Spielholz [18] was adopted. In this procedure, each subject was required to apply hand forces corresponding to different CR-10 scale levels. Levels of 2 (weak), 5 (strong), 7 (very strong) and 10 (extremely strong) were tested. Each subject was requested to grip the dynamometer to one of these levels with a grip span of 5 cm. The subject gripped for four seconds and the peak value on the dynamometer was recorded. A break of five or more minutes was arranged after the subject completed each trial so as to avoid the effects of fatigue on following trials.

2.5   Experiment Design and Data Analysis

The grip force measurements were conducted using a three-factor completely randomized design. The factors were the level of exertion, hand used, and elbow posture. A total of 1,296 (4 CR-10 levels × 2 hands × 2 elbow postures × 81 subjects) measures were collected. Both the descriptive statistical analysis and analysis of variance (ANOVA) were performed. Duncan's multiple range test was conducted if a factor was found statistically significant at $\alpha = 0.05$ level. The statistical analyses were performed using the SAS® 9.3 computer software.

3   Results

The means and standard deviations grip forces (N) under experimental conditions are shown in Table 1. The range of mean grip force for dominant hand was between 53.72 N to 223.53 N. The range of mean grip force for non-dominant hand was between 57.53 N to 209.90 N. The Pearson's correlation coefficient between the CR-10 and grip force was 0.84 ($p < 0.0001$).

Table 1. Grip force (N) under experiemntal conditions

		CR-10			
	posture	2	5	7	10
Dominant hand	90°	53.72(23.61)	130.97(34.55)	163.21(39.18)	210.82(42.79)
	180°	56.56(26.51)	126.55(38.65)	171.32(39.33)	223.52(44.61)
Non-dominant hand	90°	57.53(23.80)	125.95(30.49)	157.53(35.53)	195.58(37.26)
	180°	58.80(26.63)	128.85(35.84)	160.60(35.18)	205.90(41.27)

*Numbers in parenthesis are standard deviations

The ANOVA table for the grip force under CR level, handedness, and elbow posture conditions are shown in Table 2. All the three main factors, including the CR level ($p<0.0001$), handedness ($p=0.0107$), and elbow posture ($p=0.0063$) were statistically significant. The CR×hand interaction effect was also significant at $p=0.0035$.

Table 2. ANOVA table for grip force

Source	DF	SS	MS	F	Pr > F
CR	3	4034216.6	1344738.8	1087.0	<.0001
Posture	1	9276.0	9276.0	7.5	0.0063
CR*posture	3	7824.5	2608.2	2.1	0.0974
Hand	1	8079.8	8079.8	6.5	0.0107
CR*hand	3	168856	5628.5	4.6	0.0035
posture*hand	1	94.9	94.9	0.1	0.7818
CR*posture*hand	3	1174.1	391.4	0.3	0.8136

Fig. 2 shows the grip force under the four CR-10 levels. The grip force on the level 10 may be regarded as the grip strength of the subject.

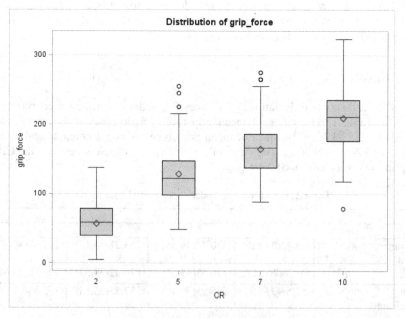

Fig. 2. Grip force (N) on the four CR-10 scale

4   Discussion

It was clear that the grip force was positively correlated with the exertion level which was administered using the CR-10 levels. This was consistent with the findings in the literature [14], [19-24].

The grip force may be converted to the %MVC if divided by the grip force at level 10 to see the deviations that they deviated from the CR-10 scales. The %MVC of the grip force at levels 2, 5, and 7 for dominant hand at 90 degree posture were 25.5%, 62.1%, and 77.4%, respectively. For dominant hand at 180 degree, the %MVC at levels 2, 5, and 7 were 25.3%, 56.6%, and 76.6%, respectively. For non-dominant hand, the %MVC at 90 degree posture for the three levels were 29.4%, 64.4%, and 80.5%, respectively. At 180 degree, the %MVC for the three levels were 28.6%, 45.6%, and 78.0%, respectively. It was apparent that the subjects applied higher grip force than they were supposed to except when applying a force at level 5 in the non-dominant hand/180 degree condition. This was consistent with the findings in the literature [14]. In other words, the subjects tended to apply a force higher than they were supposed to at 2, 5, and 7 of the Borg CR-10 scale.

References

1. Armstrong, T.J., Fine, L.J., Goldstein, S.A., Lifshitz, Y.R., Silverstein, B.A.: Ergonomics considerations in hand and wrist tendonitis. Hand Surgery 12A, 830–837 (1987)
2. Moore, J.S., Garg, A.: Upper extremity disorders in a pork plant: relationship between task factors and morbidity. Am. Ind. Hyg. Ass. J. 55, 703–715 (1994)
3. Leclerc, A., Landre, M.F., Chastang, J.F., Niedhammer, I., Roquelaure, Y.: Upper-limb disorders in repetitive work. Scan. J. Work Environ. Health 27, 268–278 (2001)
4. Silverstein, B.A., Fine, L.J., Armstrong, T.J.: Hand wrist cumulative trauma disorders in industry. British J. Ind. Med. 43, 779–784 (1986)
5. Moore, J.S., Garg, A.: The strain index: a proposed method to analyze jobs for risk of distal upper extremity disorders. Am. Ind. Hyg. Ass. J. 56, 443–458 (1995)
6. Balogun, J.A., Akomolafe, C.T., Amusa, L.O.: Grip strength: Effects of testing posture and elbow position. Arch. Phys. Med. Rehabil. 72, 280–283 (1991)
7. Bao, S., Silverstein, B.: Estimation of hand force in ergonomic job evaluations. Ergonomics 48, 288–301 (2005)
8. Bao, S., Spielholz, P., Howard, N., Silverstein, B.: Force measurement in field ergonomic research and application. Int. J. Ind. Ergon. 39, 333–340 (2005)
9. Mathiowetz, V., Kashman, N., Volland, G., Weber, K., Dowe, M., Roger, S.: Grip and pinch strength: normative data for adults. Arch. Phy. Med. Reh. 66, 69–76 (1985)
10. Casey, J.S., McGorry, R.W., Dempsey, P.G.: Getting a grip on grip force estimates: A valuable tool for ergonomic evaluations. Professional Saf., 18–24 (2002)
11. Petersen, P., Petrick, M., Connor, H., Conklin, D.: Grip strength and hand dominance: challenging the 10% rule. Am. J. Occup. Ther. 43(7), 444–447 (1989)
12. Kattel, B.P., Fredericks, T.K., Fernandez, J.E., Lee, D.C.: The effect of upper extremity posture on maximum grip strength. Int. J. Ind. Ergonom. 18, 423–429 (1996)
13. Duque, J., Masset, D., Malchaire, J.: Valuation of handgrip force from EMG measurements. Appl. Ergon. 26, 61–66 (1995)

14. Li, K.W., Yu, R.: Assessment of grip force and subjective hand force exertion under handedness and postural conditions. Appl. Ergon. 42, 929–933 (2011)
15. Borg, G.: Perceived exertion as an indicator of somatic stress. Scand. J. Reh. Med. 2, 92–98 (1970)
16. Borg, G.: Psychophysical bases of perceived exertion. Med. Sci. Sports and Exercise 14, 377–381 (1982)
17. Borg, G.: Psychophysical scaling with applications in physical work and the perception of exertion. Scand. J. Work Environ. Health 16, 55–58 (1990)
18. Spielholz, P.: Calibrating Borg scale ratings of hand force exertion. Appl. Ergon. 37, 615–618 (2006)
19. Buchholz, B., Park, J.-S., Gold, J.E., Punnett, L.: Subjective ratings of upper extremity exposures: Inter-method agreement with direct measurement of exposures. Ergonomics 51, 1064–1077 (2008)
20. Grant, K.A., Habes, D.J., Putz-Anderson, V.: Psychophysical and EMG correlates of force exertion in manual work. Int. J. Ind. Ergon. 13, 31–39 (1994)
21. Koppelaar, E., Wells, R.: Comparison of measurement methods for quantifying hand force. Ergonomics 48, 983–1007 (2005)
22. Kroemer, K.H.E.: Extra-ordinary ergonomics: how to accommodate small and big persons, the disabled and elderly, expectant mothers, and children, pp. 1–4. CPC Press, Taylor & Francis, Boca Raton (2006)
23. Park, D., Yun, M.H.: An application of psychophysical ratings to external force estimation. Computers Ind. Engng 31, 675–680 (1996)
24. Wiktorin, C., Selin, K., Ekenvall, L., Kilbom, A., Alfredsson, L.: Evaluation of perceived and self-reported manual forces exerted in occupational materials handling. Appl. Ergon. 27, 231–239 (1996)

Oxygenation and Blood Volume in Skeletal Muscle in Response to External Force

Hao Li, Chunhui Wang, and Zheng Wang

National Key Laboratory of Human Factors Engineering,
China Astronaut Research and Training Center, Beijing, China, 100094
chunhui_89@yahoo.com.cn

Abstract. Oxygenation and blood volume in skeletal muscle have been used to evaluate muscle contraction force. This paper aims to reveal the correlations between local oxygenation, blood volume and external force. Eight subjects performed isometric elbow flexion exercise of different force levels and isokinetic elbow exercise. In isometric exercise, oxygenation and blood volume indices were significantly correlated with joint torques; and their relationships could be described by linear equations. Compared with the oxygenation rate, the change of blood volume between rest and muscle contraction was more suitable to evaluate static muscle contraction force than oxygenation. In isokinetic exercise, blood volume demonstrated obvious periodicity in different motion cycles, and had low correlations with joint moments. Oxygenation indices demonstrated obvious differences between the five motion cycles. In conclusion, blood volume was found to be suitable to estimate the static and dynamic muscle contraction force, and validate musculoskeletal system biomechanical model.

Keywords: oxygenation, blood volume, near-infrared spectroscopy, isometric exercise, isokinetic exercise.

1 Introduction

Oxygen of skeletal muscle tissue is combined with hemoglobin(Hb) and myoglobin(Mb) in blood and muscle cells[1]. Near-infrared spectroscopy (NIRS) is a noninvasive method to determine local oxygenation and blood volume in skeletal muscle and brain. It was firstly used to study oxygen metabolizing of brain in 1977[2]. It is based on the relative transparency of the tissue for light in the near-infrared region and the oxygen-dependent absorption changes of Hb and Mb[3]. The reliability of NIRS has been well established. Significant correlations were observed for oxygenation and blood volume in muscles during two trials of static muscle endurance tests in healthy males[4]. NIRS can directly measure the content of oxygenated Hb/Mb(C_{oxy}), deoxygenated Hb/Mb(C_{deoxy}), total Hb/Mb($C_{Hb/Mb}$), and tissue oxygen saturation(TSI).

Oxygen of skeletal muscle have been used in evaluating muscle contraction force, validating biomechanical model. Modeling human musculoskeletal system is a sustaining research focus. Because of complexity of the model, it needs variety of methods to validate it. The muscle oxygenation and blood volume, which can be

V.G. Duffy (Ed.): DHM/HCII 2013, Part II, LNCS 8026, pp. 359–365, 2013.

measured by NIRS, were common used indices for evaluating muscle tissue activities and workload. There is growing interest in studying oxygenation and blood volume in response to exercise and external force. The oxygenation of muscle, which can be calculated by the change rate of $C_{oxy}(V_{oxy})$, $C_{deoxy}(V_{deoxy})$, and $TSI(V_{TSI})$, reflect muscle oxygen consumption situation. When muscles contract, HbO_2 and MbO_2 deoxygenated into HHb and HMb. The lager muscles contract force, the faster muscles consume oxygen. Praagman[5] reported that the change rate of HbO_2/MbO_2 is linearly related to external force in isometric elbow exercise. The relationship between V_{oxy} and external force can sufficiently be described by a linear equation. The blood volume, which can be represented by the content of Hb, reflects muscle contraction situation. Blood is extruded out of capillary vessels when muscle contracts. The content of Hb can't be measured by NIRS. But the change of $Hb(\Delta_{Hb})$ is mostly equal to the change of Hb/Mb, because the content of Mb in muscle cells is steady. Jgensen[6] reported that muscular contraction between 20% and 75% of MVC reduced or occlude erector spinae muscle blood flow.

It has been proved that the oxygenation and blood volume indices are notably correlation with joint moments in isometric movement. However, there are few comparative studies about different muscle oxygen indicators in correlation with joint moments. And it is lack of assessment in dynamic muscle contraction force. This research carried out isometric elbow flexion exercise under different force levels and isokinetic elbow exercise. Then the correlations of V_{oxy}, V_{deoxy}, V_{TSI}, and Δ_{Hb}, respectively with elbow moments were compared. This paper aims to find the suitable muscle oxygen indices to evaluate static and dynamic muscle contraction force.

2   Methods and Materials

2.1   Subjects and Instruments

Eight healthy male subjects(age 24.4±3.3 years, height 174.5±6.6 cm, and weight 71.8±10.5 kg) participated in the experiment after giving informed consent. The subjects were healthy and didn't do strenuous exercise in 24 hours before the tests.

Two instruments were used in the experiment. The instrument BTE Primus RS, which was developed by BTE of America, was used to collect elbow flexion moments. Force data was collected at 200Hz. The instrument PortaMon, which was developed by Artisnis of the Netherlands, was used to get muscle oxygenation and blood volume. PortaMon transferred data to a computer through Bluetooth technology with broadcast range of 30m. Data was collected at 10Hz.

2.2   Procedures

The subjects stood in front of BTE with their right elbow flexing 90° and hand grabbing the horizontal handle. PortaMon was attached to a subject by taping on biceps. The C_{oxy}, C_{deoxy}, $C_{Hb/Mb}$, and TSI of biceps, as well as the operation forces were recorded continuously.

Isometric elbow flexion exercise performed at four different force levels, 100%, 80%, 50%, 30% of the maximal voluntary contraction (MVC), with three minutes' rest in between. Each level repeated 3 times with one minute in between. Each elbow flexion lasted for 10s. As soon as subjects started to contract, a venous occlusion was applied in the upper arm. 80%, 50%, 30%MVC were calculated by the maximal value of repeated maximal voluntary contraction. The weight of the handle and subject's right arm was also considered, as it influenced the actual elbow moments. It could be excluded through measuring the moments when subjects were relaxed.

Isokinetic elbow exercise performed at the speed of 60°/s in the range of 30°~150°. Subjects made maximal force and repeated 5 times consecutively.

2.3   Data Processing and Statistics

In isometric elbow flexion exercise, V_{oxy}, V_{deoxy}, and V_{TSI} were determined by the linear change part of C_{oxy}, C_{deoxy}, and TSI immediately after occlusion. The slopes of the linear parts were taken as V_{oxy}, V_{deoxy}, and V_{TSI} of the muscle. Δ_{Hb} was determined by the difference of Hb/Mb between rest and exercise. The four indices were calculated from the muscle oxygen data collected in the same period. They were normalized to eliminate individual differences. For each subject and each index, the values were transformed to the percentages of the highest value of that index.

Correlation and variation of the indices were calculated. Pearson coefficients between normalized indices and different force levels, as well as the subjects' average values of coefficient of variation (*CV*) in each index were both calculated. *CV* indicates the within-subject variability derived from three repeated measurements of each force level. The equation is as follows:

$$CV\%=std.(A) \ / \ average(A) \tag{1}$$

where *A* represents the three repeated measurement values, *std.(A)* is the standard deviations of *A*, *average(A)* is the average value of *A*.

In isokinetic elbow exercise, the operation force and Δ_{Hb} during flexion movement were selected to make Pearson correlation analysis. The sampling frequency of operation force and muscle oxygen indices were different. In order to eliminate the difference of the data number between operation force and muscle oxygen indices, the uniform sampling method was used to handle operation force data.

3   Results

3.1   Muscle Oxygen Situation in Isometric Exercise

The maximal elbow flexion moments were 38.9±7.9Nm. Subjects performed obvious different maximal forces, distributing from 26.2Nm to 47.8Nm. However, each subject performed steady force in three repeated maximal elbow flexions. The average value of CVs was only 5.3.

Fig.1 showed the muscle oxygen situation of one subject during isometric elbow flexion exercise. It was similar with other subjects. Four indices were steady when subjects were relaxed. As soon as the biceps started to contract, all the indices except TSI obviously fell down. Then they performed different change. HbO_2/MbO_2 was consumed during muscle contraction. As long as the muscle contraction force was steady and the HbO_2/MbO_2 was enough, the decreasing rate of HbO_2/MbO_2 was almost linear. The changing rate fell down in a few seconds until the blood couldn't provide enough oxygen. At the same time, the consumed HbO_2/MbO_2 transferred to HHb/HMb, resulting in the increase of HHb/HMb and decrease of TSI. The changing rates of HHb/HMb and TSI were also linear in the first seconds and then fell down. Compared with HbO_2/MbO_2, HHb/HMb, and TSI, the content of Hb had little change in the period of steady muscle contraction.

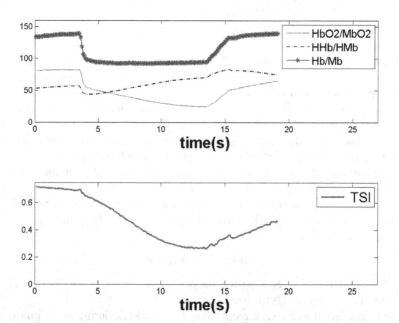

Fig. 1. Muscle oxygen content in response to isometric elbow flexion(100%MVC)

3.2   Muscle Oxygen Situation in Isokinetic Exercise

Fig.2 showed change process of the muscle oxygen of one subject during isokinetic elbow exercise. It was similar with other subjects. HbO_2/MbO_2, HHb/HMb, and TSI performed obvious differences between the five motion cycle. HbO_2/MbO_2 and TSI reduced gradually during isokinetic exercise. At the same time, HHb increased gradually. It was because that biceps didn't have enough rest during exercise, which resulted in untimely recovery of muscle oxygen. Hb/Mb performed obvious periodicity in the five motion cycle. It had more regular changes than the other three indices. Lack of muscle oxygen and rest had little influence on Hb/Mb.

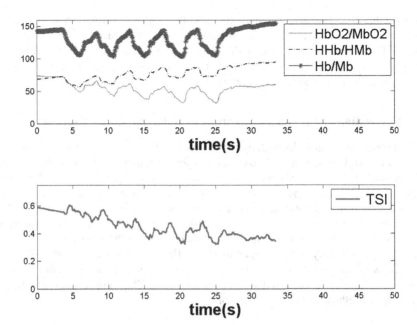

Fig. 2. Muscle oxygen content in response to elbow isokinetic exercise

4   Discussion

4.1   Correlations of Different Muscle Oxygen Indicators and Joint Torques in Isometric Elbow Exercise

All of the four indices were notably correlated with elbow flexion torques (Table 1). The coefficients of correlation ranged from 0.793 to 0.844. The CV ranged from 12.1 to 19.9. These results corresponded to previously reported findings. Praagman[5] found that V_{oxy} was notably correlated with elbow flexion torques. The correlation coefficient r =0.73, p <0.01. So both oxygenation and blood volume could be used in static musculoskeletal biomechanical mode validation. For this purpose, linear equations were made between indices and elbow flexion torques (Table 1). The equations could calculate the normalized elbow flexion torques and biceps contraction force through oxygenation and blood volume.

Table 1. Correlation and linear equation between muscle oxygen indices and external force

| Index | Pearson | | CV | a | b |
	r	p			
V_{oxy}	.801	.000	13.4	0.920	0.011
V_{deoxy}	.793	.000	19.9	0.889	0.073
V_{TSI}	.843	.000	13.1	0.788	0.164
Δ_{Hb}	.844	.000	12.1	0.978	-0.021

$Force = a*Index + b.$

Among the four indices, Δ_{Hb} demonstrated the highest correlation with external force, and the lowest variation. It corresponded to previously reported findings. Robert[4] found that Δ_{Hb} was more stable than V_{oxy} in repeated knee flexion exercise. As a result, Δ_{Hb} was more reliable to evaluate static muscle contraction force, and to validate musculoskeletal system biomechanical model.

4.2   Correlation of Δ_{Hb} and Joint Torque in Isokinetic Elbow Exercise

Workers often carry out tasks with dynamic posture and operation force. So it need to analyze the correlation of muscle oxygen and joint torques in dynamic movements. Fig.2 showed that continuous movement affected Coxy, Cdeoxy, and TSI, thereby affected Voxy, Vdeoxy, and VTSI. ΔHb was not influenced by these factors. So it was selected to evaluate the dynamic muscle contraction force.

Fig.3 showed Δ_{Hb} and elbow torques in isokinetic elbow exercise. The data came from the same subject with Fig.2. In one motion cycle, the elbow flexed first and then extended. Δ_{Hb} gradually turned larger in elbow flexion, and was largest at the end. When elbow started to extend, biceps stopped to contract and Δ_{Hb} gradually reduced. It was not completely corresponded with joint torques. The joint torques was largest at the middle of elbow flexion or extension.

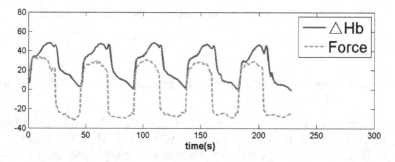

Fig. 3. Δ_{Hb} and elbow torques of one subject in isokinetic elbow exercise

Correlation of Δ_{Hb} and joint torques in isokinetic elbow exercise was analyzed. The normalized torques and Δ_{Hb} of 8 subjects during flexion movement were made Pearson correlation analysis. The correlation coefficient $r = 0.526$, $p<0.01$. Linear equation was as follows:

$$Force = 0.434 * \Delta_{Hb} + 0.335 \tag{2}$$

The correlation coefficient of Δ_{Hb} in isokinetic exercise was smaller than that in isometric exercise. The linear equations of isokinetic exercise and isometric exercise were also different. It might be because the changing joint angles during exercise influenced the muscle length. Ruiter[7] reported that muscle oxygen was influenced by the muscle length and muscle fiber architecture. As a result, the correlation coefficient decreased. Although Δ_{Hb} was influenced by joint angles, it had a small correlation with joint moments, and could be used as a reference index to evaluate dynamic muscle contraction force.

5   Conclusions

In isometric exercise, oxygenation and blood volume in skeletal muscle could be used to evaluate muscle contraction force. Δ_{Hb}, which reflects the change of blood volume, was better than other three indices. As its' correlation efficient with joint moments was the highest, and variation was the lowest. In isokinetic exercise, blood volume demonstrated obvious periodicity in different motion cycles, and had low correlations with joint moments. Oxygenation indices performed obvious differences between the five motion cycles.

In conclusion, blood volume was found to be suitable to estimate the static and dynamic muscle contraction force, and validate musculoskeletal system biomechanical model.

Acknowledgment. This work was supported by National Basic Research Program of China (2011CB711005) and Experimentation Technology Research of General Equipment Department (2011SY5405002).

References

1. Lai, N., Zhou, H., Saidel, G.M., et al.: Modeling oxygenation in venous blood and skeletal muscle in response to exercise using near-infrared spectroscopy. Journal of Applied Physiology 106, 1858–1874 (2009)
2. Jobsis, F.: Noninvasive infrared monitoring of cerebral and myocardial oxygen sufficiency and circulatory. Science 198, 1264–1267 (1977)
3. Ferrari, M., Mottola, L., Quaresima, V.: Principles, techniques, and limitations of near infrared spectroscopy. Canadian Society for Exercise Physiology 29(4), 463–487 (2004)
4. Kell, R.T., Farag, M., Bhambhani, Y.: Reliability of erector spinae oxygenation and blood volume responses using near-infrared spectroscopy in healthy males. Eur. J. Appl. Physiol. 91(5), 499–507 (2004)
5. Praagman, M., Chadwick, H.E.J., Colier, W.N.J.M., Helm, F.C.T.: Muscle oxygen consumption, determined by NIRS, in relation to external force and EMG. Journal of Biomechanics 36, 905–912 (2003)
6. Jgensen, K.: Human trunk extensor muscles physiology and ergonomics. Acta Physiol. Scand. 160, 5–58 (1997)
7. Ruiter, C.J., Boer, M.D., Spanjaard, M., et al.: Knee angle-dependent oxygen consumption during isometric contractions of the knee extensors determined with near-infrared spectroscopy. J. Appl. Physiol. 99(9), 579–586 (2005)

Simulating a Walk of Digital Human Model Directly in Massive 3D Laser-Scanned Point Cloud of Indoor Environments

Tsubasa Maruyama, Satoshi Kanai, and Hiroaki Date

Graduate School of Information Science and Technology,
Hokkaido University, Sapporo 060-0814, Japan
t_maruyama@sdm.ssi.ist.hokudai.ac.jp,
{kanai,hdate}@ssi.ist.hokudai.ac.jp

Abstract. Recently, human behavior simulations in 3-dimensional environment models have been enabled by the advance in computer performances. However, manually building the 3D models for the simulations are still costly and time-consuming, and the resultant models are sometimes inaccurate and do not necessarily reflect as-built environments. The final goal of our research is to realize the accessibility evaluation of "as-built" environments based on the human behavior simulation. To achieve the goal, in this study, we developed a technology where as-built 3D environment models could be constructed in a fully automatic way from laser-scanned 3D point clouds measured from as-built indoor environments. Additionally, we realized a basic walking simulation function in the as-built environment model represented by the point clouds. The modeling and simulation efficiency and accuracy were evaluated.

Keywords: human behavior simulation, laser scanning, 3D point clouds.

1   Introduction

Recently, studies of human behavior simulations in large-scale environments have been increasing in the area of realistic crowd animations, disaster and evacuation planning and the analyzing of crowd dynamics [1]. Also, a realistic human behavior simulation, even in a 3-dimentional environment, has been enabled by recent advances in computer performance [2]. However, manually building such 3D environment models is still costly and time-consuming, and the resultant models are sometimes inaccurate and do not necessarily reflect as-built environments. The problems become serious as the environments become large-scale. On the other hand, scanning large-scale environments as 3D point clouds was enabled by the progress of 3D laser scanning technology which realizes fast and accurate as-built modeling.

The final goal of this research was to evaluate the "accessibility" of 3D as-built environments based on the human behavior simulation results. Currently, such evaluations are greatly depending on the professionals [3] and still remain quantitative. However, the human behavior simulation could realize a more detailed and quantitative accessibility evaluation. As-built environment models are indispensable for the

V.G. Duffy (Ed.): DHM/HCII 2013, Part II, LNCS 8026, pp. 366–375, 2013.

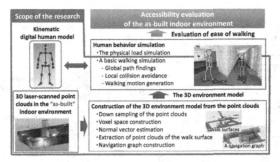

Fig. 1. Overview of the research

simulation. Therefore, as shown in Fig.1, the purpose of this paper is first to develop a technology where the 3D environment models can be constructed in a fully automatic way from laser-scanned point clouds measured from as-built indoor environments.

Moreover, a kinematics-based walk of a digital human model could be directly simulated in the models. The modeling and simulation efficiency and accuracy were evaluated.

As shown in Fig.1, a human behavior simulation consists of the global path findings, the local collision avoidance and the walking motion generation. Therefore, in this study, the walk surfaces for the walking motion generation, a navigation graph for the global path findings, and normal vectors of the down-sampled point clouds for the walking motion generation were automatically generated from the laser-scanned point clouds to build the 3D environment models.

2   Related Work

This research mainly involved three related areas: the 3D environment model construction from laser-scanned point clouds, digital human modeling for gait simulation and the crowd behavior simulation.

In the work of Nüchter [4], floors and walls were automatically recognized from laser-scanned point clouds of indoor environments. Similar work was done by Rusu [5] for recognizing household goods. However, their environment models did not include the essential data structure for the human behavior simulation such as the navigation graph for the global path findings. Many studies have been done for the digital human modeling for gait simulation. The motion-capture-based gait simulation could synthesize the variety of human gait patterns [6]. On the other hand, Chang [7] estimated a physical load in assembly tasks in the workspace using the dynamics-based digital human model. However, if their works are used for the accessibility evaluation, the walking path and footprints in the large-scale environment have to be specified manually which enforces unacceptable workload to the users of the simulation.

For the human behavior simulation, the local collision avoidance and the global path findings are indispensable. Many different methods have existed for the local collision avoidance such as social forces [8], cellular automata [9], and rule-based [2]. However, [8] and [9] did not use the 3D as-built environment models but the as-planned 2D environment ones. Kakizaki [2] proposed the local collision avoidance

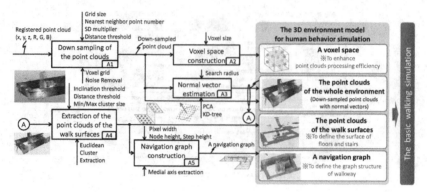

Fig. 2. Construction flow of the 3D environment model from point clouds

algorithm of the evacuation simulation which could avoid obstacles and other humans in the 3D environment models by checking the three occupation-inspection spaces in front of a human model. However, the human movements were limited only to three directions, and lacked the reality of human motion. On the other hand, Pettre [10] proposed an algorithm which constructed a navigation graph for the global path findings. The navigation graph, which represents a free-space and its connectivity, could be automatically generated from the 3D mesh model. However, their navigation graph had to be generated from the 3D mesh model of the environments which becomes hard to construct if the point clouds become too large.

3   Construction of the 3D Environment Model From Point Clouds

For the basic walking simulation, 3D environment models must be first built from 3D laser-scanned point clouds of an as-built indoor environment. Fig.2 shows the construction flow of the models. The model consists of two point clouds (the point clouds of the whole environment and the point clouds of the walk surfaces), the voxel space for efficient management of the massive point clouds and a navigation graph for defining the walkway for humans. The details are described in the following subsections.

3.1   Down Sampling Of The Point Clouds (A1), Voxel Space Construction (A2) And Normal Vector Estimation (A3)

Multiple laser-scanned point clouds were first merged to make one registered point cloud. This registered point clouds had many points, and was generally too dense to construct the model. Therefore, it was down-sampled using the voxel grid. In this research, one point per square centimeter was enough for the model. Moreover, outlier points were removed using an SOR filter [11] and Euclidian Cluster Extraction[12].

Then, a bounding box, including all down-sampled point clouds, was spatially and uniformly subdivided into a set of voxel spaces. A subset of point clouds included in a

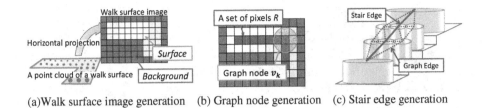

(a)Walk surface image generation   (b) Graph node generation   (c) Stair edge generation

Fig. 3. Navigation graph construction

voxel space was linked to the space. This voxel space helped quicken the neighboring point search of the simulation in the 3D environment model. Finally, normal vectors at the down-sampled points were estimated using principal component analysis of the locally neighboring points [13]. This point cloud with normal vectors was used as a part of the 3D environment model to express the geometry of the whole environment.

3.2   Extraction of The Point Clouds of The Walk Surfaces (A4)

The point clouds of the walk surfaces, such as floors and stairs, were automatically extracted from the point clouds using Euclidian Cluster Extraction. First, if the angle between a normal vector at a point and a vector $v = [0, 0, +1]$ was smaller than the threshold ε (we set $\varepsilon = 20$ deg.), then the point was extracted as one which could be placed on a horizontal plane. Finally, the point clouds of the walk surfaces were extracted by clustering the points on the horizontal plane using Euclidian Cluster Extraction, and were treated as a part of the 3D environment model.

3.3   Navigation Graph Construction (A5)

Pettre [10] proposed a navigation graph for crowd simulation which represented a free-space and its connectivity. In their graph, each graph node represented a free-space and its width, and each edge represented connectivity between two free-spaces. However, their navigation graph had to be generated from the 3D mesh model of the environments, which became hard to construct if the point clouds became too large. Therefore, the following algorithms were newly developed which could automatically create the navigation graph directly from the 3D laser-scanned point clouds.

1.   **Walk Surface Image Generation:** As shown in Fig.3 (a), a walk surface image was generated by projecting the point clouds of the walk surfaces to a horizontal plane. The image included the *surface* pixel, where at least one point of a walk surface existed, and the *background* pixel, where no points existed.

2.   **Walk Surface Image Thinning:** The thinning operation defined by equation (1) was applied to the walk surface image in order to extract the medial axis.

$$t(i,j) = \begin{cases} d(i,j) & (d(i,j) \ is \ local \ maximum \ in \ 4-neighbor) \\ 0 & (otherwise) \end{cases} \tag{1}$$

where $T = \{t(i,j)\}$ is an image after thinning, $d(i,j)$ 4-neighbor distance (Manhattan distance) between a pixel (i,j) and its nearest *background* pixel.

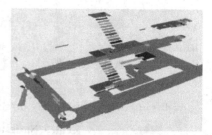

(a) The registered 3D laser-scanned point clouds   (b) The point clouds of the walk surfaces

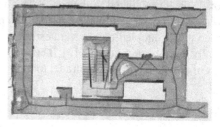

(c) The navigation graph   (d) The navigation graph (Overhead view)

Fig. 4. The result of constructing the 3D environment model for the walking simulation

3. **Graph Node Generation:** The graph node of the navigation graph was generated in the following steps. First, a set of pixels, R, which satisfies $t(i, j) > 0$ was selected from T as shown in Fig.3 (b). Then, a graph node v_k was generated according to equation (2). Also, the attributes of v_k were evaluated, which include a 2D position vector $Q(v_k)$ and attributes of a cylinder $C(v_k)$ using equation (3).

$$Q(v_k) = arg\ max_{(i,j) \in R}\ t(i, j) \qquad (2)$$

$$C(v_k) = <r(v_k), h> \\ r(v_k) = d(Q(v_k)) \qquad (3)$$

where $r(v_k)$ is a radius of cylinder $C(v_k)$, and h a height of $C(v_k)$. Then, a graph node v_k was inserted to a set of graph nodes, V. Finally, pixels contained in the $C(v_k)$ were removed from R, and these processes were repeated until $R = \emptyset$.

4. **The Graph Edges Generation:** In a set of graph nodes $= \{v_1, ..., v_n\}$, if the cylinders $C(v_i)$ and $C(v_j)$ have a common region, a graph edge $e_k = (v_i, v_j)$ is defined. A set of all graph edges $E = \{e_1, ..., e_N\}$ was generated by applying this process to all graph nodes in V.

5. **The Stair Edges Generation:** In a stairway, each stair area becomes small and many small graph nodes are generated. Eventually, many short graph edges are created among the stairs as shown in the dotted line in Fig.3 (c). For simplifying the navigation graph, these short edges were merged to one stair edge. This stair edge enabled efficient path findings on the navigation graph in the simulation.

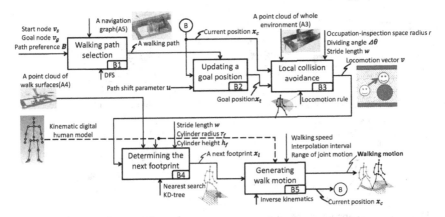

Fig. 5. A basic walking simulation flow

3.4   A Result of Constructing the 3d Environment Model

A result of the construction of the 3D environment models is shown in Fig.4. Fig.4 (a) is the registered point cloud of a building indoors including corridors and stairways. Fig.4 (b) is the point cloud of walk surfaces automatically extracted using this study's method. The stairs could be accurately reproduced as one of the walk surfaces. Fig.4 (c) and Fig.4(d) are the navigation graph. The result showed that the free-space and its connectivity could be successfully modeled in the navigation graph, even in the stairs.

4   Basic Walking Simulation in the 3d Environment Models

To realize a basic walking simulation directly in the 3D environment models expressed by the point clouds, this study used a simple kinematic digital human model [2],[14] with two legs each of which was modeled as a link mechanism with 4 degrees of freedom. As shown in Fig.5, the basic walking simulation using the digital human model is done by the following steps.

1. **Walking Path Selection:** Based on the user-defined start node and goal node, a walking path of the digital human model was automatically found. The walking path was determined by DFS (Depth-First-Search) over the navigation graph based on the path cost and user's preference for the path.

    For this purpose, first, all feasible paths from a start node v_s to a goal node v_g were extracted by DFS over the graph. Then, the path cost vector C_i which is defined by equation (4), was evaluated in each path i.

$$C_i = [d_i, \rho_i, b_i] \qquad (4)$$

where $d_i \in [0,1]$ = a normalized travel distance along path i.
$\rho_i \in [0,1]$ = a normalized crowd density on path i.
$b_i \in [0,1]$ = a normalized narrowness of path i.

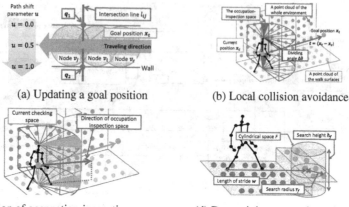

(a) Updating a goal position (b) Local collision avoidance

(c) Direction of occupation-inspection space (d) Determining a next footprint

Fig. 6. An algorithm of a basic walking simulation

Finally, a walking path j was selected by equation (5).

$$j = arg\,min_i(C_i \cdot B) \tag{5}$$

where $B = [\beta_1, \beta_2, \beta_3]$ is a user's path preference vector for the path, and each element $(\beta_1, \beta_2, \beta_3)(\beta_k \in [0,1])$ controls the degree of preferences among travel distance, crowd density, narrowness of the path.

Once a walking path j was selected, the following processes from (B2) to (B5) were repeated until the digital human model reached the goal node v_g.

2. **Updating Goal Position:** As shown in Fig.6 (a), in order to let the digital human model walk along the walking path, a goal position, x_t, which is a temporary target position of walking, was updated every time when the model walked from a current graph node, v_c, to the next node, v_i. x_t was calculated based on the path shift parameter $u \in [0,1]$ and an intersection line, l_{ij}, between graph nodes v_i and v_j by equation (6).

$$x_t = (q_2 - q_1)u + q_1 \tag{6}$$

where q_1, q_2 are position vectors of the intersected points between walls and l_{ij}. If the digital human model was made to walk in the center of the walkway, the path shift parameter u set 0.5 .

3. **Local Collision Avoidance:** A locomotion vector of the digital human model in every step was automatically determined on-the-fly by the study's locomotion rule-based local collision avoidance algorithm. As shown in Fig.6 (b), the locomotion rule determined a locomotion vector by checking obstacles represented by the point clouds of the whole environment in front of the digital human model. The fan-shaped occupation-inspection space was checked for obstacles in order from the front, and side to side. If the space was free, which meant no points existed in the occupation-inspection space, then the locomotion vector was determined as a direction of the current space, as shown in Fig.6 (c).

4. **Determining the Next Footprint:** After the locomotion vector was determined, then the next footprint was found on the point clouds of the walk surfaces. As shown in Fig.6 (d), first, a cylindrical space, F, with search radius r_f and search height h_f, was generated at a point placed on the stride length, w, a head of the current footprint. Then, the point clouds, which represent a walk surface which has a maximum point number inside of F, were extracted from the point clouds inside of F. Finally, the next footprint was determined as a centroid of these point clouds.
5. **Generating Walk Motion:** Finally, all of the leg joint angles were calculated by solving the inverse kinematics to reach the next footprint, and the motion of a walking step was generated by linearly interpolating each of the leg joint angles.

5   Simulation Results

5.1   Walking Simulation Results in the 3D Environment Models

A result of a basic walking simulation in the point clouds is shown in Fig.7. In the figure, the 3D environment models were constructed from the 3D point clouds of Fig.4 which were generated by the scans of one floor of a university building, including two stairs, by a terrestrial laser scanner (FARO Focus[3D] S120). Fig.7 (a) shows the walking simulation on stairs. This study confirmed that the kinematic digital human model could autonomously climb stairs as shown in Fig.7 (a).

On the other hand, Fig.7 (b) shows the comparison between a walking path obtained from this study's simulation and an actual human walking path in a corner. As shown in Fig.7 (b), the path difference between them was small. But the difference was mainly at the T-junction exit, because a goal position depends on the size of a cylinder, $C(v_k)$.

Fig.7 (c) shows the walking simulation results in a corridor, which contained some obstacles on the walk surface (blue objects), and its overhead view. In order to check the effectiveness of the study's local collision avoidance algorithm, a navigation graph was not intentionally used in this case. It was also confirmed that the study's digital human model could also walk directly in the 3D environment models while well avoiding the given obstacles on the walk surface. However, the basic walking simulation in the point clouds still could not work in the region where the laser-scanned point cloud is lacking. To remove this limitation, such a kind of region should be checked and corrected before simulation.

 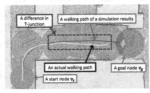 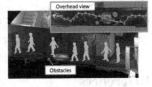

(a) A walking simulation on stairs   (b) A walking simulation in a corner (u =0.5)   (c) A walking simulation in a corridor which contained some obstacles

Fig. 7. The result of the basic walking simulation in the 3D environment models

Table 1. The elapsed time of the modeling and simulation
(CPU: Intel(R) Core(TM) i7 3.30GHz, Memory: 32GB, GPU: GeForce GTX 560 Ti)

Processing		Time [s]	Total [s]
Laser scanning (points: 7,058,731)		16,320 (272 min.)	
Registration of point clouds		2,820 (47 min.)	
Construction of a 3D environment models	Down sampling of the point clouds (points: 1,043,386)	14.36	19.1
	Voxel space construction	0.14	
	Normal vector estimation	2.40	
	Extraction of the points cloud of the walk surfaces	0.80	
	Navigation graph construction	0.50	
A basic walking simulation		0.016	
Total time of modeling and simulation		19.116	

5.2   Modeling and Simulation Performances

Table 1 shows the elapsed time of constructing the 3D environment model from original point clouds to the basic walking simulation. PCL (The Point Cloud Library) [15] was partly used for the processing of the point clouds, and the OpenGL was used for rendering. The total time of constructing the 3D environment models took 19,159s (319min.). However, the time taken for the laser scanning itself and the registration of point clouds occupied 99% of the total time, and that of constructing the 3D environment models only took 19.1s, which was significantly faster than manual modeling. Moreover, the fast rate of a basic walking simulation was archived (0.016s), and a frequency of a basic walking simulation with rendering process reached about 40 to 60 fps, which fully enabled real-time simulation.

6   Conclusions

In this study, a new method was developed which enabled automatic and efficient construction of the 3D environment models for human behavior simulation from 3D laser-scanned point clouds. In addition, a basic walking simulation was realized directly in the models using a kinematic digital human model. It was confirmed that the modeling process was quite fast and the simulation frequency was enough for real time application. However, the region where the laser-scanned point cloud was lacking should be detected. Moreover, the physical load simulation based on the dynamics [7] and the expansion of a single human walking model to the crowd simulation are needed for the accessibility evaluation. These remain as our further work.

References

1. Thalmann, D., Musse, S.R.: Crowd Simulation, pp. 3–4. Springer, London (2007)
2. Kakizaki, T., Urii, J., Endo, M.: A Three-Dimensional Evacuation Simulation Using Digital Human Models With Precise Kinematics Joints. In: Proc. of ASME DETC 2011-47075, pp. 15–22 (2011)

3. ISO21542: Building construction – Accessibility and usability of the built environment (2011)
4. Nüchter, A., Hertzberg, J.: Towards semantic maps for mobile robots. Robotics and Autonomous Systems 56(11), 915–926 (2003)
5. Rusu, R.B., Marton, Z.C., Blodow, N., Dolha, M., Beetz, M.: Towards 3D Point Cloud Based Object Maps for Household Environments. Robotics and Autonomous Systems 56(11), 927–941 (2008)
6. Troje, N.F.: Decomposing biological motion A framework for analysis and synthesis of human gait patterns. A Journal of Vision 2002 2(5), 371–387 (2002)
7. Chang, S.-W., Wang, M.-J.J.: Digital human Modeling and Workplace Evaluation: Using an Automobile Assembly Task as an Example. Human Factors and Ergonomics in Manufacturing 17(5), 445–455 (2007)
8. Helbing, D., Farkas, I., Vicsek, T.: Simulating Dynamical Features of Escape Panic. Nature 407, 487–490 (2000)
9. Tecchia, F., Loscos, C., Conroy, R., Chrysanthou, Y.: Agent behavior simulator (ABS): A Platform for Urban Behavior Development. In: Proc. of ACM Games Technology Conference, pp. 17–21 (2001)
10. Pettre, J., Laumond, J.-P., Thalmann, D.: A navigation graph for real-time crowd animation on multilayered and uneven terrain. In: First International Workshop on Crowd Simulation (V-CROWDS 2005), pp. 81–89 (2005)
11. Removing outliers using a Statistical Outlier Removal filter, http://pointclouds.org/documentation/tutorials/statistical_outlier.php#statistical-outlier-removal
12. Rusu, R.B.: Semantic 3D Object Maps for Everyday Manipulation in Human Living Environments. STAR, vol. 85, pp. 74–75. Springer, Heidelberg (2013)
13. Rusu, R.B.: Semantic 3D Object Maps for Everyday Manipulation in Human Living Environments. STAR, vol. 85, pp. 40–41. Springer, Heidelberg (2013)
14. Boulic, R., Magnenat-Thalmann, N., Thalmann, D.: A global human walking model with real-time kinematics personification. Visual Computer 6(6), 344–358 (1990)
15. PCL, http://pointclouds.org/

Modeling Body Shape from Surface Landmark Configurations

Matthew P. Reed

University of Michigan Transportation Research Institute, USA
mreed@umich.edu

Abstract. Detailed statistical models of body size and shape are valuable for wide range of statistical analyses. Most body shape models represent a single posture, usually standing. Previous efforts to model both posture and body shape have parameterized posture using joint angles. This paper presents a statistical model of body shape in supported seated postures using a posture measured derived from surface landmarks rather than internal joint locations and angles. This method is not limited by a particular kinematic linkage deformation and so is particularly well suited to model the effects on body shape of posture changes in complex linkages such as the spine or shoulder.

Keywords: body shape, laser scanning, anthropometry, posture.

1 Introduction

Advances in whole-body surface measurement and associated data processing techniques have provided the opportunity to create parametric statistical models of the human body form that allow representation of the wide range of human body shapes in digital human figure models. The parametric models allow body shapes to be predicted as a function of gender, stature, body weight, and other variables. However, the scanned postures are rarely the postures of interest for ergonomics analysis, so some mechanism for altering the posture is needed.

Several research groups have developed methods for parameterizing the external body shape in terms of posture variables defined by linkage joint angles as well as standard anthropometric descriptors [1, 2]. The development of these models requires a rich scan database containing many postures for many individuals. One limitation of this method is that the resulting models are parameterized in terms of the joint angles of a particular kinematic linkage. Generalizing such a model to a different kinematic linkage requires mapping the associated angles between the two linkages, and may be particularly challenging in the torso and shoulder, for which many different linkage definitions are in use.

This paper presents an alternative approach to modeling body shape and body shape change with posture. Conceptually, we represent posture by the 3D locations of a set of body surface landmarks, rather than by the angles of a kinematic linkage.

V.G. Duffy (Ed.): DHM/HCII 2013, Part II, LNCS 8026, pp. 376–383, 2013.

Body shape is then predicted using the landmark configuration, potentially in combination with overall target body dimensions such as stature or body weight.

To illustrate the method, we present an example application in which a kinematic linkage based on the skeleton is unnecessary and even problematic. Standard anthropometric data contain little information that is directly applicable to the design of seat backrest contours. In previous work, we used a parametric model based on scan data from a single seated posture to assess seat back fit [3] and measured multiple postures per subject to build a database that could be interpolated [4]. To improve on this approach, we used data from a recent study of body shape that included multiple supported seated postures per subject. We use surface landmark locations, or relationships among them, to predict the body shape assocated with a particular posture. An important advantage of this method is that our prediction of torso shape change across conditions is not limited by an approximating kinematic linkage. This is particularly valuable in the shoulder and spine, where the true number of degrees of freedom is much higher than that provided by a few rotational joints.

2   Methods

Data Source. The results in this paper were generated using data from an unpublished study of soldier anthropometry. Whole-body scan data were gathered using a VITUS XXL laser scanner in a range of postures. For the current analysis, data from four postures from 126 men with a wide range of body sizes were used. Figure 1 shows the four postures. The range of postures is critical, because the analysis procedure is fundamentally a data interpolation method.

Fig. 1. The four postures used for the current analysis from one subject

Figure 2 shows a flowchart of the data analysis procedure. Each scan was cleaned and processed, including hole-filling and manual extraction of up to 140 three-dimensional landmarks from each scan. Landmarks included major bony landmarks such as acromion and lateral femoral condyle that define skeletal posture. A template mesh with 38038 vertices was fit to each scan using an implicit-surface method. A principal component (PC) analysis was conducted on the vertex data to obtain a reduced-basis representation of the data. For the current work, 300 PCs were retained.

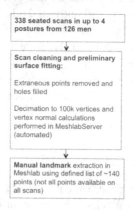

Fig. 2. Flowchart of data processing method

Figure 3 shows a flowchart of the data analysis method. Each study participant is characterized by standard anthropometric dimensions. The current analysis used stature, body mass index, and the ratio of erect sitting height to stature as predictors. The surface landmarks could be used to estimate internal joint center locations, and those joint center locations could be used to define joint angles according to a particular rotation sequence. However, an alternative is to define posture using solely external body landmarks. This avoids the need to estimate joint center locations and to use a particular joint rotation sequence.

For the current demonstration, two simple measures of torso posture were defined. Torso recline was defined as the angle of the vector from the L3 surface landmark to the C7 surface landmark with respect to vertical. Lumbar flexion was defined by the angle between lumbar and thoracic surface vectors. The lumbar vector was defined from the L3 surface landmark to the T12 surface landmark, and the thoracic vector was defined from T12 to C7. Figure 4 shows the definitions of these variables.

A linear regression was conducted to predict the principal component scores as a function of the three anthropometric and two posture variables. Exercising the model with combinations of these variables enables a wide range of seated body sizes and postures to be represented.

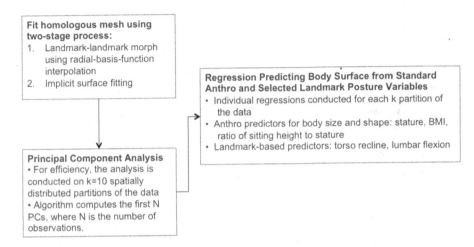

Fit homologous mesh using two-stage process:
1. Landmark-landmark morph using radial-basis-function interpolation
2. Implicit surface fitting

Regression Predicting Body Surface from Standard Anthro and Selected Landmark Posture Variables
• Individual regressions conducted for each k partition of the data
• Anthro predictors for body size and shape: stature, BMI, ratio of sitting height to stature
• Landmark-based predictors: torso recline, lumbar flexion

Principal Component Analysis
• For efficiency, the analysis is conducted on k=10 spatially distributed partitions of the data
• Algorithm computes the first N PCs, where N is the number of observations.

Fig. 3. Data analysis method

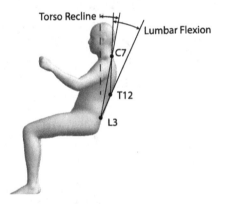

Fig. 4. Torso posture variables

3   Results

Figure 5 shows the anthropometric effects in the model, demonstrating the effects of stature, BMI, and the ratio of sitting height to stature. For these illustrations, the posture variables are fixed at the median values. Figure 6 shows the posture effects in the model, demonstrating the effects of torso recline and lumbar flexion. For these illustrations, the anthropometric variables are fixed at the median values. Figure 7 shows the combined effects of body dimensions and posture, illustrating the wide range of postures and body shapes that can be represented.

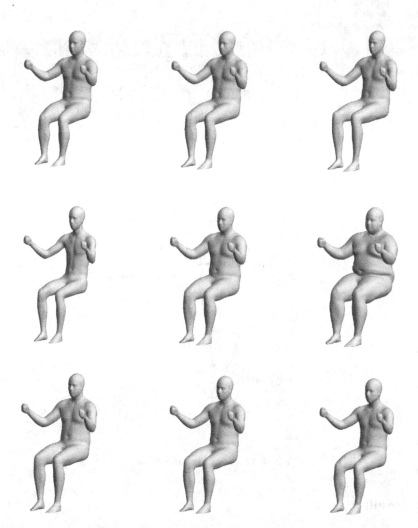

Fig. 5. Anthropometric effects. Top row: Stature 1600 to 2000 mm. Middle row: BMI 18 to 40. Bottom row: ratio of sitting height to stature 0.48 to 0.56.

Fig. 6. Posture effects: lumbar flexion (top), recline (bottom)

Fig. 7. Model results for a range of postures and body sizes

4   Discussion

The methodology presented in this paper provides a method for representing the combined effects of overall body dimensions and posture on body shape with a large range of flexibility. Previous methods for representing posture in body scan data have parameterized posture using joint angles [1]. This approach is valuable in situations in which the goal is to apply angle-based animation data to the figure. However, the method requires estimating skeletal joint-center locations and calculating joint angles using a particular rotation sequence. These calculations are straightforward for any particular linkage, but generalizing across multiple linkages with different segment and joint-angle definitions can be problematic.

The current method avoids those problems by parameterizing posture using surface landmarks that are independent of the skeletal linkage. The illustrations in this paper were generating using only two variables defined by three surface landmarks, but the calculations scale readily to use 10, 20, or more surface landmarks. The target landmark locations can be generated from other data sources, such as landmark-based posture data from environments in which scanning is not practical, such as vehicles.

The model developed in this paper can be used to create manikins for a wide range of ergonomics analyses of seated tasks. A previous torso-shape model based on scan data did not include the whole body and lacked parameterization for posture [3]. A more advanced version of that model included a posture parameterization based on four variables, but lacked extremities [5]. Importantly, generating a new model using alternative anthropometric variables and body landmarks as inputs is straightforward, simply repeating the regression analysis.

As with any empirical model, the outcomes are dependent on the range of the input data. In this case, the range of postures available in the data is critical. The current model is essentially a linear interpolation model, moving mesh node locations as linear function of the input variables, but nonlinear (e.g., squared) and interaction terms can be included in the regression models to account for more complex relationships between overall body dimensions, posture, and body shape. The terms to include can be selected using standard statistical techniques as well as domain knowledge concerning the needs of the application.

The dataset from which the current data were drawn includes a wide range of upper and lower extremity postures, as well as torso postures with lumbar flexion, twisting, and lateral bending. Extending these methods to include these postures will produce a more general model.

Acknowledgement. This research was supported in part by the Automotive Research Center, a U.S. Army Center for Excellence at the University of Michigan.

References

1. Anguelov, D., Srinivasan, P., Koller, D., Thrun, S., Rodgers, J., Davis, J.: SCAPE: Shape Completion and Animation of People. In: Proceedings of the 2005 International Conference on Computer Graphics and Interactive Techniques (SIGGRAPH), San Diego, CA (2005)
2. Allen, B., Curless, B., Popovic, Z.: The space of human body shapes: reconstruction and parameterization from range scans. In: Proceedings of the 2003 International Conference on Computer Graphics and Interactive Techniques (SIGGRAPH), San Diego, CA (2003)
3. Reed, M.P., Parkinson, M.B.: Modeling variability in torso shape for chair and seat design. DETC2008-49483. In: Proceedings of the ASME Design Engineering Technical Conferences. ASME, New York (2008)
4. Reed, M.P.: A pilot study of three-dimensional child anthropometry for vehicle safety analysis. In: Proceedings of the 2012 Human Factors and Ergonomics Society Annual Meeting. HFES, Santa Monica (2012)
5. Hu, J., Reed, M.P.: Development of a methodology for simulating seat back interaction using realistic body contours. SAE Technical Paper 2013-01-0452. SAE International, Warrendale, PA (2013)

Anatomy-Based Variational Modeling of Digital Hand and Its Verification

Yulai Xie, Satoshi Kanai, and Hiroaki Date

Graduate School of Information Science and Technology,
Hokkaido University, Sapporo, Japan
y_xie@sdm.ssi.ist.hokudai.ac.jp,
{kanai,hdate}@ssi.ist.hokudai.ac.jp

Abstract. This study proposed a method to construct an anatomy-based variational modeling of a Digital Hand model, which can be used to efficiently generate various individual hand models with different dimensions for virtual ergonomic assessments. The skin surface of a generic hand model was hierarchically partitioned into 15 segments according to the hand surface anatomy. Then it was deformed by scaling and aligning the segments so that it satisfied individual hand dimensions. Moreover, the hand models of different hand postures with markers were reconstructed using a multi-view 3D model reconstruction technique. The extracted positions of markers were used to estimate the individual bone-link structure. The proposed method was validated through comparing the generated hand skin model which fitted the hand dimensions of a subject with his MRI-measured hand surface, and comparing the generated bone-link structure, which fitted joint motion of the subject, with the reconstructed hand models based on a multi-view 3D reconstruction technique.

1 Introduction

Recently, virtual ergonomic assessment of handheld products has gotten more attention. Compared with conventional ergonomic assessment, it has many advantages such as low cost, high efficiency, and enabling to obtain quantitative evaluation of handheld products. This research group has been proposing the Digital Hand which is a virtual hand model based on MRI measurements (Endo et al., 2008; Kawaguchi et al., 2009; Shimizu et al., 2010). It has high precision and virtual ergonomic assessment functions of the quality of grasp.

However, the MRI-based hand modeling requested subjects to take a long time and difficult measurements. Also, constructing a hand model was very time-consuming, because it needs numerous manual operations. Thus, this technique could not generate a lot of hand models in such a short amount of time. However human hands have a variety of sizes depending on different individuals, ages, genders and nationalities. Therefore, a method is needed to generate different individual human hand models with variations in a relatively simpler way than that of the previous works.

V.G. Duffy (Ed.): DHM/HCII 2013, Part II, LNCS 8026, pp. 384–392, 2013.

To solve the problem, the purpose of this research was to propose a variational modeling method where a 3D hand model with a specific size could be efficiently generated from an existing reference hand model in a simple way, and where the size variation both of the surface skin model and the internal bone-link structure could be easily obtained. There have been some similar works. Kouchi et al. (2005) utilized factor analysis to evaluate 82 measurements from 103 Japanese subjects, and then found two principle factors to represent the dimensions of Japanese hands. The individual hand models could be created by scaling a generic hand by the optimization process. However, because this work only dealt with the hand skin variation in a static hand posture, there was a lack in the variation for the internal bone-link structure. On the other hand, Rhee et al. (2006) proposed a variational hand modeling method based on a palm side photo, and the finger joint centers were estimated according to the position of the main creases on the palm side. Although, the thickness of the hand was ignored in their method, and the estimated joint centers were not verified dynamically in different hand postures.

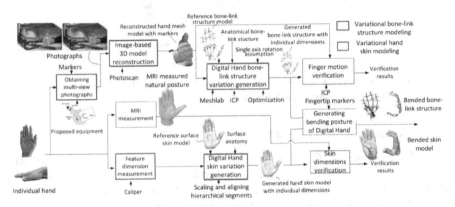

Fig. 1. Outline of the proposal method

The overview of this research is shown in Fig. 1. An anatomy-based variational skin modeling of the Digital Hand was proposed. First, the hand surface feature dimensions of individuals were measured using a caliper. According to anatomical knowledge, the main creases on palm side were used to partition the skin surface into 15 segments. Also, a hand model with size variation by scaling and aligning hierarchical segments of a reference hand was constructed. The dimension of the generated hand model with the size variation was verified by comparing it with the precise MRI measurements of the hand of the same subject.

On the other hand, an anatomy-based variational bone-link structure modeling of the Digital Hand was designed. First, multi-view photographs of a hand with markers of a subject were taken by an experimental device. Then they were used to reconstruct the models of different hand postures based on a multi-view 3D reconstruction technique. The extracted positions of markers were used to estimate the joint parameters (joint centers and their axes) of the bone-link structure. The generated bone-link structure was verified by comparing it with the reconstructed hand model. Finally, the generated bone-link structure and hand skin model were aligned at the fingertip to obtain a complete Digital Hand.

2   Variational Hand Skin Modeling Method

2.1   Hand Feature Dimension Measurement

The surface anatomy of the main creases on the palm is a common landmark in hand surgery, since the basic main creases have a strong relationship with the underlying bone structure (Rhee et al., 2006). Furthermore, they are commonly used in anthropometric measurements (Kouchi et al., 2005). Therefore, according to the main creases, as shown in Fig. 2 (a), using a sliding caliper, we could obtain the hand surface feature dimensions (length, breadth, and thickness). For one subject, we obtained 46 feature dimensions (15 lengths, 16 breadths, and 15 thicknesses).

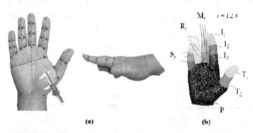

(a)   (b)

Fig. 2. (a) Hand surface feature dimensions (Red: Breadth, Blue: Length, and Green: Thickness), (b) The segments of hand model

2.2   Hierarchical Structure of Segments

Similarly, as shown in Fig. 2 (b), according to the surface anatomy of the main creases, we partitioned the general hand surfaces into 15 segments which were relatively in-dependent to each other, so that the individual segment could be scaled independently to fit the corresponding part of a real hand. The palm was treated as one segment for simplification. Furthermore, a hierarchical structure of these segments (Table 1) was constructed for the following scaling and aligning process.

Table 1. Hierarchical structure of the segments

ID	Type	Child	Parent	ID	Type	Child	Parent
P	Root	$T_2, I_3, M_3,$ R_3, S_3	-	M_3	-	M_2	P
T_1	End	-	T_2	R_1	End	-	R_2
T_2	-	T_1	P	R_2	-	R_1	R_3
I_1	End	-	I_2	R_3	-	R_2	P
I_2	-	I_1	I_3	S_1	End	-	S_2
I_3	-	I_2	P	S_2	-	S_1	S_3
M_1	End	-	M_2	S_3	-	S_2	P
M_2	-	M_1	M_3				

In the structure, each segment was assigned to at least one child, or parent segment, or both. Fingertip segments (T1, I1, M1, R1, and S1) were specified as end segments, and the palm segment (P) as a root segment.

2.3   Scaling and Aligning

As shown in Fig.3, a local coordinate frame was defined in each hand segment. All the coordinate frames have z-axes paralleled to a normal vector of a plane on which the subject's palm was laid. In each coordinate frame, the x-axis direction was defined along the direction of the creases and the wrist. An origin was defined as the middle point of the crease and wrist both of which were assumed to be placed in a 2D plane.

For each segment, it was scaled along its local coordinate axes independently along x, y and z according to the anisotropic scale factors fx, fy and fz defined in Eq.1.

$$f_x = \frac{L_{ix}^M}{L_{ix}^G}, \quad f_y = \frac{L_{iy}^M}{L_{iy}^G}, \quad f_z = \frac{L_{iz}^M}{L_{iz}^G} \tag{1}$$

where i is the ID of the segment, and L_{ix}^M, L_{iy}^M, and L_{iz}^M the measured feature dimensions of a subject respectively in the x, y, and z directions, and L_{ix}^G, L_{iy}^G, and L_{iz}^G are the corresponding feature dimensions of the generic hand skin model as shown in Fig.3.

For each segment (e.g. B in Fig.4 (a)), the scaling process along the local y-axis affected the positions of its child and successor segments (e.g. A). Therefore, alignment was needed from those segments to their parent segment (Fig.4 (c)) so that the con-nection between the segments could be kept. For all segments, according to the hier-archical structure, the one segment orderly from the root segment to end segments was arranged by the above scaling and aligning process. Finally, a variational hand skin model of the Digital Hand could be obtained from the original reference skin hand.

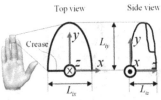

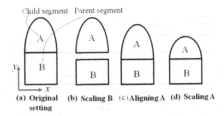

Fig. 3. The local coordinate frame and dimensions of one segment

Fig. 4. The scaling and aligning process

3   Variational Bone-Link Structure Modeling Method

In the previous study (Shimizu et al., 2010), MRI measurements of subject's phalanges were used to estimate the bone-link structure of the hand model. In order to avoid the expensive and time-consuming MRI measurements, an inexpensive and non-contact image-based measurement method was instead proposed for the estimation of the parameters of the bone-link structure.

3.1   Bone-Link Structure Model

The bone-link model in this study had the link and joint structures shown in Fig.5. The degrees of freedom (DOF) of the joint were modeled based on anatomical knowledge (Kapandji, 2005). For four fingers, each metacarpophalangeal (MP) joint of the fingers had 2DOF rotations: flexion/extension and adduction/abduction. Each proximal interphalangeal (PIP) joint and distal interphalangeal (DIP) joint had 1DOF rotation of flexion/extension. For a thumb, the MP and IP joints have 1DOF of simple rotation. The CMC joint had 2DOF where both flexion/extension and adduction/abduction accompanied pronation/supination motions.

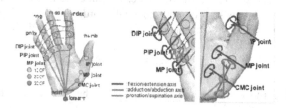

Fig. 5. Configuration of the bone-link structure model

3.2   Experiments for the Reconstruction of Hand Model

Equipment for image-based multi-view 3D modeling reconstruction was designed due to its user-friendliness and low cost. As shown in Fig.6 (a) and (b), a camera was placed on a rotatable plate. Behind the camera, LED lights were installed for illumination. Also, a subject hand was roughly placed at the pivot of the rotatable plate on the stage. By rotating the plate, a series of clear and stable photographs of the hand could be taken as shown in Fig.6 (c).

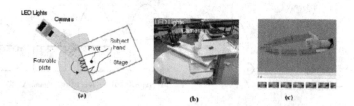

Fig. 6. (a) Experimental setting, (b) Experimental scene, (c)A series of photographs of the hand

As shown in Fig.7 (a), some dots were marked on the back side of the subject's hand as markers. A measurement of the subject's hand was performed as shown in Fig.7 (b). The relaxed natural posture and the bended postures were measured. For each posture, 10-20 photographs were taken to get a model with acceptable quality.

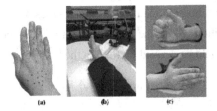

Fig. 7. (a) A hand with markers, (b) Experimental scene, (c) Reconstructed hand models

3.3   Image-Based 3D Reconstruction Technology

Based on commercial multi-view 3D reconstruction software (Photoscan), the photographs were inputted for an image-based 3D model reconstruction which includes three steps: the first step is photograph alignment. The common points on photo-graphs were searched and matched, as well as the position of the camera for each photograph was estimated. The next step is building the mesh. Based on the estimated camera position and pictures themselves, a 3D polygon mesh representing the object surface was built. Finally, after the hand mesh model was constructed, it was textured as shown in Fig.7 (c).

3.4   Deriving Finger Joint Motion of the Bone Link Structure

Joint motions were derived by comparing 3D positions and orientations of markers taken from two hand mesh models at different grasp postures. First, the marker positions at the reference posture (relaxed natural posture) and the ones at a bended posture were extracted from mesh processing software (Meshlab). Then the position and orientation of these two sets of markers were matched using ICP the algorithm (Besl and McKay, 1992) as shown in Fig.8 (a). The correspondence between the two markers' positions was picked up manually in the Meshlab. At least three correspondences needed to be specified for the right match.

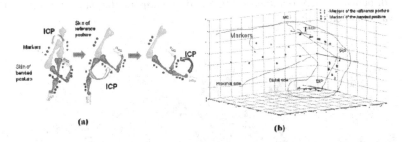

Fig. 8. (a) ICP matching of the same markers, (b) The estimation result of the single joint rotation axes in middle finger

The rigid body transformation matrix $\mathbf{T}^{ICP}$ which gives the minimum matching error between a marker position $\mathbf{v}_i^T$ at the bended posture and its corresponding one $\mathbf{v}_i^S$ at the reference posture could be derived by finding the least square solution of Eq.2.

$$\mathbf{T}^{ICP} = \arg\min_{\mathbf{T}} \sum_{i=1}^{N_s} \left\| \mathbf{T} \, \mathbf{v}_i^S - \mathbf{v}_i^T \right\|^2 \tag{1}$$

where $\mathbf{T}$ is the 4x4 rigid transformation matrix, N_s the number of markers.

If it is assumed that $\mathbf{T}^{ICP}$ can only be expressed as a single axis rotation and $\mathbf{p}_a$ as an arbitrary point on the rotational axis (a rotation center), the single axis rotation matrix $\mathbf{T}^{Axis}$ can be expressed as Eq.3 where $\mathbf{R}^{ICP}$ is a 3x3 rotational submatrix in $\mathbf{T}^{ICP}$.

$$\mathbf{T}^{Axis} = \begin{bmatrix} \mathbf{E} & \mathbf{p}_a \\ \mathbf{0}^T & 1 \end{bmatrix} \begin{bmatrix} \mathbf{R}^{ICP} & 0 \\ \mathbf{0}^T & 1 \end{bmatrix} \begin{bmatrix} \mathbf{E} & -\mathbf{p}_a \\ \mathbf{0}^T & 1 \end{bmatrix} = \begin{bmatrix} \mathbf{R}^{ICP} & -\mathbf{R}^{ICP}\mathbf{p}_a + \mathbf{p}_a \\ 0 & 1 \end{bmatrix} \tag{2}$$

Therefore, by replacing $\mathbf{T}^{ICP}$ by $\mathbf{T}^{Axis}$ in Eq.2 and by finding the least square solution of $\mathbf{T}^{Axis}$ for Eq.2, we could obtain the optimum rotation center $\mathbf{p}_a$ as $\mathbf{p}_a = (\mathbf{E} - \mathbf{R}^{ICP})^{-1} \mathbf{t}^{Axis}$, where $\mathbf{t}^{Axis}$ is the translation component of $\mathbf{T}^{Axis}$. Similarly, the optimum rotation axis direction could be derived from 3×3 rotational submatrix in $\mathbf{T}^{Axis}$ by solving a simple simultaneous linear equation. The derived single joint rotation axis from the markers at one finger is shown in Fig.8 (b).

Finally, the derived bone-link structure with finger motion was incorporated into the generated hand skin model by aligning the marker painted at the fingertip with the fingertip of the hand skin model at the extension posture of the fingers.

4   Result and Verification

A precise Digital Hand model based on MRI measurement (Fig.9 (a), Shimizu et al., 2010) from one subject (S0) was used as the reference hand model (M0). The hand skin model of M0 was deformed to satisfy the feature dimensions of another subject (S1, male, 28, right hand, Fig.9 (b)) who had smaller hand dimensions than S0. The feature dimensions were obtained using a sliding caliper. The hand skin model (M1) of S1 was obtained as Fig.9 (c).

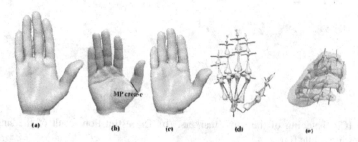

Fig. 9. (a) Reference hand model M0 from subject S0¬, (b) Hand of subject S1, (c) Generated hand model M1 with feature dimensions of S1, (d) Bone-line structure B1 of S1, (e) Bended posture of M1 and B1

For verifying variational skin modeling, a 3D mesh model of the hand of the same subject was measured by an MRI. Therefore a precise measurement of the hand surface feature dimensions could be obtained with mesh modeling software. By comparing the MRI-measured feature dimensions with those of the variational surface model by the proposed method, it was found that the average difference between the corresponding segments were 1.3 mm, 0.7mm, and 0.9 mm in x (Breadth), y (Length) and z (thickness) directions, respectively. The maximum difference that appeared in the MP crease of the thumb was 2.5mm in the x direction, as shown in Fig.9 (b). The dimension of M1 was less than that of S1. These differences came from deformation of the skin by pressure of caliper in the x and the z directions, and accuracy of measurement in the x, y and z directions.

On the other hand, the bone-link structure B1 (Fig.9 (d)) of S1 was generated based on the reconstructed 3D hand mesh model of the different postures of S0's hand. Fig.9 (e) shows a bended posture of M1 and B1. The average motion error of each set of markers moved from the reference posture to each limit posture among the four fingers B1 is shown in Table 2. For the reference, the motion errors that were only generated by using ICP are also indicated in the table, which shows inevitable lower limits of the errors. From Table 2, the average motion errors by this method (single axis rotation) were 0.37 - 0.76mm, and the difference between the ICP and the proposed method were 0.20mm or less, which may be regarded as the acceptable one.

Table 2. Average motion errors of four fingers at each limit posture motion [mm]

	Flexion posture			Abduction
Markers at	Proximal	Middle	Distal	Proximal
Errors by ICP	0.22	0.47	0.56	0.25
Errors by the proposed method (single axis rotation)	0.42	0.62	0.76	0.37

5   Conclusion

A new anatomy-based variational modeling of a Digital Hand was proposed which is simple, subject-friendly and inexpensive compared to previous work. The variation of the external skin model was generated by aligning and scaling the hierarchical segments of hand. For the variations of the internal bone-link structure, the center and the axis of each joint of the fingers were estimated by the position of markers of the reconstructed hand model by an image-based modeling technique. The finger motion could be accurately reproduced accurately. However, the CMC joint of the thumb has not been modeled in this research, because it cannot be modeled as a simple single axis rotation. In the future, the CMC joint motion of the thumb will be modeled utilizing the interpolation between the reference posture and the limit posture.

References

1. Besl, P.J., McKay, H.D.: A method for registration of 3-D shapes. IEEE Transactions on Pattern Analysis and Machine Intelligence 14, 239–256 (1992)
2. Endo, Y., Kanai, S., Kishinami, T., Miyata, N., Kouchi, M., Mochimaru, M.: Optimization-Based Grasp Posture Generation Method of Digital Hand for Virtual Ergonomic Assessment. SAE International Journal of Passenger Cars -Electronic and Electrical Systems 1, 590–598 (2008)
3. Kapandji, A.I.: The Physiology of the Joint: The Upper Limb. Churchill Livingstone (2005)
4. Kawaguchi, K., Endo, Y., Kanai, S.: Database-Driven Grasp Synthesis and Ergonomic Assessment for Handheld Product Design. In: Duffy, V.G. (ed.) ICDHM 2009. LNCS, vol. 5620, pp. 642–652. Springer, Heidelberg (2009)
5. Kouchi, M., Miyata, N., Mochimaru, M.: An Analysis of Hand Measurements for Obtaining Representative Japanese Hand Models. SAE Technical Paper 2005-01-2734 (2009)
6. Meshlab, http://meshlab.sourceforge.net/
7. PhotoScan, http://www.agisoft.ru/products/photoscan
8. Rhee, T., Neumann, U., Lewis, J.P.: Human hand modeling from surface anatomy. In: Proceedings of the 2006 Symposium on Interactive 3D Graphics and Games, pp. 27–34. ACM, Redwood City (2006)
9. Shimizu, Y., Kawaguchi, K., Kanai, S.: Constructing MRI-based 3D Precise Human Hand Models for Product Ergonomic Assessments. In: Proceedings of 2010 Asian Conference on Design and Digital Engineering, Jeju, Korea, pp. 837–844 (2006)

Simulation of Pushing the Push-Pull Rod Action Based on Human Body Dynamics

Zheng Yang, Yiyuan Zheng, and Shan Fu

School of Aeronautics and Astronautics, Shanghai Jiao Tong University,
Shanghai 200240, China
dolphinyang90@126.com

Abstract. Using the software Anybody Modeling System，a human static-standing musculoskeletal model based on inverse dynamics is presented. According to the environmental constraints of cockpit, the human body model is defined, especially the selection and design of the input parameters on muscles, bones, joints, drive, and other aspects. From the model, the design simulates the flight operations of the pilot during the plane is approaching and landing, especially the right arm pushing the push-pull rod. According to the principle of inverse dynamics, the muscle forces on the right arm will be researched to elect larger ones. And the paper focuses on muscle parametric analysis and design. On the basis of muscle metabolism which is the parameter to evaluate the muscle fatigue, the design is optimized to find where the least muscle fatigue is. Results show that metabolism can provide an experimental basis for the design layout of the cockpit instruments, operating device.

Keywords: human factors, human body dynamics, numerical simulation, AnyBody optimal design.

1   Introduction

In the field of aviation, system failure caused by human error accounted for about 70% to 90%.With the improvement of hardware, human mistakes is playing a more and more important role in the influence of system failure. With the increasing demand for the safety of the flight stability, so in the aircraft design especially the design of the cockpit, the person-centered concept is also gradually accepted. Human Reliability Analysis (HRA) [1] is the development of the Human engineering which has gradually came into being a relatively independent discipline. HRA is based on analysis, forecast, decrease and prevention of human mistakes as core research, one of the reliability of the qualitative and quantitative analysis and evaluation, so it is important for human error probability reduces to the minimum of system that can accept. And because the cockpit which is of the main places the pilot work in: the main man-environment interaction process occurs in the cockpit. Therefore, the analysis of human factors has become an important part of the plane design process.

With the development of computer technology, digital technology has become more and more extensively applied in the digital prototype stage. The simulation and

V.G. Duffy (Ed.): DHM/HCII 2013, Part II, LNCS 8026, pp. 393–401, 2013.

evaluation of the cockpit by establishing digital model of the human body for human factors gradually becomes a necessary method at home and abroad. The human body dynamics research is receiving more and more attention, on the one hand, it involves with human anatomy, human body metrology, biomechanics, robotics, and other disciplines, which is a newly emerged cross edge discipline. On the other hand, it has important research value and broad application, such as man-machine system analysis and the man-machine interface design. Because of the complexity of the pilot's human body structure, the diversity of human body action, the biological limitation and measuring instrument limitations, some parameters or index can't be measured. [2] So establishing a human body simulation model similar with a real human body system combining with related experiments and using the computer simulation technology is quite necessary to reveal and research the pilot in the mission of the characteristics and laws.

AnyBody Modeling System (AnyBody Technology Inc., Aalborg, Denmark)is a software based on inverse dynamics for the development and analysis of multi-body models, particularly those of musculoskeletal type. The system has its own language. AnyScript, which is of object-oriented type and models thus compiled can be defined in text format. Elements of the model, such as segments, joints, muscles, forces and so on, are declared in AnyScript, and grouped into different classes. Based on those classes and mathematical algorithms, muscle forces, joint reaction forces or other parameters can be obtained.

2   Parametric Modeling of Pull-Push Rod

The muscles, bones, joints, drive, environmental conditions, and other data need to be put in first in the modeling process, while muscle, bone, joint information already existed. [3] Drive and boundary conditions are required to be custom, such as importing motion capture locus data by the AnyBody solver (inverse dynamics) to obtain the results of muscles and joints, movement, function, etc. [4]

2.1   Modeling Using AnyBody Modeling System

The AnyBody modeling approach is as follows: [5]

1. Based on the established cockpit model, the three-dimensional geometry of the virtual environment must be in accord with the real ones. This results from the actual needs of the engineering problems, not brings the full range of virtual reality and really world-realistic visual experience. Importing stl file into AnyBody simulation software based on CAD, the simulation model of cockpit can be got.
2. In order to make the human body model more similar with the reality, some elements must be added. Body segments come first, which are rigid body elements and moves as the model runs. Body segments usually refer to body bone structure in the human modeling. Joints are regarded as the provider of the degrees of freedom in AnyBody Modeling System, compared with the rigid structure.
3. The next step is to define the movement. Elements at the push-pull rod fixed in this model, especially in the right arm, wrist, shoulder fixed in the seat, the elbow is the

main control movement. Elbow and wrist has remained in the same vertical plane and the body parallel to the axis.

4. Defining muscles is generally got through by some pre-defined point to reach the end; the process through the points can be defined depending on the size and length of the muscle. If the muscle is complex, some appropriate points need adding from the start to end points.

5. The final step is adding real geometry, while what obtained earlier is only the so-called stick-like shape. This is a straightforward way to view the model, which vividly reflecting the mechanical structure of the model, but does not look like a real physical body. Next the bones and other geometric model need to be added, including the bones of the 3-D graphics files.

At last, the three-dimensional musculoskeletal model of the whole biological body was developed using AnyBody Modeling System. (Fig. 1)

Fig. 1. Three-dimensional musculoskeletal model

2.2   Summary of Muscle Forces

During the operation, right hand fixed on the operating rod and right arm shoulder fixed on the seat, the pilot pushes pull-push rod. 190 muscle lines simulate right arm muscles in the AnyBody Modeling System (Fig. 2).

Fig. 2 shows that the muscle whose force is large in the process of the pushing rod is minority. To get more obvious results, larger muscle force should be elected to focus on. The muscles whose force are larger than 10N are biceps muscle, scapular deltoid, subscapularis, brachialis, brachioradialis muscle, latissimusdorsi, rhomboid muscle, teres major, left triceps, supinator, pronatorteres,musculus extensor carpi radialislongus.

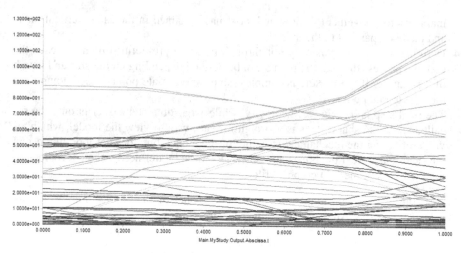

Fig. 2. Right arm muscle force simulation

2.3   Factors Selected of Muscle Force Comparison

This design focuses on where the pull-push rod locates. In a small area, the appropriate muscle force is selected as the main object of study as pull-push rod's location changes. [6]

The center of gravity of cockpit seat is centered as the origin, while the height rod layout is named as Height, the longitudinal position of rod layout is named as posX, the around position of rod is named as posZ. The position of rod initial position is Height = 0.29m posX = 0.15m, posZ =-0.6m.Every two quantities fixed, if the location of the push-pull rod changes, respectively as the initial position, the distance-increased position, the distance-reduced position ,there are three groups. Removing the same parts, a total of seven groups is shown in the following table:

Table 1. Comparison of muscle force factors conditions (unit: m)

Case number	Height	posX	posZ
1	0.29	0.15	-0.6
2	0.24·	0.15	-0.6
3	0.34	0.15	-0.6
4	0.34	0.1	-0.6
5	0.34	0.2	-0.6
6	0.34	0.2	-0.625
7	0.34	0.2	-0.575

Based on the above table, Height for the impact of each block muscle can be compared by Case1, 2, 3, posX for the impact of each block muscle can be compared by Case3, 4, 5 and posZ for the impact of each block muscle can be compared by Case 5, 6, 7.

Many fibers make up a muscle bundle. Many bundles constitute a whole muscle. So analyzing the data will be completed by maximum muscle force statistical analysis (Fig. 3) and sum of muscle force statistics analysis (Fig.4).

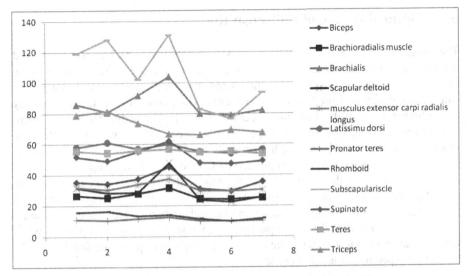

Fig. 3. Maximum muscle force statistical analysis (unit: N)

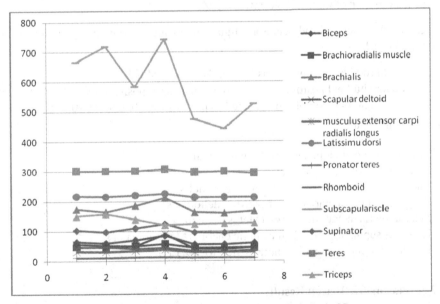

Fig. 4. Sum of muscle force statistics analysis (unit: N)

The results of two statistical analyses showed the subscapularis muscle, brachialis, triceps, humerus supination muscles, scapular deltoid, biceps change a lot as the location of push-pull rod changes, so the six muscles are selected as the main ones to research where the best location is. [7]

3   Optimal Design of Pull-Push Rod

The fatigue of muscle is evaluated by muscle metabolism. [8] The generation and consumption of human energy is defined to be metabolic energy which is reflected by the body's oxygen consumption. And the energy consumption of the body's metabolism per unit of time is called metabolic energy consumption rate. The fatigue intensity of the human body in the working process is shown by the body's energy consumption, oxygen consumption, heart rate, perspiration rate or relative metabolic rate as an index for judging, in addition, the human body need to consume a certain amount of energy in the static case, known as posture metabolic energy consumption. [9] When the pilot is operating the push-pull rod, we believe that the body's metabolic energy consumption can accordingly be divided into action metabolic energy consumption and posture metabolic energy consumption. The calculation of action metabolic energy consumption requires the action parameters of operation simulation process while the calculation of posture metabolic energy consumption requires the duration of the human body posture simulation process.

3.1   Parameter of Optimal Design

Therefore, the push-pull rod operator fatigue studies are established by the following parameters: [10]

1.   height rod layout is named as Height, Height=0.24,0.29,0.34
2.   the longitudinal position of rod layout is named as posX, posX=0.1,0.15,0.2
3.   the around position of rod is named as posZ, posZ=-0.575,-0.6,-0.625
4.   Evaluation:

Total muscle metabolic energy (Metablism_all)
Biceps metabolic energy (Met_bicep_brachii)
The brachialis metabolic energy (Met_brachialis)
Scapular deltoid metabolic energy (Met_deltoideus)
Subscapularis metabolic energy (Met_subscapular)
Humerus supination muscle metabolic energy (Met_supinator)
Left-hand triceps metabolic energy (Met_tricep_LH)

3.2   Parametric Design Results

According to the kinematics analysis and inverse dynamics analysis of AnyBody, the relationship between muscle metabolism and position such as Height, posX, posZ can be obtained.

The parameters of evaluation are so many, so the relationship between total muscle metabolic energy and position is taken as an example while others are similar with total muscle metabolic energy.

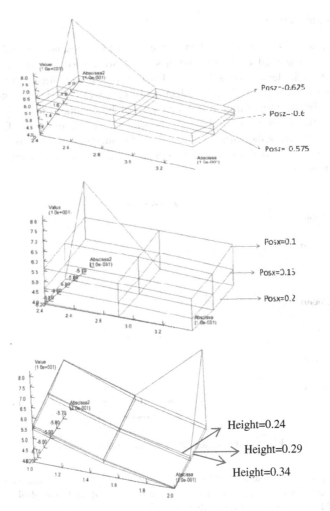

Fig. 5. The Relationship between total muscle metabolism and Height, posX, posZ

Based on the data of Fig.5, we can get:

1. Considering the three design variables, the change of posX plays the most important role in muscle metabolism.
2. In the cuboid consisted of three design variables, total muscle metabolism will suddenly change a lot in the lower right of the design space limit point (height = 0.24, posX = 0.2, posZ = -0.575).
3. As posZ changes from -0.625 to -0.575, the rod comes away from the pilot, total muscle metabolism will gradually decrease;
4. As posX changes from 0.1 to 0.2, the rod in the vertical direction moves away from the pilot, the total muscle metabolism will gradually decrease;
5. As Height changes from 0.24 to 0.34, the height of rod layout gradually increases, the total muscle metabolism will gradually decrease.

3.3   Optimal Design

Based on the six muscles selected already, the total of six muscles metabolism will be approximate as the total of all the muscles. [11] So the location of push-pull rod where pilot feel the least tired will be the least of total muscle metabolism. As posZ changes from -0.625 to -0.575, posX changes from 0.1 to 0.2, Height changes from 0.24 to 0.34, the location of min (metablism_all) can be searched out.

With two directions of the rod fixed, the other changes, minimum fixed can be obtained after changing the variable of direction. So on, the results are as follows:

The minimum of total muscle metabolism is 38.6N.m. The number of total iteration step is 19.

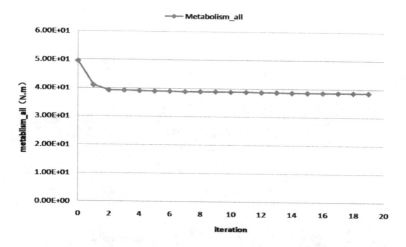

Fig. 6. Total muscle metabolism iteration diagram

According to the iteration between total muscle metabolism and Height, posX, posZ, optimal location of push-pull rod where the total muscle metabolism is least is Height = 0.319 posX = 0.2, posZ = -0.625.

4   Conclusion

This paper is based on the AnyBody modeling method of human motion of pushing and pulling push-pull rod. Faced with more than 190 muscles of right arm, six muscles are selected according to the size and the change as the location of rod changes. At the same time, as the location changes in a small room, we can get the optimal location of push-pull rod where the total muscle metabolism is least. As the result shows metabolism can provide an experimental basis for the design layout of the cockpit instruments, operating device. Furthermore, studies could continue on muscle activities, muscle forces and so on. More evaluation should be added for computing certain muscle forces. And other optimization algorithms should be used to compute muscle forces in more complicated situations.

Acknowledgements. This research work was supported by National Basic Research Program of China-(973 Program No. 2010CB734103).

References

1. Reer, B., Straeter, O., Mertens, J.: Evaluation of Human Reliability Analysis Methods Addressing Cognitive Error Modeling and Quantification (1996)
2. de Zee, M., Hanaen, L., Wong, C., et al.: A general rigid body lumbar spine model. J. of Biomeeh 40, 1219–1227 (2007)
3. Damsgaard, M., Rasmussen, J., Christensen, S.T., et al.: Analysis of musculoskeletal systems in the AnyBody Modeling System. Simul. Model. Prac. Theory 14, 1100–1111 (2006)
4. Chao, M.A., Ming, Z., Lin, Z.C.: Analysis of Human Joint Forces in Standing Posture. Journal of Beijing Institute of Technology 18(4), 437–442 (2009)
5. AnyBody Technology A/s. AnyBody Modeling System tutorials v.3.0 [EB/0L] (June 07, 2008) (August 08, 2008), http://www.anybodytech.com
6. Doehring, T.C., Rubash, H.E., Shelley, E.J., et al.: Effect of superior and super lateral relocations of the hip center on hip joint forces. J. of Arthroplasty 11, 693–703 (1996)
7. Lenaerts, G., De Groote, F., Demeulenaere, B., et al.: Subject-specific hip geometry affects predicted hip joint contact forces during gait. J. of Biomech. 41, 1243–1252 (2008)
8. Alwan, M., Wasson, G., Sheth, P., et al.: Basic walker-assisted gait characteristics derived from forces and moments exerted on the walker's handles? Results on normal subjects. Medical Engineering & Physics 29, 380–389 (2007)
9. Badler, N.: Virtual Humans for Animation, Ergonomics, and Simulation. In: Non Rigid and Articulated Motion Workshop 1997 Proceedings, pp. 28–36. IEEE (1997)
10. Gill, S.A., Ruddle, R.A.: Using Virtual Humans To Solve Real Ergonomic Design Problems. In: International Conference On Simulation, Conference Publication No.457, pp. 223–229. IEEE (1998)
11. Prilutsky, B.I., Zatsiorsky, V.M.: Optimization-based models of muscle coordination. Exercise and Sports Sciences Reviews 38, 32–38 (2002)

Higher Order Statistics Analyses
Based on the Mathematical Model of Surface
Electromyography

Yan Zhao[1,2,*], DongXu Li[1,2], and Jian Zhang[3]

[1] College of Aerospace Science and Engineering,
National University Defense Technology, Changsha, China
[2] Science and Technology on Human Factors Engineering Laboratory,
China Astronaut Research and Training Center, Beijing, China
{Yanzhao,dongxuli}@nudt.edu.cn
[3] Affiliated Hospital, National University Defense Technology, Changsha, China

Abstract. Evaluation to surface electromyographic (sEMG) of muscles is one of the important topics in human-computer interaction filed. This paper aims to quantitatively describe the difference in non-Gaussianity and non-linearity levels between the large muscle sEMG (i.e. biceps brachii, BB) and the small muscle sEMG (i.e. first dorsal interossei, FDI), which is changed with the increase of the motor unit (MU) recruitment numbers and exertion, as well the patterns of firing rate (FR). The mathematical physiology model of the BB and the FDI sEMG was developed under ten isometric maximum voluntary contraction (MVC) levels from 10% to 100% MVC for a period of 5s. Higher order statistics (HOS) detected the non-linearity and non-Gaussianity of the BB and the FDI sEMG. The Wilcoxon signed-rank test described the significant differences in non-Gaussianity/ linearity between the BB and the FDI at $p<0.05$. Results showed that the BB sEMG signals tended to a non-Gaussian distribution at 10%, 40%, 60~100% MVC and a non-linear distribution at 90%MVC. The FDI sEMG signals tended towards non-Gaussianity at 40%~60%, 80% MVC and non-linearity at 30% MVC. The BB's Gaussianity and linearity results were compared with FDI's. The linearity test showed no significant differences between two sEMG signals. However, The Gaussianity test exhibited a significant difference between them. There are three reasons for this: 1) the difference in MU recruitment range between the BB and the FDI; 2) FR and recruitment respectively play a important role in the small and the large muscles activity. 3) the difference in MUs recruitment order between small and largest muscles. The findings of this study have guiding significance on large and small muscles capability assessment.

Keywords: Higher order statistics, sEMG, Mathematical Physiology Model, Biceps Brachii, First Dorsal Interossei.

---

[*] Corresponding author.

V.G. Duffy (Ed.): DHM/HCII 2013, Part II, LNCS 8026, pp. 402–408, 2013.

1   Introduction

In the human-computer interaction field, there're a growing need that diverse consumers can use interface safely, conveniently, effectively, and enjoyable, even including people with physical constraint or disabilities. This poses great challenges and requirements to interactive products which must be handled and controlled using musculoskeletal system of human. According to users' different goal, the different muscles or muscle groups are driven to perform assignments. Some dexterous, skilful, and careful tasks are completed via small size muscles, such as, a dorsal interossei (DI), a palmar interossei, and a flexor digiti minimi brevis etc assist a hand in pressing the buttons of cell phone, calculator, and console. Beside, some heavy load tasks are completed via large size muscles, such as, a biceps brachii (BB), a deltoid, and a brachioradialis etc assist two arms in putting a full drawer into a fridge. In order to understand how the human muscle works, and reduce negative aspects (e.g. frustration, fatigue) during human-computer interaction while enhancing positive ones (e.g. effective, without engagement), we need to acquire the activity mechanism of diverse muscles. This research aims to present the activities difference between small and large size muscle in terms of the feature of surface electromyographic (sEMG).

In past researches, sEMG signals were generally regarded as having a zero mean and a near-Gaussian amplitude distribution. However, recent researches have indicated that sEMG signals have non-Gaussian and non-linear properties [1, 2]. Higher-order statistics (HOS) from the bi-frequency domain is able to recover more information from non-Gaussian and non-linear signals via higher-order moments, cumulants, and spectral representations, and does not suppress the phase relationship [3]. HOS was recently introduced as a useful method to reveal the non-Gaussianity and non-linearity of sEMG [4]. Therefore, HOS was used to test the non-Gaussianity and non-linearity levels of the BB and the FDI' artificial sEMG signals which were obtained from the simulated sEMG model . In our study, the samples of Gaussinity and linearity tests (MVC levels = 10) are small, and the population distributions of these samples are unknown. Thereby, the Wilcoxon test was used to compare the significant differences of non-Gaussianity/linearity results for two related samples at $p<0.05$.

2   The sEMG Model of the BB and the FDI

In human anatomy, the BB lies on the upper arm between the shoulder and the elbow. Both heads arise on the scapula and join to a single muscle belly which is attached to the upper forearm. its main function flexes the elbow and supinates the forearm [5]. The dorsal interossei are four muscles in the back of the hand that act to abduct (spread) and assist in flexion finger joints [6]. The first dorsal interosseous (FDI) muscle is larger than the others [7]. sEMG infects noise while it transmit though different media. A mathematical sEMG model based on a physiological property could avoid the interference noise effectively, and describe MU anatomy[8]. The artificial sEMG of the BB and the FDI were hypothetically measured using a pair of bipolar electrode. The interelectrode distance was 20 millimeter (mm). Figure 1 shows the BB and the FDI illustrations and the visual electrode locations [6].

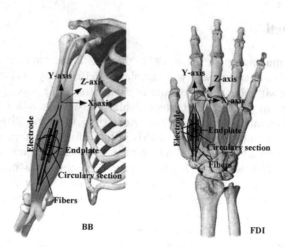

Fig. 1. The BB and the FDI muscle structures and bipolar electrode locations

The size of BB is different to the size of FDI, this lead to various physiological parameters difference between the BB and the FDI. For instance, the thickness of the BB's skin and fat layer is round 4 mm, but that of the FDI's is around 1.5 mm [6]. The muscle radius of the BB is round 15mm, but that of the FDI ranges from 30 to 45 mm[9]. During high-force contraction, the average discharge rates of MU for the BB is 26.2 ± 9.2 Hz, but that of the FDI is 31.1 ± 10.2 Hz [10]. The intrinsic hand muscle comprises about 40,500 muscle fibers that are innervated by 120 motor neurons, which yields an average of 338 fibers innervated by each motor neuron [11], the BB is comprises about 96,000 muscle fibers, that are innervated by 120 motor neurons, which yields an average of 800 fibers innervated by each motor neuron [12]. The simulation focus on the parameters difference between the BB and the FDI with the same physiology mathematic model. According to muscle physiological features and the electrode configuration, the BB and the FDI sEMG model were developed as six steps.

- Intracellular action potential simulation

  $e_i(z)$ is the fiber's intracellular action potential [13]:

$$e_i(z) = 768z^3 e^{-z} - 90 \tag{1}$$

where z is the axial direction in mm (see Fig.1); and i is an index identifying the MU.

- Extracellular action potential simulation

  This simulation at an observation point $[z_0, y_0]$ can be expressed as [14]:

$$V_E(z_0, y_0) = K[\int_{S1} \frac{\partial e(z)}{\partial z} \cdot \frac{1}{r} dS + \int_S dS \int_{-\infty}^{+\infty} \frac{\partial^2 e(z)}{\partial z^2} \cdot \frac{1}{r} dz - \int_{S2} \frac{\partial e(z)}{\partial (z)} \cdot \frac{1}{r} dS \tag{2}$$

where $\mathbf{y}$ is the radial direction in mm (see Fig.1); S_1 and S_2 are the fiber sections at the fiber ends; and r is the distance between the surface element dS and the observation point:

$$r = \sqrt{(z_0 - z)^2 + \frac{\sigma_z}{\sigma_y} y_0^2} \tag{3}$$

Here anisotropy is introduced through σ_z and σ_y, which denote the axial and radial conductivity, respectively. The part $I_m(z)$ corresponds to the transmembrane current of K'', σ_i is the intracellular conductivity.

$$I_m(z) = K'' \cdot \frac{\partial^2 e(z)}{\partial z^2} = \frac{\pi d^2 \sigma_i}{4} \cdot \frac{\partial^2 e(z)}{\partial z^2} \tag{4}$$

• Muscle fiber conduction velocity simulation

The v is the conduction velocity in meters per second [13]:

$$v = 2.2 + 0.05(d - 25) \tag{5}$$

• MU recruitment simulation

The assigned recruitment threshold excitation in the MU pool follows an exponential rule [15]:

$$RTE(i) = e^{\alpha \cdot i} = e^{\frac{\ln(RR)}{n} \cdot i} \tag{6}$$

where α is a coefficient used to establish the range of threshold values; and RR is the range of recruitment threshold values desired. This was set to be a broad MU recruitment range (at 70% of the maximum excitation) in this paper.

• MU firing rate simulation

An MU's peaking firing rate (PFR) is inversely proportional to the recruitment threshold according to [15]:

$$PFR(i) = PFR(1)\text{-}PFRD \cdot \frac{RTE(i)}{RTE(120)}, i = 2:120 \tag{7}$$

where $PFR(1)$ is the assigned PFR of the first recruited unit; $PFRD$ is the desired difference of the PFR between the first and the last units recruited; $RTE(i)$ is the recruitment threshold of the studied MU; and $RTE(120)$ is the recruitment threshold of the last recruited MU. The FR strategy of the MU was: the slope of the excitatory drive-firing rate relation of a motor unit increased with increasing recruitment threshold. All the MUs finally reached the same peak firing rate at maximum excitation [16].

• Muscle force generation model

Muscle force was modeled as an exponential form, linked to the recruitment threshold and varying over a wide range [15]:

$$F(i) = e^{\mu \cdot i} = e^{\frac{\ln(RF)}{n} i} \tag{8}$$

where $F(i)$ is the force; μ is a coefficient used to establish a range of twitch force values; and RF is the desired range of twitch force values, which is set to 100. The force was simulated at 10%, 20%, 30%, 40%, 50%, 60%, 70%, 80%, 90%, and 100% of maximum voluntary contraction (MVC).

3   Results

The Gaussianity test involves deciding whether the estimated bicoherence is zero. A non-Gaussianity assumption is accepted when the probability of a false alarm (Pfa) is less than 5% [4]. Figure 2 showed that the Pfa of the BB in accepting the non-Gaussian assumption is 0 at 10%, 40%, 60~100% MVC. Therefore, the sEMG signals of the BB at 10%, 40%, 60~100% MVC had nonzero bispectrum, i.e. they were non-Gaussianity. Beside, the FDI sEMG signals tended towards a non-Gaussian distribution at 40%~60% and 80% MVC .

The linearity test involves deciding whether the estimated bicoherence is constant in the bi-frequency domain, employing the absolute difference (dR) between a theoretical (R') and an estimated inter-quartile range (R). A non-linearity hypothesis is adopted when dR/R' > 2 [4]. As seen in Fig.2, The dR/R' value of the BB was more than 2 at 90% MVC. The dR/R' value of the FDI was more than 2 at 30% MVC. In these cases, We accept the non-linearity hypothesis.

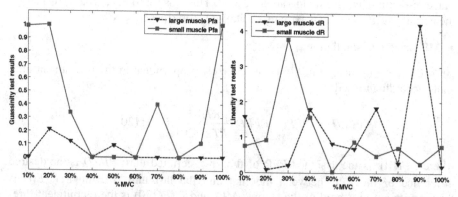

Fig. 2. The results of Gaussinity and linearity tests for large and small muscles

The Wilcoxon test was conducted to evaluate whether difference between the Gaussianity/linearity test results of BB and that of FDI. The results showed a significant difference in linearity test between the BB muscle and the FDI muscl, z = -2.197, p<0.05. Conversely, there was no significant difference in linearity test between the BB muscle and the FDI muscle, z = -0.357, p>0.05.

Table 1. Wilcoxon test statistics

	The Gaussinity comparison of the BB vs. the FDI	The linearity comparison of the BB vs. the FDI
Z	-2.197[a]	-0.357[b]
Asymp. Sig(2-tailed)	0.028	0.721

a.   Based on negative ranks; b.Based on positive ranks.

4   Conclusion

In this paper, we evaluated the Gaussinity and linearity of the BB sEMG signals vs. the FDI sEMG signals. Our purpose was to discussed the difference between large muscle — the BB activities and small muscle — the FDI activities. The findings of the research provid guiding significance on large and small muscles capability assessment. We tentatively deduced that three reasons responsible for the difference of Gaussianity between the BB and the FDI. 1) Large and small muscles have broad and narrow MU recruitment range, respectively; 2) FR plays a important role in small muscles activity, however recruitment plays a important role in large muscles activity. 3) MUs of small muscles are recruited following smallest MUs to largest MUs order, but large muscles do not. Even though the model is able to reflect the change of the BB and the FDI with exertion and recruited MU number increasing, there are still many restrictions during the sEMG signals generation. A more detailed mathematic and physiological model should be refined in the near future.

References

1. Bilodeau, M., Cincera, M., Arsenault, A.B.: Normality and stationarity of EMG signals of elbow flexor muscles during ramp and step isometric contractions. J. Electromyogr. Kines 7(2), 87–96 (1997)
2. Zazula, D. Experience with surface EMG decomposition using higher-order cumulants. In: Signal Processing 2001, pp.19-24. Poznan, Poland (2001)
3. Shahid, S., Walker, J., Lyons, G.M.: Application of higher order statistics techniques to EMG signals to characterize the motor unit action potential. IEEE Trans. Biomed. Eng. 52(7), 1195–1209 (2005)
4. Kaplanis, P.A., Pattichis, C.S., Hadjileontiadis, L.J.: Surface EMG analysis on normal subjects based on isometric voluntary contraction. J. Electromyogr. Kines 19, 157–171 (2009)
5. Lippert, L.S.: Clinical kinesiology and anatomy, pp. 126–127. Davis Company, Philadelphia (2006)
6. Carol, T., Dan, G.: Musculoskeletal Atlas: A Musculoskeletal Atlas of the Human Body, http://www.rad.washington.edu/
7. Gray, H.: Anatomy of the Human Body. Lea & Febiger, Philadelphia (1918)
8. McGill, K.C.: Surface electromyogram signal modelling. Med. Biol. Eng. Comput. 42(4), 446–454 (2004)
9. Buchthal, F., Erminio, F., Rosenfalck, P.: Motor unit territory in different human muscles. Acta Physiol. Scand. 45(1), 72–87 (1959)

10. Seki, K., Narusawa, M.: Firing rate modulation of human motor units in different muscles during isometric contraction with various forces. Brain Res. 719, 1–7 (1996)
11. Feinstein, B., Lindegård, B., Nyman, E., Wohlfart, G.: Morphologic studies of motor units in normal human muscles. Acta Anat. 23(2), 127–142 (1955)
12. Gabriel, D.A., Kamen, G.: Experimental and modeling investigation of spectral compression of biceps brachii SEMG activity with increasing force levels. J. Electromyogr. Kines 19, 437–448 (2009)
13. Nandedkar, S.D., Stålberg, E.: Simulation of sigle fiber action potentials. Med. Biol. Eng. Comput. 21, 158–165 (1983)
14. LorentedeNó, R.: Analysis of the distribution of action currents of nerve in volume conductors. Stud. Rockfeller Inst. Med. Res. 132, 384–477 (1974)
15. Fuglevand, A.J., Winter, D.A., Patla, A.E.: Model of recuitment and rate coding organization in motor-unit pools. J. Neurophysiol. 70(6), 2470–2488 (1993)
16. Zhou, P., Rymer, W.Z.: Can standard surface EMG processing parame-ters be used to estimate motor unit global firing rate? J. Neural Eng. (1), 99–110 (2004)

Author Index